THE QUEST FOR SOCIAL JUSTICE

Seal of the University of Wisconsin-Milwaukee. 1849—*Founding of the University of Wisconsin at Madison.* 1885—*Opening of Milwaukee State Normal School, which became Milwaukee State Teachers College in 1927, then Wisconsin State College, Milwaukee, in 1951.* 1956—*Merger of Wisconsin State College, Milwaukee, and the University of Wisconsin's Milwaukee Extension Center to form The University of Wisconsin-Milwaukee.*

The Key to the Future *logo and the legend "25 Years of Teaching, Research and Service" were adopted by The University of Wisconsin-Milwaukee during the 25th anniversary year.*

Published in celebration of the 25th anniversary of
the founding of the
University of Wisconsin–Milwaukee

THE UNIVERSITY OF WISCONSIN-MILWAUKEE
25 YEARS OF TEACHING, RESEARCH AND SERVICE

Morris Fromkin, 1892–1969

THE QUEST FOR SOCIAL JUSTICE
The Morris Fromkin Memorial Lectures 1970–1980

Edited by
Ralph M. Aderman

Published for
The Golda Meir Library
of
The University of Wisconsin–Milwaukee
by
The University of Wisconsin Press

Published *1983*

The University of Wisconsin Press
114 North Murray Street
Madison, Wisconsin 53715

The University of Wisconsin Press, Ltd.
1 Gower Street
London WC1E 6HA, England

Copyright © *1983*
The Board of Regents of the University of Wisconsin System
All rights reserved

First printing

Printed in the United States of America

Library of Congress Cataloging in Publication Data
Main entry under title:
The Quest for social justice.
Includes bibliographies.
1. Social justice—Addresses, essays, lectures.
2. United States—Politics and government—Addresses, essays, lectures. 3. Social problems—Addresses, essays, lectures. 4. Milwaukee (Wis.)—Politics and government—Addresses, essays, lectures. I. Fromkin, Morris, 1892–1969. II. Aderman, Ralph M.
HM146.Q43 1982   303.3'72   81-50831
ISBN 0-299-08730-1

KEY TO THE FUTURE

THIS volume of the collected Morris Fromkin Memorial Lectures, 1970 through 1980, was produced at no cost to Wisconsin taxpayers as a University of Wisconsin–Milwaukee twenty-fifth anniversary commemorative publication. Funding was provided from the Golda Meir Library Photocopy Center, the original Morris Fromkin Memorial gift, and the David R. Kotvis Trust Fund.

MEMBERS
FROMKIN MEMORIAL LECTURE COMMITTEES
1970 TO 1981

Ben Barkin
John F. Bibby
Robert Burkert
Beverly Blair Cook
Cornelius P. Cotter
Gareth W. Dunleavy
Janet Egleson Dunleavy
Lynn W. Eley
Elaine Fain
David Fromkin
Mark M. Gormley
J. David Hoeveler, Jr.
Glen Jeansonne
J. Martin Klotsche
Mark L. Krupnick
Richard Loreck
Stanley Mallach
William D. Moritz
Frederick I. Olson
Gerald Peters
Donald Pienkos
William C. Roselle
Wilbur A. Stolt
Roger H. Sundell

Contents

Foreword	xiii
Preface	xvii
Librarian's Note	xxi
Editor's Note	xxv
Introduction	xxvii
The Historic Role of Constitutional Liberalism in the Quest for Social Justice WAYNE MORSE	5
Patterns of Consumer Consciousness in the Progressive Movement: Robert M. La Follette, the Antitrust Persuasion, and Labor Legislation DAVID P. THELEN	19
The Idea of Progress in Afro-American Thought, 1890–1915 WALTER B. WEARE	51
Sentencing the Unpatriotic: Federal Trial Judges in Wisconsin during Four Wars BEVERLY BLAIR COOK	73
Politics, Religion, and Change in Polish Milwaukee, 1900–1930 DONALD PIENKOS	141
The University and the Social Gospel: The Intellectual Origins of the "Wisconsin Idea" J. DAVID HOEVELER, JR.	185

Reconstruction, Reform, and Romanism, 1865–1885: America as Seen by an Irish-American and His Irish M.P. Cousin JANET EGLESON DUNLEAVY and GARETH W. DUNLEAVY	211
The Menorah Journal Group and the Origins of Modern Jewish-American Radicalism MARK L. KRUPNICK	235
Books for New Citizens: Public Libraries and Americanization Programs, 1900–1925 ELAINE FAIN	255
Utopia Comes to the Masses: Huey P. Long's Share-Our-Wealth Society GLEN S. JEANSONNE	279
F.D.R., WPA, and Wisconsin Art of the Depression ROBERT BURKERT	299
Appendix: Third Forces in American Politics: A Symposium AUSTIN RANNEY, Moderator; THOMAS W. EVANS; W. H. FERRY; DAVID L. GRAVEN; ISABEL BACON LA FOLLETTE; CHARLES E. RICE; and FRANK P. ZEIDLER	331

Foreword

THE publication of the provocative and politically important Fromkin lectures is a welcome part of our celebration of the University of Wisconsin–Milwaukee's twenty-fifth year.

The theme of our twenty-fifth anniversary is "UWM—Key to the Future," stressing the role that our University has to play in the future of our community and its people. As we look to the future, we find strength and cause for optimism in our past. UWM's roots extend to the founding of our predecessor institution, a Wisconsin state normal school, almost 100 years ago, a time when a great surge of immigrants was entering this country. One of the strong desires they brought with them was a thirst for knowledge and education that had been denied them in their native lands. That search for knowledge and education was combined with a search for freedom and for social justice.

Perhaps the most powerful role that a university performs in our society is joining the ideas and experiences of the past to the dreams and goals of the future.

The dynamism of America has been drawn from the vigor, strength, and creativity of its people, many of them immigrants who came here in search of opportunity, freedom, and social justice. As we look at the American experience, we see major changes sweeping across the nation at well-defined intervals. A closer look at these intervals reveals that each coincides with a new wave of immigrants seeking a new life of their own but invigorating this country with their irrepressible demand for improving the quality of their life.

The vitality and strength of this nation were drawn from the men and women who departed their native lands to endure hardship and uncertainty in their travels to America. Their suffering made them more determined to pursue their dreams once they arrived. Their skills, determination, and hard work helped bring America great wealth and power. But the problem of social justice remains with us. It is the unfinished legacy of these brave men and women.

Morris Fromkin was one of those pioneering immigrants. Arriving on our shores penniless, he worked in the factories of New York City. Drawn to Milwaukee by the city's active socialist movement and ex-

Frank E. Horton, Chancellor, UWM

periments in political reform and social justice, he worked his way through law school and championed the cause of his fellow immigrants and the labor movement. This University is proud to be a part of his living memorial to the social issues confronting this nation.

The University of Wisconsin–Milwaukee has grown to meet the challenge that political and civic leaders like Morris Fromkin set for this young campus when it was created twenty-five years ago. This University was to serve the sons and daughters of the working people, many of them immigrants, who did not have access to a university education. Today, more than half of our students are among the first generation of their families to attend college. Most of these students are working their way through school, just as Morris Fromkin did. His example is a good one for current students to recognize and to follow. It would appear that today's student may well be under so much pressure to succeed economically that acquiring a broader understanding of political and social issues may not be properly prioritized. We cannot afford to lose the heritage of social progress forged out of the experiences of the past century. The danger is that we will lose the creativity and commitment to social progress that has been the driving force of our technological and economic success. Some educators go so far as to suggest that we have already lost that vitality.

Our nation's colleges and universities are not as creative as they could be and are "tired, living on the intellectual legacy of the past," according to Ernest L. Boyer, president of the Carnegie Foundation for the Advancement of Teaching. "Creative solutions follow when quality problems are identified, but the core of the creative process . . . is problem finding," Boyer recently said before a Library of Congress symposium on creativity.

The clear and present danger is that we are losing the problem finders and solvers of the future, just when we may be entering a new era of creative expansion.

Daniel J. Boorstin, Librarian of Congress, theorizes that American creativity has flourished on what he calls the "fertile verge." Boorstin defines the fertile verge as the collision point between major forces of change in our nation. The interaction at these verges—the new colonies in the wilderness, the expansion to the western frontier, the waves of immigrants over the past 100 years—is what gives America its own brand of creativity.

"Our task is to remain aware of these verges and keep the borders open—to a competitive world of new ideas, new products, new arts, new institutions," he said.

Historian Arthur Schlesinger, Jr., noted that American creativity can be linked to cycles. "In the early years of the century, the detonating issue was the concentration of private economic power in trusts. In the 1930s, it was the depression and mass unemployment. In the 1960s, it was poverty and racial injustice. As the republic gathers its forces to meet such problems, it discharges energies across the board. Sometime in the 1980s the dam will again break, as it broke at the turn of the century and in the 1930s and 1960s, with a comparable release of innovation and creativity."

Let us hope that when the dam breaks, we will be ready. One way to prepare ourselves for the future is to draw strength from the past. The causes that drew Morris Fromkin to Milwaukee are as vital and important to our future today as they were fifty years ago. The Fromkin lecture series and the research and scholarship associated with the special collection of books and papers on social justice issues will help us examine the past and evolve a new agenda for life and politics in the decades ahead.

There will be many events and projects underway during this twenty-fifth anniversary year. The Fromkin lecture series and collection will serve as an outstanding example of how the university and the community can join together to prepare for a better future. We are all proud of what the Fromkin lecture series has achieved. We are also thankful to the Fromkin family for their continuing support of our efforts on behalf of the Morris Fromkin Memorial program.

Frank E. Horton
Chancellor
University of Wisconsin–Milwaukee

April, 1981

Preface

MY father died on April 24, 1969, of a sudden stroke suffered aboard a transatlantic cruise ship at dock in New York harbor. It was the end of a long voyage, begun in another century and on the far side of the world.

Morris Fromkin was born on July 25, 1892, in a small village near Kiev, into the persecuted minority that was the Jewish community of Czarist Russia. His mother died when he still was an infant. As a child, he was brought to the United States. A penniless immigrant, he worked in factories on the lower east side of New York City. Later, he sent himself to school. Drawn to the socialist ideals of Daniel Hoan's and Victor Berger's Milwaukee, he journeyed there, worked his way through law school, and, as an active trial lawyer, specialized in defending the immigrants and the indigent, often without fee. As an early pioneer of labor law, he won courtroom victories for the labor movement at a time when it was still young, struggling, and relatively weak. His concern always was for the weak. He himself was, in every sense, strong. That was true even when he was seventy-six years old; he played a game of golf through a snow storm. Life's storms never deterred him.

From the outset, it was clear that whatever memorial we established in his memory ought to be located in Milwaukee. My mother, my sisters, and I had no doubt of that. In a sense, my father had chosen the location himself. He came to Milwaukee, not as one might relocate today to find a better job or to follow the sun, but in order to find a political environment in which his ideals could be realized. At that time, the better part of a century ago, Milwaukee was more than a city; it was a rallying point for those who believed that America needed a whole new agenda in life and politics. He came here to enlist in those causes, and so it is right that they should be remembered through him, and he, through them.

Our idea was to create a specialized collection of books and papers dealing with the sort of social justice issues with which my father and his friends were so concerned and, together with that collection, a continuing program of research and scholarship that could make a contribution to public understanding. In the autumn of 1969, our family friend Ben Barkin and I met with UWM Chancellor J. Martin Klotsche to discuss whether and how such a program could be established at the University of Wisconsin–Milwaukee. Dr. Klotsche, with his broad knowledge of Wisconsin history and of the university system, was able to give our proposal specific form. Based on our discussions and correspondence, a formal proposal was submitted on December 2, 1969, to the Board of Regents of the University of Wisconsin. That proposal was subsequently accepted.

The formal proposal outlined not merely the structure and budget of the program and the financial support that we would be able to give to it, but it also included the subject matter with which the memorial would deal: the American quest for social justice from the end of the Civil War until the coming of the New Deal.

In explanation of what we meant by this, I set forth our ideas in considerable detail for the Wisconsin Board of Regents. I referred back to the tremendous impact of the industrial revolution in America in the period following the end of the Civil War and the impact, too, of a related event: the arrival in America in that period of more than twenty-five million immigrants, bringing hopes and skills and seeking opportunities. Certainly this ferment brought great wealth, power, and progress to the United States, but there was a dark side as well. Industrialization has its cost in human terms. The problems were many. Here are some of them, as they emerged in the last half of the nineteenth century, without precedent for guidance in their solution:

—Agriculture declined in importance and increasingly became mechanized in technique. What was to become of the small farmers and now redundant farm population?

—Farmers, and millions from Europe, came suddenly to the cities in search of work. Who would produce adequate housing and sanitation? parks? schools? and, above all, jobs?

—Cities bred crime and disease. How could these ills be prevented? controlled? treated? How could prisons and hospitals be improved?

—Women and children—the weak and the vulnerable—were able to do factory work as well as men, but they could more easily be coerced into working long hours for low wages in bad conditions. Who would protect them?

—People were used to living in ancestral villages where everyone was known. Friends and neighbors helped in times of crisis. But in the new cities the forces were big—Big Business, Big Government, eventually Big Labor—and often impersonal; the individual was anonymous. To whom could a lonely and anonymous city-dweller turn for help in time of need?

Discussing those for whom these issues were foremost, I added:

"My father was one of these—the seekers after justice and mercy—and this Collection is intended to memorialize his compassion and concern. In the early years of the century he moved from the Atlantic Coast to Milwaukee because Milwaukee was then the center of movements and men seeking the answers to these social problems. That is why Milwaukee is the right place for this Collection."

In the search for solutions to these complex difficulties, many and differing ideas have been espoused. The program of the Morris Fromkin Memorial does not take sides; its function is to probe issues rather than to judge them, let alone *prejudge* them. For the members of the symposium that inaugurated the Memorial program, I posed the questions in a way intended to make clear that, for us, the fundamental questions remain open.

"What is the relevance today of the material dealt with by the Collection? What did the men and movements it deals with contribute, for good or evil, to American life? What help (if any) can studying them give us in facing contemporary problems?

"What does George Norris have to say to us today? The La Follettes? Brandeis? Holmes? Clarence Darrow? Theodore Roosevelt? Eugene V. Debs? Altgeld? Bryan?

"Assume that the so-called Welfare State achieved by the New Deal (but was it?) represented the culmination of the various movements to protect the individual by means of national legislation such as social security, minimum wages and hours laws, child labor laws, the Wagner Act, etc. Then, and if so:

a. Was this a good or a bad solution to the problems of our urban industrial society?

b. If good—why do we have so many social problems in America today? Why didn't these measures solve our problems?

c. If bad—how else could/can individuals be protected in a society such as ours? Should they be protected? Should they be protected by some entity other than the national government, or by some means other than legislation?

"What about the Brandeis phrase 'the curse of bigness'? To protect against overly big business, did we create overly big labor unions? Overly big government? Is bigness of itself a bad thing, or is it a good one?

"What is the relation between ends and means in politics? What methods (1865–1932), if any, proved successful in promoting or achieving social justice? What (if anything) does this tell us about what we should do today?

"Is social justice the right goal for a society to have? Is it illusory or can it in some measure be achieved? Is it an absolute concept, or do its contents change as society changes? What should be our goals as a society? And in what respect are they or should they be the same as or different from the various goals proclaimed by the earlier American men and movements dealt with by the Collection?"

In the final event, the program of the Morris Fromkin Memorial has been everything that we had hoped it would be. The wealth and diversity of the contributions made to America in the search for social justice are made clear by the very subject matter of the lectures, which deal with the role played by German, Irish, Polish, Jewish, and Black Americans, and by journalists, intellectuals, educators, politicians, librarians, artists, and persons from all ethnic groups and all walks of life.

For carrying out our dream and for making such a success of it, my mother, my sisters, and I are grateful to the authors whose work appears in this volume; to the director of the Golda Meir Library, Mr. William Roselle, under whose creative guidance this volume and the Memorial program it represents have developed; and to Mr. Stanley Mallach, the Morris Fromkin Bibliographer, who, from the beginning, has been the guardian of the flame. We are grateful for the leadership of Chancellors J. Martin Klotsche, Werner A. Baum, and Frank E. Horton, for the hard work of their devoted staffs, and for the dedication of the members of the annual Fromkin Lecture Committees. Indeed, we owe thanks to so many members of the UWM community that I hope they will forgive me for not mentioning them all by name, but without their support, it could never have been done.

We hope that you will enjoy, as much as we have enjoyed, the essays that follow and the striking graphic art of the posters that announced each lecture.

David Fromkin

New York City
January, 1981

Librarian's Note

THROUGHOUT my career as librarian, I have clung to a simplistic view of the university as being, at its heart, nothing more or less than the programs of instruction, research, and service that are envisioned, developed, and implemented by the faculty. That perception has been enhanced by the opportunity afforded me to serve as chair of the Morris Fromkin Memorial Lecture Committee during the past ten years.

A decade of reading the assemblage of annual Fromkin grant proposals and of interviewing those able and enthusiastic applicants has confirmed my belief in the need for higher education to reaffirm with vigor the centrality of the faculty role, despite the array of bureaucracies, agencies, departments, regulations, and committees that intrude, permeate, and, at times, needlessly dominate our environment. And, perhaps, here we realize the ultimate value of the Morris Fromkin Lectures to our University for therein is found this unique, uncomplicated opportunity for our faculty to share their research in specialized topics.

A well-attended annual lecture, publication of the research findings, interdepartmental participation and cooperation, and significant community outreach are immediate, visible benefits. The 1979 UWM symposium, "The University Library and the Arts," was a direct result of the annual Fromkin grant application process as was the appearance in 1980 of the first book published by this library, *A Climate of Creativity* by Adolph A. Suppan, Dean Emeritus of Fine Arts. It can be assumed that additional research and investigation, stimulated by the Morris Fromkin Memorial, are being conducted even now and that those findings will influence and shape aspects of scholarship in the years ahead.

Recognition and appreciation are extended to the members of the family of the late Morris Fromkin for their vision and generosity in establishing the Memorial at our Library. Throughout the planning and development of the Memorial, Mrs. Selma Fromkin, Mrs. Elliott Magaziner, Mrs. Murray Prester, and Mr. David Fromkin have become members of our university community and loyal participants in its programs. Their contributions, support, and friendship have been treasured.

Readers of this volume should know that it was our University's good friend Ben Barkin who, in the autumn of 1969, assisted David Fromkin with the development of the Morris Fromkin Memorial proposal and who placed that plan with UWM Chancellor J. Martin Klotsche. In December of that year, following a review by UWM Library Director Mark M. Gormley and his staff, Dr. Klotsche placed the formal proposal before the University of Wisconsin Board of Regents, who then accepted this uniquely significant gift.

And so, special thanks are due Chancellors Emeritus J. Martin Klotsche and Werner A. Baum for, in the first instance, ensuring establishment of the Memorial, and, in the second, nurturing and guiding it to maturity during its first decade. UWM Chancellor Frank E. Horton's direct participation in the Fromkin programs during his first years of leadership at UWM has placed the Memorial on a clear path to success during its second decade.

The selection of an annual grant recipient is a time-consuming task that demands energy and expertise in addition to the hours spent reading and discussing proposals, interviewing applicants, and negotiating the give-and-take of final committee selection. All of our colleagues who served on the Fromkin Lecture Committee during the past eleven years are listed on an acknowledgment page that has been placed in this volume.

Stanley Mallach, who has served as Fromkin Bibliographer since 1970, is due thanks for his role in building the collection and in assisting with the design of the annual lecture series. Numerous other Library staff have contributed to the Fromkin Memorial. The work of Associate Library Director William Moritz, Library Business Manager Charles MacLeod, and my assistant, Jeane Knapp, has been noteworthy.

David Fromkin, Ralph Aderman, John Solon, John Bibby, and Frederick Olson must receive much of the credit for the publication of this book, for without their work it would never have come to be. Ralph Aderman's tireless dedication to his editorial tasks has added to my indebtedness. In the 1970-71 academic year, he chaired the search committee responsible for my appointment. John Solon's expertise shaped the entire publication project. Special thanks are given Associate Vice Chancellor Russell Fenske for arranging the fiscal details of the editor's summer appointments, which spanned parts of three budget years. The typing and preparation of much of the final manuscript was patiently and effectively handled by my secretary, Charlotte Ruenzel, just as she has handled the mechanics of the annual grant application procedure.

I again will acknowledge with deep appreciation the contribution of all the Fromkin lecturers, for it was their diligent and painstaking research that brought the lecture series to today's level of recognition. Equally important and equally appreciated are all the other of our colleagues who, over the years, have sought the Fromkin Lecture grant. It was the excellence of their proposals and the strength of their competitive spirit that drove the Committee's annual selections. Without the number and quality of those application proposals, the lecture series could not exist. And, finally, a very special tribute is offered those several thousand faculty, students, staff, and community friends who have attended the eleven annual lectures. Their enthusiasm and consistent support caused us to begin planning, some half-dozen years ago, publication of this twenty-fifth anniversary record of the contributions of our faculty to a distinctive portion of our University's intellectual history.

William C. Roselle
Director of the Golda Meir Library,
Chair, The Morris Fromkin
Memorial Lecture Committee,
and Editorial Consultant,
The Quest for Social Justice

March, 1981

Editor's Note

SINCE the styles of written presentation and documentation vary from one discipline to another and since the papers in this collection represent several fields of scholarship, the form of the notes and bibliography may differ somewhat in the various essays. Wherever it was possible without violating the author's intention, the pattern of the notes and bibliography has been standardized.

Several of the essays have been revised, expanded, and retitled since they were originally presented as Fromkin Lectures. Others remain essentially unchanged from their original delivery. Consequently, readers of this volume who may have heard the original lectures will find marked differences in the scope and development of some of the essays. Whether in the brief lecture version or in a more elaborate, extended treatment, these essays reflect the careful scholarship and the continuing search for truth which the Fromkin Lecture grants have fostered during the past decade.

The Printing Services at the University of Wisconsin–Milwaukee produced the posters which introduce each lecture in this volume. The editor wishes to express his appreciation for their assistance. The photographs illustrating Robert Burkert's lecture, "F.D.R., WPA, and Wisconsin Art of the Depression," are from the Charlotte Partridge papers in the Special Collections Department of the Golda Meir Library at the University of Wisconsin–Milwaukee.

Ralph M. Aderman

April, 1981

Introduction

THE quest for social justice—equal and enhanced opportunity for all persons and a responsive, responsible, and representative government—has been a central concern of the American experience. In recognition that this search is never ending, the family of Morris Fromkin made a grant to the University of Wisconsin–Milwaukee (UWM) in 1970 for the purpose of developing a collection of scholarly materials in the UWM Library on the struggle for social justice in America. The bequest also established an annual Fromkin Memorial Lecture on the topic. This volume contains edited transcripts of the Fromkin Lectures delivered between 1970 and 1980, the twenty-fifth anniversary of UWM's founding.

It was appropriate that this Memorial be located at Milwaukee's urban university, for it was to this city that young Morris Fromkin was attracted in 1918. Milwaukee's reputation as a center for political reform and experiments in social justice programs was the magnet that drew Fromkin as a young man to Wisconsin after his birth in Russia, migration to the United States, and childhood in the tenements and factories of New York's lower east side. As a law student and later as a distinguished attorney in Milwaukee and then in New York, his commitment to social justice never flagged. He earned a national reputation for his work in the field of labor law, where he defended and extended the rights of working men and women. The annual Fromkin Lectures are a fitting and continuing memorial to a man whose life was intertwined with many of the individuals and causes discussed in this collection.

The Fromkin Lectures are, however, more than a memorial to the ideals which guided Morris Fromkin's life. They are also a testimony to the commitment of the University of Wisconsin–Milwaukee to scholarship and research on important issues of the American and Wisconsin experience. The lectures in this volume reflect the unique contributions and perspectives of a variety of academic disciplines to our understanding of the nation's progress toward the goal of social justice.

In conducting their research, lecturers have relied heavily on the special Fromkin Collection in the UWM Library which was made possible through the Fromkin family's grant. This collection features books, papers, and other materials about reform movements in America from the end of the Civil War to the New Deal era. Two recent projects that have enhanced the research potential of the Collection include the production of a guide to archival holdings in the Milwaukee area and the filming of the clipping files held by the Wisconsin Legislative Reference Service. Under terms of the grant, the Library also has retained the services of a bibliographer to supervise the Fromkin Collection and assist researchers.

The Fromkin Lecture has become an established and respected institution of the UWM campus. The annual Fromkin Lecture grant is regarded both in the University and the greater Milwaukee community as a prestigious award given in recognition of scholarly accomplishment. The award is made on a competitive basis by a Fromkin Lecture Committee composed of UWM faculty (including two prior recipients of Fromkin grants) and members of the Library's professional staff. Each applicant is required to submit a proposal outlining his research/lecture project along with a budget. The committee reviews the proposals and interviews each applicant before making the award.

Within the broad rubric of the "quest for social justice in America," scholars from a wide variety of disciplines representing the various schools or colleges of the University have submitted research proposals to the Committee. The UWM recipients of the award have therefore exhibited diverse approaches and perspectives to the study of America's social and political development. Fromkin lecturers have included three historians, three members of the English faculty, two political scientists, a specialist in library science, and an artist. They have dealt with a broad spectrum of subjects, time periods, and locations using a variety of methodologies. Four of the lectures have focused upon Milwaukee and Wisconsin, an emphasis encouraged by the bequest. The series, however, has not been parochial, for it has dealt with the South, New York City, race relations, third party movements, the immigrant experience, the roles of literature and the arts, and Irish-American relations.

Because of the breadth of academic disciplines and topics investigated by Fromkin lecturers, the lecture program has been an important impetus for scholarship and research support at the University. The annual Lecture has also been a means of recognizing the faculty's scholarly achievements.

The Fromkin Lecture series is well adapted to the urban mission of UWM and its commitment to academic excellence. The lectures, which are attended by members of the University and Milwaukee area communities, have demonstrated the relevance of scholarship to the major issues of our time and encouraged links between the University and the greater Milwaukee citizenry. The Fromkin lecturers have frequently worked closely with community leaders and organizations in doing their research, and each lecture has attracted involvement from the diverse constituencies of the University. The Fromkin Lecturers are therefore in the tradition of the University of Wisconsin System's motto, which states that "the boundaries of the campus are the boundaries of the state."

The Fromkin Memorial Lecture program began in 1970, when former Senator Wayne Morse (Oregon) presented "The Historic Role of Constitutional Liberalism in the Quest for Social Justice." His presentation was an appropriate opening for the series because it captured the spirit of the social movements in which both Morse and Morris Fromkin played an integral role. In addition, Morse, like Fromkin, approached the topic from the perspective of an attorney with extensive practical experience in politics. The two men also shared a Wisconsin heritage and were personal friends. A symposium on "Third Forces in American Politics" was also a part of the program which initiated the lecture series. Austin J. Ranney, one of the nation's foremost students of political parties, served as the moderator of the panel. At the time Ranney was a professor of political science at the University of Wisconsin—Madison, and currently he is a resident scholar at the American Enterprise Institute in Washington, D.C. Third-party movements seeking social and political change were one feature of Wisconsin that attracted the young Morris Fromkin to Wisconsin. Recent elections have demonstrated that these movements continue to be a vital force in shaping the American polity. Drawing on the experience of actual participants in the Progressive and Socialist parties of Wisconsin as well as modern day political leaders, this symposium provides unique insights into the role third-party movements have played in our history.

The second lecture (1971) was similarly focused upon the reform movements started in Wisconsin. David P. Thelen, of the University of Missouri–Columbia, provided a nontraditional view of the senior Robert La Follette in "Patterns of Consumer Consciousness in the Progressive Movement: Robert M. La Follette, the Antitrust Persuasion, and Labor Legislation." In his lecture, Thelen demonstrated La Follette's concern for consumer interests, a topic of continuing controversy in the 1980s.

The 1972 award of the Fromkin Lecture grant to Professor Walter

Weare of the UWM History Department initiated a new policy on the part of the Lecture Committee. In recognition of the University's achievement of major university status, it was decided that the Fromkin Lecture grant would be made on a competitive basis to a member of the UWM faculty. Professor Weare with his lecture, "The Idea of Progress in Afro-American Thought, 1890–1915," therefore became the first of a series of distinguished UWM faculty members to participate in the lecture program. In his lecture, Weare explored the idea of progress in Afro-American thought, thereby providing essential background for understanding the current debate over the extent of Black progress in American society.

Political Scientist Beverly Blair Cook in 1973 explored the performance of Wisconsin's Federal District Courts in sentencing draft resisters in her lecture, "Sentencing the Unpatriotic: Federal Judges in Wisconsin during Four Wars." Her analysis of sentencing patterns reveals the impact of the differing political cultures in the Eastern and Western Districts of Wisconsin on judicial decision-making. This lecture is therefore of interest not only to students of conscription policies in the United States and Wisconsin but also to persons concerned with judicial behavior more generally.

The concentration of Polish-Americans in Milwaukee has added a special ingredient to the social life and politics of the city and state. In spite of the Poles' continuing impact on the area's politics, little attention has been paid to the Polish-American community's relationship to the Progressive and Socialist parties which flourished in Milwaukee. Donald Pienkos' 1974 lecture, "Politics, Religion, and Change in Polish Milwaukee, 1900–1930," describes the involvement of the Polonia in these movements, as well as the tensions that existed between the reformers and the Polish-American leadership.

The "Wisconsin Idea," which was embraced by Robert La Follette, called for the University to join forces with state government to formulate policies for social betterment while providing services to the citizenry through its research and outreach programs. This Wisconsin approach to social reform, which was fostered by a political leader admired by Morris Fromkin, was the topic of a lecture in 1975. Historian J. David Hoeveler in "The University and the Social Gospel: The Intellectual Origins of the Wisconsin Idea" demonstrates how the Wisconsin Idea represents the secularization of social gospel ideals and their reformulation. Since the University's proper role vis-à-vis the government and the extent of its social responsibilities continue to be a point of sharp contention, this lecture provides essential background for the current debates.

Jewish intellectuals have played a major role in the twentieth-century reform movements. "The *Menorah Journal* Group and the Origins of Modern Jewish American Radicalism" by Mark Krupnick (1977) analyzes the "seed time" of these radicals of the 1920s, who had immense influence on American cultural and moral opinion during the past thirty years. Evidence of the importance of this group is the following list of journals that have spread the influence of the Jewish intelligentsia—*Partisan Review*, *Commentary*, *The New York Review of Books*, and *The Public Interest*.

The movement for social reform has been closely intertwined with the strivings of the millions of immigrants who came to our shores. In 1976 Professors Gareth and Janet Dunleavy of the Department of English through their essay, "Reconstruction, Reform, and Romanism, 1865–1885," provided an Irish-American perspective on political reform, while in 1978 the late Elaine Fain of the School of Library Science documented the little-known role of the public libraries in assimilating immigrants and working as agents of social change in "Books for New Citizens: Public Libraries and Americanization Programs, 1900–1925."

Although many would dispute whether he was indeed a reformer, the "King Fish" of Louisiana politics, Huey P. Long, was without doubt a major actor in the politics of a reform era. Historian Glen Jeansonne in his 1979 lecture, "Utopia Comes to the Masses: Huey P. Long's Share-Our-Wealth Society," sought to provide a balanced view of a masterful political leader about whose legacy there is continuing dispute.

Expression of concerns for social justice takes many forms. Robert Burkert's 1980 presentation, "F.D.R., WPA, and Wisconsin Art of the Depression," effectively demonstrates the impact of the Depression and government programs on the artistic community. Through interviews with participants in the WPA art project in Wisconsin and reproductions of their work he captured much of the spirit that characterized an era of major social change.

The lectures collected in this volume provide a basis for understanding the road we have traveled as a nation since the Civil War and give insight into the future of America's quest for social justice. This contribution to the intellectual life of UWM, the Milwaukee metropolitan area, and Wisconsin has been made possible because of the generosity of the Fromkin family and the support for the program provided by the administration of the University. A major factor in the successful implementation of this program was the decision to give the Director of the UWM Library responsibility for administration of the lectures. William Roselle, Director of the UWM Library since 1971, has been the driving force behind the program. As a member of the Fromkin Lecture Committee for eight years, I can attest to his essential contributions. His commitment to the program has been unstinting, and the high standards which he demands have helped to insure the quality and prestige of the Lectures. This volume stands as a forthright statement and testimony to Morris Fromkin's goals, Bill Roselle's leadership, and the university scholar's role in helping us understand the dimensions of Americans' unceasing search for a better life for all our citizens.

John F. Bibby
Professor of Political Science
and Member of the Fromkin Lecture Committee
University of Wisconsin–Milwaukee

Milwaukee, Wisconsin
January, 1981

THE QUEST FOR SOCIAL JUSTICE

The Morris Fromkin Memorial Collection contains approximately 6,000 books, papers, and other materials about idealistic and reform movements in America. Wilbur Stolt, University Archivist, and Stanley Mallach, Fromkin Bibliographer, are pictured in the Collection's room at the Golda Meir Library.

The Historic Role of Constitutional Liberalism in the Quest for Social Justice[1]

WAYNE MORSE

MORRIS Fromkin[2] was on the side of liberal advocates of political and economic reform because he recognized it was essential to obtain social justice for all the people rather than special privileges for the selected few. The exploitation of labor under corporate industrialization, with its mass production and repressive labor policies, brought forth the militant organized labor movement of the 1880s and 1890s and on through to the 1930s and 1940s. The right of workers to organize into unions; the right to bargain collectively for agreements governing hours, wages, and conditions of employment; and the right to withhold their services by means of a strike, first against an individual employer and later against a group of employers in the same business on a regional or industry-wide basis, were eventually won by organized labor. These rights of social and economic justice were won over the bitter opposition of organized employer groups, opposition which led to much economic suffering for workers and their families and—all too frequently—physical injuries and bloodshed inflicted by employer goons and politically directed, overzealous police. During this long struggle for the rights of groups of workers to organize into unions and to withhold their services until

---

Wayne Morse (1900–1974), who was born in Madison, Wisconsin, received a bachelor's degree from the University of Wisconsin and a master's and LL.B. from the University of Minnesota. From 1931 to 1944 he was professor and dean of the College of Law at the University of Oregon, where he established himself as an authority on criminal justice. He was named to the National War Labor Board in 1942 and served until he ran for the United States Senate in 1945. He entered the Senate as a Republican in the Progressive tradition, became an independent in 1952, and finally a Democrat. He continued to serve as a mediator in labor disputes, being named to emergency boards to mediate national disputes involving railroads and maritime industries. After he left the Senate in 1969 he returned to labor arbitration and service on various government commissions.

a collective bargaining agreement could be consummated, the representatives of labor had to oppose vigorously not only strong anti-union employer opposition, often joined in by employer-sponsored non-union employees and company police, but antilabor political administrations, city and state. Even judges, both state and federal, dishonored their robes by issuing *ex parte* antilabor injunctions breaking strikes and boycotts.

"Government by injunction" became the protest battle cry of organized labor and of political liberals throughout the progressive period from the 1880s to the 1940s. Public confidence in the impartiality of the courts was damaged by disclosures of antilabor bias, the exercise of arbitrary and capricious discretion by too many former corporation lawyers and hack politicians who had been elevated to judgeships.

The very foundation of our constitutional guarantees of democratic self-government is our judicial system, which is charged with the obligation of dispensing evenhanded justice to all litigants.

I am satisfied that throughout our history most judges have been dedicated, honest dispensers of equal justice in accordance with the law as they have found it to be applicable to the operative facts of each case coming before them. Nevertheless, in the social, economic, and political turbulence of the progressive period, with its many conflicts over social-justice legislation, it became evident that, in too many instances, the donning of judicial robes did not cover the conflicts of interest, the biases against organized labor, and the partisan political prejudices against long overdue legislative reforms. Public criticism of many decisions involving social justice spread throughout the land. Although it was not limited to labor-law jurisprudence, it was in this area that some of the strongest political attacks against the courts were made.

Under our constitutional system of government, with its three coordinate and coequal branches of government, whenever public opinion starts losing confidence in the impartiality of judges, our national stability becomes seriously threatened. Such a trend of loss of confidence in members of the bench developed in the early years of this century, and renewed itself in the 1930s. . . .

Whenever the people in large numbers come to believe that legal procedures for the administration of justice limit or infringe upon their substantive legal rights, the courts are certain to come under justifiable attack. That happened in the progressive period. It is beginning to happen again today. The people must be shown, if they do not already know, that one of the characteristics of a police state is judicial tyranny. They must be made aware that their right to social justice can never be any better than their procedural rights for obtaining it, whether through the courts, through legislation, or through executive order. . . .

Granted, today we must have more judges, police, deputy prosecutors, administrative personnel, and law enforcement facilities, but these alone will not bring about public confidence in the men and women in charge of our procedures for administering justice. We should never forget that whenever public officials, including judges, are removed from the direct check of the general public . . . public confidence in their procedures and rulings is lessened. This happened in the progressive period, and we should learn the lessons of that era before it becomes too late in our time to avoid a constitutional crisis.

The federal judiciary came under widespread criticism in that period for its alleged antiunion bias and exercise of arbitrary discretion in adjudicating labor dispute cases. Antiunion employers found it not difficult to obtain injunctive relief from many federal judges well practiced in enjoining unions from picketing, from organizing employees against employer opposition, and from engaging in other standard union practices. Many of the injunctions were obtained by employers in *ex parte* hearings based upon employer charges of alleged violence or threats of violence or coercion of one type or another. "Union busting by antiunion judges" became a political charge of organized labor. Liberal political leaders in Wisconsin and other states . . . decided that the courts in fact were abusing their powers and supported labor's demand for legislation to curb the power of the courts in labor dispute cases.

The widespread public dissatisfaction with "government by injunction" . . . produced legislation in Congress and in several state legislatures designed to restrict the jurisdiction of courts in such cases. The Norris–La Guardia anti-injunction act of 1932 was an attempt by Congress to check the courts in their abuse of the injunction power. The National Labor Relations Board legislation of July, 1935, known as the Wagner Act, was another part of the answer to public criticism of the courts. Some state legislatures adopted similar state laws applicable to state cases not subject to federal jurisdiction.

For many years, the organizational picket line, stretched in front of an employer's plant or place of business as an economic inducement for him to recognize the union and proceed to bargain collectively with the union, was enjoined by many courts on one legal theory or another or one technicality or another. It was thought by labor leaders and their lawyers that after the passage of the Norris-La Guardia

Act organizational picket lines had been placed out of the reach of court injunctions.

It was in a celebrated Wisconsin labor case which reached the United States Supreme Court in 1938, *Lauf v. Shinner & Co.*,[3] that Morris Fromkin and his colleague, A. W. Richter, successfully argued that a labor union, none of whose members worked for a given employer, could not be enjoined from picketing that employer in an attempt to force him to permit the union to organize his plant. The case editor of the *Michigan Law Review*, commenting on the significance of the case, wrote, "A freedom from the impediments of the federal equity injunction greater than at any time since the rise of the labor movement now seems assured. . . ."[4]

Thus ended many years of bitter controversy over the right of labor to stretch the organizational picket lines which were finally authorized by the Norris–La Guardia anti-injunction act and sustained by the United States Supreme Court in *Lauf v. Shinner & Co.*[5] The thoroughly researched brief prepared by Morris Fromkin and his colleague was responsible for labor's historic victory in this case. It was a great advance for social justice in the labor movement. . . .

Morris Fromkin was a dedicated constitutional liberal who throughout his professional career devoted himself to the quest for social justice. His advice was frequently sought by and given to many liberal leaders during the late 1920s and 1930s. So-called radical leaders, like Emma Goldman, valued his advice. He was politically active in supporting the campaigns of liberal candidates in Wisconsin. He supported Victor Berger in his races for Congress, many of the La Follette Progressives in their campaigns, and Daniel Hoan, for many years the Socialist mayor of Milwaukee.

Our colonial forefathers revolted against monarchic government by kings and subservient parliaments exercising arbitrary, capricious, discretionary power over a subjugated colonial populace. They sought to set up a constitutional system of government by law which would guarantee protection to the people from government by executive supremacy and secrecy. Thus, they provided for three coordinate and coequal branches of government with each exercising prescribed constitutional checks upon the other two. They recognized an ever-present human factor, frequently overlooked or ignored throughout the history of our nation and even today: that our constitutional system, which was designed to give us a government by law, is nevertheless bound to be administered by mere men, with all their human frailties. Among these frailties is the temptation to usurp power and arbitrarily deny legal rights and social justice and to justify capricious discretion with intellectually dishonest rationalizations. Thus, too frequently men in office succumb to corruptive influences and desecrate their offices and bring government into disrepute.

From Lincoln to Franklin Roosevelt, liberal leaders and their many supporters . . . sought to obtain for all the people through the guarantees of the Constitution the liberties, civil rights, and political and economic freedoms for the individual which were envisioned by the people and their leaders when the Constitution was adopted. This, to my mind, is the definition of constitutional liberalism.

These constitutional guarantees involve the basic abstract principles of self-government whence come our rights as free men and women. The denial of these rights in varying degrees to too many people was the motivating cause of dissent which grew until it produced the liberal reform movements fighting for social justice throughout the Lincoln-to-Roosevelt period. . . .

I firmly believe that the self-government guarantees of the Constitution, with its checks-and-balances safeguards against government by mere men rather than by law, if faithfully administered, will assure social justice to the American people. The provisions for amending the Constitution, the delegating of duties, and the restricting of authority granted to the people's officials in the three branches of government, if faithfully carried out, offer our people their best hope of retaining self-government through law, and of obtaining a full measure of social justice for all.

The alternative? Obviously, a form of police state under which social justice disappears along with personal liberties.

Throughout the Lincoln-to-Roosevelt era, populist movements and their leaders, regardless of their political party labels, opposed powerful, reactionary political forces that sought to deny social justice by seeking to reverse the political tenet that public officials are to serve the people, not master them.

The populist crusaders fought under the banner "constant vigilance is the price of liberty." Underlying Lincoln's faith in self-government by the people was his dedication to the commitments set forth in the Preamble to the Constitution: "We the people of the United States, in Order to form a more perfect Union, establish Justice, insure domestic Tranquility, provide for the common defense, promote the general Welfare, and secure the Blessings of Liberty to ourselves and our Posterity, do ordain and establish this Constitution for the United States of America."

Lincoln recognized that if those statements of the purposes of the Constitution ever should be allowed to become empty rhetoric, self-government in the United States would cease to exist. . . . It is not trite to quote a famous Lincoln statement of governmental obligation to the people which has become a major premise used by liberals in their advocacy of government controls, regulation, and (if necessary for the protection of the public interest) ownership and operation of facilities and projects essential to promoting the general welfare. I refer to the well-known Lincoln teaching, "The legitimate object of government is to do for a community of people whatever they need to have done but cannot do at all, or cannot do so well, for themselves in their separate and individual capacities."

I submit that from the time of Lincoln, throughout the progressive period, right up to the present, the leading spokesmen for liberal and insurgent political movements, who have fought for social justice while advocating continued self-government, have been constitutional liberals in the sense that I have used the term. . . .

It is my judgment that of all the liberal movements in the country after Lincoln to the time of Franklin Roosevelt none accomplished so much in the quest for social justice as the populist movement in Wisconsin from 1890 to 1938. It would take a one-semester seminar course to cover, even in a cursory manner, the major contributions of Victor Berger, Daniel Hoan, Robert M. La Follette, Sr., Robert La Follette, Jr., his brother Philip, and all their liberal associates in and out of office during that period of time. The liberal legislative program of the La Follette era . . . became the pacesetter for state after state, as well as for the White House and Congress. How well I remember the several conversations I had with Franklin Roosevelt about Senator Robert M. La Follette, Sr., and the legislative policies he fought for.

As a member of the War Labor Board, in addition to participation in the adjudication of cases, I was assigned the responsibility of serving as compliance officer of the Board.[6] Those duties brought me into conference with President Roosevelt two or three times a month, because all major enforcement decisions of the Board against unions or management, as in seizure cases, required his personal approval. It was a great privilege to meet with him, and frequently after we had finished our discussion of a given compliance case he would seem to enjoy relaxing into a discussion of political issues. It was on several of these occasions, knowing my early Wisconsin background,[7] that he seemed to enjoy talking about La Follette's legislative record. He told me that he had been a close follower of what he called "Bob La Follette's phenomenal liberal political record both in Wisconsin as governor and in the Senate." He did not hesitate to tell me that the La Follette Wisconsin legislative program laid the groundwork for many of his own legislative proposals both when he was governor of New York and when he and his advisors promulgated the New Deal legislative program. . . .[8]

One way to evaluate the quest for social justice of the La Follette Progressive movement is to list a few of the legislative accomplishments associated with La Follette's name when he served as congressman, as governor, and as United States senator. In the field of legislation the record of a congressman, governor, or senator should be evaluated from the standpoint not only of the public-interest legislation he sponsors or helps to pass but also of the antipublic interest legislation he helps to defeat. Both are important in serving the people in their quest for social justice. Robert La Follette was an effective leader of the Progressives in marshalling support and developing strategy for the passage of good legislation and defeating bad legislation, measured in terms of that which best serves the social justice needs of his constituents.

When he was congressman, from 1885 to 1891, he successfully opposed a bill that sought to cheat the Indians out of valuable timber lands. During his service in the Congress he opposed railroad legislation that sought to authorize land grabs by railroad companies, and he battled against unjustifiable railroad subsidies. He helped block a bad canal bill and defeat an unreasonable ship subsidy bill. He helped pass an oleomargarine tax bill, important to the Wisconsin dairy industry. He fought for the creation of the Interstate Commerce Commission, which was sorely needed to help regulate the railroads, and the bill passed. He became recognized as a keen student of tariff, railroad, and tax legislation. One of his great successes, into which he put great effort, was the law establishing United States agricultural experiment stations. . . .

Some of the progressive laws enacted while La Follette was governor, from 1901 to 1905, were the precedent-setting primary election law, child labor, income tax, inheritance tax, and civil service laws, railroad taxation and regulation, protection of women from excessive hours of work, conservation measures, insurance regulation, the regulation of state banks, and the formation of the Industrial Commission. In his message to the legislature on January 15, 1903, he recommended compensation to railroad men for injuries suffered on the job through no fault of their own, a suggestion which led to a workmen's compensation law which became a model for the nation.

As United States senator, from 1906 to 1925, Robert La Follette sought social justice through equality of civil rights and through the retention of freedom of economic choice for everyone.

In these days of misunderstanding as to the obligations which universities owe to students, faculty, the public, and the state, it is well to remember that constitutional liberals do not retreat from preserving academic freedom. The Morris Fromkin Memorial Collection and its program are in the best tradition of maintaining academic freedom and fulfilling the obligations of the university to the state. When Bob La Follette, as governor of Wisconsin, was charged with political partiality in his selection of Dr. Charles Van Hise as president of the University of Wisconsin, he expressed his strong support of the declaration of academic freedom made by the board of regents at the time Dr. Richard Ely was tried for economic heresy. . . .

In the field of foreign policy, constitutional liberals have a duty to oppose Presidential requests for authority which exceed constitutional Presidential powers. Unfortunately, many liberals, under the pressure of political expediency, have voted for resolutions requested by Presidents authorizing the use of American military forces in combat on foreign soil without a declaration of war. One of these requests was made by President Woodrow Wilson in April, 1914, when he asked Congress for approval to "use the armed forces of the United States in Mexico in such ways and to such an extent as may be necessary to obtain from Gen. Huerta and his adherents the fullest recognition of the rights and dignity of the United States. . . ."[9] It was a forerunner by many years of the Formosa, Middle East, and Gulf of Tonkin resolutions of the Eisenhower and Johnson administrations.

While the resolution was pending before Congress, President Wilson ordered Admiral Fletcher to seize Vera Cruz. During this action four American Marines were killed and twenty wounded; 126 Mexicans were killed and 195 wounded. . . .

On March 10, 1916, in a speech in the Senate, La Follette . . . said,

> I believe it to be vital to the safety and perpetuity of this government that Congress should assert and maintain its right to a voice in declaring and prescribing the foreign policy of the United States. . . . Democratic control of foreign policies is a basic principle of all organized effort looking for the future establishment of permanent world peace. . . . Shall we in this crisis of the world's history fail to assert our constitutional rights and by our negligence and default permit the establishment in this country of that exclusive Executive control over foreign affairs that the people of Europe are now repenting amid the agonies of war? . . . There never was a time in history when it was more fundamentally important that we preserve intact the essential principle of democracy on which our Government is founded—that the will of the people is the law of the land. . . .[10]

The advice-and-consent clause does not mean that the advice and consent of the Congress should be sought by the President after the fact. It means that he should seek it before the fact. Constitutional liberals should recognize that Presidents have no constitutional right to make war without a declaration of war. . . .

Presidents have no legal right to make war in the name of acting as commander-in-chief of the armed forces. They have the duty to respond to the self-defense of the republic if our nation is suddenly attacked, as the Japanese attacked us at Pearl Harbor. In that crisis, Franklin Roosevelt, as commander-in-chief, went to the immediate self-defense of our nation, but he also went to his desk and wrote his great war message calling for a declaration of war. . . .

I have mentioned the issue of the fast-growing trend in our country toward government by executive supremacy and secrecy because it is the major issue that the liberal movements since the Civil War have made the least progress in checking and solving in the interest of the people. It threatens to create a constitutional crisis. More than 44,000 American soldiers have died and more than 275,000 have been wounded in Asia because Congress has not checked Presidents from conducting an illegal, immoral, and unjustifiable war in Asia.

I would suggest that in the last decade there have developed so many changes in the life patterns of our people that mythology has come to characterize much of our American way of life. Some aspects of it are no longer relevant, or, I prefer to say, serviceable, in the solving of the crises that confront our nation. To determine what is still valid in this electronic world of computers and to discard all the rest without losing our individual liberty is the most serious problem facing us today. . . .

The Morris Fromkin Collection, in furnishing the resources for studying the contributions of the great constitutional liberals to whom we owe so much, is a magnificent conception with exciting possibilities. Its records of the liberal movements in American politics and their quests for social justice from the time of the Civil War to the era of the New Deal should provide much valuable material for historical research and analysis.

How many heroic fights, lost in the welter of day-to-day happenings, went unrecorded! How many valuable files lie hidden in attics or mouldering in basements! How many profiles of courage remain to be written! It is in reference to those battlers for social justice that the Morris Fromkin bequest, with its research and educational program, will perform a great historical service. Where did the reforms go wrong that we have so much violent protest against our institutions—even the Constitution itself? "The past is prologue." By providing the materials for examining, surveying, evaluating, and interpreting this period of ferment in our history—so little understood by most Americans—the Morris Fromkin Collection will make a significant contribution to the perpetuation of constitutional self-government in America.

NOTES

1 Stanley Mallach, Bibliographer of the Fromkin Memorial Collection, transcribed Senator Morse's lecture and edited an annotated version which appeared in the *Transactions* of the Wisconsin Academy of Sciences, Arts, and Letters 66 (1978). The present text and footnotes, which include some additions (from the taped lecture) to Mr. Mallach's text, are reprinted by permission of the Academy and Mrs. Wayne Morse.
2 Of Morris Fromkin, Senator Morse said:

> I came to know Morris Fromkin through our mutual interests and activities in the field of labor relations. When I was on the National War Labor Board, I met him first, as I recall, in Milwaukee through Joseph Padway [the legal counsel for the American Federation of Labor]. . . . He possessed a brilliant mind and a social conscience that directed him into crusades seeking social justice for individuals and groups to whom justice was being denied.
>
> Morris Fromkin was a learned lawyer who developed a flourishing law practice in Milwaukee from 1920 to 1946. He then moved to New York City where he continued to be a very successful leader of the Bar until his death, April 24, 1969. His office practice rested on a broad base of labor law, corporation law, and a general practice serving the legal and social justice needs of the rich and the poor, as well as clients of average means.
>
> He was born in Russia. After the death of his mother, when he was a young boy, his father migrated to the United States, bringing Morris and his brothers and sisters with him, and settled on the Lower East Side of New York City. Young Morris went to work with his father in a factory. It was there that he learned that urban industrialization, crowded conditions in substandard housing, low wages for long hours of work, high prices, and limited educational opportunities contributed to the denial of social justice to many immigrants and other underprivileged workers.
>
> Economic and social ruts can become deep and confining in any congested urban industrial area, even though the streets may be of asphalt and stone. Morris Fromkin came from a family that would not be rutted. The family helped each other, and Morris worked hard for his education. With scholarships and outside jobs he worked his way through Creighton University in Omaha, Nebraska, attaining his B.A. degree in 1918. He then went to Marquette University Law School in Milwaukee, where he obtained his LL.B. degree in 1920. During the First World War Morris Fromkin served in the United States Field Artillery and saw active duty in France, notably in the St. Mihiel salient.
>
> From this background, it is understandable that in his law practice he provided much free legal service to many immigrants and indigents who otherwise would have been denied justice. He was a liberal lawyer in the sense that he recognized

that if social justice and legal rights are denied to the economically disadvantaged because they cannot meet the price tag, then government by law—the foundation of political self-government—will disintegrate.

He was a liberal lawyer also in the sense that he recognized that a decent standard of living for all those willing and able to work is essential to the survival of our system of economic and political self-government. Thus, he took an active interest in many struggling social justice movements: collective bargaining for labor unions, programs of the Grange and other farmer groups, and, most particularly, the political reform proposals of liberal leaders of all political persuasions—Governor Altgeld, a Democrat of Illinois; Senator La Follette, a progressive Republican of Wisconsin; Senator Norris, a liberal Republican of Nebraska; Victor Berger and Daniel Hoan, Socialists of Wisconsin; and many leaders of the Farmer-Labor Party in Minnesota, the Nonpartisan League of North Dakota, as well as liberal leaders and organizations in other states.

3 Lauf v. Shinner & Co., 303 U.S. 323 (1938). The case involved "stranger picketing," a situation in which the picket line around a struck firm was manned by people who were not and usually never had been employees of the firm. Neither the Norris–La Guardia Act nor the Wisconsin Labor Code specifically included stranger picketing in its definition of a labor dispute. The question the United States Supreme Court confronted was whether the stranger picket in Lauf did indeed constitute a labor dispute under the provisions of the Norris–La Guardia Act and was therefore protected from being enjoined. The larger question the Court spoke on in its decision was the power of Congress to limit the injunctive power of courts in labor disputes.

The case concerned a firm that operated five meat markets in Milwaukee and a labor union to which none of the firm's employees belonged. The union came to the firm and demanded that it require its employees to join the union as a condition of employment. The firm told its employees they were free to join the union, but none did. The union then began picketing the firm's markets to force the employer to require his employees to join the union as a condition of employment or to drive the firm out of Milwaukee. In picketing Shinner's meat markets the union resorted to some unseemly tactics, such as physically intimidating prospective customers. Taking no notice of these tactics, but dealing with the question of the legality of the picket itself, a Federal District Court enjoined the picket on the ground that no labor dispute existed between the firm and the union. The Circuit Court of Appeals affirmed the decision. The Supreme Court reversed the lower court decisions by finding that a labor dispute did exist under the provisions of the Norris–La Guardia Act and the Wisconsin Labor Code and that therefore the picket could not be enjoined. On stranger picketing, see also American Federation of Labor v. Swing, 312 U.S. 321 (1941).

4 Erwin B. Ellmann, "When a 'Labor Dispute' Exists Within the Meaning of the Norris–La Guardia Act," *Michigan Law Review* 36 (May 1938): 1147. In his comment Ellmann was writing not only about Lauf v. Shinner, but

also about New Negro Alliance v. Sanitary Grocery Co., which likewise involved stranger picketing.
5 Senator Morse slightly exaggerates the importance of the Norris–La Guardia Act and Lauf v. Shinner & Co. in making picketing immune from judicial attacks. Other laws and cases were equally important. Among these were the Wagner Act, which created the National Labor Relations Board to regulate labor relations in the United States; N.L.R.B. v. Jones & Laughlin Steel Corp., 301 U.S. 1 (1937), and other cases which upheld the constitutionality of the Wagner Act; and Thornhill v. Alabama, 310 U. S. 88 (1940), in which the Supreme Court brought picketing under the protection of the First Amendment as an exercise of free speech. After the Thornhill decision, however, the Court modified its implicit position that picketing was absolutely protected as a form of communication and put the legality of pickets and injunctions against pickets on a case-by-case basis in Milk Wagon Drivers' Union v. Meadowmoor Dairies, 312 U.S. 287 (1941), and Carpenters and Joiners Union v. Ritter's Cafe, 312 U. S. 722 (1942).
6 Morse served as a public representative on the Board from 1942 to 1944.
7 Morse was born in Madison and educated at the University of Wisconsin. He taught there in 1924, after which he went to Minnesota to continue his education.
8 In an aside containing some chronological confusion and error Senator Morse reflects upon some of his education experiences:

> I shall always be indebted to the University of Wisconsin at Madison for the opportunity to study the pros and cons of many aspects of the liberal political movement in Wisconsin, with special attention to its legislative program. It was my good fortune to study labor economics under Professor Edwin Witte and Professor Selig Perlman. In one of their graduate seminars they would often ask the incomparable Dr. John R. Commons, who had retired from active teaching, to lead the discussions. For years he had been a close adviser to Robert La Follette, Sr.; and as it is recorded in the La Follette biographies, Dr. Commons made many contributions to La Follette's legislative programs. Likewise, the writings and advice of Professor Witte and Professor Perlman left their hallmark on the labor legislative program of the La Follette Progressive movement. Professor Witte became recognized as one of the architects of the Social Security System and a leading authority on workmen's compensation, labor pensions, and welfare legislation.
>
> Another teacher, among many at the University of Wisconsin who stimulated my study of political movements in Wisconsin, was my debate coach, Professor Andrew Weaver, the chairman of the Speech Department and father of the president-designate of the University of Wisconsin. These great constitutional liberals furnished much of the intellectual vitality of the period and cannot be left out of any survey.

9 Quoted in Belle C. and Fola La Follette, *Robert M. La Follette* (New York: Macmillan Company, 1953), 1:496.
10 Quoted ibid., p. 560.

PLEASE POST

HEAR
FIGHTING BOB
La Follette
~OCT. 28~

FINE ARTS TH...

THE UNIVERS...
OF
WISCONS...
MILWAU...

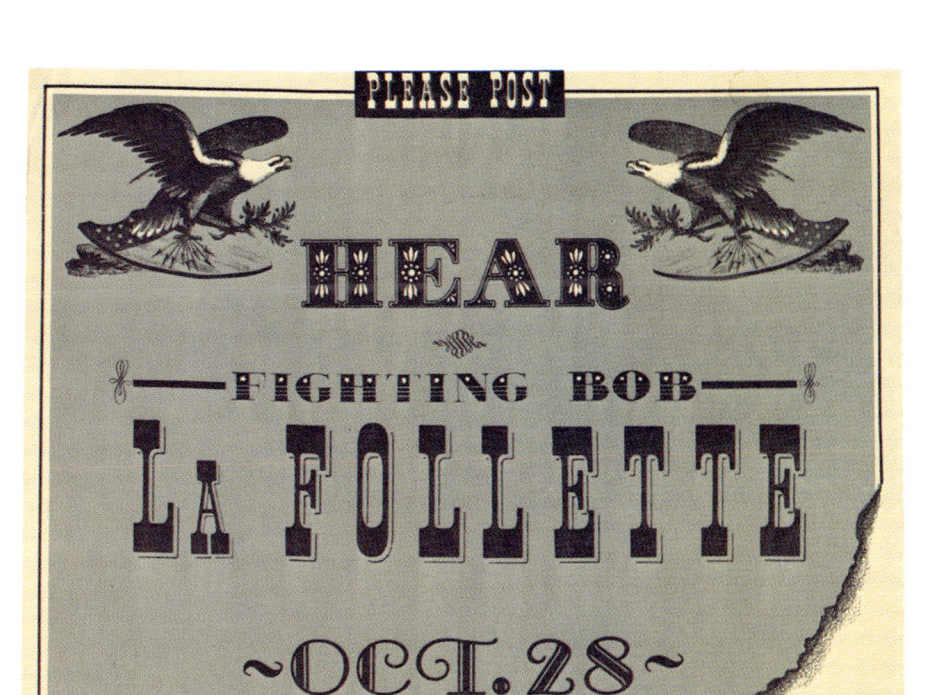

FREE
FREE
FRE...

MORRIS FROMKIN
MEMORIAL LECTURE

David P. Thelen
ASSOCIATE PROFESSOR OF HISTORY
UNIVERSITY OF MISSOURI COLUMBIA

CONSUMER MASS POLITICS:
A New Look at 'Old Bob' La Follette

FINE ARTS THEATER
THE UNIVERSITY OF WISCONSIN-MILWAUKEE

8pm Thursday, October 28, 1971
RECEPTION FOLLOWING LECTURE

SPONSORED BY THE FROMKIN MEMORIAL
COLLECTION OF THE UWM LIBRARY

NO ADMISSION CHARGE

Patterns of Consumer Consciousness in the Progressive Movement: Robert M. La Follette, the Antitrust Persuasion, and Labor Legislation

DAVID P. THELEN

INDUSTRIAL capitalism alienated production from consumption. In the preindustrial world of plantation, feudal, and self-sufficient agriculture, households united production with consumption as their members grew or made what they needed to eat or wear. While guided by the skills and traditions of their crafts, artisans expected consumers to discipline the nature, quality, and price of their products through face-to-face interchanges, community traditions, and public regulations. But when they have considered the alienation of consumption from production that accompanied the development of market agriculture and manufacturing, social scientists of all ideological persuasions have generally focused on the alienation of the producer. They have traced how workers lost ownership of their tools, skills, and pace of work to the new industrialists. Focusing on efforts by producers to escape the insecurities of the new competitive order, liberals and modernization theorists have described efforts by producers to organize into labor unions or farm groups to readjust power relationships among producing groups and to secure support from government, while Marxists have traced how workers sought to preserve their traditional values and to resist the new order by forming unique working-class cultures and institutions. Consumers,

---

David P. Thelen, who received his graduate training in American history at the University of Wisconsin–Madison, has written extensively on La Follette and Progressivism. Among his books are *The Early Life of Robert M. La Follette, 1855–1884* (1966) and *Robert M. La Follette and the Insurgent Spirit* (1976).

to the extent that they receive any attention in these analyses of industrial society, are generally viewed as passive practitioners of the new ethic of conspicuous consumption, as pawns, frequently narcissistic, to be manipulated by Madison Avenue. In these views consumption is a passive and unsatisfying process, while production is active and meaningful. When historians like Richard Hofstadter and Christopher Lasch have found consumer consciousness in movements to resist the new order, they have traced consumer alienation to the particular status insecurities of particular groups of upper-middle-class consumers who become radicals and reformers more from the experiences of their class and status groups than from the experiences of consumption itself.[1]

This essay will explore the alienation of consumption from production, but it will focus on consumers, not producers. It will examine the drive by consumers to restore discipline over productive processes, a drive that gave distinctive elements to the American progressive movement of the early twentieth century. Yearning to recover their former power to control the quality and ways that goods were made in the self-sufficient world where production and consumption were united, consumers in the early twentieth century found common ground with groups of alienated producers in attacking the new big businesses for the ways they made goods and for the unprecedented profits they extorted alike from consumers and workers. In both the movements that sought consumer control over corporations and middlemen and in their cooperative movements with alienated workers to discipline the ways goods were made, consumers tried, most fundamentally, to reunite consumption with production. In so doing, they developed a basic new critique of industrial capitalism and evolved mechanisms for mobilizing majority sentiment in democratic societies.

Robert M. La Follette served as a political focus for groups of angry consumers and workers during the progressive era. His political career revealed ways that consumer consciousness developed a strongly prolabor orientation. "The welfare of all the people as consumers should be the supreme consideration of the Government," he proclaimed in his first major speech in the Senate on April 23, 1906.[2] On this occasion he was promoting railroad regulation, but he reiterated the same basic tenet over the next decade in his campaigns for conservation, trust-busting, tariff reform, banking reform, direct democracy, tax reform, and pure foods and medicines. At the same time, however, consumer champion La Follette earned the gratitude of workers and labor unions as their best friend in the Senate. The major laws to bear the name of consumer champion La Follette were labor laws: the Lloyd–La Follette Act of 1912, which granted government workers the right of free speech and the power to form labor unions, and the La Follette Seamen's Act of 1915, which greatly strengthened the seamen's union as it freed seamen from virtual enslavement by ship owners. Recognizing a friend in this consumer champion, F. P. Lamoreux, editor of the *Fresno Labor News,* declared in 1912 that "La Follette has . . . done more for the toilers than any other living representative of an oppressed people."[3] How, then, did La Follette's consumer orientation lead him to promote and secure the enactment of legislation to help workers and unions? The answer to this question points to the need to take more seriously the alienation of consumers, to recognize that consumers generated profoundly a radical resistance to and critique of industrial capitalism, and that, on the political level, consumers were invaluable allies of alienated workers.

I

The roots of the consumer consciousness that reached organized political form in the progressive movement reached back to the earliest efforts by consumers to restore discipline over production. As consumers sought to retain control over production in an ever-expanding market economy, they drew on the economic experience of the household and its resulting values of the family. "The distinguishing feature of all democracies of consumers," wrote Beatrice and Sidney Webb, "is that their intellectual birthplace is not the factory or the workshop, but the home."[4] Rooted in the values of home and family, consumer consciousness naturally focused on the defense of neighborhood and community. Consumer consciousness was profoundly local in orientation since consumption remained a local experience whose natural unit was the home at a time when the expanding market economy made production an increasingly national and international process in which producer-oriented groups sought relief from market insecurities by federating at the national level. As the carrier of family values and the local tradition of community discipline over behavior, consumer consciousness tended to preserve a moral vision of human relationships against the secularizing, competitive, and economic thrusts of the market economy in order to preserve community-wide public control over the price and quality of goods and services. Believing in the words of Charles Gide that "the producer only exists for the benefit of the consumer," consumer consciousness has generally sought not so much lower prices as "nothing less than the destruction of capital" by "abolishing the pursuit of profit as the only real motive of economic activity."[5] In attempting to restore the traditional unity of production and consumption, consumer movements have particularly attacked the emerging layers of middlemen and the process of monopolization that grew to separate what households grew and made from what they ate and wore. Even Adam Smith conceded that English laws from the time of Edward VI to Charles II basically reflected the "popular odium" against middlemen, as consumers successfully controlled public policy over the grain and bread markets.[6] When middlemen gained growing power with the repeal of ancient public regulations over prices, usury, and middlemen, when capital became increasingly concentrated into fewer hands, consumer consciousness developed its antimonopoly and antimiddleman themes.

Uniting consumers at the community level across the ever-widening barriers of occupation, consumer consciousness also tended to generate a political outlook that reflected the recognition that consumers were the only political majority in an industrial society. Believing that minority producers increasingly controlled the representative political institutions that evolved in the eighteenth and nineteenth centuries, consumers sought political institutions that would respond directly to majority pressures and thereby permit consumers to discipline producers. Frustrated by the growing tendency of political institutions to reward minority and powerful producers, consumer movements soon developed the weapons of exposure, publicity, and mass pressure through oratory, petitions, and mass media that united readers or listeners across class and ethnic barriers. Exposure was one thing minority producers could not endure, because it implied that the majority in its common capacity as consumers was rallying to reassert the older family and community disciplines.

Modern patterns of consumer consciousness began to appear when the "invisible hand" of competition increasingly replaced local and public controls as the basic regulator of economic behavior. "In urban and rural communities alike, a consumer-consciousness preceded all other forms of political or industrial antagonism," wrote E. P. Thompson in his path-breaking social analysis of industrialization.[7] By the end of the eighteenth century, consumer protests had become organized direct action. In English and French communities consumers attacked middlemen and rulers who seemed to drive up the price of bread, culminating in the Parisian riots that heralded the

French Revolution. Hatred of government-sponsored monopoly that interfered in traditional consumption patterns led tea drinkers in Boston to board the ships and destroy the tea of the monopolistic East India Company. Anger at taxes on consumption levied by remote and unresponsive political elites helped trigger the American Revolution.

As the emerging market economy stimulated the development of industrial capitalism, nineteenth-century consumers developed new patterns to assert the old yearnings for local and community control, family and moral yardsticks to regulate social relationships, hatred of monopoly, reunification of production with consumption, and direct action. Although ethno-religious identity and to a lesser degree class affiliation bordered some of these patterns, consumers from all backgrounds created remarkably similar agencies to restore control and supplant middlemen. The most popular and persistent agency was the consumer-owned cooperative that served its members with higher quality, lower prices, or more responsive services than the new private middlemen. Purchasers of homes, for example, sought to escape private bankers and their high mortgage rates by creating building and loan societies through which members pooled their savings and lent money to each other to purchase homes. In Missouri, for example, the first building and loan society was formed by a group of thirty German immigrants in Kansas City in 1868, and within a quarter of a century the state had 313 separate building and loan associations with 71,578 members and resources that totalled almost a third of those in all the private banks.[8] Local groups of homeowners similarly pooled their resources to insure their members against fire, lightning, and wind damage in county-level, consumer-owned, mutual insurance companies that charged their policyholder-owners a third the rate of private fire insurance companies. Such consumer-owned mutuals first appeared in Missouri, for example, in the 1870s, and by 1906, 120 separate companies had 100,000 members and insured risks of over $200 million.[9] Hoping to bring "the producers and consumers of agricultural implements and products together," the Granger movement of the mid-1870s established cooperative stores where their members could receive lower prices than from private merchants. Within two years of its founding, the Missouri Grangers' wholesale store in St. Louis did over a million dollars in business.[10] The most famous of the drives to escape the high prices and interest rates of private middlemen centered in the network of farmer organizations that came together in the Populist movement of the late 1880s and early 1890s. The movement developed a vibrant culture that centered around local cooperative stores through which farmers hoped to preserve their very lands and independence against credit merchants and bankers whose prices and interest rates drove them into tenancy.[11] Echoing a century-old lament by consumers that middlemen who intervened between production and consumption added eighty percent to the cost of living, H. J. Bowen, manager of the Producers and Consumers Co-operative Market at St. Joseph, Missouri, put the issue simply in 1913: "The middleman is the vermiform appendix attached to the bowels of civilization and . . . he should be cut out."[12]

The formal consumer cooperatives that best revealed many strands of consumer consciousness in nineteenth-century America were the fraternal insurance lodges that grew from pre–Civil War origins—in orders like the Masons and Odd Fellows—to embrace hundreds of orders, tens of thousands of local lodges, and, in Missouri alone, 703,232 members in 1914.[13] By 1885 residents of the Bollinger County, Missouri, village of Lutesville, population 235, could choose among local lodges of the Masons, Odd Fellows, and Ancient Order of United Workmen, and that year the 1394 residents of Farmington could choose among the Knights of Pythias, Knights of Honor, Masons, Odd Fellows, and A.O.U.W.[14] The new brotherhoods offered the doctrine and economic means of mutual assistance to members in times of greatest need. Defying the capitalist approach of permitting stockholders to make a profit from the daily operation of mutual aid, of permitting wealthier policyholders to purchase more insurance than poorer policyholders, the fraternal orders required each member to contribute equally to the resources of the order and to share equally in its benefits in those times of distress—illness, accident, death, loss of job—when no single individual could bear the burden. Like other consumer movements, the fraternal movement originated in the traditional paternal and fraternal obligations of the male family head toward his brothers and dependents. Fraternalism rose to such popularity because it used fraternal obligations and discipline to preserve the paternal responsibility to insure that children would survive their father's death, illness, or unemployment to live healthy lives. Rejecting control over behavior by the impersonal "invisible hand" of the market or the very visible hand of their employers, fraternal orders carefully guarded admission to their lodges while practicing elaborate rituals and following rules that would preserve feelings of brotherhood and family responsibility. And they could never be good family members within the lodge if they were not good family members at home. Palmyra, Missouri's Amicitia Lodge 32, Knights of Pythias, dismissed James S. Spear in 1885 for neglecting his family; and the Springfield, Missouri, Lodge 85 of the same order suspended J. H. Fishpool in 1891 for a year because he assaulted his wife.[15]

The fraternal movement sought to preserve local communities by admitting members according to the traditional criteria of people's moral, social, and neighborly qualities rather than the modern criterion, their jobs. The Modern Woodmen of America's Russell Camp 2065, Sedalia, Missouri, included among its members in 1901 Mayor Walter C. Overstreet, laborer James D. Creegan, butcher Joseph Paradis, architect E. A. Strong, machinist George R. Fletcher, Baptist preacher James M. Plunnett, clerk Joseph Kraus, grocer Sol Rosenthal, mason James Wilkerson, teacher Charles A. Deppe, driver Perry C. Huntsman, and shoemaker Thomas J. Solon. Reflecting the preference for the criterion of neighborliness rather than occupation, 26 percent of the members of Odd Fellows Lodge 26 at Hannibal, Missouri, in 1901 were laborers, 42 percent were artisans, 13 percent were merchants, 5 percent were manufacturers and managers, 8 percent were engaged in sales and clerical occupations, and 5 percent were professionals.[16] By the turn of the century Americans had experienced in their fraternal orders a cooperative challenge to monopolistic middlemen that had united consumers in their local communities across class lines by criteria that focused around preservation of the family, the taproot of consumer consciousness.

II

Modern consumer consciousness began to take the organized political shape of progressivism in response to new threats that forced consumers to enter the political arena. This new shape resulted from rapid urbanization and the resulting development of a new type, the urban consumer, who was completely dependent on others to perform the traditional household activities that in the past had defined household self-sufficiency. The classic consumer-oriented statement of the problem was written by Edward A. Ross in 1907: "Nowadays the water main is my well, the trolley car my carriage, the banker's safe my old stocking, the policeman's billy my fist. . . . I let the meat trust butcher my pig, the oil trust mould my candles, the sugar trust boil my sorghum, the coal trust chop my wood, the barb wire trust split my rails."[17]

There lay the challenge. By the early twentieth century, monopolistic corporations had acquired control of the basic services required by the urban consumer, particularly the utilities that provided consumers with transportation, heat, light, water, and sewage removal. And these private utilities maintained their control by dominating local politics and obtaining long-term, monopolistic franchises from local governments. These private utilities responded to the revenue crisis that accompanied the disastrous depression of 1893–97 by curtailing services, raising fares and rates, and refusing to accommodate consumers' basic needs for health and safety. Failure to provide healthful drinking water translated into epidemics of disease and death. Failure to install bumpers on streetcars translated into thousands of injuries and hundreds of deaths in most cities for the passengers and pedestrians who were mangled under the streetcars' wheels. When consumers sought redress in the political process, they ran straight up against a tight alliance of utility executives and political leaders. In Milwaukee, for example, the two top officials of the transportation and lighting monopoly were the statewide bosses of the Republican and Democratic parties. As a result, desperate consumers were forced to develop radical political and economic alternatives to the prevailing arrangements. These grassroots protests by utility consumers across class and ethnic lines became the origins of the progressive movement. Frustrated when consumer protests were ignored by city councils and state legislatures who were more interested in the money of the utilities and the patronage of utility-oriented political leaders than in their constituents, the consumer-conscious progressives developed political methods that provided for direct policymaking by voters (including the initiative and referendum, direct primary nominations of candidates, and popular votes on utility franchises), for local home rule (which would permit angry local citizens to deal with utility issues in their home communities instead of leaving them to remote state legislators who never seemed to understand the local anger), and for radical economic programs (like public ownership of utilities which would put control over urban services in the hands of consumers and taxpayers instead of stockholders and profit-oriented managers).[18]

Originating in these local crusades against utilities, the consumer-conscious drive against privileged and concentrated wealth moved to the national political arena in the early twentieth century as consumers experienced the corrosive effects of inflation for the first time in their lifetimes. For the first time in two generations prices rose faster than incomes. From 1865 to 1897 wage earners had gained from a general deflationary trend: Wages had fallen less than 10 percent while prices in general had fallen 35 to 40 percent and prices of necessities had fallen even more sharply—food by 61 percent, fuel by

70 percent. Blue- and white-collar workers were stunned by their sudden experience with inflation. From 1897 to 1909 wages rose about 22 percent while prices in general rose about 35 percent and prices on necessities rose even faster—food by 37 percent and fuel by 53 percent. Consumer-oriented Americans quickly concluded that the basic cause of soaring prices was the rapid growth of monopolistic businesses which raised their prices as they absorbed their competition. In the six years ending in 1897, forty-two important "trusts" were formed, but in the six years following 1897, 317 important "trusts" were launched, including United States Steel, International Harvester, and Standard Oil. The total capitalization of all million-dollar corporations jumped 120 times from 1897 to 1904, from $170 million to $20 billion.[19] "The real power emerging to-day in democratic politics is just the mass of people who are crying out against the 'high cost of living.' That is a consumer's cry," concluded Walter Lippmann in 1914. "We hear a great deal about the class-consciousness of labor; my own observation is that in America to-day consumers'-consciousness is growing very much faster."[20]

This basic grassroots revolt by consumers incorporated the traditional patterns of consumer consciousness as it evolved new ways for consumers to recapture control over producers and policymaking. During its heyday, from the antiutility crusades of the mid-1890s until it perished in the engines of wartime production in the mid-1910s, the consumer revolt created progressive spokespersons with a distinctive ideology and style of political leadership. The basic problem for all who sought to direct the consumer revolt toward basic changes in the political economy resulted from the historic contradiction for consumers in democratic societies: They were, on the one hand, the vast majority of citizens whose will ought by definition to prevail when they agreed on a particular solution, and they were, on the other hand, very poorly organized when compared to other groups. The prevailing structures and traditions of politics and government had evolved to respond to producer-oriented groups, ethno-religious voting blocs, and patronage needs. These structures and traditions created political leaders who believed that production was the highest good, that well-organized groups of producers, particularly corporations, had the only programs worth considering because they could deliver the money, votes, and information required to reelect politicians, and that the mass base of American politics rested on ethnic, religious, and sectional conflicts which politicians needed to heed.

Robert M. La Follette wrestled with these problems as he evolved into the most prominent consumer champion in the national political arena in the early twentieth century. During his terms as county district attorney (1881–85) and Congressman from Wisconsin (1885–91), La Follette always differed from other politicians in his acute sensitivity to the wishes of his constituents and his eagerness to build political organizations that were devoted exclusively to his own political career instead of relying on established party machines. To his natural responsiveness to majority sentiments, La Follette in 1897 added a consumer-oriented program in response to the antiutility crusades that echoed from one Wisconsin community to the next. In this initial championship of progressive measures he was, as Wisconsin's leading newspaper observed, one of "the party leaders who try to find out what the popular current is, what the people want. . . . They may give effect to forces already at work and they may profit, too, by their recognition and understanding of these forces."[21] Replacing the caucus and convention system of nominations with the direct primary, La Follette maintained, "brought the business of choosing candidates back to the basic principle of pure democratic government. It eliminated the boss and the machine. . . . It proclaimed to the world that the people proposed to take charge of the business of government for themselves."[22] From his initial championship of the direct primary in 1897, to his successful shepherding of the measure through the Wisconsin legislature in 1903 and its ratification by Wisconsin voters in 1904, to his national promotion of presidential primaries that culminated in the first presidential primaries in the election of 1912, La Follette pushed a new political method that would simultaneously "emancipate the majority from its enslavement," thereby giving power to the unorganized majority of consumers, and produce the nomination of popular candidates who, like him, would not let minority producer and ethnic groups and established party organizations stop them from advocating popular, consumer-oriented issues.[23]

Although La Follette concentrated on converting popular issues into legislative policies, he came by 1910 to embrace the initiative and referendum system of elections whereby voters could enact laws directly at the ballot box. From its origins the movement for the initiative and referendum was seen by both proponents and opponents as a way to mobilize poorly organized majorities against corporations. "Over the heads of the politicians in conventions and legislatures and councils we may make our appeal to the people direct," declared Cincinnati's antimonopoly advocate Herbert S. Bigelow. "The corporations . . . will have to come out in the open and meet us, not with bribes and lawmakers, but with arguments to the people."[24] Opposition to an initiative and referendum proposal for the Michigan Constitutional Convention of 1908 was led by F. E. Carter, president of the Michigan Businessmen's Association and the Michigan National Bank. A corporate spokesman at that convention attacked the initiative and referendum because "it is democracy pure and simple. Opening the door for pure democracy is something I very much deplore."[25] Corporate leaders profoundly feared a mobilized majority of consumers who could make policy directly. When conservative senators walked off the Senate floor to protest La Follette's demand for a strong antitrust measure to protect consumers from monopoly in 1911, he digressed: "Need anyone marvel that there is a great uprising throughout this country for a restoration of government to the people? . . . They demand the initiative, the referendum, and the recall in order to insure" that the United States remain "a people's government."[26]

Like previous consumer champions, La Follette and other progressives depended heavily on exposure of the ways in which corporations were using the structures and traditions of representative government to frustrate campaigns by consumers and majorities. Over his five years as governor, as he faced mounting opposition from a corporate-oriented faction in his party, La Follette gradually modified his approach to political leadership from a dependence on a loose confederation of lieutenants throughout the state to deliver the vote to a dependence on newspapers like the *Milwaukee Free Press* that he controlled and the national popular magazines. As his own organization began to crumble in his 1904 campaign for renomination and reelection, La Follette came to rely on the national muckrakers to convince Wisconsin voters that he truly represented majority sentiment. La Follette believed that Lincoln Steffens' article in *McClure's* was the most important cause of his reelection.[27] Trying to compel legislators to heed majority sentiment in their districts, La Follette devised the method of exposing to a representative's constituents the legislative votes in which their representative sided with corporations and against consumers. Beginning in his second term by "reading the roll call" in Wisconsin communities whose representatives had voted against his railroad regulation bill, La Follette carried this technique of exposure to the national level when he moved to the Senate in 1906. On speaking tours between sessions of Congress he exposed the votes of his audiences' senators against consumer measures, and the "Roll Call" became an important feature of *La Follette's Weekly Magazine* when he launched it in 1909.

Consumer champions like La Follette concluded that the most effective way they could secure consumer-oriented, antimonopoly legislation was not by negotiating with conservative fellow politicians to produce compromised measures but by cooperating with other major consumer champions, the journalists who wrote exposures for the popular daily "yellow" newspapers and muckraking magazines. "The great volume of the cheaper magazines which are circulating among the people and which have become the people's literature have wrought almost a mental and moral revolution among the people," concluded Indiana progressive Senator Albert J. Beveridge to his Kansas colleague, Joseph L. Bristow, in 1910.[28] Maintaining that "the press and the platform" were the "only two agencies that in any way can reach the whole people," La Follette maintained for the rest of his life that the muckraking magazines of the early twentieth century uniquely permitted consumers to penetrate corporate control over politics: "The free and independent periodical . . . opened the closed doors of the secret caucus, the secret committee, the secret conference, behind which United States Senators and Members of Congress betrayed the public interest into the hands of railroads, the trusts, the tariff mongers, and the centralized banking power of the country."[29] After spending a full day with Lincoln Steffens in 1906, La Follette confided to his wife that he had finally found "a friend who is in full sympathy."[30] When President Theodore Roosevelt led a conservative attack on the muckrakers for too radically criticizing political traditions with David Graham Phillips' "Treason of the Senate" series, La Follette took the Senate floor to reply that corporations and senators, not journalists, created the situation that called forth exposure.[31] During the Ballinger-Pinchot controversy of 1909–10 that revealed the apparent willingness of the Taft Administration to betray Alaska coal lands and the conservation movement to the Morgan and Guggenheim interests, muckraking journalists from *Hampton's, McClure's,* and other popular magazines met frequently with La Follette and other progressive senators to determine which information should be exposed in magazines and which on the Senate floor since both were forums for reaching consumers.[32] Conservatives like Pennsylvania Senator Boies Penrose fully understood that the alliance between progressive journalists and political leaders threatened corporate-conservative control over government. On one occasion Penrose excoriated La Follette for canceling an appointment he had made to address the Senate so that he could instead go "openly abroad upon the streets consulting with the editors of yellow journals and the agents of uplift magazines."[33]

Aided by the muckraking journalists and the new mechanisms for direct democracy, angry consumers found in their progressive spokespersons politicians who redefined old issues and created new ones that would shift wealth and power from wealthy producers, particularly monopolistic corporations, to consumers. The Senate debate on the Payne-Aldrich Tariff of 1909 revealed the full fury of consumers, the recognition and fear by corporate supporters that consumer revolts threatened their world more deeply than other protests, and the ways that consumer-oriented progressives redefined issues—for the tariff was one of the oldest issues in American politics—to create a basic challenge to concentrated wealth. Middle-class women organized the most obvious consumer pressures to lower tariff duties. Behind their organized campaigns for lower tariff duties was the old cry of the united community as it sought to reunite production with consumption and assert consumer control. Since the home was the basic unit of consumption and they were the chief defenders of the home, these clubwomen took the lead. They collected hundreds of thousands of signatures on petitions that demanded that Congress lower the duties on cotton goods, gloves, hosiery, ribbons, and other "necessaries of life." The petitions came from Detroit, Chicago, and Denver and from small communities like Berlin, Wisconsin.[34] Behind such organized drives "there has been a powerful but less definite movement of the public mind springing from the conviction of the great wrongs inflicted by the tariff on those least able to bear them," observed the *New York Times*.[35] The *Washington Post* lumped clergymen with ditch-diggers as a part of a "mighty army of consumers" who believed, in the words of the *Chicago Daily News*, that "the interests of the people as consumers should be paramount."[36]

Riding this wave of consumer protest, consumer-conscious progressives redefined the old issue of the tariff to meet the challenges of industrial capitalism. As a congressman in the late 1880s, La Follette had echoed century-old arguments that a high tariff encouraged economic growth and created opportunities for American farmers, workers, and businessmen.[37] As they felt the consumer revolt of the early twentieth century, progressives like La Follette came to believe that the protectionist Dingley Tariff of 1897 had been a major cause of the rapid growth of monopolies as larger firms drove out their smaller competitors and then raised their prices without fear of foreign competition. Albert Cummins of Iowa, who had long championed lower tariffs as a means for consumers to discipline monopolistic American corporations, trumpeted the new faith: "The right of the consumer of any article or any commodity to competition is dearer and higher and more sacred than the right of the producer to protection, and therefore . . . I say invite the competition of the whole world rather than suffer the monopoly of our own country."[38] "Greed tempered by absolute control," declared La Follette, had created "exorbitant prices and inferior products," for the corporate managers' "plan of destroying competition at home was devised so that the prices fixed for the American consumer should be regulated not by home competition nor by foreign competition, but regulated by these combinations of combinations organized and reorganized until they constitute a single power with a single purpose in control of production, transportation, and finance."[39] Reflecting the moral view of economic relationships that sprung from family and community, Moses Clapp of Minnesota charged that "in all human history there never has been such absolute, inexcusable greed as is shown to-day in some of these great combinations" of corporate protectionists.[40] Greed, profit, oligopolistic control, and freedom from foreign competition had led the new corporate middlemen constantly to cheapen and lower the quality of products below consumers' familiar expectations. "The same spirit which necessitated the enactment of a pure-food law to prevent the adulteration of food," Oklahoma's Thomas Gore observed, required the adoption of lower tariff duties if consumers were to restore the traditional control over price and quality that oligopolies had usurped.[41]

Conservative defenders of corporations in the Senate simply pretended that they did not hear any revolt by consumers, adamantly denied that consumers had rightful claims to discipline producers, and proceeded to draft the tariff bill to meet the demands of large corporate producers. Senator Henry Cabot Lodge of Massachusetts attacked "this myth of a consuming public": "Where is this separate and isolated public of consumers? . . . This is a Nation of producers."[42] Underscoring the traditional obligation of legislators to serve only well-organized groups, Charles W. F. Dick of Ohio urged the Senate to ignore consumers since "I have no communication from them."[43] When progressives insisted that the Republican party fulfill its 1908 platform pledge to revise the tariff and thereby to make the party platform a means for unorganized majorities to control legislation, conservative leader Nelson Aldrich proclaimed that the only majority that mattered was the majority of Republican senators that he controlled.[44] Consumers were outraged when Aldrich and the conservatives used traditional Senate disciplines to enact the high Payne-Aldrich Tariff in 1909. When voters in the pivotal state of Indiana were polled a few months later as to whether people in their state were "satisfied" with the Payne-Aldrich Tariff, 14 percent said yes, 78 percent said no, and 8 percent were unsure.[45] Angry consumers slaughtered the conservative Republicans in the election of 1910 by using the new direct primary system of nominations to replace conservative with progressive Republican nominees in some states and by electing Democrats to replace conservative Republicans in the general election.[46]

Believing, as La Follette put it, that the new trusts intervened between producer and consumer,[47] progressives sought to narrow the distance between producer and consumer, to curb the economic and political power of large corporations, and to restore consumer control with a wide variety of public controls at the federal level. As the creators of the new industrial market economy, the railroads were the most obvious middlemen between producers and consumers and, as oligopolies controlled by Wall Street investment bankers, the railroads added significantly to the cost of living by charging rates that served banker profits rather than consumer needs. "Consumers do not deal directly with the carrier, and yet they pay practically all of the fifteen hundred millions collected by the railway companies annually for carrying the freight of the country," declared La Follette during the 1906 debate on the Hepburn Act to regulate railroad rates. Angered that the proposed law provided a mechanism for well-organized shippers to get relief from discriminatory railroad rates while it did nothing for the unorganized "helpless consumer, for the millions who pay the freight," La Follette unsuccessfully maintained that consumers would receive redress only when the Interstate Commerce Commission geared rates to the actual physical property of the roads rather than the complaints of shippers or the profits of their banker owners.[48] When Congress finally enacted physical valuation of railroad properties in 1913, La Follette hoped that "it will then be possible to determine whether the general government can truly control and regulate interstate rates and services in the public interest" through a regulatory commission.[49] By the time that he achieved his major objective for regulation, however, La Follette had come to question whether regulation by commission could ever work as long as there was no competition for the six financial syndicates that owned the railroads. When the Interstate Commerce Commission late in 1914 granted the eastern railroads a 5 percent rate increase based on their watered stock instead of their physical properties, La Follette concluded that public ownership was the only effective way for consumers to control the railroads.[50]

La Follette also established an independent position as the consumers' champion in the debate over conservation and the use of public lands. President Theodore Roosevelt wanted the federal government to control access to public mineral lands in order to preserve economic growth by insuring a future supply of coal, lignite, oil, gas, asphalt, and other minerals. La Follette, on the other hand, introduced a resolution in 1906 that would serve "the coal and oil consumers" by insuring that "free and fair competition," not the needs of the large energy corporations, would determine access to public mineral lands. His great fear was not the supply of resources but "the monopolization of these great mineral and oil deposits" that would mean high prices to consumers who kept warm by burning coal.[51]

As La Follette evolved an approach to the general problem of monopoly, he incorporated older themes of consumer unrest that he tried to apply to restore to consumers and competition their historic control. Since "the control of credit and banking is the greatest power that the trusts possess to keep out competitors," La Follette concluded by 1908 that the Standard Oil and Morgan investment banking empires—what he called the Money Trust—"dominate and control the business and industrial life of this country against the interest of the great mass of the people" by earning speculative profits from arranging the mergers of other businesses into monopolies that the bankers controlled. By insisting on seats on the boards of directors of the new holding companies they formed as the price for lending capital, investment bankers like J. P. Morgan and James Stillman controlled the nation's industrial life by sitting on the boards of more than fifty corporations each.[52] The bankers quite naturally had "little or no sense of a personage with whom the rich and powerful must at last deal fairly or fall, and that is the 'ultimate consumer,'" Ida Tarbell wrote.[53] Consumer champions agreed on the problem and disagreed on the solution. John D. Works of California sought to replace investment banker control over credit with a national, publicly owned bank.[54] La Follette believed that the most important first step was to prohibit interlocking directorates and then to establish a flexible, decentralized, publicly controlled banking and currency system. But they all agreed that Woodrow Wilson's Federal Reserve System failed to protect consumers because, as La Follette mocked, it "turned that Money Power over to the unrestrained fury of the Big Banking Interests."[55] Echoing the consumers' traditional antimonopoly theme, La Follette believed by the 1910s that any corporation that exceeded over 30 percent of its market ought automatically to be broken into smaller, competing units.[56] He continued to believe, as he told an audience in 1912, that the Sherman Anti-Trust Act, "the wisest statute that has been framed in our time," had failed only because presidents had failed to enforce it.[37]

In addition to consumers' traditional suspicion of monopoly and credit, La Follette drew on other themes from consumer consciousness as he grappled with the new corporate giants. His 1911 antitrust bill "places the burden of proof on the trust to show that any restraint of trade it practises . . . benefits the community."[38] Just as consumers had historically disciplined producers by dealing directly with them, La Follette repeatedly sought to "fix the blame" directly on corporate officers, to fine them and imprison them, when their behavior threatened the community. He placed greater faith in prosecution than in regulation, for he believed that the community ought to regard and punish antisocial corporate behavior in the same way it treated individual lawbreakers. Once convicted, corporations should pay reparations to consumers. Believing, like other consumer movements, in exposure, La Follette maintained that the best feature of Woodrow Wilson's Federal Trade Commission was its broad mandate to investigate and expose corporate wrongdoing. "Publicity," he said, agreeing with Louis Brandeis, "will go far toward preventing monopoly."[39]

III

As part of the drive to reunite production with consumption, the consumer consciousness of the progressive movement sought not only to secure better products at lower prices but also to improve the conditions under which those products were made. Far from viewing workers or trade unions as simply another group of selfish producers, consumer-conscious progressives tended to view employers as middlemen who intervened between workers and consumers. Workers were guided in making products by traditional human qualities like their knowledge of how to do a job, their community traditions, or simply the need to support their families, while employers were guided by the thirst for profit. Consumers, in short, were natural allies of workers if they could only devise mechanisms and programs of mutual support.

The National Consumers' League of the early twentieth century sought to use the consumers' ultimate weapon to compel employers to let consumers' concerns, not profits, determine how employers would treat their workers. No amount of legislation could ever discipline producers as fully as an effective consumer boycott. In turning to the boycott, the National Consumers' League adopted a weapon that trade unions had devised in the 1880s to force employers to recognize unions and accept their demands. Members of all trade unions pledged to use their purchasing power as consumers to boycott products made by employers regarded as unfair by any constituent union and to purchase products that bore the union label that told consumers that the employer treated his workers fairly. Printers and cigar-makers had proven particularly effective in using the boycott and union label to make employers accept union demands out of their fear of consumer wrath. Conscious of their power as consumers, labor unions thus blazed the path that organized consumers adopted when they formed the National Consumers' League in 1899.

The National Consumers' League proclaimed that consumers had an obligation not as members of trade unions but simply as consumers seeking to restore a more just community to use their purchasing power to discipline the ways employers treated their workers. Believing that "the interests of the community demand that all workers shall receive fair living wages and that goods shall be produced under sanitary conditions" and that "the responsibility for some of the worst evils from which producers suffer rests with the consumers who seek the cheapest markets regardless how cheapness is brought about," the League declared in its formal Principles that "it is . . . the duty of consumers to find out under what conditions the articles they purchase are produced and distributed, and insist that these conditions shall be wholesome and consistent with a respectable existence on the part of workers."[60] "The consumer is practically the producer and is responsible for the conditions under which the articles consumed are produced," declared Mrs. Charles Henrotin, president of the Illinois Consumers' League in 1901.[61] The League told consumers whether workers were fairly treated by permitting employers to display the official label of the League if they complied with four requirements. The League inspected each employer, checked his record with the local board of health and the state factory inspector, and then awarded him the right to affix the label if his factory had obeyed state factory legislation, produced goods only on the premises instead of sending some to homes for manufacture, prohibited overtime work, and employed no workers under sixteen.

The Consumers' League dream of helping workers through consumer purchases appealed very largely to women, in part because the act of consumption originated in the home and not the workplace. And the League concentrated on using its purchasing power to help women and child workers, in part because male trade unionists were relatively uninterested in organizing them. In the spirit of female consumers helping female workers, the League directed its campaigns toward the women who made women's garments and who worked as retail clerks. In Cleveland, for example, the Retail Clerks' Union gave major credit to the local consumers' league for mobilizing consumer pressure in 1902-3 to create shorter hours, higher pay, and better workrooms and lunchrooms for women who worked in stores.[62] League organizers had little trouble recruiting middle-class women to use their purchasing power to help poorer women. Talks to local branches of the Ladies Catholic Benevolent Association in western Pennsylvania or the California General Federation of Women's Clubs, or the local Congress of Mothers, the Association of Collegiate Alumnae, or the Women's Christian Temperance Union soon produced a local consumers' league or the support of other women's groups for campaigns by existing consumers' leagues. By 1902 the General Federation of Women's Clubs had made Consumers' League General Secretary Florence Kelley the chair of its Committee on the Industrial Question as it Affects Women and Children.[63] Women consumers accepted the special obligation defined by Florence Kelley in her 1904 plea for garment workers: "A body of working-girls between the ages of fourteen and twenty-one years of age can neither form stable organizations to defend their own wages and hours of work, nor can they influence legislation in their own behalf—they are singularly dependent upon the intervention of the purchasing public in their behalf."[64]

While the Consumers' League enjoyed initial success because it encouraged women to direct their traditional roles as consumers charged with the defense of home and children toward a feminist sense of sisterhood, its success soon spread in many directions. Local branches used the boycott against retailers who sold adulterated milk, meats, oils, and candies, and they campaigned for the enactment and enforcement of pure food and drug laws at the federal and state levels. The sponsors of the Pure Food and Drug Act of 1906 maintained that the Consumers' League "assisted materially in creating public sentiment in favor of this legislation."[65] Soon boycotts by female consumers spread to include hastily formed housewife boycotts to force lower meat prices early in 1910 and to the more formal Housewives' League to compel wholesalers and retailers to lower food prices.[66] Although at the outset the consumer boycott may have provided women with a traditionally female weapon as an alternative to involvement in the traditionally male world of politics, the Consumers' League soon entered politics to demand better conditions for women workers and the abolition of child labor. The National Consumers' League persuaded Louis Brandeis to defend the cause of overworked female employees in the Oregon and United States Supreme Courts. Although Brandeis provided the basic outline for his defense, he relied on a team of ten Consumers' League researchers, coordinated by Josephine Goldmark, to collect and arrange the facts that became the "Brandeis Brief" in the landmark case of *Muller v. Oregon*.[67] Originating in the use of the act of consumption to reunite producer with consumer, the National Consumers' League revealed one pattern in which consumer consciousness encouraged a prolabor orientation.

Robert M. La Follette earned the gratitude of labor unions for directing consumer consciousness toward a second pattern of helping workers and unions. In appealing to the self-interest of consumers on labor issues, the basic question was whether consumers would insist on preserving their traditional expectations about the quality and safety of a product or service or whether they would accept the new market definition of consumers which encouraged them to buy the cheapest product or service. In order to defeat competitors in an ever-widening market, employers could survive and make the profits they wanted for growth only by constantly cheapening production costs and most particularly labor costs. As a believer in competition and cheap products, La Follette had originally endorsed management techniques for cheapening labor costs like Frederick W. Taylor's system of "scientific management," but by the early 1910s he came to see that the result was to rob workers of skills, "grind the last ounce of work" out of them by constant speedups, and produce premature old age. By 1916 he successfully led the Senate fight against the application of Taylorism to army-supervised plants.[68] By this point La Follette also believed that monopolization, not competition, led to unnaturally high prices for consumers and low wages for workers, that profit as the unnatural intermediary between producer and consumer was extorted equally from workers and consumers.[69] But a common ideological objection to profit based on the memory of times when production and consumption were more integrated was hardly the easiest way to mobilize consumer consciousness to assist workers.

La Follette concentrated his efforts to mobilize consumers behind labor legislation by trying to persuade consumers to replace the employers' emphasis on cheap prices with a consumers' traditional insistence on quality and safety. The Railway Hours Act of 1907 was a spectacular example. The railway brotherhoods, including engineers, firemen, conductors, trainmen, and telegraphers, suspected that La

Follette's hatred of railroad owners that he had expressed as governor of Wisconsin would make him a natural supporter of their legislative issues when he came to the Senate in 1906. The brotherhoods' chief lobbyist, H. R. Fuller, persuaded La Follette in 1906 to introduce union bills that would impose employer liability on railway companies for accidents to their workers and that would prohibit railway workers from working more than sixteen consecutive hours. Giving routine support to the first bill, consumer champion La Follette immediately saw the possibility of getting consumer support for the sixteen-hour bill and spent the next nine months working strenuously for its passage by the Senate. La Follette promoted it as a passenger safety law that would curtail the tens of thousands of injuries and deaths to passengers in train wrecks. "Its main purpose," he wrote, "is the protection of the public . . . from accidents and casualties resulting from overwork of men in charge of trains." During the Senate recess from June 1906, when the Senate buried the bill, until the new session in January 1907, muckrakers helped to sharpen the railway hours bill as a consumer issue. "The most serious railway accidents are in many cases traced to an overworked employee," La Follette explained as he tried to convince passengers that railroad greed had produced the exhausted railroad worker who, at the crucial moment, would fall asleep at the switch and unknowingly send the passengers to their doom. The issue became more consumer oriented in 1907 than it had been in 1906 because railroads produced petitions signed by hundreds of railroad workers in opposition to the hours bill. La Follette charged that railway managers, like a division superintendent of the Southern Railway, had extorted these signatures from workers as the price for keeping their jobs. The basic issue, he reminded passengers who were alarmed at the escalating number and severity of train wrecks, was "the quality of the service rendered to the public." When Congress enacted the sixteen-hour law early in 1907, the *New York Times* proclaimed it "the most important act of greatest practical importance to most people."[70]

The railway brotherhoods recognized that La Follette's appeals to consumers had won them a far broader constituency for their legislative program than they had ever won by promoting their bills as union bills. John F. McNamee, editor of the *Brotherhood of Locomotive Firemen's Magazine*, warmly thanked La Follette for consumer appeals that added up, from the union's perspective, to "your magnificent advocacy and defense of the interests of American Railroad men and their loved ones." It was an appeal that railway workers would use with great success. From the state of Washington a local of the Order of Railway Conductors wrote La Follette in 1907 that "what you have done in our interest at Washington was of great assistance to us in this State in securing the passage of laws for the benefit and protection of the railroad employees."[71] For the rest of his life La Follette had a special relationship with the railroad unions. They warmly supported his campaigns for the Senate and presidency. He promoted union bills in ways that appealed to consumers. The brotherhoods favored passage of "full crew" laws in part to create more jobs for their members, but La Follette defended the laws in 1908 because they provided "for the protection of the public."[72] While La Follette was clearly more empathetic to the daily problems of railway workers in 1916 than he had been a decade earlier, he supported the Adamson eight-hour law for railroad workers with appeals to passengers.[73]

La Follette's greatest achievement in directing consumer consciousness toward a union issue was one that the National Consumers' League had also made a high priority, the La Follette Seamen's Act of 1915. The achievement was particularly remarkable because of the political differences between railway workers and seamen. Well organized with locals across the country, mature, having a long tradition of political involvement with their votes and money, the railway brotherhoods naturally inspired respect from politicians. Train travel was a common feature of life; passengers feared wrecks as daily occurrences. Seamen in the merchant marine were, by contrast, young and itinerant, politically invisible, and the International Seamen's Union was politically powerless. Few passengers traveled on ships.

The Seamen's Act originated as a classic union bill. Andrew Furuseth, president of the West Coast–based International Seamen's Union, had long sought a law that would give seamen a measure of independence in dealing with autocratic ships' captains, would make ships more seaworthy, and would preserve jobs for American seamen in an industry that was increasingly turning to cheaper workers. In December of 1909 Furuseth brought his proposal to La Follette and urged the Wisconsin senator to make it his cause. The bill sought to end the "involuntary servitude" of sailors to ship companies and captains. It permitted seamen to quit ships in ports where cargoes were unloaded and abolished the prison sentences that ship companies could impose on sailors who quit before their one-year contracts had expired. It sought to replace Chinese, Japanese, and Turkish sailors with Americans by requiring that 75 percent of a ship's crew be able to understand the language of the captain and by requiring that an increasing percentage (rising to 65 percent) of the crew be skilled seamen with three years of training on deck. La Follette took up the bill and urged Furuseth to add measures that would make it more attractive to passengers who feared death by drowning in a raging sea. Reflecting La Follette's pressure, the final act required that there be enough lifeboats on the ship for every passenger and crewman, that there be mandatory fire drills, and that there be two skilled seamen for each lifeboat. The language requirement would reassure passengers that the crew would be able to follow the captain's orders in an emergency.[74]

La Follette, the Consumers' League, and other consumer-conscious progressives then set out to show why the seamen's cause was the cause of all Americans. They showed that disasters at sea resulted from shipowner greed that sent ships to sea with unskilled seamen and insufficient lifeboats. Nearly thirteen thousand people had lost their lives in sea disasters from 1900 to 1914. La Follette and Consumers' League Secretary Florence Kelley repeatedly insisted that the bill would greatly assist the "traveling public." Each sea disaster provided the opportunity to mobilize consumers. When the *Titanic* went down in 1912, La Follette proclaimed: "Sixteen hundred human beings sacrificed to greed and avarice. Many call it murder. We cannot find a less ugly word to characterize wholesale killings by Business." He went on to link ship passengers to consumers who suffered in more everyday ways from the decline in safety and quality that resulted from cheapened production: "Because there are dividends in adulterated foods and 'doped' drugs, there is a sordid indifference to public health."[75] As a passenger on the *Kronland,* one of the ships that came to the aid of the sinking *Volturno,* Florence Kelley described the horror of watching people drown because there were not enough skilled seamen to man the lifeboats.[76] The wreck of the *State of California* off the Alaska coast proved to La Follette that "existing laws are not adequate to furnish protection to the public."[77] In one of the most moving speeches of his life, La Follette portrayed the "hour of supreme danger" as people milled around "a lifeboat, perhaps one into which, say, your daughter or your son is to go; you can not go with them; the conditions may be such that they must go alone, with the fury of an ocean storm all about them, with the vessel every moment settling lower and lower. . . ." Whom would the listener prefer to have in charge of that lifeboat—unskilled workers who could not understand the captain or skilled seamen who knew how to "catch the wash just right"? Because of the "judgment and experience and intelligence" of the seamen, "the boat does not crash against the side of the vessel and crumple like an eggshell; she goes where she should go; she gets away."[78] The basic reason to pass the Seamen's Act was, as La Follette put it, "Safety first."[79]

Passage of the Seamen's Act was a dramatic tribute to the success with which La Follette, the National Consumers' League, and other consumer champions convinced consumers to retain their traditional concern for the quality and safety of services and goods in the face of an enormous media campaign by ship companies and allied business groups that sought to frighten consumers with the fear of higher prices that would accompany enforcement of the act.[80] When consumers shunned ship company and railroad appeals to their fears of higher prices, they revealed the depth of their desire not to let corporations usurp consumers' ancient control over the quality and safety of services they used. They, not corporations, had the traditional right to control the conditions under which workers created goods and services. And they would pay higher prices, if necessary, to preserve that right.

IV

The alienation of production from consumption that accompanied the loss of household self-sufficiency in the face of the market economy and industrial capitalism drove people to try to preserve their traditional consuming patterns as well as their producing patterns. As corporations tried to persuade workers to accept higher wages in exchange for loss of worker control over production, they tried to persuade consumers to accept lower prices in exchange for loss of consumer control over consumption. The drive for workers' control centered around control of tools, skills, pace, and wages, and the drive for consumers' control centered around quality, service, and prices. The common cause that workers and consumers mounted in the Progressive Era reflected their common inheritance in the belief that profit was extorted from both as the basic cause of the alienation of production from consumption.

Liberals and radicals since the death of progressivism have paid a high political price for their intellectual failure to treat consumers and consumption with the same care and dignity that they have given to workers and production. Realizing that their ultimate hegemony over the culture, to say nothing of their economic survival, depends on convincing consumers to acquiesce in their production techniques and values, corporations have developed sophisticated and expensive mechanisms to try to make consumers feel resigned to their loss of control. Liberals and radicals have simply accepted the corporate definition of consumers. As a result, corporations and conservative politicians have been able to exploit consumer-oriented values like family and community with no challenge. The faith in direct majority rule as the way for consumers to recover control, the hallmark of consumer-conscious progressives, has ebbed along with the traditional faith in democracy.

Greater attention to the alienation of consumers might create a fresh approach for those who believe that people should control their own lives democratically.

NOTES

1 Richard Hofstadter, *The Age of Reform: From Bryan to F.D.R.* (New York: Alfred A. Knopf, 1955), chs. 4–6; Christopher Lasch, *The New Radicalism in America, 1889–1963: The Intellectual as a Social Type* (1965; New York: Vintage Book ed., 1967), ch. 2.
2 *Congressional Record,* 59th Cong., 1st sess., p. 5701.
3 F. P. Lamoreux to Medill McCormick, January 22, 1912, National Progressive Republican League papers, Manuscripts Division, Library of Congress, Washington, D.C.
4 Beatrice and Sidney Webb, *The Consumers' Co-operative Movement* (London: Longmans, Green, 1921), p. 390.
5 Charles Gide, *Consumers' Co-operative Societies* (New York: Haskell Publishers, 1921), pp. 8, 12, 56.
6 Adam Smith, *An Inquiry into the Nature and Causes of the Wealth of Nations* (New York: Modern Library, 1937), pp. 493–507, esp. p. 494. See also C. R. Fay, *The Corn Laws and Social England* (Cambridge: Cambridge University Press, 1932); and Donald Grove Barnes, *A History of the English Corn Laws from 1660–1846* (1930; New York: Augustus Kelley ed., 1961).
7 E. P. Thompson, *The Making of the English Working Class* (New York: Vintage Books, 1963), p. 63.
8 Robert J. Richardson, "Missouri," in *History of Building and Loan in the United States,* ed. H. Morton Bodfish (Chicago: United States Building and Loan League, 1931), pp. 460–67; *Fifteenth Annual Report of the Bureau of Labor Statistics and Inspection of the State of Missouri . . . 1893,* pp. 109–274.
9 S. G. Mead, comp., *Mutual Insurance Manual: A Hand Book* (McPherson, Kansas: National Association of Mutual Co-operative Fire Insurance Companies, 1906), pp. 491–95; Missouri State Board of Agriculture, *Eleventh Annual Report . . . 1875,* pp. 32–33, and *Thirtieth Annual Report . . . 1898,* p. 333.
10 Missouri Bureau of Labor Statistics, *Second Report* (1880), pp. 213–17; William E. Parrish, *A History of Missouri,* vol. 3, *1860 to 1875* (Columbia: University of Missouri Press, 1973), pp. 285–86.
11 The classic account is Lawrence Goodwyn, *Democratic Promise: The Populist Movement in America* (New York: Oxford University Press, 1976).

12 Quoted in *Cooperation* 5 (August 1913): 315.
13 Missouri Bureau of Labor Statistics, *Thirty-Sixth Annual Report* (1914–15), p. 46.
14 *Goodspeed's History of Southeast Missouri* (1888; Cape Girardeau: Ramfre Press, 1955), pp. 442–43.
15 *Journal of the Proceedings of the Grand Lodge, Knights of Pythias of Missouri, 1885*, p. 231; and *1891*, pp. 143–44.
16 *By-Laws of Russell Camp, No. 2065, Modern Woodmen of America* (1901); *M. H. McCoy's Sedalia, Mo., City Directory for 1898–1899; Hoyte's Sedalia City Directory for 1903; By-Laws of the Constellation Lodge No. 26 I.O.O.F., of Hannibal, Missouri* (1901); *Hackman & Wallin Hannibal City Directory 1905*.
17 Edward A. Ross, *Sin and Society: An Analysis of Latter-Day Iniquity* (1907; New York: Harper Torchbooks ed., 1973), p. 4.
18 See, for example, David P. Thelen, *The New Citizenship: Origins of Progressivism in Wisconsin, 1885–1900* (Columbia: University of Missouri Press, 1972), pt. 3.
19 David P. Thelen, *Robert M. La Follette and the Insurgent Spirit* (Boston: Little, Brown, 1976), p. 71; Charles Forcey, *The Crossroads of Liberalism: Croly, Weyl, Lippmann, and the Progressive Era* (London: Oxford University Press, 1961), p. xiv.
20 Walter Lippmann, *Drift and Mastery: An Attempt to Diagnose the Current Unrest* (1914; Englewood Cliffs: Spectrum Books ed., 1961), pp. 54–55.
21 *Milwaukee Sentinel*, August 3, 1898.
22 La Follette's Veto Message, May 10, 1901, reprinted in *The Political Philosophy of Robert M. La Follette*, ed. Ellen Torelle (Madison: Robert M. La Follette Co., 1920), p. 44.
23 Quotation is from 1897, as reprinted, ibid., p. 57.
24 Herbert S. Bigelow, "From Pulpit to Stump," *Independent* 61 (November 1, 1906): 1036–37.
25 *Detroit News*, January 3, 8, 1908.
26 "Speech of Hon. Robert M. La Follette . . . August 19, 1911," p. 6, reprinted from *Congressional Record*, in Robert M. La Follette papers, Manuscripts Division, Library of Congress, Washington, D.C. All subsequent references to La Follette papers are to this collection.
27 Lincoln Steffens, "Wisconsin: A State Where the People Have Restored Representative Government—the Story of Governor La Follette," *McClure's* 23 (October 1904): 563–79.
28 Albert J. Beveridge to Joseph L. Bristow, July 19, 1910, Albert J. Beveridge papers, Manuscripts Division, Library of Congress, Washington, D.C.
29 Address to Periodical Publishers' Association, February 2, 1912, reprinted as appendix to Robert M. La Follette, *La Follette's Autobiography* (Madison: Robert M. La Follette Co., 1913), pp. 793–94, 796. See also *La Follette's Magazine* 9 (June 1921):1.
30 Robert M. La Follette to Belle Case La Follette, December 16, 1906, La Follette papers.

31 *Congressional Record*, 59th Cong., 1st sess., 1906, p. 5723.
32 Robert M. La Follette to Benjamin B. Hampton, May 29, 1909; Hampton to La Follette, June 1, 1909; George K. Turner to La Follette, December 17, 1909, La Follette papers.
33 *Congressional Record*, 61st Cong., 1st sess., p. 2707.
34 Ibid., p. 3176; *Washington Post*, March 21, 28, April 3, 4, 7, June 13, 18, 1909.
35 Quoted in *Washington Post*, March 15, 1909.
36 *Washington Post*, April 3, May 5, 17, 1909.
37 *Wisconsin State Journal* (Madison), January 7, February 17, 1886, January 11, July 19, 26, 1888; *Congressional Record*, 51st Cong., 1st sess., pp. 4474–77.
38 *Congressional Record*, 61st Cong., 1st sess., p. 4313.
39 Ibid., p. 2660.
40 Ibid., p. 3497.
41 Ibid., p. 3365.
42 Ibid., p. 1857.
43 Ibid., p. 3865.
44 Ibid., p. 4314.
45 *Washington Post*, June 5, 1910.
46 For two examples, see *Washington Post*, April 20, 1910.
47 *La Follette's Weekly Magazine* 3 (June 24, 1911):6.
48 *Congressional Record*, 59th Cong., 1st sess., p. 5695. See also *La Follette's Autobiography*, pp. 773–76.
49 *La Follette's Weekly Magazine* 5 (April 26, 1913):1.
50 *La Follette's Weekly Magazine* 5 (July 26, 1913): 1; *La Follette's Magazine* 7 (January 1915): 1–2; 7 (April 1915): 4; 9 (January 1917): 3. Robert M. La Follette to Belle Case La Follette, April 9, 1914, La Follette papers.
51 *Congressional Record*, 59th Cong., 1st sess., p. 8763; Robert M. La Follette to Theodore Roosevelt, January 28, 1907; La Follette to Claude Stephenson, April 24, 1906; La Follette to W. Reid, April 6, 1906, La Follette papers.
52 *Congressional Record*, 60th Cong., 1st sess., pp. 3434–53; *La Follette's Autobiography*, pp. 776–93.
53 Ida Tarbell, "The Hunt for a Money Trust," *American Magazine*, reprinted in *La Follette's Weekly Magazine* 5 (April 26, 1913):3.
54 John D. Works to Stoddard Jess, December 26, 1913, John D. Works papers, Bancroft Library, University of California at Berkeley.
55 *La Follette's Weekly Magazine* 5 (August 2, 1913): 1; 5 (September 17, 1913): 1; 5 (December 27, 1913): 1; 6 (January 3, 1914): 1. Robert M. La Follette to Rudolph Spreckels, December 26, 1913, La Follette papers.
56 *La Follette's Weekly Magazine* 5 (June 21, 1913): 11.
57 Manuscript of speech at Orchestra Hall, Chicago, 1912, in box B215, La Follette papers.
58 *La Follette's Autobiography*, pp. 787–88.

59 Thelen, *La Follette and the Insurgent Spirit*, pp. 85–86, 113–14; *La Follette's Weekly Magazine* 5 (June 21, 1913): 11; 5 (September 27, 1913): 3; 5 (October 11, 1913): 3; Robert M. La Follette to North Dakota Volunteers, March 1, 1912, La Follette papers.
60 National Consumers' League, *Second Annual Report* (1901), p. 3.
61 Ibid., pp. 18–19.
62 National Consumers' League, *Fourth Annual Report* (1903), pp. 50–54.
63 National Consumers' League, *Second Annual Report* (1901), pp. 15–16; *Third Annual Report* (1902), p. 26; *Fourth Annual Report* (1903), pp. 6–7, 16; *Fifth Annual Report* (1904), pp. 34–36.
64 National Consumers' League, *Fifth Annual Report* (1904), p. 9.
65 National Consumers' League, *Seventh Annual Report* (1906), pp. 50–71; *Tenth Report* (1909), pp. 53–60.
66 *Washington Post*, January 25, 28, 1910; *La Follette's Weekly Magazine* 6 (August 29, 1914): 7.
67 National Consumers' League, *Tenth Report* (1909), pp. 41–45; *The National Consumers' League: First Quarter Century, 1899–1924* (New York: National Consumers' League, n.d.), pp. 13–14, 17.
68 H. D. Block to Robert M. La Follette, March 26, 1911, including enclosures, in La Follette papers; *La Follette's Magazine* 8 (August 1916): 5–6.
69 *La Follette's Weekly Magazine* 3 (December 30, 1911): 9.
70 *Congressional Record*, 59th Cong., 1st sess., pp. 6811–12, 6821, 7590, 7659–61, 7696, 7920, 9269–70, 9370–72, 9683–85, 9789; 59th Cong., 2d sess., pp. 811–19; Robert M. La Follette to C. Shuster, July 9, 1906; La Follette to J. C. Roberts, January 8, 1907; La Follette to S. G. Baker, April 29, 1907, La Follette papers; *New York Times*, March 5, 1907; *Washington Post*, March 2, 1907.
71 John F. McNamee to Robert M. La Follette, August 11, 1906; Mt. Tacoma Division No. 249, Order of Railway Conductors, to La Follette, April 22, 1907, La Follette papers.
72 Robert M. La Follette to George Reed, June 10, 1908, La Follette papers.
73 *La Follette's Magazine* 8 (April 1916): 1; Belle Case La Follette to Dear Ones, June 26, 1916, Belle Case La Follette papers, Manuscripts Division, Library of Congress, Washington, D.C.
74 Belle Case and Fola La Follette, *Robert M. La Follette* (New York: Macmillan, 1953), 1: 521–31. Robert M. La Follette to Robert M. La Follette, Jr., October 24, 1913; Robert M. La Follette to Belle Case La Follette, October 24, 1913, July 31, 1914; Senate Bill 468, 62d Cong., 1st sess., April 10, 1911, all in La Follette papers.
75 *La Follette's Weekly Magazine* 4 (April 27, 1912): 3; 5 (March 29, 1913): 4; International Seamen's Union, "Some of the Reasons Why the Seamen's Act Was Passed" (1915), p. 15, in La Follette papers.
76 Article from *The Survey*, reprinted in *La Follette's Weekly Magazine* 5 (November 22, 1913): 4.
77 *La Follette's Weekly Magazine* 5 (August 30, 1913): 1.

78 *Congressional Record*, 63d Cong., 1st sess., pp. 5715–20.
79 *La Follette's Weekly Magazine* 6 (August 8, 1914): 1.
80 *New York Times*, October 18, 1915; *American Industries* 16 (November 1915): 11–12; "Our Natural Waterways and the La Follette Seamen's Bill," *The Survey* 33 (December 12, 1914): 282–83; Philip B. Kennedy, "The Seamen's Act," *The Annals of the American Academy of Political and Social Science* 63 (January 1916): 233; *La Follette's Weekly Magazine* 5 (November 1, 1913): 1–3; *La Follette's Magazine* 7 (July 1915): 1; 7 (October 1915): 1–3; R. P. Schwerin to Robert M. La Follette, July 30, 1915; Robert M. La Follette to Belle Case La Follette, October 24, 1913, both in La Follette papers.

MORRIS FROMKIN MEMORIAL LECTURE

Sponsored by the Fromkin Memorial Collection of The University of Wisconsin—Milwaukee Library

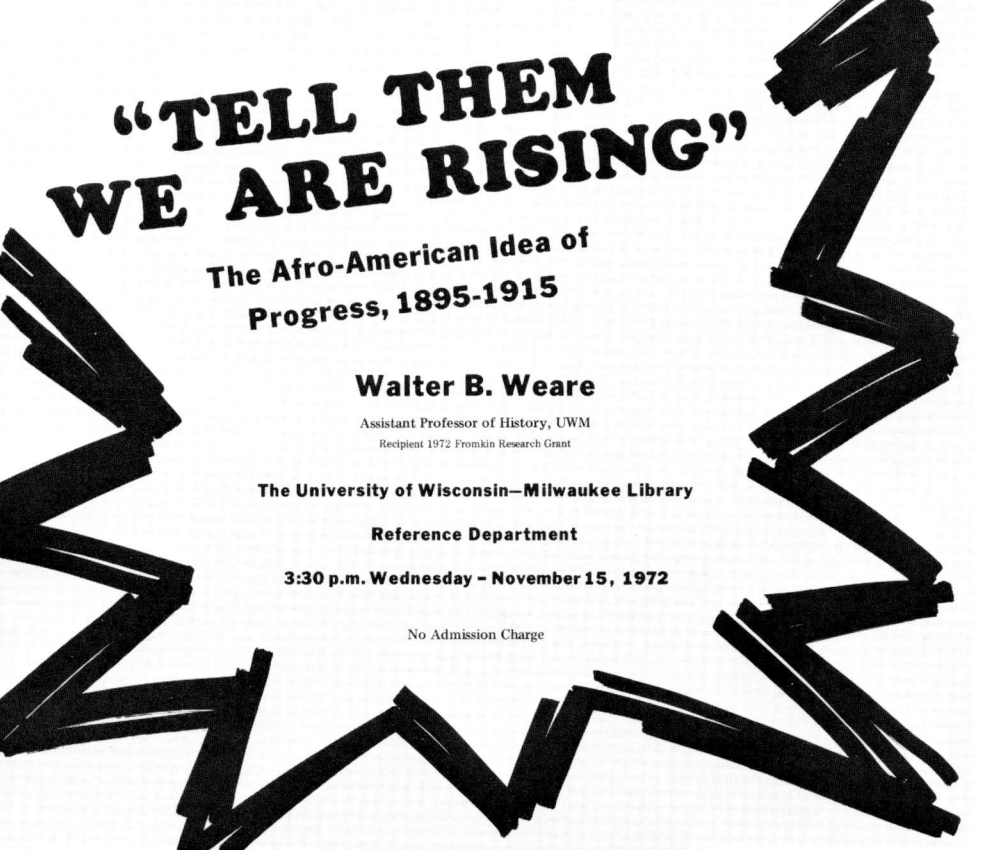

"TELL THEM WE ARE RISING"

The Afro-American Idea of Progress, 1895-1915

Walter B. Weare

Assistant Professor of History, UWM
Recipient 1972 Fromkin Research Grant

The University of Wisconsin—Milwaukee Library

Reference Department

3:30 p.m. Wednesday – November 15, 1972

No Admission Charge

The Idea of Progress in Afro-American Thought, 1890–1915

WALTER B. WEARE

ON a spring afternoon in 1908, a group of white citizens of Detroit, Michigan, staged a debate on what the local press described as a "red hot American problem": "Resolved that the Negro of the South is in a worse condition today than before the war." Black Americans, argued the affirmative, had made no progress since slavery.[1]

What took place in Detroit stands as one of the little events of history symbolic of the great event—a microcosm of the national debate over racial progress. If white Americans found the issue an absorbing one, black Americans found it obsessive, intrinsic to their survival. The black press overflowed with a harvest of statistics marshalled under sensational headings painting the era of Booker T. Washington as a golden age of progress with the black man in the vanguard. Indeed, if one were to submit black publications of the period to computerized content analysis, the word "progress" would print out near the head of the list. Washington, the high priest of the progress movement, rejoiced in the "remarkable advancement" of his race and declared at the turn of the century that "the future of the Negro never looked brighter." But while he spoke, black Americans were enduring the most evil days since slavery, the "nadir of the Negro's status in American society," wrote the black historian, Rayford Logan; the climax of the career of Jim Crow, said C. Vann Woodward, and by all modern accounts a blatant betrayal of those dreams born in the halcyon years of Reconstruction.[2]

Walter B. Weare, who received his B.A. and M.A. degrees at the University of Colorado and his Ph.D. degree in American history from the University of North Carolina, has taught at the University of Wisconsin–Milwaukee since 1968. His specialties are Afro-American history and the history of the South, and he has written *Black Business in the New South: A Social History of the North Carolina Mutual Life Insurance Company* (1973).

Yet, the idea of progress dominated Afro-American society and thought during those oppressive years between Washington's celebrated Atlanta Compromise in 1895 and his early death in 1915. The progress movement with its emphasis on self-help, struggle, and the Yankee virtues of thrift and enterprise was largely a Washington-led effort to accommodate, but it could voice protest as well, and it contained, moreover, a strong undercurrent of black nationalism. The nadir of race relations, far from having a deadening effect on the black community, provoked creativity and ferment, most of which found expression through the idea of progress.

In a very direct sense, black leaders mobilized one thoroughly American ideology—progress—to do battle against another thoroughly American ideology—racism. In retrospect they had little choice, for the two social forces lived in symbiosis. Whites concluded that the proof of racial inferiority lay in the lack of Negro progress; blacks concluded, therefore, that if they could convince whites of the freedmen's astounding progress since slavery, at least one rationale for racism would fall to the ground. The challenge was an awesome one, for these were the years that produced the peak of ideological racism. Hundreds of volumes of racist literature, much of it published under the guise of science, poured forth to attack the racial integrity of non-whites, black Americans in particular. Idus A. Newby and George M. Frederickson, among a host of other scholars, have catalogued and analyzed this literature, most of which can be characterized under three popular racist themes of the period: "The Negro a Beast," "The Negro a Menace to Civilization," and "The Negro a Vanishing Race." Negrophobes employed pseudo-anthropology to make the first assertion; statistics on crime and disease the second; and mortality figures the third. Social Darwinism, already much in vogue as a racial justification for imperialism, provided the intellectual fabric of these various strands of racist thought. The white prophets of black doom portrayed Negroes as child-like and pointed to rising mortality rates along with a decline in the proportion of black population from 10 percent of the total in 1860 to 8 percent in 1900 as proof that blacks could not survive without the parental supervision and care enjoyed under slavery. Frederick Ludwig Hoffman, a statistician whose calculations betrayed his German-American *volkgeist*, declared that the Negro race would die out by 1950, and all for the good because blacks were a parasitic weight on the progress of the Republic. A black Georgian, who chose to look at absolute figures rather than percentages, noted that the black population had increased from four million in 1860 to over eight million in 1900, and thus suggested to Hoffman: "If Negroes are going to die out they will have to stop doubling their numbers every 40 years."[3]

For the most part this was a war of words carried on between elites. Progress, after all, was the universal religion of the bourgeoisie, and the incipient black middle class proved no exception. Moreover, the black "talented tenth" had a personal stake in the quarrel. Their individual achievements, often against great odds, should count for something, they argued. And they deeply resented the white tendency to lump them with the "meaner sort" of the race.

Journalists, scholars, preachers, physicians, attorneys, and an irrepressible group of non-professionals stepped forward to represent the race and supply the rhetoric of rebuttal; black businessmen and the founders of all-black towns served as the leading illustrations of racial self-fulfillment in a highly conspicuous world proudly sustained by blacks only; black farmers, craftsmen, inventors, artists and musicians—anyone who might reflect credit on the progress of the race—became a symbol, a symbol very likely to be placed on elaborate display at hundreds of black expositions.

Apart from its great volume, the most arresting feature of the Afro-American progress literature was its great zeal. "We have astonished the world," declared the *Chicago Defender*. "Less than a generation ago we lived in chains. Today we have the Negro in business. Can you beat it!" Self-adulation abounded in black newspapers. One headline asked the rhetorical question, "Is the Negro growing rich?" The *New York Age* proclaimed in bold type, "Afro-Americans own millions," while the *Amsterdam News* listed its data on wealth under the heading "Not A Child Race."[4]

Doubtless the style of the white adversaries shaped the style of the black journalists, but it would be a mistake to characterize any aspect of Afro-American history as simply a response to racism. The internal will to maintain a sense of community and racial pride often worked in perfect harmony with the external world of white hostility and rejection. The idea of progress emerged as another means of resisting the white man's definition of the black man, even if it meant embracing the white man's criteria to do so. Also it must be remembered that in the early years of the twentieth century, millions of black people could still remember slavery; thus the contrast between 1863 and 1913 stood on more than lifeless census statistics. "Up from slavery" success stories became favorites among blacks and whites alike. Progress, like status, always a scarce commodity in the black community, became all the more dear during peaks of oppression. Because there was little to cheer about, each achievement became proportionately more to cheer about. A black reporter confessed that he was so overcome with racial pride from observing the operation of a Negro bank in Norfolk one busy afternoon that "I just went out on the street singing 'Praise God' and I was praising him so loud . . . until the police talked about locking me up, but I told them I was rejoicing over what I had seen my people doing." Similarly the masses of black folks took to the streets during this period to celebrate the success of Jack Johnson, as they would again during the depression for Joe Louis. The point is that black success—progress—was highly symbolic, and it is the celebration of the progress, not the substance, that demands our attention. Every statistic stood as a symbol, and every symbol in turn supported the emerging mythology of progress.[5]

Unlike the larger American gospel of success, which pictured the country boy leaving the farm to make good in the city, the Afro-American mythology left many of its Algers on the farm—an element of realism within the myth, for Negro farm ownership did increase between 1900 and 1910, and urban industrial opportunity for blacks amounted to little before World War I. The theory emerged that blacks might literally inherit the earth as whites flocked to the city. Staying on the farm, moreover, positioned the black man on even higher mythological ground, because rural existence promised moral progress while the city threatened moral decay. In his wistful moments, Booker T. Washington dreamed of a Jeffersonian society held together by the moral fiber and horse sense of black husbandry. Black newspapers never tired of extolling the black farmer, and it is interesting that journalists cited a disproportionate number of such examples from Oklahoma and Kansas, perhaps because of the utopian character of the black agrarian exodus to those areas, climaxing at the turn of the century in a movement to make Oklahoma Territory an all-black state.[6]

If much of the progress literature was an accommodative effort to put the best face on a bad situation without answering white hostility in kind, another genre of the literature, more northern than southern, eagerly sought confrontation, and took no pains, as Washington and others felt they must, to disguise the hostility. A black minister in Boston reminded the white detractors, "Verily you are a splendid improvement of your forefathers whom Julius Caesar found running about in the forests of Britain, living upon the roots of trees, and occasionally offering up a human sacrifice under the Druid Oak. . . ." The *Amsterdam News* wondered how blacks could be classified as a child race when Africans had fathered "the great dawn of civilization while the ancestors of the present-day haughty and supercilious caucasians were enjoying the blessings of cave existence." Progress and the capacity for self-government were "not purely western European traits," the editor continued, and "the colored American, given a state of his own, could doubtless give the white American a few pointers [on civilization]." For one thing, "we would do away with lynching."[7]

The progress movement provided opportunities to gibe the "dominant race" and to give vent to black hostility. A businessman boosting black enterprise at the 1901 National Negro Business League Convention ended his address by asking only that the white man stand aside and allow a clear field for economic progress. "There is not a colored man in this audience who wants to marry Ben Tillman's ugly daughter. We ask nothing from him." The Grand Master of the Negro Masons in Mississippi similarly pitted black progress against the politics of white supremacy: "Our organization has $19,132 in three colored banks, and we have also recently purchased 1000 acres of land. Governor Vardaman and all other devils this side of Hades cannot stay this kind of prosperity." Afro-American progress, hypothesized the editor of a black business journal, would take the race issue away from red-neck politicians. "With such prosperity facing the country, the spell binder . . . will have to get a new theme. Shouting 'nigger' has become a little threadbare. When it comes to the vital issues of progress, cheap politicians who can only appeal to passion dwindle away like mist before the sun."[8]

Since the days of slavery the gift of irony and humor had served blacks well as a means to preserve their humanity and to channel their aggression. The era of progress only added new possibilities for such expression. When a small community of prosperous black farmers in the Mississippi Delta heard the rumor that whites were thinking about taking up land in the area, a spokesman jested with his neighbors that they ought to discourage the whites: "For God's sakes, boys, don't you know that we black folks already got just as many white people in this county as we can support?"[9]

Traditionally, most American ethnic groups have relieved their frustration and pent up aggression at the expense of other ethnic groups. Frederick Douglass remembered that during slavery, "somebody was always whipping somebody," but the slaves could whip only the mule or each other. Under the mantle of race progress, however, a number of alternatives appeared. A favorite target for invidious comparison was the Russian serf. In 1913, the semi-centennial anniversary of emancipation, a black professor at Tuskegee published a special progress volume expressing the ubiquitous theme, "Fifty Years of Negro Progress," in which he asserted that "No other emancipated people have made so great a progress in so short a time." As proof for his assertion he cited the Russian serfs who with a two-year head start on the American slave had accumulated only half the wealth, and remained comparatively illiterate. Every black newspaper picked up the comparison, and the progress literature grew full of other such dubious references.[10]

After a trip to Europe in 1910, Booker T. Washington rushed into print *The Man Farthest Down,* in which he argued that not only had blacks outstripped the former slaves of Russia, but that in his opinion all European peasants ranked well below Afro-Americans on the scale of progress. The most tempting comparison, however, pitted the black American against the red American. The relationship between blacks and Indians is an interesting one historically, clearly marked with ambivalence for blacks, who were both enslaved and befriended by Indians, and who both respected the Indian's struggle against the white man and yet looked askance at the lesson of genocide it taught. But the relationship took on another meaning at the turn of the century. As the most oppressed and least powerful of American minorities, the Indian stood as a convenient bottom rung on which blacks might stand a little higher in American society.

There would seem to be a large measure of displaced aggression at work in the reported practice of black students at Hampton Institute teaching Indian students English and urging them to recite far into the night, "We Savages, We Savages." Washington himself never tired of pointing out the amount of taxes paid by blacks, part of which, he alleged, went "to support the American Indian whose welfare was costing the government 10 million dollars annually." A black businessman reporting on the 1914 National Negro Business League Convention at an all-black town in Oklahoma summarized the telling attitude. The local Indians, he observed, were "half nude and gaily painted, . . . remaining uncivilized, . . . ignorant, idle, and dependent on the United States Government. Unlike the Negro, they have no banking institutions, neglecting their opportunity, they are fast losing their birthright, while on the other hand, NEGRO INDUSTRY, THRIFT, AND SELF-INITIATIVE have given to our race 10,000 mercantile enterprises, 63 banking institutions, 400 drug stores, 20 million acres of land, and material wealth exceeding $700,000,000."[11]

Although expediency characterized much of the progress movement as it fastened itself at random to whatever ideology fit its social and psychological needs, including social Darwinism, it increasingly moved toward a coherent ideological home in history and religion. The notion that religion has served blacks only as an opiate is a vast oversimplification—surely it performed that function for some, but black religion even under slavery, looked as much to this world as to the other world. The progress movement reinforced that tendency as it openly advocated that the City of God might yet appear on earth as a truly egalitarian America; or better yet as a fallen America redeemed by black people.

Religion, history, and industrial progress commingled to assure material as well as spiritual salvation. Sweet Jesus and mighty Jehovah marched side by side in support of black progress. The image of an angry Old Testament God delivering his people from bondage remained almost as functional as it had under slavery. "Learn to imitate the Jews," Washington repeated time and again, and in so doing he invoked not only one of the most persistent themes in black religion, but a plea for commercial progress through ethnic solidarity. "Fifty years of Negro progress," preached a black minister, has already made "the world's flesh quiver on its bones, [but] give us a century and these dusky sons and daughters of Ham . . . will make the very earth tremble at our coming." Black progress, proclaimed another preacher, was proof that injustice had been "slapped by an omnific hand, telling to the world that a powerful nation is in the land."[12]

The gospel of progress linked the Old Testament deliverance of a chosen people by a wrathful god to the New Testament deliverance of those who appear in the Sermon on the Mount, those who had suffered—the Christlike. The last would come first; the meek and humble would inherit the earth—this earth—and if Jehovah had his way it would be black over white. "Southern whites," warned a black churchman, "seem to believe that the earth is the Anglo-Saxons and all that dwell therein. Despite the Anglo-Saxons . . . the Almighty is going to cause *us* to dwell in this land that we have made rich through the labor of our ancestors." A leading Georgia preacher advised his audience at a black exposition that the Sermon on the Mount and aggressive economic behavior posed no contradiction: "The Bible says, 'Blessed are the poor in spirit,' but it doesn't say 'Blessed are the poor in pocketbook.'" A prominent preacher-banker in Alabama avowed that "We teach our people to use two books—the Bible and the Bank Book." Because the black church served as the matrix of Afro-American institutional development, it is no coincidence that preachers often took the lead in black business, particularly in banking and insurance.[13]

Like black religion, the black history movement of the progress era drew no sharp distinctions between the secular and the spiritual. History as progress is, of course, not a theme peculiar to Afro-American thought, but a theme central to all Western thought—at least since the Enlightenment. Black intellectuals undoubtedly fell under the influence of the larger idea of progress, but metaphysics has often been a luxury in the black community. The idea of progress could not rest as idle philosophy; rather, it had to go to work for the race. Thus the black history movement within the black progress movement fashioned an historiography which put every example of achievement on literary display, the rationale being that an exalted image would break down white prejudice and build up black pride. The result was often another version of "cherry tree" history—"a long column of America's dark sons moving steadily and surely up the hills of progress," said J. W. Gibson in his aptly titled *Progress of a Race: Or the Remarkable Advancement of the Colored American from the Bondage of Slavery, Ignorance and Poverty to the Freedom of Citizenship, Intelligence and Affluence*. G. F. Richings, in his *Evidences of Progress among Colored People*, thought it a tribute that his biographical sketches "read like romances"; William N. Hartshorn's *An Era of Progress*, Joseph R. Gay's *Life Lines of Success*, and countless others constituted a genre of popular literature. W. L. Hunter, a black physician from Brooklyn, spoke more pointedly in a 1901 publication entitled *Jesus Christ Had Negro Blood in His Veins*, a tract which went through nine editions by 1913. An important outgrowth of the Negro history movement was the effort to replace racist textbooks and to revise the European view of Africa. As early as 1890, E. A. Johnson, a black attorney from Raleigh, North Carolina, introduced black students to his *School History of the Negro Race in America;* by 1913, Benjamin Brawley had produced a much better classroom text, *A Short History of the American Negro*. Interestingly, it was Booker T. Washington, in the early chapters of his two-volume *Story of the Negro* (1909), who pioneered in revising the white distortions of black Africa. Amateurs gave way to professionals, however, as the history movement became institutionalized. In 1897 W. E. B. Du Bois began the rudiments of a Negro studies program at Atlanta University which soon offered courses in Afro-American history and sociology and by 1916 had produced a twenty-volume study of Afro-American life. In 1915 Du Bois synthesized existing research on Africa in a volume entitled, simply, *The Negro;* and in that same year, Carter G. Woodson, another Harvard trained Ph.D. in history, gathered this first black history movement into a formal professional organization, the Association for the Study of Negro Life and History, which along with its *Journal of Negro*

History remains an important legacy of the intellectual ferment born out of the era of progress.[14]

If black historians spent much of their energy celebrating progress, it was black businessmen who provided the *cause célèbre*. Black capitalism became a crusade, a middle-class millenarian movement under the pressures of prejudice in the early years of the twentieth century. Booker T. Washington's National Negro Business League, founded in 1900, acted as the ecumenical administrative center for all denominations of the progress movement, and its annual conventions resembled camp meetings with businessmen issuing testimonials of racial salvation under the gospel of progress. Washington drained the last ounce of inspiration from the delegates as he called them forth to testify on the altar of race progress—the shoemaker from Memphis, the ice cream dealer from Danville—and then sent them away euphoric to spread the good news. "Don't make a speech," he admonished the witnesses, "just tell us the size of your bank account five years ago and now," and inviting the exaggeration, he persisted, "*now* tell us how much you plan to make next year?"[15]

There was scarcely a skeptic among the black leaders. Du Bois worried that black folks, the single "oasis of faith and reverence in a dusty desert of dollars and smartness," might lose their souls to Mammon; but he, like other "anti-Bookerites," acknowledged that Washington had captured the spirit of the age—"triumphant commercialism." John Hope, President of Spellman College and an archenemy of Washington and the Tuskegee machine, said it best:

> We are now under the immediate sway of business, more than humanity has ever been before. We are living among the so-called Anglo-Saxons and . . . they are a conquering people who turn their conquests into their pockets. Business seems to be not simply the raw material of the Anglo-Saxon Civilization, but almost the civilization itself. Living among such a people is it not obvious that we cannot escape its most powerful motive and survive?

"BUSINESS IS KING," proclaimed a black editor in Detroit, and his counterpart in Norfolk echoed the sentiment: "We have got to do business just like the white people if we are ever to amount to much in the scale of advancement and progress."[16]

There was talk of a "New Negro in a New Era," black captains of industry marching as the vanguard, their business success serving as a cutting edge on the frontier of racial progress. "You must stand behind these Negro enterprises," commanded the *New York Age;* "this is the call of the hour, this is the call of your race." Obviously black business represented more than economic activity. It was a social and political movement. It promised a solution to the race problem. Nobody pronounced this idea more persistently than Washington. "I do not believe," he wrote in 1907, "that the world ever takes a race seriously . . . until a large number of that race have demonstrated, beyond question, their ability to develop business enterprises. The Negro will be on a different footing when it becomes common to associate the possession of wealth with a black skin." One of Washington's colleagues went so far as to say that "this much talked of Negro problem is merely a business problem." The lore of progress now looked to the secular Jew rather than the spiritual Jew. "Money power," said one source, "will raise the Negro as it has the Jew, who was once as much persecuted as the Negro is now. Let us hammer away. The almighty dollar is the magic wand that knocks the bottom out of race prejudice and all the humbugs that fatten on it."[17]

The American dream came forward to repress the American reality, with mythical black industrialists following in the footsteps of mythical European immigrants who went from rags to riches in one generation. "Let us not forget," reminded the *New York Age*, "that Cornelius Vanderbilt and nearly all of the magnates in the United States began on the farm or in crude huts." The Afro-American idea of progress seized the ruling myths of the larger American culture and used them with a vengeance. Within very pragmatic limits black businessmen found social Darwinism more to their liking than did white businessmen. Certainly struggle formed the centerpiece of their ideology. "No race of people," argued Booker T. Washington, "ever got upon its feet without severe and constant struggle." And if, as Herbert Spencer insisted, progress came only out of struggle, then the black man ought to have an advantage. Indeed, the phrase "Take Advantage of the Disadvantages" became one of the slogans of the progress movement.[18]

A giant rationalization began to emerge: Slavery was but part of a larger plan to prepare blacks for the current struggle. "The history of this race of ours in America in the intense and direct competition with the most powerful forces that the world has ever known has been the very thing we needed to insure our development," affirmed a black Virginian. "Rough treatment is the very thing to start us on the road to success." This espousal of struggle transformed discrimination into a positive challenge, disfranchisement and segregation into economic opportunity and racial pride, despair into hope. In Boston, a black editor agreed that "disfranchisement of the colored man" might be a blessing in disguise as it would "stimulate the Negro to accumulate wealth and education, while the poor white man in the South will sink lower in the scale of human existence." Similarly, exclusion from white labor unions might not be an unmixed evil if it steered the black wage slave back to farming or into business as a producer of wealth and progress. "Everywhere one goes now," wrote a black newspaper man in Newport News, "the spirit of race cooperation has possessed the race. The white man's meanness and prejudice are working wonders for the Negro." A black businessman in Indiana complained to the white journalist, Ray Stannard Baker, "The trouble here is that there is not enough prejudice against us. You see we are still clinging too much to the skirts of the white man. When you hate us more it will drive us together and make us support colored enterprises."[19]

Of course the dubious benefits of oppression had a point of diminishing returns, and one could not be consistent on the matter of struggle and progress without applying it within the race as well as between the races. Moreover, none of the black ideologues could rest comfortably as the bed-fellow of the white scientific racists who concocted racial Darwinism in the first place. Black writers employed social Darwinism with an air of pragmatism at the same time they drew their ideas from a traditional Afro-American mechanism of defense—the cultural necessity of finding the good in the bad. The middle class merely added the ideological gloss of struggle and progress, and it mattered very little if their thought revealed inconsistency and contradiction, for they always held an ace—actually another contradiction: God, after all, not Darwin or Spencer, contrived this struggle; and while blacks were destined to see it through, in the end they couldn't lose. According to R. R. Moton, Booker T. Washington's heir-apparent, it was simply a matter of "crossing the wilderness before we reach the promised land."[20]

The overweening pride and all-consuming zeal within the business movement suggest that the crusade for black capitalism during the age of Booker T. Washington was in itself a form of protest thought as was the larger idea of progress. The general response of the black leadership, when confronted with the nadir of race relations, was nothing short of a sublimation into the world of business—progress—as a substitute for politics and protest. Washington, in his *Story of the Negro*, entitled one chapter "The Negro Disfranchisement and the Negro in Business," leaving no doubt about the reciprocal relationship. "They [Negroes] began to see," he observed, "that there was still hope for them in economic, if not political directions."[21]

John Merrick, a devoted Bookerite and founder of the nation's largest black business, the North Carolina Mutual Life Insurance Company, offered the typical rationale for taking leave of politics (as if there were much choice in the matter) and entering business. In the wake of the North Carolina white supremacy campaign highlighted by the 1898 Wilmington race riot, Merrick lamented that whites had "turned their attention to making money and we turned ours to holding office and paying debts of gratitude to the Republican Party." One of Merrick's business colleagues put it more eloquently: "We have turned from pursuing the phantom of political spoils to learning the secret of successful accumulation. With such a wise determination we may safely say we are gliding out among the shoals and our view opens to a clearer deeper sea." Such language proved enormously pleasing to most whites, and most blacks experienced an inner pleasure in understanding what whites did not—that economic progress was not the ultimate aim, but rather a trojan horse, an "economic detour," as another insurance executive put it, on the road to full civil and political equality. Of the six men who joined John Merrick in this business venture, five had been active in politics; and in the 1930s when black politics became possible again, a new generation would use the company as a political base.[22]

The formation and subsequent success of the North Carolina Mutual stands as a symbol of the racial flight from the politics of protest to the politics of progress, but it is interesting that the white South, in the wake of the Civil War, saw itself pursuing a similar course vis-à-vis the North. Indeed, there are intriguing parallels between the rhetoric and rationale of the black disciples of progress and that of the white prophets of an industrial New South who, in response to their post-war loss of political power, launched a fervent campaign to become a competing industrial power. The central problem from the white point of view was the place of the black man in this new society. For most whites, caste and peonage provided the solution, but Booker T. Washington put a better face on it. Blacks and whites could build a new South together and yet remain apart, he promised in his famous Address at the 1895 Atlanta Cotton Exposition.[23]

That blacks as well as whites might exploit the industrial opportunities of the New South became a cardinal principle in the Afro-American idea of progress. "In a material sense," said Washington in 1907, "the South is still an undeveloped country . . . and in the matter of business there is very little obstacle in the Negro's way." No one can miss the ideological kinship between white New South nationalism and black bourgeois nationalism. The aura of industrial enthusiasm spilled over into the black community and when grafted to the black cult of progress, produced a hybrid of incredible vigor.

Henry W. Grady, Atlanta's white apostle of a New South, could scarcely have been more exuberant than a black editor in Durham, North Carolina, who in 1903 captured the uncritical zeal of the New South creed:

> Everything here is push, everything is on the move. The Negro in the midst of such life has awakened to action. . . . Durham! The very name has become a synonymous term for energy, pluck and business ability. . . . When you say Durham! the wheels begin to turn, the smoke rolls in massive clouds from every stack and the sweet assuring music of busy machinery is heard. Durham! and as if by magic, everything springs into new life, the veins and arteries of business throw off their stagnation and the bright sun of prosperity sends its radiant beams out upon the world. . . .[24]

If a black editor in a white town could engage in such New South boosterism, one can imagine the enthusiasm that emanated from all black towns. By 1910 there existed over fifty such Southern towns, each theoretically connected with the commercial life of the New South, but otherwise separate—each symbolizing a kind of Utopian apartheid. By all odds the most famous was Mound Bayou, Mississippi, founded in 1887 by Isaiah T. Mongomery, an ex-slave of the Jefferson Davis family. By 1910 he presided as mayor over a community of 5,000 which boasted a full range of institutions including three schools, six churches, a large hotel, two saw mills, and four cotton gins, all surrounded by 30,000 acres of prime delta cotton land, all owned by black farmers.[25]

Needless to say, in the eyes of the progress movement, this was the black jewel of the New South. "This is a town owned and operated by our people," exulted a black reporter, a town where "a black mayor with his black aldermen sit in the council chambers making laws," where "a black marshall carries the billy, a black postmaster passes out the mail, a black ticket agent sells the tickets, and the white man's waiting room is in the rear." Perhaps the single most celebrated event of the progress era occurred at Mound Bayou in the winter of 1912, when the town dedicated its new $100,000 cotton seed oil mill. Nearly 10,000 persons made the pilgrimage to see Booker T. Washington christen this symbol of black progress in the New South. That Mound Bayou represented more than a city and the mill more than a machine is an understatement if measured by the assessment of the black journalist who reported the dedication ceremony. "The beauty of the whole thing," he began, "is that it is in its entirety the product of the Negro's genius, designed and erected by Negroes, illustrating the possibilities of the race. Here in this monumental city is born a new era in the development of the race—that of utilizing the resources of the South and placing upon the market the finished products of the soil." In his best progress prose the reporter continued: "The crowd of 10,000 came to feast their souls upon the most notable creation of the race since emancipation, and when Dr. Washington pulled the cord that blew the whistle that started on its productive career this mighty concept of the people, cheer after cheer rent the balmy Indian summer air. Strong men wept and the women cried for joy. A glimpse of the millennium seemed to have vouchsafed them."[26]

Mound Bayou, the North Carolina Mutual, and other autonomous institutions became the showcases of racial progress, and black folks did indeed make pilgrimages to see them and still do; but since not everyone could go to Mound Bayou or to Durham, the progress movement took its message to the people through fairs and expositions. Afro-American expositions, while representative of the idea of progress, were a social movement in their own right and as an important piece of social history deserve a separate study. It is enough to say here that they institutionalized the idea of progress, translating it into graphic display. By the time the movement peaked in 1913 with scores of expositions and jubilees sounding the theme, "Fifty years of Negro progress," every Southern state had its black counterpart to the annual white state fair, in addition to hundreds of smaller exhibitions, usually staged at county fairs. W. E. B. Du Bois prepared a special Negro progress exhibit for the Paris Exposition of 1900; larger exhibits appeared in the Pan American Exposition at Buffalo in 1901 and at the St. Louis World's Fair in 1904; but the greatest single display appeared at Jamestown, Virginia, in 1907 as part of the 300th anniversary celebration of the founding of Jamestown. Congress appropriated $100,000 for a separate black exposition hall, a testimony to the lasting appeal of Booker T. Washington's Atlanta Compromise. The message of the exposition movement was steady and clear: self-help and racial pride. "Let us all go to work and prove something," commanded the *Journal of Industry,* the monthly publication of the Negro Fair and Exposition Company. "The character of a *nation* is judged by the value of its production. Therefore to establish any valid claim to progress among the great nations of the earth, we must, despite our disadvantages, make a favorable comparison of our products." The effusive editor instructed "every colored man with the slightest vestige of race pride [to] interest himself in this movement, and when we learn to stand together, we can date our upward march to that destiny which God has in reserve for all the finally faithful."[27]

However inflated the rhetoric, there can be little doubt that the thousands of black expositions held throughout the South inspired racial pride (in addition to their being important social events), but that they changed white attitudes is another question. Whites after all could have it both ways: they could argue that there had been little progress and that the expositions represented the exception rather than the rule; or they could agree that there had been great progress, but that such progress only proved the *absence* of racial discrimination.

The idea of progress did much to sustain the jubilant mood expressed in the expositions. After what appeared to be the climax of the expositions in 1913, a great flurry of oratory and display arose in 1915 to celebrate "Fifty Years of Negro Progress" all over again, measured this time from the ratification of the Thirteenth Amendment in 1865. But the spirit began to wane. Based on symbol, as much of it was, the progress movement unavoidably lost some of its vitality with the death of Washington in 1915. He and the exposition platform had been made for one another.[28]

But larger forces were at work as well. World War I set off vast social and economic changes in Afro-American life: the great migration, urbanization, rising expectations, and hence a new militancy that turned a deaf ear to the facile assumptions of progress. And well before Washington's death, one could discern a shift from self-help to interracial protest as demonstrated in the growth of the NAACP, whose Supreme Court victory over the Grandfather Clause in 1915 presented another approach to racial progress. Nonetheless, the idea of progress that Washington popularized was so basic to Afro-American thought that it would live at least a generation beyond his death. Much of his boosterism simply migrated from the New South to the black metropolis where it took on added enthusiasm under the direction of editors like Robert S. Abbott of the *Chicago Defender,* who pictured the northern city as the rising black Utopia. Chicago and Harlem became an extension of the hopes and dreams of Mound Bayou a million times over. But if the masses of black migrants entertained any such vision, it quickly faded in the gloom of postwar race riots, declining economic opportunity, and the pathological side of city life. Undoubtedly the high hopes and the broken dreams provided the ferment in the 1920s for the Harlem Renaissance and the back-to-Africa movement of Marcus Garvey. But even Garveyism, for all its hostility toward the black bourgeoisie, borrowed a good deal from the older progress movement. Garvey acknowledged that much of his inspiration came from Booker T. Washington and that his initial purpose in coming to the United States was to visit Tuskegee. It is striking, moreover, that Washington's personal secretary, Emmett J. Scott, became a Garveyite, and that Washington's editorial spokesman through the *New York Age,* T. Thomas Fortune, became the editor of Garvey's *Negro World.* And certainly Garvey's Black Star Shipping Line and his Negro Factories Corporation were more adventures in black capitalism than efforts in African repatriation.

Whenever the idea of opportunity has been threatened in American history a social movement has arisen to meet the threat. Populism, Progressivism, and the New Deal are ready examples, but these were largely white reform movements which brought little progress and sometimes retrogression to black Americans. The Afro-American idea of progress could not be an instrument of reform because it had no political power, but it could challenge the intolerable white assumption that blacks might go down rather than up from slavery. Against this assumption an emerging black middle class searched for social justice when there was none and thus exaggerated what it found to take its place. Out of desperation it looked for cracks and footholds in the white monolith and out of necessity imagined them as great ladders to the sky. Given the failure of the various black nationalist movements to leave America and the failure of internal politics to remake America, a zealous belief in material progress, despite or perhaps because of the oppression, became the obvious alternative to total despair.

NOTES

1 *Detroit Informer,* March 28, 1908, in Hampton Institute Clippings, "Negro Progress and Prosperity," vol. 1.
2 Rayford W. Logan, *The Negro in American Life and Thought: The Nadir, 1877–1901* (New York: Macmillan Company, 1954); C. Vann Woodward, *The Strange Career of Jim Crow,* 3d ed. (New York: Oxford University Press, 1974). Although Woodward's interpretation of the origins of segregation in the South has met with a good deal of dissent, there is general agreement among scholars that the 1890s witnessed a deterioration of race relations (both in the North and the South) that was to continue into the twentieth century.
3 Idus A. Newby, *Jim Crow's Defense: Anti-Negro Thought in America, 1900–1930* (Baton Rouge: Louisiana State University Press, 1965); George M. Frederickson, *The Black Image in the White Mind: The Debate on Afro-American Character and Destiny, 1817–1914* (New York: Harper and Row, 1971); see also, Thomas F. Gossett, *Race: The History of an Idea in America* (Dallas:

Southern Methodist University Press, 1963); Claude H. Nolen, *The Negro's Image in the South: The Anatomy of White Supremacy* (Lexington: University of Kentucky Press, 1967); Lawrence J. Friedman, *The White Savage: Racial Fantasies in the Postbellum South* (Englewood Cliffs, N.J.: Prentice Hall, 1970); and John S. Haller, Jr., *Outcasts from Evolution: Scientific Attitudes of Racial Inferiority, 1859–1900* (Urbana: University of Illinois Press, 1971); Frederick Ludwig Hoffman, *Race Traits and Tendencies of the American Negro* (New York: Macmillan Company, 1896). *Macon Telegraph*, November 24, 1910, in Hampton Clippings, "Negro Mortality," vol. 1; *Chicago Defender*, January 18, 1913.

4 *New York Age*, April 4, 1907, in Hampton Clippings, "Progress and Prosperity," vol. 1; *Amsterdam News*, June 7, 1916, in Hampton Clippings, "Progress and Prosperity," vol. 2; *Detroit Informer*, December 28, 1907, in Hampton Clippings, "The Negro in Business," vol. 1.

5 *Norfolk Journal and Guide*, February 11, 1920.

6 Booker T. Washington and W. E. B. Du Bois, *The Negro in the South: His Economic Progress in Relation to His Moral and Religious Development* (Philadelphia: G. W. Jacobs, 1907), pp. 105–8; Louis R. Harlan, *Booker T. Washington: The Making of a Leader, 1856–1901* (New York: Oxford University Press, 1972), pp. 198–203; August Meier, *Negro Thought in America, 1880–1915* (Ann Arbor: University of Michigan Press, 1963), pp. 105, 117, 123–24; Jack Temple Kirby, *Darkness at the Dawning: Race and Reform in the Progressive South* (Philadelphia: Lippincott, 1972), chs. 6–8; William L. Bittle and Gilbert L. Geis, "Racial Self-fulfillment and the Rise of an All-Negro Community in Oklahoma," *Phylon* 18 (Third Quarter 1957): 247–60; *New Bedford* (Massachusetts) *Standard*, November 16, 1914, in Hampton Clippings, "Negro Progress and Prosperity," vol. 2; *New York Age*, April 4, 1907.

7 W. H. Crogman, *Talks for the Times* (Cincinnati: Jennings and Pye, 1896), p. 169; *Amsterdam News*, June 7, 1911, in Hampton Clippings, "Progress and Prosperity," vol. 2; *Afro-American Ledger*, May 18, 1907, in Hampton Clippings, "Negro Expositions."

8 National Negro Business League, *First Proceedings*, Boston, 1900; W. E. B. Du Bois, *Economic Cooperation Among Negroes*, Atlanta University Publications, no. 12 (Atlanta: Atlanta University Press, 1907), pp. 109–11; *Durham Negro Observer*, August 4, 1906.

9 *New York Age*, February 28, 1901, in Hampton Clippings, "Negroes in Business," vol. 1.

10 Monroe N. Work, *The Negro's Progress in Fifty Years* (Philadelphia: American Academy of Political and Social Science, 1913); see also Work, "Fifty Years of Negro Progress," *Southern Workman* 42 (January 1913): 9–15; and Hampton Clippings, "Progress and Prosperity," vol. 2, and "Negroes in Business," vols. 1 and 2.

11 Booker T. Washington, *The Man Farthest Down: A Record of Observation and Study in Europe* (New York: Doubleday, Page and Company, 1912); Louis

R. Harlan, "Booker T. Washington in Biographical Perspective," *American Historical Review* 75 (October 1970): 1592; National Negro Business League, *Fifteenth Proceedings*, Muskogee, Oklahoma, 1914.

12 *New York Age*, March 14, 1901; Meier, *Negro Thought in America*, pp. 57, 105, 249; *The Star of Zion*, January 29, 1914, in Hampton Clippings, "Progress and Prosperity," vol. 2; *Afro-American Ledger*, May 18, 1907, in Hampton Clippings, "Negro Expositions."

13 *Afro-American Ledger*, May 18, 1907; *Augusta Chronicle*, November 13, 1912, in Hampton Clippings, "Negro Expositions."

14 John W. Gibson, *Progress of a Race* (originally published in Atlanta: J. L. Nicols, 1897, under the title, *Colored American*; the later title was adopted in 1901, and two subsequent editions were published in 1920 and 1929); G. F. Richings, *Evidences of Progress among Colored People* (Philadelphia: G. S. Ferguson Company, 1902); William N. Hartshorn, *An Era of Progress and Promise, 1863–1910: The Religious, Moral and Educational Development of the American Negro Since His Emancipation* (Boston: The Priscilla Publishing Company, 1910); W. L. Hunter, *Jesus Christ Had Negro Blood in His Veins* (Brooklyn: Nolan Brothers Printery, 1901); Edward A. Johnson, *A School History of the Negro Race in America* (Philadelphia: Sherman and Co., 1893); Benjamin Brawley, *A Short History of the American Negro* (New York: Macmillan Company, 1913); Booker T. Washington, *The Story of the Negro*, 2 vols. (New York: Doubleday, Page and Company, 1909); W. E. B. Du Bois, *The Negro* (New York: Holt and Company, 1915); Meier, *Negro Thought in America*, pp. 52–53, 260–63.

15 Booker T. Washington, *The Negro in Business* (Boston: Jertel, Jenkins and Company, 1907); Louis R. Harlan, "Booker T. Washington and the National Negro Business League," in *Seven on Black: Reflections on the Negro Experience in America*, ed. William G. Shade and Roy C. Herrenkohl (Philadelphia: Lippincott, 1969), pp. 73–91; National Negro Business League, *First Proceedings*, Boston, 1900; *New York Age*, August 14, 1902.

16 W. E. B. Du Bois, *Souls of Black Folks* (London: Archibald Constable and Co., 1903), pp. 11, 12, 41–43, 50; quoted in Du Bois, *The Negro in Business*, Atlanta University Publications, no. 4 (Atlanta: Atlanta University Press, 1899), pp. 58–59; *Detroit Informer*, December 28, 1907; *Newport News Star*, October 25, 1918, in Hampton Clippings, "Negroes in Business," vol. 2.

17 Booker T. Washington, N. B. Wood, and Fannie Barrier Williams, *A New Negro for a New Century: An Accurate and Up-to-Date Record of the Upward Struggles of the Negro Race* (Chicago: American Publishing Company, 1900), pp. 176, 232; *New York Age*, April 22, 1909, in Hampton Clippings, "Negroes in Business," vol. 1; *Washington Post*, August 15, 1900, and the *New York Age*, March 14, 1901, both in Hampton Clippings, "Negroes in Business," vol. 1.

18 *New York Age*, March 14, 1901, in Hampton Clippings, "Negroes in Business," vol. 1; Booker T. Washington, *The Future of the American Negro* (Boston: Small, Maynard and Company, 1899), p. 206.

19 *Colored Virginian*, November 4, 1915; *New York Age*, February 28, 1901, in

Hampton Clippings, "Negroes in Business," vol. 1; National Negro Business League, *First Proceedings,* Boston, 1900; *Newport News Star,* February 26, 1920, in Hampton Clippings, "Negro Banks," vol. 2; Ray Stannard Baker, *Following the Color Line* (New York: Doubleday, Page and Company, 1908), pp. 228–29.

20 *Norfolk Journal and Guide,* November 18, 1916.
21 Washington, *Story of the Negro,* vol. 2, p. 191.
22 R. McCants Andrews, *John Merrick: A Biographical Sketch* (Durham: Seeman Printery, 1920), pp. 158–61; *North Carolina Mutual,* January, 1906; Walter B. Weare, *Black Business in the New South: A Social History of the North Carolina Mutual Life Insurance Company* (Urbana: University of Illinois Press, 1973), chs. 1, 2, 3, 8.
23 Weare, *Black Business in the New South,* ch. 1; the best analysis of Washington's Address is in Harlan, *Booker T. Washington,* pp. 217–28.
24 Washington, *Future of the Negro,* p. 225; *Durham Negro Observer,* June 23, August 4, 1903.
25 Meier, *Negro Thought,* pp. 147–49; Hampton Clippings, "Negro Towns."
26 *Afro-American Ledger,* December 3, 1910; *New Orleans State,* June 7, 1910; *Star of Zion,* Dec. 19, 1912, in Hampton Clippings, "Negro Towns."
27 The Hampton Institute Clippings contain several volumes of material on Negro expositions and fairs. See volumes catalogued under "Negro Fairs and Expositions," "Jamestown Exposition," and "Emancipation Jubilees," 2 vols. Copies of the *Journal of Industry* are in the Charles N. Hunter papers, Manuscript Division, Duke University Library. Hunter was an ex-slave from Raleigh, North Carolina, who along with his brother launched the *Journal of Industry* in 1879 and made a career of organizing expositions and putting "Negro Progress" on display. See, for example, Hunter to U.S. Senator, Joseph Foraker, January 12, 1907, in regard to the Jamestown Exposition.
28 Hampton Clippings, "Emancipation Jubilees," vol. 2.

BIBLIOGRAPHIC NOTE

In its more direct and self-conscious form, the ubiquitous theme of progress in Afro-American writing at the turn of the century was a genre of literature worthy of study in its own right. The theme also dominated the everyday documents of Afro-American life: in sermons, speeches, correspondence, school books, pamphlets, and most especially in newspapers. The black press not only generated its own progress literature, but it reprinted, often in their entirety, the popular addresses of the period that invariably spoke to this theme. Moreover, the news of the day, much of it bad news, necessarily inspired a counterpart of good news. Racial progress, as a cultural and psychological necessity, also became the news of the day.

Among extant sources, the best register of this overall mood is the five-hundred-volume clipping file at Hampton Institute. This mine of information, drawn from black periodicals of the period, is arranged in scrapbooks under headings that in themselves reveal the topical concerns of the time. Surely it is significant that the librarians at Hampton chose progress as a major subject heading, and more significant that they found such a wealth of material. In addition to these rich clipping files, there are voluminous official proceedings, reports, and institutional publications stressing racial progress. Prominent examples would include the *Proceedings* of the Hampton Negro Conferences, along with Hampton's *Southern Workman*, the *Atlanta University Publications*, the *Occasional Papers* of the American Negro Academy, the *Negro Yearbook*, and the *Proceedings* of the National Negro Business League. *Alexander's Magazine* and the *Colored American Magazine* aimed less at academic or professional audiences in their celebrations of progress.

There is little point in repeating the footnotes here, but the writings of Booker T. Washington, especially his *Story of the Negro* (New York, 1909), should be reemphasized as a key source; and despite W. E. B. Du Bois's dissent against the uncritical assumptions of material progress, especially in his *Souls of Black Folk* (London, 1903), he, too, would champion the theme when it came to defending the race against scientific racism and its claims of Negro retrogression; see, for example, his various writings in the *Atlanta University Publications* (1896–1914), *The Negro* (New York, 1915), and the *Gift of Black Folk* (Boston, 1924).

In addition to these primary sources and those cited in the footnotes, one should also consult the bibliography and footnotes of August Meier's *Negro Thought in America, 1880–1915* (Ann Arbor, 1963) and the author's *Black Business in the New South* (Urbana, 1973). Two contemporary bibliographies remain particularly valuable: one by Du Bois, *A Select Bibliography of the American Negro* (Atlanta, 1905), the other by Booker T. Washington's researcher, Monroe N. Work, *A Bibliography of the Negro in Africa and America* (New York, 1928), in which Work set aside an entire section under the heading "progress."

4th Annual Morris Fromkin Memorial Lecture
Sentencing the unpatriotic.
Federal Trial Judges in Wisconsin During Four Wars

Beverly Blair Cook
Associate Professor of Political Science
The University of Wisconsin—Milwaukee
Recipient of the 1973 Fromkin Research Grant

Wednesday, November 7 at 3:00 p.m.
Reference Reading Room/UWM Library
Students, faculty and the public are cordially invited.
A reception will follow.

Sentencing the Unpatriotic: Federal Trial Judges in Wisconsin during Four Wars

BEVERLY BLAIR COOK

OVER four modern wars federal judges in the Western District of Wisconsin consistently sentenced defendants accused of unpatriotic illegal acts more harshly than the federal judges in the Eastern District. Political culture provides a fundamental explanation for the central tendencies and boundaries of this kind of judicial behavior. Previous empirical work has related judicial behavior to the psychodynamics of individual judges, to their socialization to legal and political roles, to their ambitions, and to their response to internal and external environmental pressures. The forces of national and local opinion also press heavily upon federal trial judges because of their national roles and work location within their home communities. But the political culture of a jurisdiction stimulates, reinforces, or modifies the substantive effect of such factors upon judicial decisions.

A CULTURAL-ROLE FRAMEWORK

Political scientists and anthropologists have not often probed the direct relationship between cultural differences and the substantive outcome of cases (Merry, 1979).[1] Rather, culture has been associated

---

Beverly B. Cook, who took degrees at Wellesley College, the University of Wisconsin–Madison, and Claremont Graduate School, is a political science professor who specializes in judicial behavior. Her work on sentencing and public opinion and on women judges was most recently published in *American Journal of Political Science, International Political Science Review*, and the *1981 Yearbook* of the U.S. Supreme Court Historical Society. She has chapters in *Women in the Courts* (1978); *The Study of Criminal Courts* (1979); *Women in Local Politics* (1980); *Courts, Law, and Judicial Processes* (1981); and *Women, Power, and Political Systems* (1981).

with a method of selecting officials or of resolving disputes and the characteristics of the officeholder and of the process then used to explain decisional patterns. Several political scientists have implicitly tested the relationship of culture to judicial output. In his classic description of the dilemma of southern federal judges caught between the expectations of the Supreme Court for egalitarian race decisions and their local communities for support for segregation, Peltason (1961, 1971) does not explicitly employ a cultural framework. He does examine the relationship of beliefs and prejudices in the southern tradition to the resistance of federal judges to the enforcement of new legal norms and offers a general hypothesis that "judicial decisions here, as elsewhere, are not likely to make any major departure from the norms of the community" (253). Vines (1964) compared the racial makeup of southern counties to the school segregation decisions in southern federal courts; his population measure was one indicator of the degree of cultural traditionalism in the counties. Levin (1977) compared the criminal sentence patterns in Minneapolis and Pittsburgh, cities with different structures of judicial selection, recruitment, and socialization. He could have conceptualized the structural and other variations as indicators of political culture.

A number of studies have described a relationship between the geographical location of courts and the severity of criminal sentences. Sentencing has been compared across counties in California and across districts in the federal Fifth Circuit (Harries, 1974, 102–3). The purpose of these studies has not been to explain variation in judicial decisions but to identify and prescribe remedies for "disparity." The authors argue that where the same penal code, the same criminal procedure, and the same court structure exist, the outputs (for similar cases) should also be alike (Sutton, 1978). Their implicit claim is that legal culture should control legal products, but since geographically distinct judicial districts with the same legal culture may have distinguishable political cultures, sentence variation may be treated as a political phenomenon with political correlates.

CULTURE CONCEPT

Political culture can be defined as a set of deeply rooted, historically conditioned beliefs about the nature of political authority, the relationship of the political elite and the mass, the criteria for membership in the political community, and the organization and procedure for making political decisions. Legal culture is distinct although related to political culture, and federal judges work within the confines of both cultures. The two Wisconsin federal district courts share the same national political and legal cultures associated with national politics and the federal judicial hierarchy but operate within different local political and legal cultures. Culture is an appropriate framework to examine how these Wisconsin trial judges controlled political dissidents, since patriotism is an effect universally associated with political cultures. Patriotism identifies the survival of a political entity with its entire package of values, customs, and interests (Doob, 1964, 128–33).

The role expectations for elites, such as judges, are defined by the major orientations of the political and legal cultures, including the ubiquitous cultural norm of patriotism. Federal judges, whose positions are a prized reward of the political system, showed little patience with antiwar defendants during the four wars through the end of the Vietnam period, when a majority of the public questioned the congruence of that war with national values and its necessity for national survival.

The political culture categories used in this study derive from Elazar's (1966, 1975) description of three political subcultures in the United States—the traditional, the individualist, and the moralist. Each political culture has a different pattern of orientation to political action, which affects the type of people attracted to political office and influences the way they make public policy (Sharkansky, 1969, 67). In the model moralist (M) culture the function of politics is the pursuit of the common good, recognized by a broad consensus. Government is a positive instrument to achieve social goals, and a consensual or nonpartisan political process selects and supports the regime. Participation of citizens in politics is high in M areas (Sharkansky, 1969, 83). The substantive content of judicial policy depends upon the contemporary values of the M culture, which could pursue pacifist or chauvinist values with the same intensity.

In the model individualist (I) culture government is a limited purpose corporation, which operates like a marketplace, with law and policy the product of bargaining. The proper scope of political authority and the claim of government to citizen obedience are problematic in the I culture. Private ends are valued above most public purposes. Partisan organizations provide a mode of combining private interests and channeling their struggle over control of patronage and other resources. In the model traditional (T) culture, an ascribed elite, who epitomize the historical values of the community, monopolize the public positions, including the judiciary. Public policy serves the ends of the elite, who see the close relationship among the stability of the political system, the continuity of its historical values, and

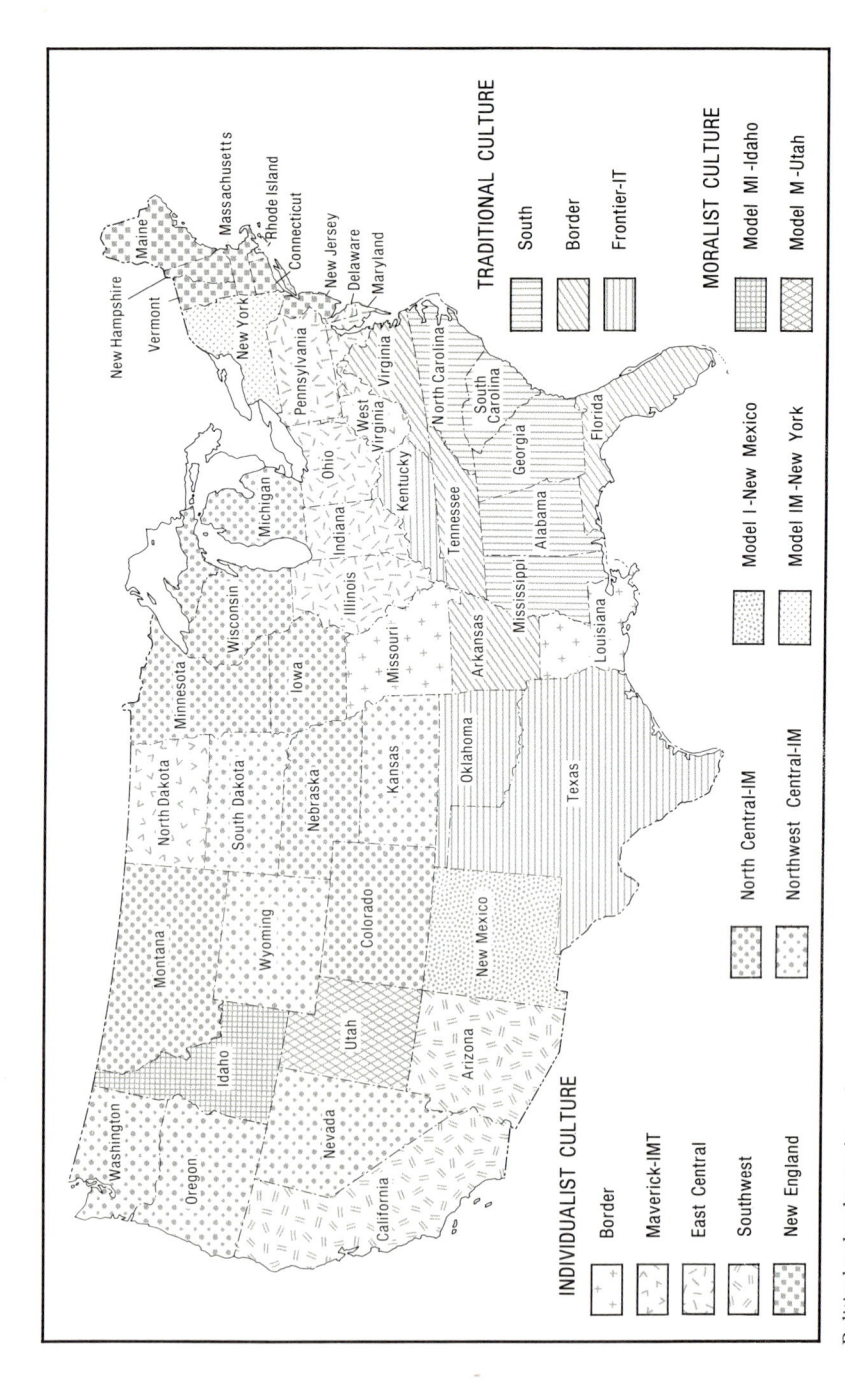

Political subcultures in regions

their own tenure in office. One-party dominance is typical of T culture politics.

UTILITY OF THE ROLE CONCEPT

A concept which fits nicely into a cultural framework is "role," or the expectations for the behavior of a person in a systemic position. For our purposes judicial role is defined by the expectations generated by a culture for the performance of persons in the federal judge position in war cases. The formal norms which constrain the judges are in the legal culture, specified in federal law and procedures which affect the entire federal judiciary. But broader cultural norms also set limits to their interpretation of that law and the use of their discretion. To avoid anthropomorphizing "culture," we should keep in mind that cultural expectations reach the judges through past or present human intermediaries. Role implies reciprocal expectations, so that a judge who creates "extra-judicial" roles must receive some supportive feedback to persist in creative performances (Sheldon, 1974).

Judicial role is often defined by judges' use of their legal tools. A judge exercises restraint by construing a law "strictly," i.e., by following precedent, by choosing narrow meanings, and by relying on historical judgments. An activist judge construes a law flexibly, i.e., by broadening word and phrase meanings, by developing or breaking with precedent, and by taking standards from extra-legal sources.

Activism finds its outlet not only in the interpretation of law but also in the performance of (largely) discretionary acts, such as jury charges and sentencing. Policy preferences appear boldly in statements to jurors and defendants or less obviously in sentences. What is acceptable in the homilies offered as jury charges or sentencing orders is unclear. The practices indulged by Federalist judges during an early cold war have been adopted by other judges with strong political feelings throughout U.S. history (Warren, 1922, vol. 1, 164–67). Some federal judges in every war reiterate in the courtroom, during jury charges and at sentence hearings, their loyalty to the country, support for the war, and solidarity with war leaders.

This example shows that activism is not necessarily in defense of minority rights; another form of activism is in support of the majority point of view and carries the policy legitimatized by law to its extreme. This type of activism is little noted or disapproved because it comports with governmental stability. The legal literature describes judges who accept legislative policies and executive practices as exercising "judicial restraint." Minority-focused activism can be a threat to system stability, but majoritarian activism may be contrary to the constitutional principle of separation of power and the judicial norms of objectivity and neutrality. The only study to examine judges as "crusaders" in the implementation of existing public policy explains this activism in terms of ambition but also asks a number of interesting questions about the linkage between acceptable judicial styles and local legal cultures (Galanter, 1979). War is an environmental condition favorable to the increased scope and vitality of judge power, in harness with other authorities to achieve the common goal. This study compares the boundaries imposed by different cultures in different judicial districts upon this majoritarian judicial activism.

Within the cultural-role framework one would expect judges to approach their law-jobs in the style characteristic of the culture. These law-jobs have been categorized by Hoebel (1954, 11ff.) as social control, norm enforcement, conflict resolution, and adaptation/social change. As applied to wartime cases, *M* judges in a nationalistic community would engage in social control by coercing defendants into patriotic behavior and by punishing harshly those who refused their duty. Judges in the *M* culture take on a general responsibility to higher principle with their position on the bench and generally expect citizens to meet at minimum the mandatory legal requirements of citizenship. Similarly, the *M* judges would uphold precedents (norms) which give broad scope to the other branches in military matters and would enforce the rules vigorously enough to deter potential delinquents. The judge in the *M* culture would see consistent punishment for disobedience of the same law regardless of the interests of the defendant to be a positive judicial duty in a principled political system.

Since the *I* culture leaves room for compromise and disagreement on principle, the judge may be more sympathetic and flexible in setting penalties for members of ethnic or religious minority groups who resist military service. *I* judges would be satisfied with an imperfect level of enforcement, perhaps dismissing cases to allow more individual expression and action. The *I* judges, less certain of the rightness of any government policy, would be more moderate and less didactic. Since judges in the *I* culture recognize their own self-interest in accepting public office, they are more likely to accept the self-interest of others as a legitimate reason for accepting or refusing civic obligations, such as the draft.

Conflict resolution is generally more central to the abilities of the *I* judge, who would look for compromises to suit the unusual sects and philosophical objectors and to make the patriots feel that national symbols were properly honored. The M judge would decide definitively for the "right" side rather than approve any compromise with principle. In respect to adaptation and social change the I judges would move with the tide, while the M judge might move dramatically ahead or stubbornly adhere to *stare decisis* to protect an ideal. The M judge would be as vigorous in enforcing the principle of pacifism, if that were the community preference, as patriotism.

Extra-Judicial Roles

During a war or emergency period persons in specialized roles tend to focus upon the primary goal of system survival. Diverse public officials, with discrete roles in normal times, become integrated into a war "machine" and concentrate upon the defeat of the common enemy. In Wisconsin during the First World War, professors, ministers, local officials, and judges made national defense their common function. University professors taught prowar courses, and police chiefs rounded up workers for war industries (Pixley, 1919; Stewart, 1919). Ministers gave sermons urging parishioners to join the Loyalty Legion to purify the country of dissent (Carey, 1965). One prosecution in Wisconsin's Western District was based on the defendant's unpatriotic complaint that churches were turning into recruiting stations (Janick, 1918). Instead of different standards for appropriate behavior in different roles, patriotism became the primary measure for all roles.

During the wartimes covered in this research, federal judges in Wisconsin assumed more or less responsibility for the function of system survival, i.e., national defense. They justified their behavior in doing their part for victory in terms of its purpose: national persistence. During the Korean War, one Wisconsin judge explained his enforcement of the draft act in terms of the "survival of this country" (Scheel, 1954) and "the defense of the country" (Nichols, 1952). Even during the Vietnam War a judge explained to a defendant that "The government's interest in national defense must be deemed superior to an individual's . . . opposition to military service" (*United States v. Kuchnau*, 1972). The judges did not carry out their defense function only through their traditional roles of law interpretation and application but also added "extra-judicial" roles.

Not all federal judges slipped into special wartime roles. But like the La Follettes and Bergers, judges who refused to put aside traditional role restraints found themselves accused of disloyalty. In handling cases against people who refused to give personal or financial contributions to the cause, judges had an opportunity to expand their repertoire of roles. Some judges dropped the standard of "neutrality" in processing wartime cases and quite openly took on the prosecutor role. Other judges elaborated their roles beyond trial umpire to act like army recruiters, manpower mobilizers, and fund raisers.

Expectations for Trial Judge: Circuit Supervision

A new role assumed by a public official is not viable without the approval or neutrality of others in the same political system. Federal trial judges work in a hierarchy subject to the supervision of appellate judges and cannot press their sentence discretion to the limit or create new recruiter or fund raiser roles without the implied if not explicit consent of their superiors. Even if their local constituency encourages and approves the extra-judicial roles, trial judges cannot pursue them unless they also fulfill the expectations of their appellate supervisors. The Sixth Circuit, for example, restrained the patriotic zeal of a trial judge in the Great War, noting that his jury charge "contains in several places rich and inspiring expressions of patriotism and of the nobility of our aims in the war, which could hardly have failed to increase the patriotic feeling that was already aflame in the heart of every juryman" (*Stokes v. United States*, 1920, 26).

The Seventh Circuit in Chicago monitored the prosecutor role of Wisconsin judges several times in World War II, in appeals from the conviction and sentencing of Jehovah's Witnesses (*United States v. Mroz*, 1943; *United States v. Messersmith*, 1943). The appellate judges specified the standard, that "a defendant is entitled to be tried by an impartial and fair judge, who shall maintain his role of judge and not assume that of prosecutor" (*United States v. Domres*, 1944, 479). But they did not find that the trial judge's "lively interest in the trial . . . was prejudicial in view of the clear case of guilt proved." The circuit judges also applauded the contribution of trial judges to the mobilization of men for the armed forces (479). The appellate bench corrects only clear-cut violations of legal expectations, giving trial judges a generous implied permission to experiment with extra-judicial roles which fit their local political cultures.

Appellate courts also supervise the introduction by trial judges of new legal standards for the treatment of the unpatriotic, through their interpretation of statutes or expansion of constitutional rights. In the Vietnam period the higher courts were as hesitant about the expansion of the trial judges' power over draft policy made by the executive as they had been liberal in ignoring their extra-judicial power over offenders.

FEDERAL JUDICIAL DECISIONS AND THE THREE CULTURES

In order to justify the comparison of judicial sentences in two districts with cultures which differ modestly, we will begin with a more general examination of the arrangement of cultures by state throughout the continental United States and to establish their relationship to draft case sentences during the Vietnam War. Figure 1 shows the location within regions of the cultures defined by Johnson's (1976, table 1) operationalization of Elazar's impressionistic categorization of cultural mix. Only two states are clearly moralist: Utah is 93 percent M and Idaho 68 percent M. One state is an ideal I—New Mexico with a score of 92 percent. The individualist and moralist migrations can be traced from the New England states, through the East Central and North Central states, then spreading to the Northwest and Southwest corners of the country. The traditional migration moves from the Deep South to the border and frontier states and slightly infiltrates the East Central area, but does not reach to the North Central, or Far West. Only two states are mixtures of the three cultures, West Virginia and North Dakota.

Table 1 shows the changing percentage of prison sentences given by judges in seven cultural areas, where a substantial caseload of draft cases in each time period insured stable percentages. The seven groupings are based on similarity of scores in the major and the minor culture. The five states omitted (Idaho, Utah, West Virginia, North Dakota, and New Mexico) could not be included in a larger category because of their extreme culture scores and insufficient cases to be considered separately. The national pattern of draft sentencing is increasing leniency, from the 82.2 percent imprisoned in 1967–68 to 24.4 percent in 1973–74, which correlates with changing national opinion about participation in the Vietnam War (Cook, 1977, table 3). Each cultural area, like each major geographical region and each judicial circuit, shows the same pattern of less severe sentences over time (Cook, 1977, table 1).

The aggregation of sentences by culture type indicates that the boundaries of sentence variation differ by culture. The traditional states, in the Deep South and the Border, imprisoned as many as 90 percent of the convicted offenders. The states with a moralist component, in the Northwest, North Central and New York, and Southwest and the states in the East Central with a traditional component reached their most severe point at just over 80 percent incarcerated. But the most typical of the individualist states in New England did not exceed 75 percent prison sentences. Judges who were selected

Table 1. Prison Sentences in Draft Cases by Cultural Areas

	Scale	\multicolumn{4}{c}{Percentage of Convicted Sent to Prison}	Average	Case N
		1967–68	1969–70	1971–72	1973–74		
South/Border T (9)	T = 84–78 I = 14–19 M = 01–04	89.2	73.3	47.1	34.2	60.9	1002
Frontier/Border IT (5)	T = 46–23 I = 47–69 M = 05–10	90.1	69.4	47.4	28.6	64.3	519
East Central I (7)	T = 11–01 I = 71–87 M = 12–21	81.1	41.7	22.4	18.1	37.1	1406
New England I (6)	T = 00–00 I = 75–82 M = 18–23	73.4	45.0	24.7	7.0	33.9	413
Southwest I (2)	T = 02–02 I = 75–76 M = 22–23	78.8	44.0	25.2	20.7	38.4	2157
North Central IM (7)	T = 03–01 I = 81–68 M = 18–29	81.0	50.7	40.1	25.9	44.0	1581
Northwest/NY IM (7)	T = 05–00 I = 70–50 M = 30–40	80.7	45.4	39.5	31.1	47.7	1157
Averages Case N		82.2 1608	50.7 1943	32.6 2843	24.4 1841	39.3	8235

NOTE: T shows the range of scores on the traditional dimension for the states within the cultural area. I shows the range of individualist scores; M shows the range of moralist scores. Each successive group increases on one or more dimensions and decreases on one or more dimensions. Number of states in parentheses.

and worked within a culture which appreciated political compromise gave more moderate sentences, even during a period when their colleagues in other parts of the country were insisting upon full enforcement of the law and the tradition of wartime patriotism and honor. By the last time period, 1973–74, the most individualist section had reached a minimal 7 percent to prison, while the most traditional area and the most moralist area did not reach 30 percent. The individualist states were not willing to demand complete conformity of individual members of society to public policy, even on national security, and so revealed a range of punishment from moderate to very lenient. The traditional and the moralist areas were willing to subordinate their constituents to governmental policy and moved from very harsh to reasonably lenient.

The range of adaptation also differed, with the most individualist area showing the greatest range and the most traditional and moralist the least. In the order in which the cultural areas are listed on the table, the ranges are South/Border 55, Frontier/Border 61, East Central 63, New England 66, Southwest 58, North Central 55, and Northwest/New York 50. The individualist areas responded in much more flexible fashion to changing public opinion than the areas with fixed traditions or moral positions. I would expect traditional jurisdictions to maintain high boundaries for punitiveness and low ranges but would predict that moralist jurisdictions in certain situations would move through a wider range than individualist areas, in response to a major cultural revision of values.

Since there appears to be a difference in the response of judges in different cultural areas to the unpatriotic offenders during the Vietnam War, it seems feasible to examine the reactions of judges in two judicial districts with different cultures in Wisconsin across four wars. In the next section the difference in culture in the Eastern and Western Districts will be described in the context of the Civil War. The following three sections will examine and compare the traditional and extra-judicial roles of the Wisconsin federal judges in the two districts from the First World War through the Vietnam War.

WISCONSIN'S TWO CULTURES IN THE CIVIL WAR

Wisconsin contains two of the three political cultures recognized by Elazar (1966, 1975)—the moralist and the individualist. The third culture, traditionalist, was not carried by migrants into Wisconsin. Elazar associates the location of cultures with patterns of ethnic and religious migration across the nation. In the first major immigration into Wisconsin territory, New Englanders and northern Europeans brought a moralist culture to the western part of the state. The second major immigration from the middle colonies and central Europe carried the individualist culture across the state. Elazar considers Wisconsin a mixed state, primarily moralist, but Johnson (1976) concludes from his use of census indicators of religious membership that the state is predominantly individualist.

CULTURAL DISTINCTIONS BETWEEN THE FEDERAL DISTRICT COURTS

At admission to the union in 1848 Wisconsin had a single federal judicial district coterminous with the state line, with one judge authorized to hold court in Milwaukee, the population center of the *I* culture, and also in Madison, the population center of the *M* culture. In 1870 Congress created two districts, each with one judge, divided by a north-south boundary generally congruent with the separate settlements of the ethnic and religious groups carrying the two cultures. The number of judges in the Eastern District increased from one through World War II to two in the Korean War, and three in the Vietnam War (up to four by 1980), while one judge served the Western District (until a second position was created in 1979). (See appendix A for the list of Wisconsin federal judges serving during the four twentieth-century wars.) The Eastern District covers twenty-seven counties with court sites in Milwaukee, Green Bay, and Oshkosh, and the Western forty-four counties with court centers in Madison, Eau Claire, LaCrosse, Superior, and Wausau.

Table 2 describes the distinctive populations of the two judicial districts by their ethnic and religious composition in the 1920s. People of the Eastern District include descendants of German and Polish immigrants and of adherents to the Catholic Church and the Lutheran Synods of Missouri and Wisconsin. People of the Western District include descendants of Scandinavian countries and of Congregational and Lutheran denominations. A more rigorous approach to the categorization of Wisconsin by culture is to examine the religious makeup of the population by county and to measure the contribution of all three cultural elements to the political unit. Johnson (1976, table 1) reports that Wisconsin, based upon the average religious composition of the state in 1906, 1916, 1926, and 1936, is 80 percent individualist, 20 percent moralist, and 1 percent traditional. The data

Table 2. Ethnic and Religious Roots of Wisconsin Subcultures

	Religious Population in State, 1920s	Percentage of Group in Federal Judicial Districts	
		Eastern	Western
Lutheran Synods			
Missouri/Wisconsin	269,719	67.1	32.9
Catholic Church	657,511	65.0	35.0
German-born	151,250	68.0	32.0
Polish-born	50,558	74.4	25.6
Congregational	35,013	45.8	54.2
Norwegian Lutheran	101,480	16.0	84.0
Swedish-born	22,896	25.2	74.8
Norwegian-born	45,433	18.1	81.9

SOURCES: U.S. Bureau of the Census, *Census of Religious Bodies: 1926*, vol. 1, table 32, "Members in Selected Denominations, by Counties: 1926, Wisconsin"; U.S. Bureau of the Census, *14th Census* (1920), vol. 3, table 12, "Country of Birth of Foreign-Born Whites for Counties—Wisconsin."

from the 1926 Department of Commerce census of religious affiliation (vol. I, table 32), aggregated by county into judicial districts, show the Eastern District is 90 percent individualist, 9 percent moralist, and 1 percent traditional and the Western District 72 percent individualist, 26 percent moralist, and 2 percent traditional.[2] For simplicity of contrast, the Eastern District will be called individualist and the Western moralist.

The ideals of the wars in which Wisconsin participated carried different meanings for the people of the eastern and western sections. In the Civil War the goals of union and abolition had little practical attraction to the recent immigrants from Europe. For the *M* culture of the western part of the state the issues were abstractions from their immediate life experience on Wisconsin prairies and forests but a part of their intellectual heritage from the New England colonies. World War I was "a war to end all wars" by defeating the Kaiser and establishing a permanent framework for peace. The notion of one world community under law fitted the highest ideals of the moralistic commonwealth. The moralists could treat the Civil and World Wars as crusades.

On the other hand, the German people in the *I* section of Wisconsin saw no psychological or economic benefits in neglecting their farms and businesses to fight their own relatives in Europe. The world government ideal had little appeal to people concerned with personal and group interests. The war was a tragedy in which *I* types did not want to play a role. World War II in principle was a reenactment of the first with more emphasis on the negative impact of losing to the totalitarian Nazis than on any positive hope of world government and peace. While the sentiment in the Eastern District was not so closely tied to personal associations with Germany, the benefits of a personal investment in the war were as doubtful to individualists as in the previous war.

The wars in Asia did not provoke mixed loyalties in the Eastern District, but neither did they offer any practical rewards to a soldier or taxpayer. Without an industrial base dependent on military needs, the pragmatic Eastern District had no material incentive to support these Asian wars. The goals were essentially negative—to stop communism in Asia. The hope of world peace which aroused support in the World Wars was missing and in its place an explicit appeal to American world domination. Although another moralistic culture might respond to the ideal of national supremacy, western Wisconsin was not ready to shift quickly from the ideal of democracy to power. The court decisions of the two districts would be expected, on the basis of this analysis, to differ considerably during the World Wars but to move toward similarity in the Asian wars when neither principle nor materialism could be served by patriotism.

CONSCRIPTION ISSUES IN THE CIVIL WAR

In the Civil War period no comparison of federal judicial behavior is possible since only one federal judge with statewide venue served Wisconsin. The skeletal federal law enforcement was one indicator of the frontier condition of the state, which was only loosely connected with the seat of national government through primitive communication and transportation systems. The federal government had no alternative to reliance on the good will and cooperation of state officials and citizens in producing manpower and supplies for the Northern armies. Wisconsin residents in the two cultural sections reacted differently to war mobilization.

Wisconsin was a state of recent immigrants, persuaded by state agents on duty at New York harbor to buy land in Wisconsin. Thirty-six percent of the population was foreign born, and many had left Europe specifically to avoid military conscription. Active and passive resistance to the Civil War focused on the draft and dissatisfaction with the military leaders whose ineptitude created new demands for conscripts. There was little opposition based upon the moral purpose of the war or upon personal ties with the enemy. Only 1 percent of the state residents were southerners (Klement, 1962, 72–73). The Yankees and the Forty-Niner liberals who fled Germany were abolitionists in principle, but the nonintellectual laborers from Germany and Ireland had a self-interested fear that emancipation would produce cheap labor and cut their own living standards (Klement, 1962, 74).

The laws and the legal structure, like patriotism, were less well developed in Wisconsin in the Civil War than in the World War sixty years later. State officials acted under national authority, carrying out presidential directives and accepting reimbursement for services and expenses from the national treasury. Governors and sheriffs, who were state and county elected officials, and enrollment officers and draft commissioners, appointed by the governor, all engaged in national duties. The federal and state war roles were not distinct, and the unpatriotic seldom faced national authority except through the buffer of state officialdom.

There was room for resistance to the draft in the Civil War because the traditional theory that the duty to "muster" and the penalty for refusal were local was in transition. During the Civil War, Congress authorized the president to make all necessary rules and regulations for enrolling the militia in states which lacked such provisions (July 17, 1862). The Wisconsin legislature found it politically expedient to accept the president's order rather than pass its own draft law. In 1863 Congress spelled out the details of calling up the "national forces" in the Conscription Act (12 Stat. 731, March 3, 1863). The power to define and control the state militia was beginning to move from the state to the national government.

Opposition to the draft festered in the eastern counties of the *I* culture, where recent immigrants were concerned about working to pay off their farm mortgages. They avoided the draft in legal ways, e.g., by signing into volunteer fire companies, by filing exemptions as aliens, and by providing personal or monetary substitutes, and in illegal ways, e.g., by avoiding registration, by feigning illness, or by hiding in the woods or in Canada. A variety of public and private programs gave opponents in the Civil War options which they did not enjoy in later wars. Federal law allowed the payment of a commutation fee of $300 during the early part of the war. Throughout the war the draftee could avoid muster by presenting a qualified substitute at the rendezvous point. Draft insurance companies collected membership fees from enrolled men in return for finding substitutes for those actually drafted. The first such association in the country was formed in Wisconsin (Schoonover, 1915, 45). These companies prospered in the eastern *I* section among Germans, Democrats, and voting aliens. Those loyal to the war, mostly Republicans, formed clubs called Union Leagues to show their disapproval of the legal as well as the illegal forms of war resistance.

There were also public and private incentives to participate in the war. Conscripts received $100 in 1863. Volunteers received larger bounties from their communities; and as the war dragged on, the amount increased. The city of Eau Claire paid $100, Madison $200, and Port Washington by 1864 offered $300. In Milwaukee the bounty failed to attract recruits (Schoonover, 1915, 67). Taxpayers were willing to pay to encourage volunteers since their number reduced the local draft quota. These various compromises of the principle of universal service did not entirely defuse resistance.

Since volunteers did not fill the quotas set by the governor in the eastern counties, the first official drafts occurred in the individualist section most opposed to war participation. Opponents organized "no draft" marches, blocked the house to house progress of the enrollment officers, and threw stones and eggs at draft officers (Murdock, 1967; Klement, 1962). A full-scale riot in Port Washington in November 1862 provided the grist for a number of cases before the Wisconsin Supreme Court. In that dramatic incident a mob stoned and beat the draft commissioner, broke up the ballot box stuffed with names of eligible draftees, destroyed the property of prowar Republicans, and set up a cannon on the pier to impede retaliation from the militia. Local authorities sympathetic to the draft resisters did not punish the rioters by enforcing available state and local laws forbidding property destruction or disturbance of the peace.

The statistics on the results of the 1863 draft in Wisconsin (table 3) show clearly the difference in response from the region of individualist culture and the region of moralist culture. Although the western area was more sparsely populated and had a lower quota, it actually provided more draftees (480) than the eastern zone (312). The same proportion in both sections was discharged prior to muster under the family and medical exemptions. The eastern individualists provided more personal substitutes than the western moralists, but a larger proportion of the settled westerners were able to buy out from service. Over one-fifth of the eastern draftees disappeared, but only 6.5 percent of the western draftees disappeared. The proportion of western draftees actually mustered into service was over three times the proportion of eastern draftees.[3]

TRADITIONAL JUDICIAL ROLE: LAW INTERPRETATION

Federal and state court jurisdiction over war cases overlapped, and the location of responsibility for enforcement of the draft was uncertain and fluid. The fact that forms of disloyalty short of treason, from

Table 3. 1863 Draft in Wisconsin by Cultural Section

	Individualist Culture	Moralist Culture
Congressional Districts	1, 4, 5	2, 3, 6
Total drafted	10,136	4,799
Discharged prior to muster	4,299	2,022
Percentage	42.4	42.1
Substitutions		
Persons	224	28
Commutation money	3,153	1,928
Total percentage	33.3	40.8
Disappearances	2,148	314
Percentage	21.2	6.5
Mustered into service	312	480
Percentage	3.1	10.0

SOURCE: Lynn Schoonover, "A History of the Civil War Draft in Wisconsin" (M.A. thesis, University of Wisconsin, 1915), pp. 55–56, from the Adjutant-General Report, 1864, p. 512.

violence against draft officials to subversive speech, were not defined in federal law at the beginning of the Civil War caused problems for the dual court system. The maintenance of order during registration and drafting depended upon the attitudes of local law enforcement agencies. When local officials lost control, the military—under state and/or federal direction—sometimes intervened to stop the mobs, protect the conscription process, and lock up the culprits. The inadequacy of the local forces and the questionable legality of the military action gave legal space for the growth of opposition.

Congress wrote the first criminal laws which applied to interference with the draft immediately after passage of the first federal conscription act (1863). The application of this criminal law in Wisconsin was at issue before the United States Supreme Court after the war upon certification by a split federal circuit court. The question was whether assault upon an enrollment officer was included as a crime in the 1863 act, when the amended act of 1864 separately described that offense. The Supreme Court concluded that federal criminal law did not cover resistance to registration in 1863, and the case was dismissed from the federal court (*United States v. Murphy,* 1866).

After the Civil War, Congress expanded and embroidered on the inadequate federal criminal laws applying to civilian behavior in wartime. Gradually federal judges accumulated the legal instruments for protecting the country against internal opposition. The state governments, which were unprepared to deal with subversion in the Civil War, also filled their codes with provisions to punish un-Americanism of various kinds. Between the Civil War and the World Wars, forty-four of the states drew up statutes to protect the United States government from unpatriotic words and acts. State judges used these laws to control persons with unacceptable ideologies during and after World War I. The preeminence of the federal government in prosecuting crimes against national security was recognized by the Supreme Court after World War II (*Pennsylvania v. Nelson,* 1956). The Court found that "Congress has occupied the field to the exclusion of parallel state legislation," almost one hundred years after the chief justice of the Wisconsin Supreme Court urged that the federal government assume such exclusive responsibility (*In re* Kemp, 1863).

Resisters in the Civil War (and later in the Vietnam War) took the initiative in the courts to challenge draft policy on constitutional grounds. In the World Wars and Korea the assertive party was the government, which turned to the courts to coerce resisters to do their duty or pay an appropriate penalty. But without criminal laws as enforcement tools, the federal government was on the defensive in the judicial process during the Civil War. War opponents had traditional due process rights at their disposal. In a series of cases the antiwar groups challenged the legality of the presidential draft order of 1862, of the governor's power under that order to suppress draft riots, and of the president's power to suspend the writ of habeas corpus.[4] The state Supreme Court approved the national power to conscript and the governor's power to arrest draft rioters and disapproved presidential suspension of habeas corpus without legislative authorization.

Recruiting and Constitutional Interpretation

Draftees in Manitowoc County challenged the authority of the draft commissioner to call them up and deliver them into military custody, by applying for habeas corpus to gain their release from military camp. The state Supreme Court, which consisted of three justices sitting in Madison, found that Congress had authorized the presidential order of 1862 which established rules for the administration of the draft in states without their own provisions. The Wisconsin state judges found no improper delegation of legislative power to the president. The Court said that: "The federal government is clothed with ample powers of self-preservation and self-defense, whether assailed by traitors at home or enemies abroad" (*In re* Griner, 1863, 466–67). Judges were no more willing to declare the draft unconstitutional in the Civil War than in the Vietnam War.

The Wisconsin justices also assisted the recruitment process through its ruling on draft eligibility. They found that a resident alien who declared intent to become a citizen, since treated as a citizen under Wisconsin law, therefore was subject to the draft (*In re* Wehlitz, 1862).

Fund Raising and Constitutional Interpretation

In the first flush of enthusiasm for the Northern side in the war, the Wisconsin legislature in special session 1861 passed a statute authorizing the issuance of bonds and the borrowing of money or credit up to one million dollars for war purposes. The state constitution allowed this degree of indebtedness only to repel invasion, suppress insurrection, and defend the territory of the state. Concerned about the constitutionality of the measure, the governor asked the Supreme Court for an advisory opinion. The Supreme Court had no authority to give an advisory opinion by statute or custom. Nevertheless two justices signed a letter to the governor assuring him that they had no doubt as to the constitutionality of the highly questionable statute (Winslow, 1912, 200).

Loyalty on the Home Front and Constitutional Interpretation

Although the state Supreme Court gave legitimacy to recruiting and fund raising for the war, the justices stopped short of approving the suspension of habeas corpus for civilians in an area far removed from hostilities. The first habeas corpus case arose from the Port Washington riot. The governor ordered the militia to pick up the rioters and turn them over to the military, in conformity with the 1862 executive order that "all persons discouraging volunteer enlistments, resisting militia drafts, or guilty of any disloyal practice" be subject to martial law (Gen. Orders No. 141, War Dept. September 25, 1862). The Supreme Court issued a writ of habeas corpus to the general in charge of the prisoners, who was holding them without any official complaint or judgment of any court. Since the president had suspended habeas corpus for military prisoners in 1862, the general did not respond to the state court writ.

The Wisconsin Supreme Court then decided that only Congress could pass a law suspending the writ and that the president could not make criminal law or impose martial law in an area where civilian government was using ordinary judicial processes. The Court was embarrassed by its jurisdiction over presidential action, particularly when its conclusions might appear to hamper the war effort. Under the circumstances, rather than issue an attachment to the general, the Court agreed to delay in order to allow the federal officials to extricate themselves from the situation (*In re* Kemp, 1863). The Lincoln administration did not want the case appealed to the United States Supreme Court, where Chief Justice Taney, the author of the *Merryman* opinion (1861), would have an opportunity to affirm the unconstitutionality of Lincoln's order. The rioters were quietly released.

Although the Wisconsin court would not stretch constitutional principles to empower the president, the justices would not allow the rioters to collect damages from the governor for his part in their arrest. When a rioter brought a civil action for false imprisonment against the governor after the war, the Wisconsin Supreme Court decided that their resistance had been treasonous and that the governor was justified in ordering the arrests (*Druecker v. Salomon*, 1867, 626).

In 1863 Congress passed new legislation delegating to the president power to suspend the writ when in his opinion the public safety so required; President Lincoln acted under that authority to suspend the writ for persons held by the military as prisoners or soldiers. The Wisconsin Supreme Court ruled on the validity of this delegation when the father of a minor son who enlisted without permission asked for a writ to reclaim the son from the military. The Court refused to issue the writ, obeying the presidential order despite their serious doubts about the constitutionality of the delegation of power (*In re* Oliver, 1864). The Court went along with the war powers when the national legislature as well as the president agreed on the rule and when the person involved was in a military rather than a civilian role.

During the Civil War in Wisconsin the state judges rather than the federal judges played a significant role in making war policy and controlling the unpatriotic. The state judges in the Civil War suffered the same kind of personal distress over conflicts between patriotism and judicial standards of neutrality and objectivity that the federal judges felt in later wars. Justice Paine salved his conscience over his early states' rights attitude by resigning from the state court in 1864 and entering service as a colonel (Winslow, 191, 231–32). The discomfort involved in finding that the president acted unconstitutionally shows clearly in the opinion written by Chief Justice Dixon in 1863 (*In re* Kemp, 370).

> Penned at the gloomiest period of our public misfortunes, when over fifty thousand of the noblest of the land, answering the summons, had fallen a sacrifice to the cause of our nationality . . . when the only way to national life, honor and peace, lay through the fire and blood of battle . . . instead of the utmost loyalty and patriotism . . . there was . . . factious and disloyal opposition—the proclamation in question is not a welcome subject of criticism.

In the following section we will see how differently the judges of the Eastern and Western Districts of the federal courts handle the strains imposed by cases involving unpatriotic acts in four twentieth-century wars.

WISCONSIN CULTURE AND JUDICIAL DECISIONS IN WORLD WAR I

Federal trial judges during the Great War had direct encouragement from their own superiors and from their constituents to become active partners with the president and Congress in the war effort. The tone set by the Supreme Court and the attorney general could only have legitimated for inferior judges the harsh treatment of war offenders. Chief Justice White jumped from his seat and led the cheering when President Wilson asked a joint session of Congress for a declaration of war in 1917.[5] The attorney general, who supervises the federal prosecutors and until 1939 had administrative control over the district courts, warned all opponents of the war: "May God have mercy on them, for they need expect none from an outraged people and an avenging government" (Peterson & Fite, 1957).

Federal judges outside of Wisconsin provided examples of active judicial support of the war and punitive treatment of persons opposed to the war.[6] Judges in the Middle West were among the most punitive. Judge Wade in Iowa "developed a sort of mania for denouncing traitors on all possible occasions" (Peterson & Fite, 1957, 36). In Chicago, Judge Kenesaw Mountain Landis before pronouncing a twenty-year sentence on Wisconsin Socialist leader Victor Berger, announced: "One must have a very judicial mind, indeed, not to be prejudiced against the German-Americans in this country. Their hearts are reeking with disloyalty" (*Berger v. United States*, 1921).

This kind of open patriotism from the bench permeated the system. G. B. Shaw summed up the performance of trial courts in the allied nations (quoted in *Ex parte* Starr, 1920, 147):

> [T]he courts in France, bleeding under German guns, were very severe; the courts in England, hearing but the echoes of those guns, were grossly unjust; but the courts of the United States, knowing naught save censored news, . . . were stark, staring, raving mad.

Powerful private groups, e.g., the American Defense Society, the National Security League, and the American Protective League, were organized to suppress opposition to the war and were imitated by smaller groups such as the Anti–Yellow Dog League, the Sedition Slammers, and the Boy Spies of America. Members of the American Protective League in Wisconsin volunteered as detectives to help the Justice Department find slackers. In the Eastern District, League members investigated 2400 possible violations of the espionage act and 6500 violations of the draft act (Hough, 1919, 405). In the Western District, League members investigated the pacifist Russellite sect, assisted United States marshals in arresting draft dodgers, and helped FBI agents to collect evidence of disloyalty (Hough, 1919, 406; Carey, 1965, 69–70). The Wisconsin Council of Defense ordered people to keep their eyes and ears open and to report every suspicious act or word. The Wisconsin Loyalty Legion helped with recruiting, and their 100,000 state members took a pledge: to encourage enlistment, to hold up slackers to public contempt, and to practice a vigorous American patriotism (Kull, 1919).

Wisconsinites who questioned the motives, the tactics, or the consequences of the war, were on trial throughout the conflict, in or out of a courtroom. Wisconsin vigilantes arranged for informal punishments of those branded disloyal, from ostracism to a parade around the town square inside a cage. A mob in Ashland kidnapped and tarred and feathered a professor whom they suspected of subversion.

The judges on both Wisconsin federal benches worked within the same superpatriotic national and state atmosphere. Unlike their Civil War predecessors, the judges had detailed criminal laws on the draft and subversion to apply to the flood of similar complaints brought to their attention by the United States attorneys in the two districts. Yet the number of cases which the judges took to trial and their dispositions of the guilty were quite different. Although the hotbed of war resistance was in the Eastern District, the Western District had almost three times as many subversive cases and four times as many draft cases on the dockets. Judge Geiger in the Eastern District often refused to hear cases after the United States attorney brought in the indictments. He dismissed one-third of the draft registration cases and 86 percent of the sedition or espionage cases, thus discouraging the prosecutor from filing such charges. In contrast, Judge Sanborn and Circuit Judge Evans, who was assigned to help him in the western district, dismissed only 17 percent of the draft and 16 percent of the subversion cases.

The World War I judges worked out their policies primarily through their discretionary powers to select cases, to sentence, and to teach contemporary patriotism. They made little use of their authority to articulate for a wider public the reasoning behind their interpretations of the criminal law. However, the judges began to develop the extra-judicial roles which were played so extensively by their successors during the next two wars.

DISCRETIONARY ROLES: SENTENCING AND TEACHING

Draft Cases

Those who failed to register for the draft received token sentences from the federal courts; offenders charged with crimes after registration and sentenced by military courts martial were treated much more severely. Of those draft offenders imprisoned by Wisconsin judges, Judge Geiger gave 62.5 percent and Judge Sanborn 45.7 percent two months or less in jail. The draft opponents handled by the military received an average sentence of eighteen years, and 42 percent received twenty years or more in prison (Wright, 1931, 241). All of Judge Geiger's incarceration sentences were less than one year, and Judge Sanborn gave only a single one-year sentence. The judicial bark was worse than the bite in the Western District: the toughness was more apparent in verbal behavior toward jurors and defendants than in actual sentences. The Western judge performed as a father figure—reiterating proper standards and threatening dire consequences but giving token penalties for draft offenses. (See Martin, 1952.)

Subversion Cases

Upon conviction for "espionage," the judges in the Western District, particularly visiting Judge Evans, gave harsh penalties. Since Judge Geiger in the Eastern District sentenced only three offenders, his decisions cannot be compared with the Western judges. The longest sentence given by Judge Geiger was one year, and by the Western judges two years. Table 4 shows that Judge Geiger in the Eastern District dismissed most of his cases, while Judge Sanborn took defendants to trial and then sentenced 11 percent of those not fined to one year or more in prison. Visiting Judge Evans sentenced three times that proportion to the same term. The Wisconsin judges were more lenient than their brothers in other federal districts, since 86 percent of those imprisoned by all district courts were sent away for three to twenty years (Chafee, 1920, appendix 2).

A more detailed assessment of the relative behavior of the judges in the two districts considers the subversive speech cases under four broad headings—antidraft, isolationist, economic, and pro-German. The talk for which defendants were indicted often covered more than one of these topics. The antidraft, economic, and isolationist arguments were publicly articulated by leaders of two important political forces in Wisconsin, the Progressives and the Socialists. Senator La

Table 4. Subversion Cases in Wisconsin—World War I

	Eastern District %	Western District %		National* %
Dismissed	85.7	16.2		—
Convicted	75.0	88.0		90.9
		Sanborn	Evans	
Fined	—	64	25	2.7
Prison over one year	—	11.1	33.3	98.6

*Data on espionage cases in 1917–18 involving free speech issue from Zechariah Chafee, Jr., *Freedom of Speech* (New York: Harcourt, Brace & Howe, 1920), appendix 2.

Follette for the Progressives and Representative Berger for the Socialists provided much of the rhetoric used by the war and draft resisters and were indirectly responsible for prosecutions of those who parroted their speeches in conversations at home, in factories, and in taverns. La Follette was more fortunate than Berger in avoiding prosecution himself, but their adherents paid a high price for repeating their ideas in front of patriotic friends.

La Follette, a "mouth of sedition" to his detractors, opposed preparedness, advocated strict neutrality, and later voted against the declaration of war. He viewed compulsory conscription for service abroad an unconstitutional assumption of power by Congress, which allowed the president "violently to lay hold of one million of our finest and strongest boys . . . and deport them across the seas . . . to wound and kill other young boys like themselves . . . " (La Follette, 1953, 734). The Socialist party platform passed in St. Louis in 1917 called for unyielding opposition to conscription, and Berger's newspaper (*Milwaukee Leader,* June 4, 1917, p. 3) called the draft "the national shame and disgrace of selecting men to be butchered for the financial benefit of the capitalist class."

La Follette held the same view that war was the product of commercial and imperial rivalry, which would benefit the wealthy while delaying economic reforms, such as unemployment insurance and utility regulation. The Socialists also saw war as an interruption of economic reform from which capitalist investors profited. Indiscreet people repeated a popular slogan found in the *Milwaukee Leader* (March 30, 1917, p. 6): "the rich man's war, and the poor man's fight." La Follette assured his audiences that they had the first amendment right to oppose the war, but those who took his advice and were indicted found out that moral rights and practical rights applied by judges are not the same.[7]

Antidraft Speeches

Any speech critical of the draft was taken much more seriously in the Western than the Eastern District as an interference with mobilization. Only when Judge Geiger was convinced that the talk was purposive counsel to behavior and that the listener was eligible for the draft did he proceed to trial and sentence (*United States v. Brinkman,* 1918). The Western District judges tended to incarcerate speakers regardless of motive or of audience. Following are examples of similar conversations reported in indictments in the two districts and the respective dispositions.

Eastern District	Western District
"The U.S. has no right to ship drafted men across the ocean. I would not go across if I were drafted." Dismissed (Tegge, 1918)	"The Constitution of the U.S. says that the government of the U.S. cannot compel a person to go to another country to fight. . . ." Prison 15 months (Balcer, 1918)
"The Conscription Act is unconstitutional. Congress has no right to send American boys to other countries to fight." Dismissed (Pergande, 1918)	". . . they are getting all of our boys and many of them will be God damn lucky if they get out of this draft." Fine $300 (Rogers, 1918)
"They can't draft the boys and make them go across." Dismissed (Enders, 1918)	"Young men subject to the draft are foolish not to claim exemption . . . those who go are likely to get drowned on the way." Prison 18 months and fine $3,500 (Schilling, 1918)
"There go the cattle cars to haul our boys to be slaughtered . . . " Fine $200 (Drager, 1918)	"What do they mean by putting these boys in cars like cattle and shipping them off." Fine $500 (Biederman, 1918)

Judge Geiger considered the statement that drafted men were being taken away from home in cattle cars intimidating enough when spoken to potential draftees to warrant punishment for the speaker. His fine was less than that for similar speech not directed to eligible draftees in the Western District. During the Civil War the persons who physically interfered with the enrollment and draft avoided punishment, but during the Great War even talk about interference brought penalties. The man who said: "We ought to get a bunch of men together and not let them take a man out of this town to enter the army" received a fine of $500 from Judge Sanborn (*United States v. Ochsner*, 1919).

Isolationist Speeches

To Judge Geiger the war policy was open to debate, but to the Western District judges those who opposed the government's declaration of war and war aims did not have the right to express themselves openly, as the following paired cases show.

Eastern District	Western District
"We have no business in this war. We ought not to go over there." Dismissed (Klest, 1918)	"We have no business in this war." Prison one year, fine $1000 (Yearous, 1918)

"I hope that every man who goes to France will never return . . . We have no business over there." Dismissed (Knopke, 1918)

"This government has no right to send an army to Europe to fight Germany." Dismissed (Snell, 1918)

"To hell with the boys over there. They got no business over there." Fine $100 (Hoerner, 1918)

"This is an unjust and wicked war which will surely lead to a bad end. Here the people are told we are gone to war to bring peace to the world. A lovely peace that." Prison 18 months (Auer, 1918)

Many of those with isolationist beliefs were concerned about the participation of their own children. One Eastern District resident who said that the country had no business in the war added that "I will never allow my son to serve in the U.S. Army," and Judge Geiger dismissed the case (*United States v. Hempe*, 1918). But when a Western District resident said, "I would shoot my own boys before allowing them to serve," Judge Sanborn gave him eighteen months and fined him $3,500 (*United States v. Schilling*, 1918).

Economic Speeches

The materialist objection to the war was considered fair comment in the Eastern District. But the moralist culture put great stock in the high purpose of the war and did not appreciate the idea that greed was one motivation of American entrance. The penalties for calling the Great War a "rich man's war" were very high in the Western District and nonexistent in the Eastern District.

Eastern District

"This is a rich man's war. Let the rich man pay. The millionaires are making all the money and they don't care about us fellows." Dismissed (Warnke, 1918)

"This is a rich man's war and the rich are getting richer and the poor poorer." Dismissed (Keller, 1919)

Western District

"This is a rich man's war." Fine $250 (Kohlapp, 1919)

"The big pups of millionaires in the U.S. caused this war." Prison one year (Sternberg, 1918)

Some of the defendants who complained that the war was for the profit of industrialists also refused to invest their own money in war bonds or to contribute to private groups supporting the war effort. How the judges treated this group of resisters is examined in the section on the judicial role of fund raiser.

Pro-German Speech

Since a large proportion of the immigrants who contributed to the spread of the individualist culture in Wisconsin were German, their family loyalties reinforced their inclination against spending their resources on any war effort. In isolated rural communities and in enclaves in the cities, Germans maintained their attachments to their homeland through the use of their own language, books, schools, churches, and clubs. United in opposition to the war and visible because of their speech and customs, the German immigrants were vulnerable to the suspicions of their prowar neighbors and of the authorities. Various German-American societies pragmatically closed shop during the war. But individual Germans who spoke of their fears and allegiances were indicted under the Espionage Act, often turned in by patriotic acquaintances. The movement to assimilate ethnic groups and the declining number of first-generation immigrants reduced the antiwar activities and visibility of Germans by the Second World War. In the Civil War and in the Korean and Vietnam wars there were no ethnic minorities associated both with the enemy nations and with the establishment of the local cultures in Wisconsin to provide articulated resistance and to serve as targets for the homefront prosecutors.

The following pairs of statements from indictments show that expressions of love and admiration for the fatherland received more repressive treatment in the Western District than in the Eastern District, which housed their mixed cultural and national heritage. Judge Geiger considered pro-German remarks *de minimis* as an interference with the war effort and dismissed all the cases. Statements of pride in the German nation were taken more seriously as impediments to the war in the Western District, and the speakers were convicted and punished.

Eastern District	Western District
"The Kaiser will never lose this war. . . . Hurrah for the Kaiser." Dismissed (Schultz, 1918)	"I do like the Kaiser. I am a German and I will fight for Germany. . . ." Fine $100 (Hendricks, 1919)
"Germany has better soldiers than America." Dismissed (Klug, 1918)	"If the U.S. sends a million over there, it will do no good. . . ." Jail 3 months (Lunardi, 1919)
"Germany is too strong for us . . . the U.S. could never reach Berlin." Dismissed (Tegge, 1918)	"We will never lick the Kaiser. It's impossible." Fine $1,250 (Lueck, 1919)
"Germany is right and will win." Dismissed (Keller, 1919)	"I want Germany to win the war." Fine $500 (Noacks, 1918)

The Western judges were particularly upset by defeatist talk which was printed in foreign language papers. The defendant who wrote in Polish that "President Wilson will have to crawl on his knees to kiss the Kaiser's feet" received six months in jail and a fine of $500 (*United States v. Deachman*, 1918). The Germans in the Western District discovered that they could not make the same comments as their fellows in the Eastern District with impunity: The statement "I have just as much right to stick up for my country and the Germans as you" brought a fine of $200 (*United States v. Bergerschmidt*, 1919). Judge Evans felt much more strongly than Judge Sanborn about anti-American talk. He gave a sentence of two years to the poor fellow who said: "I wish the war would end and the Kaiser would win . . . we will never have good times until the Kaiser wins" (*United States v. Emil Schiller*, 1918).

SYMBOLS OF NATIONAL PRIDE AND SECURITY AT RISK

The judges in the Western District were particularly disturbed by disrespect toward two symbols of national pride and security—the president and the flag. Mild complaints in the Eastern District were dismissed, while in the Western District similar statements resulted in fines.

Eastern District	Western District
"President Wilson was a damn fool, and if it had not been for such a damn fool, the U.S. would not be in this war." Dismissed (Pergande, 1918)	"I voted for Wilson to keep us out of war and then he went and put us right into the war." Fine $1,250 (Lueck, 1919)
	"Wilson is worse than the Kaiser." Fine $350 (Boebel, 1918)

Others who said that they would hang or shoot the president, if they could, received from thirty days to six months in jail from Western District judges (*United States v. Kmetz*, 1919; *United States v. Williams*, 1918; *United States v. Gilberts*, 1918).

The judge in the individualist culture did not take abuse of the flag as seriously as those in the moralist culture. Two Wisconsinites who happened to live in different judicial districts made very similar obscene comments about the flag, as reported below from the indictments, but the case in Judge Geiger's court was dismissed, while the defendant in Judge Sanborn's court paid $500.

Eastern District	Western District
"You know what I'll do with the American flag . . . (here using language too vile, obscene, and scur-	"The American flag is only good enough for me to wipe my ass on." Fine $500 (Noacks, 1918).

rilous to be set forth)." Dismissed (Keller, 1919)

"God damn flag." Fine $100 (Crevits, 1919)

Judge Geiger found on his court calendar a controversy over the flag which was such a *cause célèbre* that he was not able to dismiss the charges. The facts of the case constitute a comic opera which makes sense only if the flag is understood as a powerful symbol. The episode described in the indictment occurred on August 17, 1917, after the townspeople of the village of Corliss in Racine County prepared for a Red Cross rally by hanging a huge American flag, five or six feet wide, less than ten feet above the main street (*United States v. Harmon*, 1918). Farmer Harmon drove his thresher from a field on one side of town toward a field on the other side. As he moved along the shoulder of the main street, a strong wind caught the flag and blew it into the governor of the thresher engine. Harmon's hired hand pulled out the chewed-up piece of flag, about a foot square, and threw it on the pavement. Local citizens carried the flag remnant to a deputy sheriff in the grocery store, and he stopped the thresher down the road. Harmon told the sheriff: "You can take the damned flag out of there. That is a public highway."

At the federal grand jury hearing witnesses from the village testified that Harmon was not patriotic. Before the United States entered the war, he bet his farm that the Kaiser would win in debate with friends. He said he wanted to keep his money for his own business instead of buying bonds. The courtroom provided a forum for the patriots to vent their resentment and anger over the desecration of their symbol of national strength and goodness. Wisconsinites who were sacrificing children, money, and energy in the war effort were naturally upset by disparagement of the flag, which implied that the virtue of the nation and the reasons for the war were subject to question. By assessing a token penalty against Harmon of $200, Judge Geiger showed his understanding that the complainants were trying to defend the country by protecting its symbols.

The punishments selected for guilty offenders involved judgments of common sense and experience rather than of legal interpretation. Following long practice, appellate courts refused to monitor the sentences selected by trial judges, as long as they exercised their discretion within statutory limits. Nor did the circuit set a standard for the minimum case facts which would have reduced the disparity in the proportion of indictments carried to trial in the two districts.

By dismissing most of the war cases, Judge Geiger had fewer opportunities to take a position on the war to jurors, to express himself through the choice of sentence, or to offer his views of standards for citizen loyalty to offenders. On the other hand, by taking a large number of cases through trial, the Western judges showed their policies directly through their courtroom interchanges with lawyers and defendants and indirectly through their sentences. Although the World War I judges wrote fewer opinions than their successors, their law interpretation revealed the same attitudes toward the war as their discretionary decisions.

TRADITIONAL JUDICIAL ROLE: LAW INTERPRETATION

The state appellate judges in the Civil War concentrated on issues of constitutionality of federal law and of executive and military behavior, but the World War I federal trial judges accepted the new federal laws as legitimate. The United States Supreme Court provided them with minimal guidance, upholding the constitutionality of the war acts but waiting until after the war to review the application of these laws in particular cases. The trial judges in every federal district developed their own interpretations of the draft and subversive control statutes, based upon their own attitudes and their reading of legislative intent. Under minimal circuit supervision, the trial judges worked with the available "law-stuff" to support the war effort or to protect the offenders.

The Espionage Act provided room for expanding or contracting the pool of offenders through interpretation of its vague language about "wilfully attempting to cause insubordination, disloyalty, mutiny and refusal of duty in the military and naval forces" and "obstructing the recruiting and enlistment service." Judge Sanborn in the Western District broadly interpreted military and naval forces to include men registered for the draft (*United States v. Yearous*, 1918) and interpreted attempts to cause disloyalty to include critical and unpatriotic comments about the war. Nearly all the district judges who interpreted the statute broadly and used similar instructions were upheld by their circuit panels (*Rhuberg v. United States*, 1919, 870–71).

Judge Sanborn did not rationalize his interpretations of the law in published opinions, but Judge Evans, sitting by assignment from the Seventh Circuit, explained why he included the YMCA and the Red Cross within the meaning of the military forces of the United States. In the case of a man indicted for saying, "I do not believe in the work of the YMCA or the Red Cross, for I think they are nothing but a bunch of grafters . . . I won't give you a cent," Judge Evans found that the home defense groups were so interrelated with the fighting forces that they could also be protected from scurrilous attack under federal law. The judge extended federal protection against criticism to other private groups not involved in the case—the Knights of Columbus, the Salvation Army, and the Jewish Relief engaged in war work (*United States v. Nagler,* 221).[8]

In contrast, Judge Geiger in the Eastern District narrowly interpreted the law, insisting that men who are registered are still civilians and become part of the armed forces at induction and that espionage has a simple meaning covering betrayal and injury but not social talks about war causes (*United States v. Henning,* 1918). Based on their conflicting interpretation of the criminal law, charges which Judge Geiger dismissed Judge Sanborn carried to trial.

The draft law also provided the judges with opportunities for narrow or broad interpretation. Judge Geiger accepted the contemporary view that draft boards are executive agencies, empowered by Congress and the president to carry out the important function of raising military forces, and that their errors in the use of discretion are not subject to judicial review (*In re* Kitzerow, 1918). However, he made clear in 1918 that the courts are open to any claim of lack of jurisdiction over the person. When a registrant in federal custody who had applied for deferred classification after receiving notice to report asked for a hearing, the judge accepted the invitation and ordered his release. He found that the registrant was still in civilian status, and "until a man has been selected as the law prescribes . . . he retains his function as a civilian" and must have a civilian tribunal to establish his status and its rights (*Ex parte* McDonald, 1918, 103).

Naturalization examiners in the Justice Department objected to conferring citizenship upon aliens who had claimed exemption from military service on grounds of that status during the war. Judge Geiger, unlike other federal trial judges, insisted that the enjoyment of a legal exemption could not become the basis for rejection of a subsequent application for citizenship, in the absence of clear statutory direction (*In re* Naturalization of Aliens, 1924, 601). He argued that Congress "could not have intended to vest in such tribunals [district courts] a sort of undefined judicial grace, to be granted or withheld without restraint. It is not possible that granting or withholding naturalization can proceed upon considerations of mere personal views, regardless of evidence which may be offered. . . ." Judge Geiger construed the naturalization law strictly, thus preventing the government from using the denial of citizenship as a punishment. The Wisconsin judges were able to use the law as well as their discretion to reach quite different results for the unpatriotic.

EXTRA-JUDICIAL ROLE: THE FUND RAISER

During the Great War judges used their sentencing power to finance the war, by fining the unpatriotic who failed to buy bonds or contribute to the Red Cross.[9] The discretionary nature of the sentence power allowed the judges to become active participants in the war effort, with little fear of interference. Chafee (1920, p. 74) reported at the time that judges "felt it to be their duty to deliver stump speeches to the jury as if they were soliciting subscriptions to a Liberty Loan." However, the judges went beyond persuasion and accomplished the equivalent of the superpatriotic citizens who raised money for the fourth Liberty Bond drive by threatening slackers with ropes or yellow posters on their houses (Stewart, 1919). Just as citizen boards gave themselves the role of assessing contributions from fellow citizens, called the "mob rule by the rich," the judges took on a new role of raising money from the convicted "subversives."

The performances of the judges in the Eastern and Western Districts were entirely dissimilar. Judge Geiger simply dropped charges against the defendants indicted for saying:

"The Liberty Bonds are no good. What's the use of buying them." (Czelski, 1922)

"The men in charge of this Liberty Loan campaign are nothing but grafters and are all well paid for what they are doing." (Riehl, 1918)

In contrast, Judge Sanborn provided a scale of fines for the following remarks or actions:

$200—"U.S. Liberty Bonds are no good for the poor man."
   (Peterson, 1919)

$300—Refusal to buy war bonds
   (Cole, 1919)

$500—"Fuck the Liberty Bonds." "Fuck the War Savings stamps." "Only 10% of the money given to the Red Cross gets to the soldiers."
   (Clauson, 1919)

$500—"The government can't force me to take the Bonds."
   (DeSombre, 1919)

$500—"The U.S. Government Bonds are worth less than forty cents on the dollar."
   (Schubring, 1918)

$500—"The U.S. Liberty Bonds will soon be worth nothing but $45—and then nothing."
   (Sternberg, 1918)

$600—"I am not going to buy any Bonds and they can't make me buy any bonds."
(Petry, 1919)

$1250—"I won't buy any Liberty Bonds no matter how it goes."
(Lueck, 1919)

$3500—"Private subscriptions for war purposes are liable to remain in private hands." (Schilling, 1918)

In the next world war the federal judges were even more inventive in their development of extra-judicial roles.

WORLD WAR II AND KOREAN CASES

Subversive conversations did not provide the occasions for federal judges to show their patriotism (Elliff, 1945, 79, n23). The draft cases were the dramatic focus of war resistance from World War II through the Vietnam War. Since draft resisters were prosecuted in civilian courts until their induction, judges considered a larger range of issues than they had faced in the Great War. World War II and the Korean War can be treated together for the purpose of examining judicial behavior, since the Western District judge remained on the bench through both wars and the issues did not change.

Wisconsin judges in the two districts played extra-judicial war roles with some enthusiasm, encouraging defendants to enlist or to work in war factories. For those who persisted in their disobedience of the law, the judges developed different sentence goals. The major purpose of Eastern District Judge Duffy in sentencing to prison was to deter others subject to call. Western District Judge Stone, however, followed an equity principle, and Judge Tehan accepted both approaches during his tenure. There was no necessary relationship, however, between the sentence goal and the actual length of prison term selected. The two Eastern District judges were much less harsh than Judge Stone during both wars.

Judge Stone proposed to the Seventh Circuit Judicial Conference in 1942 that the judges agree upon a uniform sentence for selective service violators.[10] The matter was discussed, but it is evident from the statistics on sentences given by the judges during the last two years of the war that they were unable to agree on a uniform sentence policy. Table 5 compares the treatment of all draft resisters sentenced by Seventh Circuit trial judges during 1944 and 1945. The average prison sentences (of those judges who sentenced at least ten offenders to prison) ranged from nineteen months for Judge Lindley of the Eastern District of Illinois to fifty-seven months for Judge Stone.

Table 5. Relative Severity of Draft Sentences, 1944–45, of Seventh Circuit Trial Judges

	District	N Cases	On Probation (%)	Average Prison Sentence (months)
Lindley	ED Ill.	48	35.4	19.2
Sullivan	ND Ill.	35	14.3	25.0
Duffy	ED Wis.	64	31.2	28.2
Wham	ED Ill.	50	34.0	30.2
LaBuy	ND Ill.	23	8.7	34.3
Igoe	ND Ill.	33	18.2	36.0
Barnes	ND Ill.	34	2.9	39.4
Campbell	ND Ill.	18	11.1	42.0
Baltzell	SD Ind.	53	20.8	55.6
Stone	WD Wis.	28	17.9	56.9

SOURCE: Statistics prepared by circuit staff for internal court use, filed in Office of Clerk, Northern District of Illinois, Chicago.

Only two judges gave shorter average sentences than Judge Duffy. Judge Stone gave the longest average sentence, very close to the statutory maximum of sixty months. Judge Duffy's average sentence declined from 33.8 months in 1943 to 28.2 months in 1944–45, but Judge Stone increased his average from 49.6 to 56.9 months (U.S. Bureau of Prisons, 1944). Although five other trial judges sent a larger proportion to prison, Judge Stone kept them there longer. As in World War I, the Western judge was considerably more harsh.

DEFENDANT TYPES

The typical defendants in draft cases could be categorized as "losers" and COs (conscientious objectors). Losers were draftees with minor criminal records (*United States v. Vicklund*, 1945; *United States v. Petelle*, 1945), migrant farm workers (*United States v. Estrada*, 1946), or marginal people in marital or financial difficulty (*United States v. Sadowski*, 1946; *United States v. Gloy*, 1947). They were usually poorly educated, mentally deficient, or minor delinquents, whom the military would probably reject.

The COs were quite different—students or working men with a moral purpose and a good reputation. The largest proportion of the CO defendants were Jehovah's Witnesses (JWs), who claimed minister exemptions and who refused to go to a CO camp where there would be no consumers for their evangelism. In the Eastern District JWs constituted 85 percent of the CO defendants and in the Western District 52 percent.[11]

The judges were antagonistic toward the JWs since they stubbornly refused to give either military or alternative service. Judge Duffy used the sentencing process to shame the objectors for not meeting their military obligations. He told a JW upon giving him a three-year sentence that "waiting in the other room . . . are nearly 100 applicants for American citizenship . . . among the things they have agreed to do is to bear arms for their adopted country" (*United States v. Herauf*, 1944). Judge Duffy admitted in 1946: "Well, I have had, I will confess, not too much patience at times with members of the Jehovah Witnesses who refused to do their duty by their country in time of war." Judge Stone was much more cold. He responded to a JW who insisted he would obey God's law before men's regardless of the consequences that: "In the court's opinion, you are just a plain draft dodger, and nothing else" (*United States v. Baron*, 1945, 3). Judge Stone gave the maximum five-year penalty to every JW, regardless of plea or circumstance, except for one of several convicted brothers whom he gave three years (*United States v. Domres*, 1943). JW defendants in both districts asked the judges to disqualify themselves for bias.[12] (Letter to Stone from Anna Mae Davis, December 30, 1942, in Stone Papers.)

The number of draft cases on the docket and the similarity of claims made by the COs allowed the judges to develop a routine way of handling them. The judges considered the time used by defendants to raise legal issues and to make personal explanations of their beliefs wasted. Judge Duffy was accused in an affidavit of prejudice of calling COs an expense and burden to the court.[13] The judges tried to expedite the procedure by taking a number of JW cases on the same day or week. One trial to the court in the Western District took exactly twenty minutes, from the time trial began at 11:25 until the prison sentence was pronounced at 11:45 (*United States v. Alvin Domres*, 1943). A jury trial from the moment the jury was drawn to the five-year sentence lasted for one half hour, from 11:30 until noon (*United States v. Furrer*, 1945). The uniform sentence adopted by the respective judges in the two districts was the final aspect of the routinization of the entire process.

DISCRETIONARY JUDICIAL ROLE: SENTENCING

Table 6 shows how differently the "losers" and the COs were treated by the Wisconsin judges and the national judiciary. Judge Duffy gave 69 percent of the losers probation, more than twice as high a percentage as the national figure. Judge Stone with 38 percent probation also exceeded the national percentage. In contrast, Judge

Table 6. Treatment of COs and Other Draft Resisters in Wisconsin and the Nation, 1940–46

	CO Sentences			Other Sentences		
	ED Wis.	WD Wis.	U.S.A.	ED Wis.	WD Wis.	U.S.A.
% of Convicted Probation/Fine	6.1	0	4.6	68.9	38.3	29.1
N to Prison	(62)	(27)	(5805)	(23)	(29)	(6857)
1–12 months (%)	1.6	0	11	60.9	20.7	41.0
13–24 months (%)	6.5	0	20.5	26.1	3.4	27.1
25–36 months (%)	56.5	7.4	31.8	8.7	24.1	22.3
37–48 months (%)	24.2	14.8	10.3	0	0	4.9
49–60+ months (%)	11.3	77.8	26.3	4.3	51.7	4.7

SOURCES: Director of Selective Service, *Enforcement of the Selective Service Law*, (Washington, D.C.: Government Printing Office, 1951), p. 93, table 14, p. 94, table 16. Records of Wisconsin Eastern and Western Districts in Federal Records Center, Chicago.

Stone did not give probation to a single CO, while the national percentage was almost 5 percent and Judge Duffy gave probation to 6 percent. The terms of incarceration of the losers were shorter than those of the COs. Judge Duffy sent away about 70 percent for one year or less, higher than the national average, and Judge Stone sent away only 21 percent for the shortest period, only half the national proportion. The non-COs were more apt to escape prison, and if sentenced to prison they served considerably shorter terms.

The personal sentence policy of Judge Duffy was three years; he told a defendant in a proceeding in 1946 that: "If you were a wilful evader, we customarily impose a three-year sentence" (*United States v. Estrada*, 1946). The average for all sentences in the circuit was thirty-five months in 1945, very close to Judge Duffy's sentence of choice (AO Report, 1951, table 11). After the war, when deterrence was no longer a rational goal, Judge Duffy gave lighter sentences. He was explicit about his purpose in several sentencing proceedings in 1947:

". . . we don't have to impose sentence to deter others because the defense is no longer important . . ." (Messner, 1947, 3)

"I am imposing a six-month sentence instead of the usual three-year sentence because the war is past now and that feature of deterring others isn't present . . ." (Schrank, 1947, 7)

The personal sentence policy of Judge Stone was four or five years, depending upon the basis of their resistance. At one point he asked the United States attorney in disbelief, ". . . under what circumstances did I ever sentence a draft dodger to six months?" (*United States v. Crimmins*, 1945, 3). Judge Stone followed an equity rather than a deterrence principle. He tried to balance the scales between those men who contributed their time (or lives) for national interests and those who refused to answer the draft call. The criminal case was not an obvious vehicle for the equity principle, since those in service were not parties to the case and could receive no material compensation for their loss of time, health, or opportunity. Yet Judge Stone and Judge Tehan in the Korean War had a sense of achieving some kind of social justice by making the resisters pay with the same length of time in prison as others contributed in the armed forces.

Judge Stone explained his policy in a letter to the director of the Bureau of Prisons after he sentenced several JWs to five years in prison:

> "The defendants are all strong, able-bodied men, and should be rendering some military service to this country at this time. . . . It was the Court's intention, when sentence was imposed, that they be confined to prison until at least six months after the end of the War. They should not be permitted to enjoy their liberty one day sooner than the boys in the Army and Navy . . ." (Stone to Parole Board, September 21, 1942, Stone Papers, Box 1)

Judge Tehan copied Judge Stone's reasoning during the Korean War. He explained that his consistent policy was to give a jail sentence similar to the probable term of service if drafted (*United States v. Swenson*, 1952, 5–6; *United States v. William Schlueter*, 1953, 8; *United States v. Schoebel*, 1952, 158). His statements in several cases follow:

> ". . . the measure of punishment must be in line with those who do respond to the call of their country." (Albrecht, 1952)
> "You shall get as a sentence an amount equal to that which you would have had you been conscripted and consented to join the Armed Forces." (Ray Schlueter, 1954)

The judges also felt that the men who remained in civilian life illegally should not gain any economic or political advantage over those doing military service away from their communities. Although the motive of many Wisconsin residents for refusing to serve in the Civil War and the Great War was to give priority to their own family farms or businesses, those prosecuted in World War II were of a different type. The COs and the "losers" were unlikely to challenge returning veterans for economic or social prominence. The losers had no resources to displace the veteran who came back to the community with honor and entitlements. The JWs belonged to a small and stigmatized minority, with no interest in or hope of attaining worldly power. Judge Stone, however, saw the JWs as a threat to those in uniform, telling one offender: "You can let the other boys do the fighting while you enjoy the profits" (*United States v. Baron*, 1945). The judges put the JWs out of this imaginery competition with the veterans by sending them to prison for long terms.

Probation Policy

Wisconsin judges treated draft defendants differently from ordinary criminals, for whom they individualized the sentence. The general policy was to release on probation a first offender considered harmless to society and unlikely to repeat the offense. But the draft defendants, particularly the conscientious objectors (COs) who posed no danger to society, rarely received probation.

Until the end of World War I, federal judges were generally unfamiliar with the technique of putting offenders into their communities under court supervision. Their only alternative to incarceration was the fine. By the Second World War, the innovation of probation had produced its own specialized personnel and spread throughout the federal judiciary (Bates, 1950). For all draft resisters, Judge Duffy used probation almost in the same proportion as the Eastern District of Illinois judges (also in an individualist culture) who most favored probation in the Seventh Circuit. (See table 5.) Judge Stone used probation half as often as the maximum in the circuit, but more than several Chicago judges. Judge Duffy gave exactly the same percentage of probation as the national average in 1945, and Judge Stone less.

During the Korean period, Judge Tehan established a policy of not offering probation in cases involving national defense (*United States v. Swenson*, 1952). When a defense counsel brought to his attention the use of probation in draft cases in other districts, the judge responded that he was not adopting probation (*United States v. Doering*, 1952). He insisted that "those who fail to bear that burden shall not be allowed to have the full liberty and all of the comforts of society without being penalized" (*United States v. William Schlueter*, 1953, 8).

TRADITIONAL JUDICIAL ROLE: LAW INTERPRETATION

Judge Duffy did not expand upon the power of the courts to oversee the draft boards beyond the point reached by Judge Geiger in the Great War. He repeated in a number of cases that "the courts do not have any supervisory power over the local draft boards" (*United States v. Paulos*, 1943, trial transcript, 23). In 1943 Duffy pointed out that according to circuit precedent an offender could raise the issue of a fair hearing or procedural due process before the draft board only after induction through habeas corpus. He forcefully told the counsel for a Jehovah's Witness that "I don't take any stock at all in this constitutional argument, and you don't need to spend any time on behalf of the defendant arguing it. These and similar laws in the last World War were declared to be constitutional, and I have no idea but what the Courts will hold the same."

Despite this firm statement, Judge Duffy permitted evidence to go in the record on the question of a fair hearing, but then he rejected counsel's argument that standards for procedural due process should include keeping proceedings in written form and the passage of a formal motion to order induction for each draftee (*United States v. Messersmith*, 1943, transcript, 90). Judge Duffy predicted correctly that his appellate superiors on the Seventh Circuit would continue to deny district courts the authority to examine the internal processes of draft boards. The reviewing panel said that Judge Duffy showed "greater liberality toward defendant than we think the law extends to him" by receiving evidence on the arbitrariness of the board, and it affirmed the conviction (*United States v. Messersmith*, 1943, 601).

After the Second World War, the Supreme Court ruled that courts had minimal power to review draft classifications if there was "no basis of fact" for the classification (*Estep v. United States*, 1946, 122–23). The Court developed this line of reasoning during the Korean War by allowing trial judges to require "some proof" for the board's decision (*Dickinson v. United States*, 1953, 396). Judge Grubb in the Eastern District accepted this interpretation by finding defendants not guilty when there was no basis in fact for the classification (*United States v. Krueger*, 1956) and when the registrant was denied a procedural stage which was mandatory (*United States v. Thomas*, 1956). Judge Tehan handled most of the criminal cases for the Eastern District in the Korean War and did not expand far beyond Judge Duffy's understanding of the limits of the court's supervisory authority. He was aware of the fact that other district judges around the country were looking into the nature of the evidence before the draft boards, but waited for reversal from the Seventh Circuit before protecting procedural rights of offenders (*United States v. Nelson*, 1955).

In the Western District, counsel raised the defense of mistakes during the draft process to Judge Stone, relying on the circuit's and the Supreme Court's approval of limited supervision. In *United States v. Kannenberg* (1956) counsel argued that the board must show in court some factual basis for disagreement with the proofs offered by the registrant, particularly when the board made no record of its findings. Judge Stone persisted in his refusal to supervise draft boards during the Korean War despite the movement by his appellate supervisors to require minimal due process.

EXTRA-JUDICIAL ROLES

Prosecutor Role

Judge Stone in the Western District took on the role of prosecutor, by urging the United States attorney to bring in more draft cases. He was displeased when the prosecutor recommended leniency in sentencing (Davis, interview, 1973). The judge even managed cases from the filing of a complaint to the issue of parole. In one instance he personally saw Jehovah's Witnesses peddling their *Watchtower* publication with antiwar articles in his hometown of Wausau. He checked into their draft status, and after their conviction for refusing to report to civilian camp, he vented his irritation by giving maximum prison penalties plus fines. The letter to the parole board discussed above named these defendants as well as others. Although Judge Duffy was under pressure from patriotic United States attorneys in the Eastern District, no evidence of his stepping into the prosecutor role appeared.

Recruiting Officer Role

The judges understood that the intent of the draft law was to raise an army and not to incarcerate resisters. Penalties were on the books to serve as deterrents and to win compliance, and the Wisconsin judges were anxious to redirect the defendants from resistance to the nearest induction center before, after, or during trial. The judges treated the offenders like those who break economic regulations, until they proved implacable. At that point, the judges used their penalties to punish and to balance the books for the soldiers.

During World War II Judge Duffy in the Eastern District and Judge Stone in the Western District used their power to dismiss cases to persuade offenders to submit to induction or to alternative service. Of the cases dismissed (omitting those of missing persons), Judge Duffy sent 63 percent to be inducted and Judge Stone 72 percent, although some of these were rejected as unfit. Very few were persuaded to report to CO camp (*United States v. Monson*, 1942).

A typical order follows:

> It appearing that the above named . . . have been indicted for violation of the Selective Training and Service Act of 1940 and are now under arrest and in the custody of the U.S. Marshal in the Dane County Jail at Madison, Wisconsin . . . and that each of the above named persons has volunteered for

immediate induction into the land or naval forces of the U.S. and that it is necessary that they appear for final physical examination in Milwaukee . . . for the purpose of such induction,
IT IS ORDERED that the U.S. Marshal for the Western District of Wisconsin safely keep and conduct . . . to the office of the examining physicians . . . and in the event any or either of said persons shall fail to pass the physical examination for induction . . . that he return such persons to said Dane County jail . . . (Stone Papers, Box 30, 1942)

During the Korean War Judge Tehan in the Eastern District and Judge Stone in the Western District continued the practice of dismissing or continuing cases to allow offenders to join the armed forces (*United States v. Horban*, 1953; *United States v. Martin*, 1953).

The judges after trial would suspend prison terms and place convicted defendants on probation conditional upon their compliance with registration or induction (Eastern District: *United States v. Nielsen*, 1945; *United States v. Held*, 1942; *United States v. Duesterhoeft*, 1943; *United States v. Kloss*, 1943; *United States v. France*, 1942; Western District: *United States v. Andrzeyeski*, 1942; *United States v. Machling*, 1942; *United States v. Drury*, 1943). Judge Duffy was even successful in getting a few COs into service. He suspended a three-year prison sentence for a CO who said that his conscience would be at ease in the Merchant Marine (*United States v. Schmidt*, 1944). One of the few Jehovah's Witnesses who was willing to compromise offered to enlist for eighteen months in 1946, but the judge and the United States attorney pointed out that with the heat of the war over a short service would be unfair to those who served earlier under fire.

Judge Stone managed to persuade convicted defendants whose only crime had been failure to register or to keep their board informed of a current address to join up (*United States v. Rineck*, 1943; *United States v. Clark*, 1943; *United States v. Johnson*, 1945). Judge Duffy persuaded convicted defendants who were not eligible for induction to avoid the penalty for their draft evasion by enlisting (*United States v. Marciniak*, 1943; *United States v. Obenberger*, 1944). When one offender was sent for induction and rejected, Judge Duffy gave him the option of enlisting or serving three years in prison (*United States v. Guerraro*, 1946). In one case the induction center had closed and the deputy marshal had trouble finding someone to take the recruit off his hands (*United States v. Felder*, 1946).

Judge Stone carried through his responsibility for manpower with great determination. He continued a case involving registration, not satisfied merely to have persuaded the defendant to register, "until the time you are required to report, and then if you report for service, then this case will be dismissed" (*United States v. Johnson*, 1945). Many file folders in the Western District ended with the notation—"transported and inducted."

Manpower Mobilizer Role

When the defendants before the court were not qualified for military service, the judges channeled them into civilian work in defense plants or on farms. The judges also took steps to insure their good citizenship, since their personal habits affected their productivity in war work.

Judge Stone in the Western District suspended sentence for men who would take defense jobs (*United States v. Rowley*, 1943; *United States v. Alderman*, 1943; *United States v. Adams*, 1943). He developed a standard order of the court directing defendants to obtain employment at Badger Ordnance Works (*United States v. Lane*, 1942). When a defendant failed to get work in a defense plant, the judge revoked probation and sent him to prison (*United States v. Smith*, 1943; *United States v. Jackson*, 1942). Judge Stone encouraged good moral standards which would make a good war worker and set probation conditions against the use of intoxicating liquor and for the support of the family (Stone Papers, Box 305). In one revocation hearing, the judge changed the original prison sentence of a man convicted of false registration from six months to three years. The defendant, appearing without counsel, protested inadequately. The conversation between the judge and probationer from the transcript of the revocation proceedings follows:

JUDGE: It is the judgment of the Court that this sentence be amended, and this defendant be sentenced to serve a term of three years in a federal penitentiary instead of six months . . .

DEFENDANT: But, your honor, that wasn't for trying to get out of the army . . . It was just using an assumed name. I registered . . . I never tried to duck the army; I tried to get in.

JUDGE: You heard the statement of the District Attorney about the manner in which you treated this girl.

DEFENDANT: Well, all right . . . I plead guilty to the charge.(*United States v. Crimmins*, 1945, 4)

Several months later the judge discovered that he did not have the power to revise the sentence on the basis of new charges of immorality not covered by the federal criminal code and without trial on those charges (Order for Amendment of Sentence, *United States v. Crimmins*, 1946).

Judge Duffy also set up conditions of probation to guarantee war workers with good habits (*United States v. Zientek*, 1942). He suspended an eighteen-month prison term on condition of war work or enlistment and family support (*United States v. Musel*, 1942). Another defendant received a one-year suspended sentence and probation conditional upon draft registration and child support payments (*United States v. Sadowski*, 1946). Those who failed in their jobs or family life went to prison (*United States v. Kloss*, 1943). During the Korean War Judge Tehan revoked probation of an offender who was irresponsible, didn't work regularly, and was convicted in a bastardy case (*United States v. Sanchez*, 1950).

Fund Raiser Role

During the Second World War the federal tax levy was high enough that the public was less exercised by laxity in contributions to war funds than during the Great War. Moreover, the draft act was less appropriate for this purpose than the sedition acts. However, the two judges sitting during World War II, both of whom served in the military in World War I, acted as fund raisers using the selective service law, particularly for those who were unlikely candidates for service.

Judge Duffy used a question to test the good faith of a draft dodger, an illegal immigrant who hid on a farm during the war: "Did you buy any bonds while you were here?" He answered no, and his sentence included a fine of $300 (*United States v. Gloy*, 1947, transcript, 8). Judge Stone raised the same issue in the Western District. A trial transcript reveals the following interchange between a draft delinquent and the Western judge:

JUDGE: How many war bonds did you buy during the last few years?

DEFENDANT: Well, I didn't buy many bonds.

JUDGE: Did you buy any?

DEFENDANT: Well, I donated money to the Red Cross and different things like that.

JUDGE: Oh yes, maybe a dollar or two now and then, but how many war bonds did you buy?

DEFENDANT: No, I didn't buy any bonds.

JUDGE: No—it didn't make any difference to you whether we won this war or not. (*United States v. Petelle*, 1945, transcript, 7)

The Second World War and the Korean War saw the greatest expansion of extra-judicial roles. In the Vietnam period the traditional and discretionary judicial roles were more important and continued to distinguish between the judges in the *I* and *M* cultures.

VIETNAM CASES

The purpose of the government in prosecuting draft cases during the Vietnam war remained the same as in previous wars—to maintain national defense. The draft resisters during the Vietnam war, except for the ubiquitous "losers" who appear in all criminal categories, had more in common with their predecessors of the Civil War and Great War than those of World War II and the Korean War. The philosophical objectors did not present the trial judges with a dilemma once the Supreme Court provided a way to categorize them with the religious pacifists (*United States v. Seeger*, 1965; *United States v. Bova*, 1969; *United States v. Foran*, 1969). The defendants who presented new problems to the judges were those who disapproved of the specific war in Southeast Asia (*United States v. Shermeister*, 1968).

The new settlers in frontier Wisconsin during the Civil War and the German immigrants with home ties during the Great War also disagreed with the war policy, but they had strong personal motives for opposition. The young Americans who objected to the Vietnam involvement did not have either economic or familial reasons for refusing their support. They simply carried the national debate over the nondeclared war into the judicial arena, refusing to accept the decision of legitimate executive and legislative authorities on the matter. (*United States v. Pluim*, 1971). A defendant before Judge Reynolds in the Eastern District filed a letter which he had written to President Johnson, stating, "for quite some time I have felt very deeply that our policies in Vietnam . . . are completely wrong, morally, politically, and against the traditional American concepts of Foreign Affairs" (*United States v. Kurki*, 1966, 166).

By the Vietnam period the federal judiciary had discovered a technique for dealing with the JW defendants, who had been so mercilessly punished during the earlier wars. The JWs were still prosecuted, but after the finding of guilt the judges themselves issued the order for alternative civilian service (*United States v. Hasmuk*, 1968). JWs who would not obey their "neighbors" on local draft boards often would accept judicial authority as a legitimate instrument of the sovereign (Solomon, 1970, 487). The JWs, however, continued to be litigious and to search for legal ways of avoiding civilian service (*United States v. Matz*, 1971; *United States v. Schuster*, 1971; *United States v. Kuchnau*, 1972; *United States v. Waller*, 1970; *United States v. Gast*, 1970).

The stubborn defendants of the Vietnam period were not the JWs but the political opponents of the war (*United States v. Gargan*, 1970).

There were also some modern-day anarchists, who simply refused to cooperate with a government from which they felt alienated because of its unresponsiveness to problems of social equality (*United States v. Lewis*, 1967; *United States v. Cassidy*, 1972). The reaction of the Wisconsin judges to their obduracy showed the historical pattern of milder punishment in the Eastern District. However, the more significant differences for the first time appeared in the playing of their traditional law roles rather than their discretionary or extra-judicial roles.

JUDICIAL ATTITUDES TOWARD THE UNPATRIOTIC

The attitudes of the judges in the two districts were similar in all the wars; the different cultures allowed the expression of the intensity of feelings to different degrees through the dispositions. Just as the Wisconsin judges were patriotic, but translated their attitude differently by culture, so were all the judges somewhat sympathetic with the Vietnam war opponents.

Judge Gordon in the Eastern District said: "The drafting of young men for military service is a difficult and often painful matter. The Congress has set a thorny path before any young man who seeks to challenge his draft classification in a court of law" (*Foran v. Weinhoff*, 1968, 499). In refusing to review the civilian work assignment made by a draft board, Judge Reynolds noted that his restraint "is compelled by the present status of the law in this area" and not an indication of approval of the board's treatment of the defendant (*Schuster v. Selective Service Board 76*, 1971, 707n). Judge Reynolds acquitted a young man after finding that the draft board had "no basis in fact" for its conclusion that he did not qualify for CO classification, saying, "The Court is convinced that the defendant is sincere in his opposition to all violence and any participation in war" (*United States v. Foran*, 1969, 1326). His recognition of "sincerity" in the defendant contrasts sharply with the frequent finding of "insincerity" by his World War predecessors; it might seem that a judge is likely to recognize sincerity when he has not rejected the views of the claimant as illegitimate.

Judge Doyle in the Western District, unlike his brothers in the Eastern District, had a national reputation for understanding the problems of the draft resister, although he did not translate that sympathy into less severe sentences. He described the dilemma of a conscientious objector as "a solemn personal choice . . . which a young man, motivated by deep, conscientious convictions, must exercise between two years of hospital work, a task which may conflict with those convictions, and probable confinement in prison . . ." (*Hestad v. United*

States, 1968, 1194). He was determined that the draft resister would have the full protection of procedural law.

DISCRETIONARY ROLE: SENTENCING

During the Vietnam period the environment did not exude the intense chauvinism which encouraged judges during World War II and the Korean War to apply deterrence or equity policies. The type of objector in this war was unlikely to be deterred by sentence length since his antiwar commitment was as vigorous as the Loyalty Legion patriotism of the Great War. Table 7 provides the data for a comparison of districts. The judges in the individualist culture dismissed a larger proportion of cases, continuing the pattern of the earlier wars. Of those convicted (1967–74) the Eastern District judges put almost half of the offenders on probation, while Judge Doyle did not give a single probation sentence. Neither did he employ the "split" sentence which combines a short prison term with probation. Of those sent to prison, the Eastern judges sent away slightly larger proportions for a year or more. Judge Doyle refused to differentiate among those convicted in his court; in the same time period, he gave all offenders the same sentence. In following this policy he rejected the advice of one experienced federal judge who recommended for the purpose of deterrence the imposition of longer sentences on prominent leaders of the antidraft movement, i.e., two years, and shorter sentences for the nonmilitant (Solomon, 487–88). Judge Doyle refused to enter into the power struggle over the war policy, instead applying sentences automatically after the offenders had received their full legal protections.

In their use of probation and in their employment of a variety of sentence lengths, the Eastern judges were more similar to the circuit and national pattern than Judge Doyle. As befits their culture, the Eastern judges tried to be fair and reasonable in balancing the defense interests of the government against the specific situation of the defendant. Judge Doyle was serving the institution of the law with the same vigor that previous Western judges had served nationalism. Law was not a simple ideal, however, but included a respect for precedent, the law made by his superiors on the federal appellate bench, as well as reverence for broad constitutional principles of due process and free speech (and conscience).

TRADITIONAL JUDICIAL ROLE: LAW INTERPRETATION

On some major issues the Wisconsin federal judges agreed with the state Supreme Court Justices of one hundred years earlier—that the national government had the power to conscript. They also fol-

Table 7. Treatment of Draft Resisters in Wisconsin,
the Seventh Circuit, and the Nation, 1967–74

	ED Wis.	WD Wis.	7th Circuit	U.S.A.
Defendants (N)	315	123	1762	20348
Cases Dismissed (%)	71.7	60.2	58.1	54.4
Trials to Judge (%)	44.9	51.0	38.8	45.6
Probation of Convicted (%)	46.8	0.0	52.7	55.9
Imprisoned (N)	41	40	319	3490
Split (%)	4.8	0.0	4.7	13.3
1 month–1 year, 1 day (%)	12.3	27.5	11.3	7.2
1–3 years (%)	80.5	72.5	37.3	30.0
3–5 years + (%)	2.4	0.0	46.7	49.2

SOURCE: U.S. Bureau of Prisons, *Federal Offenders in U.S. District Courts, 1972* (Washington, D.C.: Administrative Office of the U.S. Courts, 1975), table H10, "Selective Service Act, 1945–1974."
NOTE: Split sentences in short prison term followed by probation.

lowed World War I decisions of the Supreme Court that drafted soldiers could be sent abroad (Selective Draft Cases, 1918). Judge Doyle accepted the law of his superiors on the Seventh Circuit and the Supreme Court, who found the same authority in effect in the absence of a declared war. He indicated that he might be willing to reconsider old precedents but could not "ignore so recent an expression by the Supreme Court" (*United States v. Lonsdorf*, 1970, 414). A defendant in the Eastern District tried to persuade Judge Gordon that alternative service could be required only during a declared war or a national emergency. But the judge found such a close relationship between military and civilian work that the precedent on conscription into the military applied to alternative service (*United States v. Kuchnau*, 1972). Judge Reynolds refused to rewrite the draft law to cover those with a conscientious objection to a particular war. He decided, "This court cannot adopt such a test which . . . defies the intent of Congress when it sets up the conditions for the conscientious objector exemption" (*United States v. Kurki*, 1966, 165).

The Eastern District judges did not take the same risks of reversal as the Western judge in applying constitutional or statutory law to the facts of draft offenses. One of the clearest examples of the cultural differences occurred when identical claims for fatherhood exemptions were made before the two courts. Judge Doyle decided that the registrant was a member of a class covered by a favorable Detroit decision (*Schrader v. Selective Service Board 76*, 1971). Within the same month Judge Gordon rejected the same claim, concluding that the Detroit federal judge was wrong in treating the deferment as a statutory right rather than a discretionary matter and that without proper representation and notice the Wisconsin claimant was not a member of a class in any event (*McCarthy v. Director of Selective Service*, 1970). Judge Doyle argued, "I see no good reason why the government should be permitted continual relitigation of an issue already judicially determined" (967).

When the Sixth Circuit reversed the Detroit judge (*Gregory v. Tarr*, 1971), Judge Doyle ordered the draft board to reopen the registrant's case to consider his paternity claim (*Schrader v. Selective Service Board 76*, II, 1971). Judge Doyle felt very strongly about the "lawlessness" of the actions of the Director, writing, "In its brief the government reminds me that 'the court is not to sit as a super-draft board.' It is equally true, that the National Director of Selective Service is not to sit as the Court of Appeals for the Sixth Circuit" (892). Judge Doyle was reversed two-to-one in an opinion written by the World War I trial judge of the Eastern District, Judge Duffy. Duffy followed the reasoning of one of his successors, Judge Gordon, and rejected the Doyle conclusions. Judge Doyle was concerned about the principle of separation of powers, specifically the authority of the court over bureaucrats, while the judges in the individualistic culture were willing to compromise with those who were actually running the draft machinery.

The judges also disagreed on the rigor of procedural due process required in the process of classifying registrants. Judge Doyle insisted that the evidence of the refusal to submit to induction presented by the prosecution in his court could not be hearsay unless there was a routine followed which would serve to guarantee the trustworthiness of the reporting system (*United States v. Knudsen*, 1971, 882 n.4). Judge Doyle noted in a footnote that if he were free of controlling precedent, he would go farther and reject letters and memos embodying hearsay in criminal draft cases. He suggested that such a trial by affidavit was the last of a series of procedural failings which included lack of counsel and judicial review. He refused to accept the corroborating testimony of the FBI agent about admissions made by defendant, "since it is clear that an accused may not be convicted on his own uncorroborated confession" (882). Judge Doyle allowed testimony on the claim to counsel (*United States v. Wierzchucki*, 1965). In contrast, Judge Reynolds admitted the written confession of a draft defendant, refusing to suppress on Miranda grounds, since the registrant was "not in custody" at the induction station (*United States v. Shermeister*, 1968).

Judge Reynolds found the procedures of the board to be lawful when the clerk rather than the board issued the order and prepared the induction lists (*United States v. Buckley*, 1969; *United States v. Lewis*, 1969). The judge saw the clerk's action as ministerial, following the exercise of judgment and discretion by the board. But Judge Doyle insisted that "the essential element is that a duly constituted majority of the board deliberate upon and approve a reasonably definite and precise proposition. . . ." He believed that expecting a registrant to rely upon an "implication" that the board made a particular order would raise serious constitutional questions. Judge Doyle interpreted the term "order" in the statute to mean "an express and reasonably definite and specific motion or resolution deliberated upon and approved by a majority of the local board . . . and set forth clearly and understandably in some readily accessible record maintained by the local board" (*Hestad v. United States*, 1968; *Cupit v. United States*, 1968). Judge Reynolds said plainly: "I do not agree with the latter construction of the regulation" (*United States v. Buckley*, 995).

While Judge Doyle was ahead of the Seventh Circuit appellate bench in setting high standards for due process, the Eastern District judges were behind. In a number of cases, Judges Reynolds and Gordon bowed to appellate ruling that lateness of a CO claim, after receipt of notice or after date of induction (*United States v. Shermeister*, 1968; *United States v. Hinjosa*, 1970; *United States v. Johnson*, 1970; *United States v. Dougan*, 1971), is not sufficient basis for board refusal to reopen the classification (*United States v. Freeman*, 1967). Judge Doyle went a step farther; he attempted to build a legal edifice from the refusal to reopen a classification to the pre-induction judicial review of classification. His reasoning was that the improper denial of a hearing on the CO claim prevented the registrant from taking an administrative appeal. The failure to provide the appeal was a deprivation of procedural due process, and the denial of an essential Fifth Amendment right is the kind of blatantly lawless behavior which invites judicial intervention in the bureaucratic process. Judge Doyle emphasized the procedural failures which give the court entry to substantive matters (*Fallon v. Selective Service Board 11*, 1971). He developed the same line of reasoning in the Schrader case, when he argued that the Director of Selective Service, in ignoring the Detroit order, acted in a lawless way, which provided the basis for judicial review of classification before induction. He ordered the reopening of the registrant's classification to allow him subsequent procedural rights, with the implied alternative of his looking into the matter (*Schrader v. Selective Service Board 76*, 1972).

In the Eastern District Judge Gordon showed no interest in expanding his authority over classification (*McCormick v. Selective Ser-*

vice Board 41, 1970; *Bresette v. Knutson*, 1971). A three-judge court in the Eastern District decided a direct claim of the constitutional right to judicial review prior to induction against the plaintiff two to one. The draft resister argued that the choice of indictment or induction against his conscience was a denial of due process of law. Judge Gordon rested his opinion on clear Supreme Court precedent. Judge Reynolds dissented, but, unlike Judge Doyle, he did not write an opinion to try to persuade the lawmakers on the appellate courts (*Foran v. Weinhoff*, 1968).

EXTRA-JUDICIAL ROLES

The extra-judicial roles were either institutionalized or discarded by the Vietnam War period. The recruiter role had become routinized; draft resisters were given time to enlist or to appear for induction at each stage of the process. Judge Reynolds of the Eastern District explained that "In selective service cases it is the policy of this court to give the defendant every opportunity to reconsider his decision to refuse induction" (*United States v. Lewis*, 1969, 511).

The Wisconsin judges did not act as if they belonged to the prosecutor's office or to an employment or social welfare agency during the Vietnam War. Neither did they help to finance the war by collecting fines from the war opponents. They did not levy any fine—only sentences during the Vietnam War, in line with the practice of the entire federal judiciary which levied such fines in less than 1 percent of the convictions. Those judges who felt that it was appropriate to use their powers to express a war policy worked through their discretionary sentencing authority or their traditional responsibility to elucidate the meaning of statutes and constitutional phrases in new contexts.

THE SIGNIFICANCE OF CULTURE TO WARTIME CASES

The argument of this paper is that culture is a necessary but not a sufficient explanation for judicial behavior. Alternative explanations, which have generally been tested without any controls for culture, may be broadly categorized as personal, process, and environmental. My contention is that judges fit the culture of the geographic area they serve. It has not been possible to treat individual attributes as a linking variable in this research because of the small size of the Wisconsin federal bench. The very smallness of the Wisconsin bench did not provide room to accommodate anyone who deviated from the cultural norms, in the way large metropolitan benches can provide representation for minority cultures.

The methodological barrier to the introduction of judge variables into the study did not restrict the use of some process variables as controls. It has been established in criminal disposition studies that certain case events, such as the type of legal counsel, the plea of the defendant, and the form of the trial have an effect upon the sentence. The question which needs to be answered, then, is whether a significant difference in case processing by district, rather than culture, could explain the differences in judicial output.

A substantial majority of World War cases were decided after guilty pleas. (See table 8.) During World War II and the Korean War a less substantial majority of sentences followed admission of guilt. But during the Vietnam War the percentages dropped below 50 percent in both districts. Although the defendant seldom denied commission of the illegal act, the legal meaning of that act, the appropriateness of procedures, the basis of administrative orders, and the validity of statutes were issues which could not be reached without a trial.

Many defendants could not hope for relief from their untenable situation without a change of precedent at the circuit or Supreme Court level. To gain that review they had to go to trial. The defendants, however, paid a price for their public forum. As in ordinary criminal cases in federal courts, the sentence was more severe after a trial than after a plea. The severity index for draft cases which went to trial in the World Wars and the Korean War was 6.42, while the severity index after plea was only 2.96. The severity index after trial to the judge was 5.67 and after jury trial 7.17. The difference in both comparisons was significant ($p < .001$). Of the subversive cases in World War I there was a significant difference in severity between those sentenced after guilty plea, with an index of 1.74, and those after jury trial, 2.92 ($p < .05$). Few cases were tried to the court, since the defendants were looking for jury sympathy to result in acquittal.

During the Great War the trial type does not explain sentence differences by district, since the same percentage in each district pled guilty and used the jury. The judges plainly told defendants that they did not care to provide a public forum for treason. The World War II

Table 8. Case Types by District and War

	N	Guilty Pleas (%) ED	Guilty Pleas (%) WD	Jury Trials (%) ED	Jury Trials (%) WD
World War I	101	72.7	73.3	66.7	66.7
World War II	214	62.1	48.6	49.1	57.9
Korean War	33	52.2	50.0	18.2	40.0
Vietnam War	138	48.3	36.7	13.0	19.4

judges faced defendants less willing to take their just deserts than those in the Great War. During the Second World War the Western District took fewer pleas and in the Korean War provided more jury trials; but it is probable that the relationship of process and sentence was in the opposite direction, with the defendants knowing the reputation of Judge Stone deciding to take a chance on acquittal by jury. In the Western District the following interchange occurred at the plea stage:

JUDGE: You certainly can get a jury trial, and you will get one fast, too.
DEFENDANT: Well, I wanted a jury trial. (Baron, 1945, Stone Papers, Box 309)

Since Judge Stone had a fixed policy of five years for JW offenders, these COs had nothing to lose before a jury. The small proportion of guilty pleas in the same district during the Vietnam war is not the explanation for sentence, since Judge Doyle also had a firm policy of treating defendants alike during a time period regardless of trial process or defense.

The constitutional right to counsel in federal criminal trials made the offer of a lawyer mandatory, but the judges expedited the trial of war offenders despite this limitation. During the Great War, the judges routinized their inquiry about counsel to the point that the intimidated defendants ordinarily signed a waiver. Three of Judge Geiger's defendants had retained counsel, and of the much larger number of defendants in the Western District, none had counsel. Twenty-five percent of Judge Duffy's and Judge Stone's defendants in World War II had their own lawyers, and Judge Duffy appointed lawyers for another 22 percent, leaving 53 percent without legal aid. Judge Stone made appointments in 10 percent of his cases, leaving 65 percent without aid. The appointment of counsel during the World Wars was almost entirely ritualistic. For example, typical of Judge Stone's attitude was this remark in a 1945 case: "Any man that has been farming as long as you have can pay for your own lawyer. You shouldn't have the nerve to ask the government to provide you an attorney."

In the Korean War, Judge Tehan took the need for counsel much more seriously, following a new trend in the federal court system. In his court 56 percent of the draft offenders had their own counsel, and he provided lawyers for 22 percent more, leaving only 22 percent without counsel. By the Vietnam period the provision of counsel was almost automatic.

There was a significant difference in the disposition of defendants with and without counsel. Those who waived counsel during the World Wars and the Korean War received less severe sentences than those who hired their own or accepted appointed counsel. The severity index was 3.89 after waiver of counsel, 4.32 for their own counsel, and 5.27 for appointed counsel (p < .01). These findings are opposite to the relationship between employment of counsel and severity of sentences in ordinary crimes, where counsel can engage in plea bargaining. The judges in both districts penalized the offenders for appearing with counsel. The judges treated the request for an attorney in the same fashion that they treated the demand for a trial, as an unnecessary cost imposed by the unpatriotic on the government they refused to support. By the Vietnam War the connection between the presence of counsel and a fair trial was firmly established; only the difference in quality of representation between assigned and private counsel could affect the outcome.

Judges may also be influenced by other participants in the judicial system with whom they come into regular contact (Jacob & Eisenstein, 1977). Within a cultural framework it would be predicted that other "repeat player" participants in the authoritative process, like the judges, would reveal attributes and attitudes congruent with cultural expectations. There is some evidence from the transcripts of the war cases that the prosecutors and the defense counsel in the two districts did not differ as much as the judges. The JW defense lawyers worked in both districts. The United States attorneys, who also received policy directions through the Justice Department hierarchy, were generally patriotic. For example, during the Second World War the United States attorney in the Western District recommended the maximum sentence, saying to Judge Stone, " . . . the defendant has got a yellow streak in him" (*United States v. Vicklund*, 1945). The United States attorney in the Eastern District used sarcasm and innuendo and urged Judge Duffy to apply the equity principle in several cases (*United States v. Schrank*, 1947; *United States v. Kovatz*, 1946).

This discussion of intervening variables leads to the conclusion that there is an interaction between the judge's attitudes and previous behavior (personal variables) and the use of plea, jury, and counsel (process variables), and that any complete understanding of judicial decisions must include these and environmental intervening variables such as public opinion. Culture probably defines the boundaries of action and reveals comparative differences across geographic lines, but the more rapidly changing personal, case, and, environmental variables explain the variation within cultures over time.

Although the legal issues, the type of defendant before the court, the economic and political environment in which the judges worked, and the goals and enemies changed in each period, the behaviors of successive judges in the two districts retained the same significant differences. The Great War judges handled more subversion than draft cases and vigorously contributed to the war effort through their extra-judicial roles. The World War II and Korean War judges faced uncompromising religious objectors and the Vietnam War judges equally immovable political resisters. The issues of due process which defense counsel raised in the Second World War and the Korean War became serious legal questions for the Vietnam War judges to address. The judges gradually extended the scope of their supervision over the procedures of the draft system and cracked the door to preinduction review. There is no need to describe the many other differences in the political, economic, and social features of the four wars from 1918 to 1974 in Wisconsin.

When the entire period is treated as the time unit, the sentence severity index in the Western District (4.99) is significantly higher than in the Eastern District (3.65 [$p < .001$]). When each war is treated as the unit of analysis, there is also a significant difference in the statewide treatment of defendants by war ($p < .0001$), with the World War II and Korean War sentence levels considerably higher than the Vietnam War and Great War levels. Most important for our purposes is the difference between districts for all periods shown on table 9. The Western District judges sentenced draft offenders more harshly than the Eastern judges across time periods ($p < .0001$); the relative severity of the two districts remained consistent despite the changing issues and environment.

The analyses do not lead to the conclusion that judges in a moralist culture are necessarily more severe toward draft offenders than those in an individualist culture. The conclusion is that moralistic judges will act to achieve the currently predominant ideals of their jurisdiction (or themselves in the unusual case that they differ from the culture) with energy and determination, whether those ideals are patriotism or due process, victory in war or protection of personal conscience. On the other hand, judges in the more individualist culture would be expected to act in moderation, following rather than leading in the development of law or the playing of extra-judicial roles. The individualist culture supports an official stance of compromise among competing interests and ideas, while the moralist culture looks for a judge who will vindicate high principles through judicial behavior or even extra-judicial activities. These conclusions, which rest on the data from a single state, are obviously tentative and serve as hypotheses to be tested in the diverse cultures of the states and counties.

If the cultural framework is to be generally useful, then it should fit with other approaches suggested in the literature. Packer (1968) has described the criminal process in terms of two models, the crime control and the due process models. Since the cultures approach the basic law-jobs differently, Packer's models should fit particular cultures. The crime control model emphasizes efficient adjudication of criminal defendants, providing minimal rights and appeals, and weighing the scales in favor of the social interest in public safety. The due process model insists upon proof of "legal" guilt rather than merely factual guilt and weighs the scales in favor of individual liberty.

Since the government of the traditional culture is elitist and the historical norms incorporated into law, the crime control model should fit the treatment of the nonelite offender in that culture. However, one would expect that a more flexible, due process model would be followed when members of the elite or their cherished values were at stake in a case. The due process model, after all, leaves space for delay, for reexamination of interests, and for environmental change. The traditional culture would probably have two models, a flexible one for the elite and a rigid one for the constituents.

The government of the moralist culture, as Elazar defines it, is a participatory democracy. Status as an authority revolves among the competent citizenry. Without an elite only one criminal process

Table 9. Sentence Severity in Draft Cases Decided by Wisconsin Federal Judges over Four Wars

	Eastern District			Western District		
	Judge(s)	Severity	N	Judge	Severity	N
World War I	Geiger	—	8	Sanborn	2.13	40
World War II	Duffy	3.69	140			
Korean War	Tehan	3.91	23	Stone	6.36	84
Vietnam War	Reynolds/ Gordon	2.51	77	Doyle	3.73	40

KEY: Sentence Severity Index formula in B. Cook, "Sentencing Behavior of Federal Judges: Draft Cases—1972," *Cincinnati Law Review* 42 (1973), 597–633, appendix A.
SOURCES: Case files in federal court clerk offices, Milwaukee and Madison, Wisconsin, and Federal Record Center, Chicago.

model is required. Neither the crime control nor the due process necessarily fits a moralist culture. The value of consensus would suggest a more rigid enforcement, but the value placed upon individual contribution to society might suggest reasonable protection for their rights.

The individualist culture would seem appropriate for the due process model, because that culture emphasizes individual enterprise and the continuing problem of restricting government. The appreciation of the marketplace form of decision-making also suggests some satisfaction with a criminal process which provided numerous plays in the game. However, the individualist culture also stimulates competition among antagonistic interests, and one might expect the crime control model to be used for the political enemies of those in office. The patronage and winner-take-all customs of the culture would exist in harmony with a punitive justice system for the political opposition.

The use of cultural variables does not require the elimination of other interesting variables from a research design. In fact, the cultural approach has the advantage of suggesting linkages with a variety of contemporary models and popular concepts and also recommends itself to cross-national work on judicial behavior.

APPENDIX A

LIST OF FEDERAL DISTRICT JUDGES IN WISCONSIN DURING FOUR WARS

	District	Judge	Tenure as Active
World War I	Eastern	Ferdinand A. Geiger	1912–39
	Western	Arthur L. Sanborn	1905–21
World War II	Eastern	F. Ryan Duffy	1939–49
	Western	Patrick T. Stone	1933–63
Korean War	Eastern	Robert E. Tehan	1949–71
		Kenneth P. Grubb	1955–67
	Western	Patrick T. Stone	1933–63
Vietnam War	Eastern	Robert E. Tehan	1949–71
		John W. Reynolds	1965–date
		Myron Gordon	1967–date
	Western	James E. Doyle	1965–1980

APPENDIX B

WORLD WAR I CASES IN WISCONSIN*

EASTERN DISTRICT

United States v. Bergen	404 Crim G	1918
United States v. Brinkman	289 Crim G	1918
United States v. Czelski	393 Crim G	1922
United States v. Drager	394 Crim G	1918
United States v. Enders	391 Crim G	1918
United States v. Engle	366 Crim G	1918
United States v. Harmon	381 Crim G	1918
United States v. Hempe	408 Crim G	1918
United States v. Henning	398 Crim G	1918
United States v. Keller	422 Crim G	1919
In re Kitzerow	252 F. 865	(1918)
United States v. Klest	367 Crim G	1918
United States v. Klug	372 Crim G	1918
United States v. Knopke	339 Crim G	1918
United States v. McDonald	253 F. 99	(1918)
In re Naturalization of Aliens	1 F. 2d 594	(1924)
United States v. Pergande	406 Crim G	1918
United States v. Riehl	396 Crim G	1918
United States v. Schultz	405 Crim G	1918
United States v. Snell	410 Crim G	1918
United States v. Spiegel	392 Crim G	1918
United States v. Tegge	390 Crim G	1918
United States v. Warnke	389 Crim G	1918

WESTERN DISTRICT

United States v. Amborn	88 Crim K	1918
United States v. Auer	139 Crim K	1918
United States v. Balcer	100 Crim K	1918
United States v. Bergerschmidt	206 Crim K	1919
United States v. Biederman	207 Crim K	1918
United States v. Boebel	209 Crim K	1918
United States v. Clauson	228 Crim K	1919
United States v. Cole	239 Crim K	1919
United States v. Crevits	221 Crim K	1919
United States v. Deachman	131 Crim K	1918
United States v. DeSombre	225 Crim K	1919
United States v. Gilberts	96 Crim K	1918
United States v. Hendricks	234 Crim K	1919
United States v. Hoerner	236 Crim K	1919
United States v. Janick	15 Crim K	1918

United States v. Keyson	230 Crim K	1918
United States v. Kmetz	242 Crim K	1919
United States v. Kohlepp	223 Crim K	1919
United States v. Lueck	355 Crim K	1919
United States v. Lunardi	224 Crim K	1919
United States v. Naffz	134 Crim K	1918
United States v. Noacks	213 Crim K	1918
United States v. Ochsner	202 Crim K	1919
United States v. Peterson	398 Crim K	1919
United States v. Petry	220 Crim K	1919
United States v. Rogers	211 Crim K	1918
United States v. Emil Schiller	133 Crim K	1918
United States v. Schilling	89 Crim K	1918
United States v. Schubring	219 Crim K	1918
United States v. Sternberg	95 Crim K	1918
United States v. Williams	94 Crim K	1918
United States v. Yearous	115 Crim K	1918

*Case files, arranged by docket number, are stored in the Federal Records Center, Chicago.

APPENDIX C

WORLD WAR II AND KOREAN WAR CASES

EASTERN DISTRICT

United States v. Albrecht, 14 Crim U, 1952. Transcript of Sentence Proceedings.
United States v. Block, 297 Crim S, 1946. Transcript of Sentence Proceedings.
United States v. Doering, 15 Crim U, 1952. Transcript of Sentence Proceedings.
United States v. Duesterhoeft, 254 Crim R, 1943.
United States v. Estrada, 409 Crim S, 1946.
United States v. Felder, 301 Crim S, 1946.
United States v. France, 109 Crim R, 1942.
United States v. Gloy, 447 Crim S, 1947. Transcript of Sentence Proceedings.
United States v. Gormly, 195 Crim R, 1943.
United States v. Guerraro, 302 Crim S, 1946.
United States v. Held, 193 Crim R, 1942.
United States v. Herauf, 38 Crim R, 1944.
United States v. Kloss, 259 Crim R, 1943.
United States v. Kovatz, 167 Crim S, 1946. Transcript of Sentence Proceedings.
United States v. Krueger, 286 Crim U, 1956.

United States v. Marciniak, 254 Crim R, 1943.
United States v. Messner, 444 Crim S, 1947. Trial Transcript.
United States v. Musel, 187 Crim R, 1942.
United States v. Nichols, 22 Crim U, 1952. Transcript of Sentence Proceedings.
United States v. Nielsen, 176 Crim S, 1945.
United States v. Obenberger, 469 Crim R, 1944.
United States v. Paulos, 265 Crim R, 1943. Trial Transcript.
United States v. Sadowski, 49 Crim S, 1946.
United States v. Sanchez, 285 Crim T, 1950. Revocation Hearing.
United States v. Scheel, 306 Crim U, 1954. Transcript of Sentence Proceedings.
United States v. Ray Schlueter, 206 Crim U, 1954. Transcript of Sentence Proceedings.
United States v. William Schlueter, 146 Crim U, 1953. Transcript of Sentence Proceedings.
United States v. Schmidt, 446 Crim R, 1944.
United States v. Schoebel, 17 Crim U. 1952. Trial Transcript.
United States v. Schrank, 448 Crim S, 1947. Transcript of Sentence Proceedings.
United States v. Swenson, 21 Crim U, 1952. Transcript of Sentence Proceedings.
United States v. Thomas, 55 Crim 13, 1956.
United States v. Woodrick, 54 Crim S, 1944.
United States v. Zientek, 181 Crim R, 1942.

WESTERN DISTRICT
United States v. Adams, 27 Crim 12117, 1943.
United States v. Alderman, 27 Crim 12072, 1943.
United States v. Andrzeyeski, 26 Crim 12001, 1942.
United States v. Baron, 28 Crim 12563, 1945. Trial Transcript.
United States v. Brieske, 26 Crim 12151, 1941.
United States v. Clark, 26 Crim 11985, 1943.
United States v. Crimmins, 26 Crim 11874, 1945. Revocation Transcript.
United States v. Davison, 27 Crim 12145, 1943.
United States v. Domres, 27 Crim 12063, 1943.
United States v. Alvin Domres, 27 Crim 12060, 1943.
United States v. Drury, 26 Crim 11911, 1943.
United States v. Furrer, 28 Crim 12509, 1945.
United States v. Horban, 30 Crim 13296, 1953.
United States v. Howe, 27 Crim 12143, 1943.
United States v. Jackson, 26 Crim 1190, 1942.
United States v. Johnson, 28 Crim 12564, 1945.
United States v. Kannenberg, 30 Crim 13442, 1956.
United States v. Lane, 27 Crim 12151, 1942.

United States v. Machling, 26 Crim 11875, 1942.
United States v. Martin, 30 Crim 13455, 1953.
United States v. Monson, 26 Crim 11994, 1942.
United States v. Petelle, 27 Crim 12036, 1945.
United States v. Rineck, 27 Crim 12194, 1943.
United States v. Rowley, 27 Crim 12077, 1943.
United States v. Smith, 27 Crim 12140, 1943.
United States v. Vicklund, 28 Crim 12516, 1945.
United States v. Weston, 27 Crim 12068, 1942.

APPENDIX D

VIETNAM WAR CASES IN WISCONSIN

EASTERN DISTRICT

Bresette v. Knutson	330 FSupp 828	(1971)
Foran v. Weinhoff	291 FSupp 498	(1968)
McCarthy v. Director of Selective Service	322 FSupp 1032	(1970)
McCormick v. Selective Service Board 41	316 FSupp 974	(1970)
Schuster v. Selective Service Board 76	330 FSupp 702	(1971)
United States v. Bova	300 FSupp 936	(1969)
United States v. Buckley	300 FSupp 991	(1969)
United States v. Cassidy	337 FSupp 473	(1972)
United States v. Dougan	323 FSupp 162	(1971)
United States v. Foran	305 FSupp 1322	(1969)
United States v. Gargan	314 FSupp 414	(1970)
United States v. Hasmuk	282 FSupp 60	(1968)
United States v. Hinjosa	307 FSupp 797	(1970)
United States v. Johnson	310 FSupp 624	(1970)
United States v. Kuchnau	349 FSupp 1323	(1972)
United States v. Kurki	255 FSupp 161	(1966)
United States v. Lewis	275 FSupp 1013	(1967)
	302 FSupp 510	(1969)
United States v. Matz	324 FSupp 846	(1971)
United States v. Pluim	323 FSupp 164	(1971)
United States v. Shermeister	286 FSupp 1	(1968)

WESTERN DISTRICT

Cupit v. United States	292 FSupp 146	(1968)
Fallon v. Selective Service Board 11	321 FSupp 988	(1971)
Hestad v. United States	302 FSupp 1188	(1968)
Morin v. Grade	301 FSupp 614	(1969)
Schrader v. Selective Service Board 76	329 FSupp 966;	
	328 FSupp 891	(1971)

United States v. Gast	314 FSupp 414	(1970)
United States v. Knudsen	320 FSupp 878	(1971)
United States v. Lonsdorf	314 FSupp 413	(1970)
United States v. Matz	324 FSupp 846	(1971)
United States v. Waller	314 FSupp 414	(1970)
United States v. Wierzchucki	248 FSupp 788	(1965)

APPENDIX E

APPELLATE CASES

UNITED STATES SUPREME COURT
Berger v. United States, 255 US 22 (1921)
Dickinson v. United States, 346 US 389 (1953)
Estep v. United States, 327 US 114 (1946)
Pennsylvania v. Nelson, 350 US 497 (1956)
Selective Draft Cases, 245 US 366, 247 US 3 (1918)
United States v. Murphy, 70 US 217 (1866)
United States v. Seeger, 380 US 163 (1965)

WISCONSIN SUPREME COURT
Druecker v. Salomon, 21 Wis 621 (1867)
In re Griner, 16 Wisconsin 423 (1863)
In re Kemp, 16 Wisconsin 359 (1863)
In re Oliver, 17 Wis 681 (1864)
In re Wehlitz, 16 Wis 443 (1862)

FEDERAL CIRCUIT CASES
Gregory v. Tarr, 436 F. 2d 513 (1971)
Rhuberg v. United States, 255 F. 865 (1919)
Schrader v. Selective Service Board 76, 470 F. 2d 73 (1972)
Ex parte Starr, 263 F. 145 (1920)
Stokes v. United States, 264 F. 18 (1920)
United States v. Domres, 142 F. 2d 477 (1944)
United States v. Freeman, 388 F. 2d 246 (1967)
United States v. Messersmith, 138 F. 2d 599 (1943)
United States v. Mroz, 136 F. 2d 221 (1943)
United States v. Nagler, 252 F. 217 (1918)
United States v. Nelson, 221 F. 2d 623 (1955)
United States v. Shermeister, 425 F. 2d 1362 (1970)

NOTES

1 The term *culture* is used loosely in some literature. Nagel (1969), in his chapter on cultural patterns and courts, measures "cultural characteristics" by economic and political environmental data, without specifying how the variables link with culture.
2 The computation applies Johnson's (1976) categorization of major religious denominations by culture on his table A, p. 493, to the religious makeup of each county in the two Wisconsin districts, reported by the Census Bureau in *Religious Bodies: 1926,* vol. 1, table 32, "Members in Selected Denominations, by Counties: 1926, Wisconsin."
3 Wisconsin was not unique. In Illinois, which includes all three Elazar cultures, the disappearance of draftees also reflected cultural values. During the 1864–65 drafts, 25.1 percent of the draftees in the moralistic culture, 30.5 percent in the individualist, and 40.8 percent in the traditional (southern) culture disappeared. The percentages are drawn from figures in Sterling, 1971, 258.
4 Counsel for petitioners in the cases involving presidential power was Edward G. Ryan, a Democratic leader and later chief justice of the state court, who had opposed state interference through habeas corpus with enforcement of the Fugitive Slave act (Beitzinger, 1960).
5 *New York Times,* April 3, 1917, p. 2. Sugrue, 1946, 87. The Supreme Court members present when President Roosevelt gave his war message in 1941 expressed no elation; *New York Times,* December 9, 1941, p. 1. During the arguments before the court on the validity of the draft, the chief justice reprimanded a lawyer for making "a very unpatriotic statement"; Swisher, 1958, 118.
6 The Espionage Act trials were the first experiences of federal judges with sedition since the prosecutions for antigovernment views under the Sedition Act of 1789; Swisher, 1958, pp. 82–83.
7 A federal judge in Texas told grand jurors that La Follette and five other "traitors" in Congress should be prosecuted, and then "this country should stand them up against an adobe wall tomorrow and give them what they deserve . . . I wish that I could pay for the ammunition." Belle Case La Follette and Fola La Follette, *Robert M. La Follette* (New York: 1953), vol. 2, p. 784. The senator was better equipped to protect himself against judges who took on extra-judicial roles than ordinary citizens, particularly members of "discrete minorities."
8 However, the 8th Circuit reversed the trial judge who included speech directed toward mothers, sisters, and sweethearts, because of their effect upon the morale of the men in the military; United States v. Stokes, 264 F. 18 (1920).
9 State as well as federal judges played the fund-raising role. A Milwaukee County judge levied a fine of $25 on a German resident who said, "To hell with Liberty Bonds"; Carey, 1965, 69.

10 Minutes of the Seventh Circuit Judicial Conference, Chicago, December 11–12, 1942, p. 2. Judges in Philadelphia had adopted a uniform district policy for first offenders; see Sibley and Wardlaw (1945, p. 8, n.15).
11 Of those convicted sent from all federal courts to federal institutions from 1941 to 1946, 77.1 percent of the COs were JWs; U.S. Bureau of Prisons, 1946, p. 10, table 3.
12 Judge Stone was also displeased by the Taliesin defendants, whose objections to service were quite frankly based on their personal conscience and on their evaluation of their own worth as architects. They asked to be assigned to "interior defense" as a group. During the trial Judge Stone made disparaging remarks about Frank Lloyd Wright and then sentenced the offenders to three or four years in prison (West, 1942; Davison, 1943; Howe, 1943).
13 It was costly for the court system to send judges from Illinois to take cases for disqualified Wisconsin judges. The use of the affidavits was discouraged by the practice of visiting judges to give the same or longer sentences than the average Wisconsin sentences. Judge Duffy specifically asked the senior judge to assign Judge Campbell from Chicago to a JW case in which an affidavit was filed against him. Judge Campbell gave the defendant a five-year sentence, two years longer than Duffy's normal policy (letter to Evans from Duffy, January 7, 1943, in United States v. Gormly, 195 Crim. R., February 5, 1943).

BIBLIOGRAPHY

PRIMARY SOURCES

Anna Mae Davis. Interview at Madison, Wisconsin, on October 12, 1973, 3:00–4:45 p.m.

F. Ryan Duffy. Papers deposited at Wisconsin State Historical Society, Madison, Wisconsin.

Patrick Stone. Papers deposited at Federal Records Center, Chicago, Illinois.

SECONDARY SOURCES

Aubert, Vilhelm. 1963. "Competition and Dissensus: Two Types of Conflict and of Conflict Resolution." *Journal of Conflict Resolution* 7:26–42.

Bates, Sanford. 1950. "The Establishment and Early Years of the Federal Probation System." *Federal Probation* 14:16–21.

Beitzinger, Alfons J. 1960. *Edward G. Ryan: Lion of the Law.* Madison, Wis.: State Historical Society of Wisconsin.

Carey, Lorin L. 1965. "Wisconsin Patriots Combat Disloyalty: The Wisconsin Loyalty Legion and Politics." M.A. thesis, University of Wisconsin–Madison.

Chafee, Zechariah, Jr. 1920. *Freedom of Speech.* New York: Harcourt, Brace and Howe.

Cook, Beverly B. 1977. "Public Opinion and Federal Judicial Policy." *American Journal of Political Science* 21:567–600.
Devine, Donald. 1972. *The Political Culture of the United States.* Boston: Little, Brown & Co.
Doob, Leonard W. 1964. *Patriotism and Nationalism: Their Psychological Foundation.* New Haven, Conn.: Yale University Press.
Ehrmann, Henry Walter. 1976. *Comparative Legal Cultures.* Englewood Cliffs, N.J.: Prentice-Hall.
Elazar, Daniel J. 1966. *American Federalism: A View from the States.* New York: Crowell.
Elazar, Daniel, and Joseph Zikmund, eds. 1975. *The Ecology of American Culture.* New York: Crowell.
Elliff, Nathan T. 1945. "The War in the Courts: A Review of the Lawyers' Wartime Work." *The Federal Bar Journal* 7:75–85.
Fish, Peter Graham. 1973. *The Politics of Federal Judicial Administration.* Princeton University Press.
Galanter, Marc, F. S. Palen, and J. M. Thomas. 1979. "The Crusading Judge: Judicial Activism in the Trial Courts." *Southern California Law Review* 52:699–741.
Harries, Keith D. 1974. *The Geography of Crime and Justice.* New York: McGraw-Hill.
Hoebel, Edward A. 1954. *The Law of Primitive Man.* Harvard University Press.
Hough, Emerson. 1919. *The Web.* Chicago: Reilly & Lee Company.
Hutcheson, John D., Jr., and George A. Tayler. 1973. "Religious Variables, Political System Characteristics, and Policy Outputs in the American States." *American Journal of Political Science* 17:414–21.
Jacob, Herbert, and James Eisenstein. 1977. *Felony Justice.* Boston: Little, Brown.
Jacobs, Clyde E., and John F. Gallagher. 1967. *The Selective Service: A Case Study of the Governmental Process.* New York: Dodd, Mead, and Company.
Johnson, Charles A. 1976. "Political Culture in American States: Elazar's Formulation Examined." *American Journal of Political Science* 20:491–509.
Klement, Frank L. 1962. "Wisconsin in the Civil War," in *Wisconsin Blue Book*, 1962, pp. 72–180. Madison: Wisconsin Legislative Reference Library.
Kull, George F. 1919. "Wisconsin Loyalty Legion," in *Wisconsin Blue Book*, 1919, pp. 415–16. Madison: Wisconsin Legislative Reference Library.
La Follette, Belle Case, and Fola La Follette. 1953. *Robert M. La Follette.* 2 vols. New York: Hafner Press.
Leach, Jack F. 1952. *Conscription in the U.S.* Rutland, Vt.: E. Tuttle Publishing Co.
Levin, Martin A. 1977. *Urban Politics and the Criminal Courts.* Chicago: University of Chicago Press.
Luttbeg, Norman R. 1971. "Classifying the American States: An Empirical Attempt to Identify Internal Variations." *Midwest Journal of Political Science* 15:703–21.

Martin, Lawrence J. 1952. "Opposition to Conscription in Wisconsin, 1917–1918." M.A. thesis, University of Wisconsin–Madison.
Merry, Sally Engle. 1979. "Going to Court: Strategies of Dispute Management in an American Neighborhood." *Law and Society Review* 13:891–925.
Murdock, Eugene C. 1967. *Patriotism Limited, 1862–1865: the Civil War Draft and the Bounty System.* Youngstown, Ohio: Kent State University Press.
Nagel, Stuart A. 1969. "Culture Patterns and Judicial Systems," in *The Legal Process from a Behavioral Perspective.* Homewood, Ill.: Dorsey Press.
Packer, Herbert. 1968. *The Limits of the Criminal Sanction.* Palo Alto, Calif.: Stanford University Press.
Patterson, Samuel. 1968. "The Political Culture of the American States." *Journal of Politics* 30:187–209.
Peltason, Jack. 1971 (1961). *Fifty-Eight Lonely Men: Southern Federal Judges and School Desegregation.* Urbana: University of Illinois Press.
Peterson, H. C., and Gilbert C. Fite. 1957. *Opponents of War, 1917–1918.* Seattle: University of Washington Press.
Pixley, R. B. 1919. *Wisconsin in the World War.* Milwaukee: The Wisconsin War History Company.
President's Commission on an All-Volunteer Armed Force. 1970. Studies Prepared for the Commission. 2 vols. Vol. 2, ch. 1, "U.S. Experience with Volunteer and Conscript Forces."
Rohde, David W., and Harold J. Spaeth. 1976. *Supreme Court Decision Making.* San Francisco: W. H. Freeman & Co.
Rosenbaum, Walter A. 1975. *Political Culture.* New York: Praeger Publishers.
Russell, R. R. 1952. "Development of Conscientious Objector Recognition in the United States." *George Washington Law Review* 20:409–48.
Schoonover, Lynn. 1915. "A History of the Civil War Draft in Wisconsin." M.A. thesis, University of Wisconsin–Madison.
Sharkansky, Ira. 1969. "The Utility of Elazar's Political Culture: A Research Note." *Polity* 2:66–83.
Sheldon, Charles H. 1974. "Role Models," in *The American Judicial Process: Models and Approaches.* New York: Dodd, Mead and Co.
Sibley, Mulford Q., and Philip E. Jacob. 1952. *Conscription of Conscience.* Ithaca: Cornell University Press.
Sibley, Mulford, and Ada Wardlaw. 1945. *Conscientious Objectors in Prison, 1940–1945.* Philadelphia: Pacifist Research Bureau.
Solomon, Gus J. 1970. "Sentences in Selective Service and Income Tax Cases." *Federal Rules Decisions* 52:481–88.
Sterling, Robert E. 1971. "Civil War Draft Resistance in Illinois." *Journal of the Illinois State Historical Society* 64:244–66.
Stewart, Charles D. 1919. "Prussianizing Wisconsin." *Atlantic Monthly* 123:99–105.
Sugrue, Thomas. 1946. *Starling of the White House.* Chicago: Simon & Schuster.
Sutton, L. Paul. 1978. "Federal Sentencing Patterns: A Study of Geographical

Variations." Report No. 18 of Utilization of Criminal Justice Statistics, LEAA, Department of Justice.

Swisher, Carl Brent. 1965 (1958). Chapter 4, "The Place of the Military," in *The Supreme Court in Modern Role*. New York University Press.

U.S. Administrative Office of the U.S. Courts (AO). Report of the Director. 1951.

U.S. Bureau of the Census. 1930. *Census of Religious Bodies: 1926*. Washington, D.C.: Government Printing Office.

U.S. Bureau of Prisons. *Federal Prisoners*. Washington, D.C.: Administrative Office of the United States Courts, 1944, 1946.

U.S. Director of Selective Service. 1951. Enforcement of the Selective Service Law, Special Monograph 14. Washington, D.C.: Government Printing Office.

Vines, Kenneth N. 1964. "Federal District Judges and Race Relations Cases in the South." *Journal of Politics* 26:338–57.

Warren, Charles. 1922. *The Supreme Court in United States History*. 3 vols. Boston: Little, Brown & Co.

Winslow, John Bradley, 1912. *The Story of a Great Court*. Chicago: T. H. Flood & Company.

Wisconsin Blue Book. 1919. "Wisconsin's War Activities." Madison: Wisconsin Legislative Reference Library.

Wright, Edward N. 1931. *Conscientious Objection in the Civil War*. Philadelphia: University of Pennsylvania Press.

PROGRESSIVES, SOCIALISTS, and the MILWAUKEE POLES

**FIFTH ANNUAL
MORRIS FROMKIN MEMORIAL LECTURE**

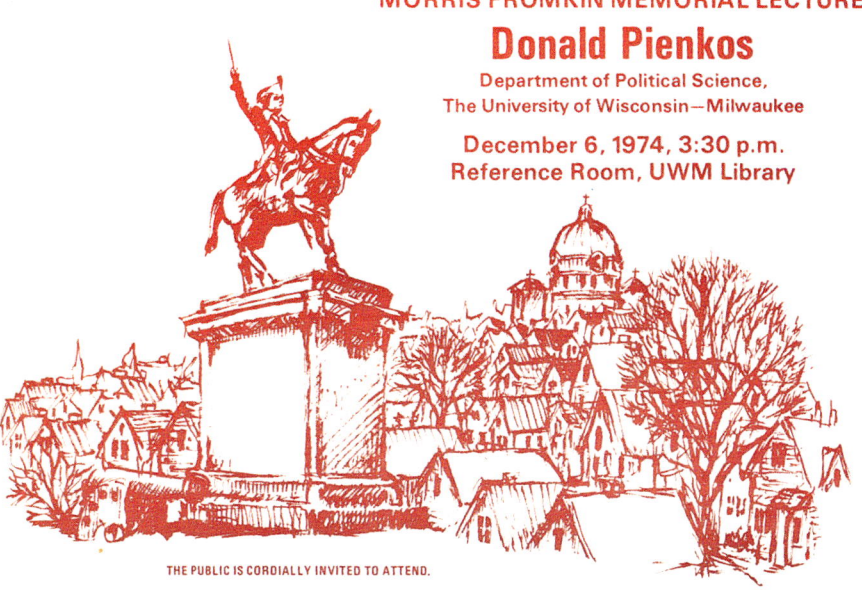

Donald Pienkos

Department of Political Science,
The University of Wisconsin—Milwaukee

December 6, 1974, 3:30 p.m.
Reference Room, UWM Library

THE PUBLIC IS CORDIALLY INVITED TO ATTEND.

Politics, Religion, and Change in Polish Milwaukee, 1900–1930

DONALD PIENKOS

PRIOR to the Civil War, not more than a few dozen residents of Milwaukee were of Polish origin, but as a result of the massive emigration that began in the 1870s, the Poles became a sizable, if little understood, factor in both Wisconsin and Milwaukee.[1] In 1906, roughly 68,000 of Milwaukee's 313,000 inhabitants were Polish, either by birth or ancestry. They constituted some 22 percent of the city's population—second only to the Germans, who accounted for 54 percent of the total.[2] The Poles of Milwaukee differed in several significant ways from Poles who settled in other American cities. By and large they had come from the German-controlled provinces of Poland, which were politically repressed but industrially more advanced than the regions under Austrian and Russian rule.[3] Few Polish emigrants from these economically more backward sections of the partitioned country settled in Milwaukee. Rather, they went to Chicago, Pittsburgh, and Detroit—cities where unskilled work in the stockyards, steel mills, and automotive assembly plants was more plentiful. Fewer jobs like these were available in Milwaukee, which was well known for its many small precision-toolmaking firms and breweries, though many unskilled Poles did find work in the tanneries, rolling mills, and meat-packing houses. The Polish community in heavily German Milwaukee thus became more tightly knit and more parochial than the more diverse, more cosmopolitan Polish settlements (usually called *Polonia* by the Poles themselves) in other American cities. "America's Poznan," one writer called it, alluding to

---

Donald Pienkos, who has degrees from DePaul University and the University of Wisconsin–Madison, is a specialist in comparative government and international relations. He has investigated aspects of communism in eastern Europe, social problems affecting Russian and Polish peasants, and ethnicity and Polish-Americans of Milwaukee. This essay, which originally appeared in the *Wisconsin Magazine of History* 61 (Spring 1978), is reprinted by permission.

the common origins of so many Milwaukee Poles in the German provinces of their partitioned homeland.[4]

Because Polish migration to Milwaukee occurred earlier than the movement of Poles from Austrian and Russian Poland to other American cities, the institutional development of *Polonia* in the Cream City was virtually complete by 1910. By then Milwaukee's Polish community possessed a stability and degree of organizational completeness that would endure for many years. In the heavily Polish neighborhoods of the city's South Side stood a number of Roman Catholic parishes, which were historically the centers of life in *Polonia*. These included the oldest parish, St. Stanislaus', erected in 1866, St. Hyacinth's (1882), St. Josaphat's (1888), St. Vincent's (1888), Sts. Cyril and Methodius' (1893), St. John Cantius' (1907), and St. Adalbert's (1908). In the smaller *Polonia* on the city's Northeast Side were St. Hedwig's (1871), St. Casimir's (1894), and St. Mary of Czestochowa parish (1907). Attached to each parish was an elementary school administered by an order of Polish sisters. In addition, several banks and loan associations and scores of small shops and businesses, real estate firms, and two newspapers run by Poles were by then in operation. A large number of Polish fraternal societies, including one founded in Milwaukee, were active.[5]

Into the early 1900s it was Catholic clerics who provided much of the leadership among Milwaukee's Poles. These early priests, nearly all of whom were well-educated and foreign-born, had come to America's immigrant community imbued with a sense of missionary zeal which is difficult to appreciate fully today. They were "confessors, teachers, counselors, social directors, alms givers, and even political leaders. . . ." They gave voice to Polish hopes and aspirations, and when they spoke on secular as well as religious matters, it was with authority.[6] One such priest—an example among many—was the Reverend (and later Monsignor) Hyacinth Gulski. Pastor of St. Stanislaus' parish between 1876 and 1883, Gulski built St. Hyacinth's church and became its first pastor in 1883. A diocesan consultant to the archbishop—and thus the ranking Polish clergyman in Milwaukee—Gulski championed the creation of additional parishes to serve the burgeoning number of Polish immigrants on the South Side. From 1909 to 1911 he was also pastor of St. Hedwig's parish on the North Side. Chaplain for many local fraternal organizations and well known throughout the community, he was politically influential, although, as he put it, he was "a Democrat, but not active."[7]

Outside their own neighborhoods, of course, the Poles of Milwaukee were a distinct minority whose dealings with non-Poles were usually with Germans. In a city that was noticeably less ethnically cosmopolitan than, for example, Chicago, it was understandable that Poles tended to be defensive in their dealings with the German majority and to be responsive toward expressions of anti-German rhetoric in the Polish press and pulpit. The self-containment of the Poles— what was called their "clannish" ways—was a phenomenon upon which outsiders frequently remarked.

The Poles were distinct from their fellow Milwaukeeans in class and status as well. The predominantly Polish wards had a decidedly working-class character and a much higher proportion of factory hands and common laborers than of tradesmen and machinists. According to a state census conducted in 1905, only 15 percent of the residents in the two Polish wards were engaged in proprietary, professional, or clerical occupations, compared with a citywide figure of 32 percent. In the city, 34 percent of the inhabitants were listed as skilled workers and 30 percent as unskilled; for the Polish wards, 29 percent were skilled and 54 percent were unskilled.[8] Among the Poles, clergymen played a far more important role as community leaders than they did among non-Poles, who tended to be dominated by lawyers, businessmen, and other professional persons. Religion, like ethnicity, inclined the Milwaukee Polish community toward the Democratic party, which was historically the party of the immigrant and the Roman Catholic.[9]

What follows is intended to describe more precisely the political behavior of the Polish voters of Milwaukee during the progressive era and to examine their response to progressive and socialist ideas and movements in terms of four general themes. 1) Between 1900 and 1940 the Polish population of Milwaukee was far more "progressive" than has been generally acknowledged, in that large numbers of Poles voted for socialist candidates, particularly when the Socialist party was a viable force in city politics or when Polish socialists were nominated; and a sizable contingent of Polish socialists attained prominence and was able to win elections between 1910 and 1932. 2) Most Milwaukee Poles remained outside the organized labor movement before the New Deal, primarily because the Milwaukee Federated Trades Council was a crafts-oriented union which by definition excluded most Polish factory workers; but in fact there were Polish trade-unionists in Milwaukee, a number of whom had close ties with the Socialist party. 3) As early as 1900, some Polish leaders in Milwaukee were attracted to Robert M. La Follette's progressive wing of the Republican party, although it was only during the 1920s, when La Follette's sons carried on the progressive tradition, that the Republican party assumed much significance in Polish politics. 4) Far from remaining a monolithic structure of ethnics who thought and acted as one, *Polonia* was deeply divided over several important issues, including the proper role for Polish clerics within the Catholic hierarchy and the proper response of Polish voters toward the newly forming socialist and progressive movements which challenged the Democratic party. These conflicts within both the ecclesiastical and secular domains, occurring at practically the same time in history, profoundly altered the character of traditional Polish-American life. Over time, the concerns of the Polish community increasingly mirrored the political, cultural, and economic pluralism to be found within the larger Milwaukee environment, and hence the process of the Poles' assimilation into that environment accelerated.[10]

The Poles first achieved recognition as a factor in Milwaukee politics following the suppression of a Polish workmen's strike at the Bay View rolling mills by the Wisconsin National Guard in May, 1886. Nine persons were killed in the confrontation, which was part of the citywide effort led by the Knights of Labor to achieve the eight-hour workday. The incident produced a crisis within *Polonia*, since a Polish unit of the National Guard had taken part in suppressing the strikers; more important, it also provoked a large Polish voter turnout in support of the People's party, whose candidates swept all the county races in the spring election of 1886.[11] In 1890, the Catholic sentiments of the Poles roused them against the Republican party, whose leaders were held responsible for passing the Bennett Law the previous year. The law stipulated that certain subjects in all Wisconsin schools (including Catholic and Lutheran parochial schools) must be taught in English, thus arousing the ire of several ethnic groups. In the next election, Democrats swept the state for the first time in many years. Their victory usually is credited to the Germans, who, despite previous party membership, united to defeat the Republican party which had foisted the Bennett Law upon them. But the Poles, too, enjoyed political advancement in the election. A number of them, including Michael Kruszka (running for a state assembly seat), won office, again demonstrating the Poles' political potency.[12]

Two reasons can be given which explain the Poles' recognized significance in local politics. On the one hand, it was widely appreciated that the Poles, when voting as a bloc, were capable of delivering huge pluralities for their favorites. As early as 1892, one Milwaukee newspaper concluded that since the German and native-born voters did not behave as a solid group, the "Poles [already possess] the balance of power that will soon make them by far the most important element" in city politics.[13] The staunch support they gave to David Rose, a five-term Democratic mayor of Milwaukee between 1898 and 1910, served to reinforce this opinion.[14]

Equally important, however, was the Poles' ability to elect "their own" to public office. Wenceslaus Kruszka proudly asserted in his 1906 history of Milwaukee's *Polonia* that "as far back as 1892, we in Milwaukee had Poles in every level of public service, from policeman to state senator. . . . Nowhere in any other Polish settlement in all America did Poles so frequently achieve so many high offices as in Milwaukee, not in Buffalo, nor Detroit, not even Chicago where the largest number of Poles lived."[15]

August Rudzinski had won a place on the county board of supervisors as early as 1878. His son Theodore became Milwaukee's first Polish alderman in 1882, and later that year Francis Borchardt became the first Pole to represent a Milwaukee district in the Wisconsin Assembly. Between 1890 and 1940, thirty-one Polish-Americans were elected to the lower house in Milwaukee legislative districts. Indeed, the most heavily Polish district of Milwaukee, encompassing the South Side's fourteenth ward, was represented by a Pole for forty-two of those fifty years. Nine Polish-American state senators were elected from Milwaukee County constituencies beginning in 1892.[16] As for the city's common council, a large number of Polish-Americans became aldermen. Between 1908 and 1940, twenty-four Poles won seats. Poles were also able to win as candidates for important city-wide administrative positions: between 1890 and 1933, four Polish-Americans created a kind of local tradition by winning the comptroller's office (whose incumbents were jocularly known as "the Polish mayor"). The first Pole to hold this prestigious post was Roman Czerwinski, who served two terms between 1890 and 1894. Peter Pawinski held the office between 1902 and 1906, followed by August Gawin in 1908–10. Most notable among Milwaukee's so-called "Polish mayors" was the American-born Louis Kotecki, who served as comptroller between 1912 and 1933 and won eight consecutive elections.[17]

The affinity of Milwaukee's Poles for the Democratic party has been acknowledged by numerous historians, who have tended to discount the Polish role in socialist and progressive reform movements. Thus, Bayrd Still, in his history of Milwaukee, wrote: "The predominance of workingmen among the Poles inclined the group most consistently to the Democratic Party, their coolness toward the Socialists being motivated by both the attitude of the church and the Socialists' opposition to fighting the battles of Poland in World War I."[18] And David

Shannon, in his history of American Socialism, concluded: "The Socialists [in Milwaukee] had tremendous strength among the Germans, substantial influence among the Yankees, and their least power among the Poles."[19]

To a certain extent these generalizations are true. Class, religion, and ethnicity did incline the Poles of Milwaukee toward the Democratic party. But for the years 1900 to 1930—that is, in an era of tremendous political ferment—even a cursory glance at the election returns from the heavily Polish wards shows that the socialists made major inroads within Milwaukee's most heavily Polish districts. In every presidential election between 1908 and 1924, the socialist standard-bearer ran better in wards with substantial Polish populations than in Milwaukee as a whole. In 1912, Eugene V. Debs received a plurality of the vote in those wards.[20] The socialists demonstrated similar strength in the Polish wards for all sixteen gubernatorial elections between 1900 and 1930. In nine such contests—the elections of 1902, 1904, 1906, 1908, 1910, 1914, 1916, 1926, and 1928—Socialist *and* Democratic party candidates ran better in Polish wards than in the city as a whole. In 1900 and 1918 the Democratic nominees outpolled the Socialist party candidates, but in 1912, 1920, and 1924 the reverse was true in the Polish wards.

These same Polish voters were also more supportive of La Follette progressivism than has generally been recognized. In 1922, for example, Senator Robert M. La Follette carried Milwaukee with an 84 percent majority—and by an 88 percent majority in the four Polish wards. In 1924, as a presidential candidate, La Follette's 56 percent majority in the Polish wards equalled his showing in Milwaukee as a whole. And in 1930 La Follette's son Philip, a gubernatorial candidate, won 59 percent of the vote in the Polish wards, compared to 53 percent in the city as a whole. In short, both socialist and progressive Republican candidates enjoyed considerable success in Milwaukee wards having large numbers of Poles.[21] Why, then, do historians continue to describe the Polish voter as conventionally Democratic in politics, and therefore unworthy of detailed analysis?

Research about Milwaukee's Polish community during the progressive era has been deficient because of a general reliance upon English-language sources. Recent studies show little evidence that their authors were familiar with the city's Polish-language dailies, the *Kuryer Polski* and *Nowiny Polskie*. Similarly, few interviews seem to have been conducted with members of the Polish community whose recollections could add immeasurably to what is available in printed sources.[22] And finally, although a number of scholars have begun to perform statistical analyses of voting behavior during the progressive era and have made much use of aggregate data in correlating election results with census information about the ethnic and class composition of the Wisconsin electorate, their work (insofar as it has touched upon Polish political behavior) has as yet yielded little that challenges, much less contradicts, conventional wisdom about the Poles in Milwaukee.[23] Why should this be so?

For one thing, in depending upon census enumerations of foreign-born populations in order to determine the identity, size, and location of ethnic voting groups, scholars have made two false assumptions. The first has to do with the fact that censuses themselves name as members of ethnic groups only those persons born on foreign soil (the "first generation" Americans), and they do not identify the native-born descendants of the immigrants as members of the ethnic groups. Some scholars who have relied on such data have tended to write about the political behavior of the entire ethnic group when they really can only consider the political orientations of the foreign-born. This practice is justified by assuming that the voting behavior of second- and third- generation Americans will resemble the voting behavior of the foreign-born parents or grandparents, the only persons counted as ethnic group members in the census. But this assumption is false, since it is precisely these American-born ethnics who were more likely to be active politically, because they (unlike their immigrant forefathers) were automatically eligible to vote. Hence, the traditional methods of analyzing ethnic voting behavior by relying upon enumeration of the foreign-born must be rejected, unless it can be shown that membership in a given ethnic group was synonymous with foreign birth and that foreign birth was in fact not a serious impediment to political participation.

A second false assumption which scholars have made is that what was true in Milwaukee's single most heavily Polish ward (the fourteenth on the South Side) was true for all Polish voters throughout the city. But, since Poles were found in substantial numbers elsewhere in Milwaukee, it cannot be assumed that all Poles behaved alike, regardless of where they lived.

In order to identify and isolate Polish voting patterns, I decided to forgo the traditional examination of census returns and election results from Milwaukee's Polish wards and turn instead to the lists of registered voters which have been kept by the city since 1888.[24] These lists hold several advantages over election returns in permitting the researcher to determine the shape and thrust of ethnic voting behavior. For one thing, all Poles actually eligible to vote are included, regardless of their country of birth. In addition, since the lists are for precincts having as few as 200 and rarely more than 800 eligible voters, they enable one to pinpoint the most densely Polish precincts, which are usually far more homogeneous (that is, far more Polish) than so-called "Polish" wards containing 15,000 to 25,000 residents.

Table 1. Size and Location of Milwaukee Precincts with Voting Population at Least 50 Percent Polish, 1904

\multicolumn{3}{c}{1904 Precincts (Total = 112)}	Total	Percent
Ward	Precinct	Location	Voters	Polish
14	6	South	648	93.2
12	4	South	505	89.7
14	3	South	465	88.0
14	5	South	576	84.7
14	4	South	602	79.1
14	2	South	863	76.4
14	1	South	579	72.7
17	4	South	383	70.5
18	2	North	712	56.6
13	6	North	592	56.1

Total vote in Milwaukee mayoral election: 59,604.
Total eligible Polish voters: 5,856.
Percentage of Polish voters residing in Polish precincts: 79 percent.

Table 2. Size and Location of Milwaukee Precincts with Voting Populations at Least 50 Percent Polish, 1914

\multicolumn{3}{c}{1914 Precincts (Total = 141)}	Total	Percent
Ward	Precinct	Location	Voters	Polish
14	1	South	616	82.5
14	2	South	518	82.0
14	3	South	244	80.3
24	4	South	206	78.6
14	4	South	260	65.4
17	4	South	257	64.7
8	5	South	438	63.9
8	6	South	542	58.5
8	4	South	586	58.5
12	4	South	539	57.4
13	1	North	674	53.9
1	5	North	523	51.4

Total vote in Milwaukee mayoral election: 66,795.
Total eligible Polish voters: 5,694.
Percentage of Polish voters residing in Polish precincts: 58 percent.

By carefully checking for Polish surnames on the precinct lists of registered voters for the mayoral elections of 1904, 1914, and 1924, I was able to identify a number of Milwaukee precincts containing at least 50 percent Polish voters. (See tables 1, 2, and 3, and the map of Milwaukee for 1924). From this it was possible to determine that in 1904, 1914, and 1924 the vast majority of all the Polish voters in Milwaukee was concentrated into ten, a dozen, and two dozen precincts out of 112, 141, and 242 precincts respectively. In 1904 and again in 1924, nearly four-fifths of all of Milwaukee's Polish voters resided in these few precincts.

My analysis of voter-registration lists at the precinct level raises serious doubts about the validity of studies of ethnic voting behavior derived from census data. When a comparison was made between

Table 3. Size and Location of Milwaukee Precincts with Voting Populations at Least 50 Percent Polish, 1924

Ward	Precinct	Location	Total Voters	Percent Polish
14	1	South	749	91.5
14	3	South	687	83.7
8	8	South	540	83.5
14	4	South	899	80.0
24	1	South	493	78.7
24	6	South	609	78.3
14	2	South	705	77.2
1	5	North	661	74.7
14	5	South	795	73.5
17	4	South	551	73.3
14	6	South	301	72.3
12	7	South	675	70.7
8	4	South	564	68.6
13	5	North	681	62.3
12	8	South	650	61.8
8	6	South	628	61.1
13	1	North	660	60.0
8	5	South	795	59.9
8	7	South	750	56.4
21	8	North	727	55.9
12	4	South	515	55.3
13	6	North	537	51.8
24	2	South	547	51.2
1	4	North	660	50.2

Total vote in Milwaukee mayoral election: 131,412.
Total eligible Polish voters: 13,412.
Percentage of Polish voters residing in Polish precincts: 78 percent.

the ward-based census figures about Milwaukee Poles and the actual number of voters having Polish surnames on precinct registration lists, the unreliability of the census data became evident. (See table 4.)

While Poles comprised upwards of 20 percent of Milwaukee's population during the progressive era, the number of actual Polish voters seems not to have exceeded 6 or 7 percent of the electorate. This disparity is explained partially by the fact that a larger proportion of the Polish population was made up of women and children than was true for the city as a whole.[25] Furthermore, since many Poles originally came to America with no intention of remaining permanently, American citizenship, with its right to the franchise, may have held little appeal initially.[26] But among those Poles who did register to vote, participation at the polls was quite high. In the mayoral election of 1914, for example, a count of the names of actual voters who were systematically ticked off the registration lists throughout the city showed that 86.7 percent of the eligible Polish voters cast ballots—slightly higher than for the city as a whole.

Table 4. Milwaukee Wards with Large Polish Populations
(Comparing census findings with precinct-based information on registered Polish voters, 1904–24)

Ward	Location	Foreign-Born Poles (from Wisconsin census) (1905)	Registered Voters with Polish Names (1904)
14	South	34%	81.9%
12	South	13	26.9
18	North	10	20.0
11	South	8	15.7
13	North	11	15.3
17	South	8	11.0

Ward	Location	Foreign-Born Poles (from U.S. census) (1920)	Registered Voters with Polish Names (1914)	(1924)
14	South	24%	70.9%	80.4%
8	South	18	37.8	48.0
12	South	11	29.7	29.5
24	South	16	25.4	25.8
13	North	7	16.0	19.1
1	North	7	15.8	18.7
11	South	14	11.8	21.8
21	North	5	9.0	10.4
17	South	6	6.0	7.5

Analysis of voter registration lists and election returns at the precinct level confirms what is evident from larger, ward-based aggregate statistics: that Polish voters in significant numbers moved away from the Democratic party during the progressive era. Socialists were the major beneficiaries of this trend; however, the La Follettes and other progressives such as John J. Blaine also won large numbers of Polish voters to their side during the 1920s. For example, Blaine received 37.0 percent of the vote cast in the city's Polish precincts, a figure nearly equaling his citywide share of 37.4 percent. In 1930, Philip La Follette carried Milwaukee with 52.7 percent of the total vote; but in the Polish precincts he did even better, winning 59.9 percent. Polish support of socialist candidates for state and local office was even more pronounced during this era, but the precinct-level data also point up significant differences between the larger South Side Polish community and the smaller enclave on the North Side.

Polish support for socialist candidates was confined exclusively to the *Polonia* on the South Side; the Polish voters of the North Side remained overwhelmingly Democratic in their preferences.[27] For example, in 1914 Emil Seidel, Milwaukee's first socialist mayor, received 55.1 percent of the vote in the South Side Polish precincts; his opponent carried the North Side precincts by a margin of more than two to one while winning re-election with 55.4 percent of the total vote. In 1916 Daniel W. Hoan, another socialist, was elected to the first of his seven terms as mayor when he won 51.3 percent of the total vote. Again, the outcome on the Polish South Side was strongly favorable to the socialist, with Hoan gathering 62.7 percent of the vote. The North Side, however, was divided exactly between Hoan and the Democratic incumbent. Thereafter, Polish support of socialist candidates tailed off, largely because of the Socialist party's strong opposition to World War I (which Poles interpreted as opposition to Poland's independence), but Polish South Siders continued to provide much stronger support for the socialists than did those on the North Side. In 1924, for example, when the irrepressible David Rose unsuccessfully challenged Hoan, the socialist incumbent still won 39.1 percent of the South Side precinct vote, but only 22.1 percent on the North Side. In 1928, Hoan won 44.5 percent of the votes cast in the South Side precincts, but only 26.2 percent of those from the North Side, while winning 58.2 percent of the total vote.[28]

The impact of residence upon the political preferences of Milwaukee Poles is most evident when one considers elections in which the candidate for comptroller (chief financial officer for the city) was Polish. In the elections of both 1902 and 1904, Peter Pawinski, a Democrat, overwhelmingly carried both the South Side and North Side precincts (even outdistancing the popular Mayor Rose), although he trailed his running-mate in the mayoral race in both elections. In the elections after 1914 for which detailed precinct-level data are available, the victorious Polish candidate for comptroller, Louis Kotecki, was far less successful in the South Side Polish precincts than in the traditionally Democratic stronghold of the North Side. In all these elections, socialist candidates for comptroller captured at least one-third and usually something approaching 40 percent of the South Side vote, while on the North Side, Kotecki's total generally exceeded

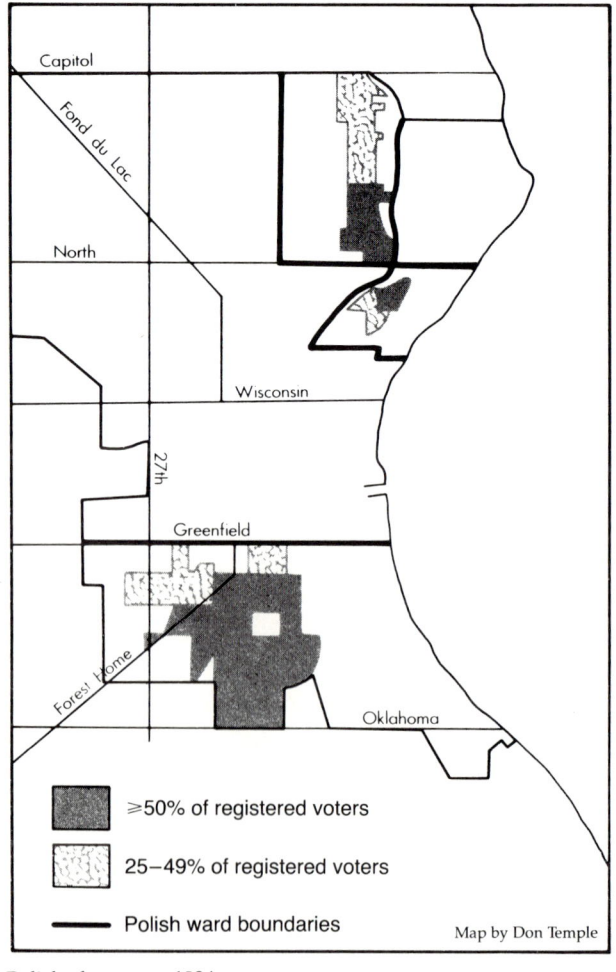

Polish electorate, 1924

75 percent of the total. Perhaps the most interesting contest took place in the spring election of 1916, in which the race for city comptroller pitted two Poles against each other: the incumbent Democrat Kotecki and the socialist challenger, alderman Leo Krzycki. In the two North Side precincts, the Democrat destroyed the socialist, winning 72.8 percent of the 1,030 votes there. But in the two South Side precincts, a great degree of ambivalence as to the relative merits of two "favorite sons" was obvious from the election results. Here, Krzycki received 50.3 percent of the vote—a majority of twenty-five votes out of 3,949 cast.

From these returns it is possible to detect a significant trend in favor of the socialists on the South Side as early as 1910. (See tables 5 and 6.) Indeed, almost from the time that the Milwaukee socialists became a significant factor in the political life of the city, Polish activists were to be found among them. Most were workingmen, up from

Table 5. Polish-Americans Elected to Wisconsin Legislature, by Decade and Party Affiliation, 1891–1940

	Assembly			Senate		
	Democrats	Republicans	Socialists	Democrats	Republicans	Socialists
1891–1900	6	0	0	1	0	0
1901–1910	4	0	0	0	1	0
1911–1920	3	0	3	0	1	0
1921–1930	1	3	4	0	1	1
1931–1940	7	1	1*	3	1	1

*Elected on Progressive party ticket.

Table 6. Total Man-Years Served by Polish-American Legislators, by Decade and Party Affiliation, 1891–1940

	Assembly			Senate		
	Democrats	Republicans	Socialists	Democrats	Republicans	Socialists
1891–1900	10	0	0	4	0	0
1901–1910	10	0	0	0	2	0
1911–1920	10	0	6	0	4	0
1921–1930	2	6	8	0	4	8
1931–1940	24	2	2*	16	4	4

*Elected on Progressive party ticket.

the ranks, with ties to organized labor. Martin Gorecki, a brewery worker who was elected alderman-at-large in the elections of 1910—the first in which a socialist became mayor—was among the first of many. Gorecki was subsequently elected to the state assembly in 1912, representing the heavily Polish fourteenth and twenty-fourth wards of Milwaukee; and he was involved in the founding of a short-lived Polish-language socialist weekly, *Naprzod* (*Forward*).[29] Another important early Polish socialist, Casimir Kowalski, had worked as a coal miner in Pennsylvania before settling in Milwaukee in 1906. With his wife, he organized several socialist units among Milwaukee's Poles, including a women's branch of the party.[30] An unsuccessful candidate for a number of city and county offices, Kowalski was elected alderman-at-large from 1918 to 1922 and later served as one of Mayor Hoan's secretaries. A third early Polish socialist was Michael Katzban. Born in Illinois, a molder by occupation and a long-time unionist, he was the first Polish socialist elected to the Wisconsin legislature, where he represented Milwaukee's fourteenth ward between 1911 and 1913. A socialist throughout his long life, Katzban ran unsuccessfully for an assembly seat in 1930 and served for six years on the Milwaukee Board of Election Commissioners beginning in 1950.[31]

While several other Polish socialists were elected to the state assembly and Milwaukee county board and aldermanic offices after 1910, perhaps the most prominent Polish-American in the entire movement up until the late 1930s was Leo Krzycki. Born in Milwaukee in 1881, Krzycki was active in organized labor throughout his long life, becoming a vice-president of the Lithographic Press Feeders Union at the age of twenty-three and ultimately serving as a national vice-president of the Amalgamated Clothing Workers Union. For a number of years, Krzycki was a Milwaukee County Socialist party secretary and was the party's state secretary at its 1932 convention.[32] A major political figure in the fourteenth ward Socialist party organization, he was the ward's alderman for two terms beginning in 1912 and later was deputy sheriff of Milwaukee County. A serious, forceful, and deliberate thinker, his speeches demonstrated his capacity to discuss American political conditions within a rather sophisticated Marxian framework. For example, in his keynote speech to the Socialist party's state convention in 1934, Krzycki called for an alliance between unorganized Wisconsin farmers and urban laborers under the socialist banner, its purpose being to overthrow the bankrupt capitalist system.[33]

Most successful of all the Milwaukee Polish socialists in winning elective office was Walter Polakowski. He was born in Buffalo in 1888, but he came to Milwaukee as a boy. Like Krzycki and most other Polish socialists, Polakowski was self-educated. An upholsterer by trade and an energetic unionist, he became one of his union's representatives in the Federated Trades Council at age nineteen. In 1920, he won a seat in the state assembly, representing Milwaukee's eighth ward, and in 1922 he was elected to the state senate from the city's third district, which included the heavily Polish eighth, fourteenth, twenty-fourth, and eleventh wards. (In that same election, his younger brother John won a seat in the state assembly, representing the eighth and fourteenth wards.) Walter Polakowski served three consecutive terms in the state senate before a narrow defeat in a four-cornered race in 1934. Physically large and imposing, Polakowski was universally regarded as an effective public speaker, with a booming "lion's roar" oratorical style. A competent legislator, he became known as "the father of Wisconsin's unemployment compensation law," having first proposed this measure as an assemblyman in 1921. The bill became law in 1932. In 1937, he left the Socialist party when it divided over its relationship vis-à-vis Philip La Follette's new Progressive party. He later joined the Democrats and eventually became chairman of their fourteenth ward unit.[34]

Among other notable Polish socialists was a printer, Martin Cyborowski, who unsuccessfully sought public office as early as the 1890s as a populist, later edited a progressive newspaper, *Glos Ludu* (*Voice of the People*), and worked for Michael Kruszka's liberal daily, the *Kuryer Polski*. Cyborowski fought for the teaching of Polish in Milwaukee's public schools and served as the first president of the Federation of Polish Catholic Laymen, a group which mobilized thousands of Milwaukee Poles in favor of nominating a Polish bishop to serve in the Catholic archdiocese.[35] Other notable figures in the party included Louis Rutkowski, who served one term as county treasurer, the highest county office ever won by a Polish socialist, and Frank Boncel, a twelfth ward alderman between 1932 and 1936 who wrote the so-called Boncel Ordinance, a prolabor measure which empowered the city to intervene in labor disputes with private businesses to settle strikes—a burning issue in depression-era Milwaukee.[36]

What prompted these Milwaukee Poles to become active in a political movement so much at odds with the views of the traditional secular and religious leaders of *Polonia*? As already noted, many Polish socialists were active in the trade-union movement in an era when very few Polish workers even belonged to labor organizations.

The spirit of trade unionism probably played a larger role in their lives than was the case for other Poles, or for workers in general. John Polakowski recalled that one of his uncles had been active in the Knights of Labor organization in the 1880s. Walter Polakowski was known as "a strong union man, but too radical." Leo Krzycki named his two eldest sons Victor and Eugene, in honor of the socialist labor leader Eugene V. Debs.[37]

Polish socialists in Milwaukee were undoubtedly influenced by working-class German socialists with whom they had considerable contact. Polakowski remembered that "our family was the only Polish one on the block. Everyone else was German." Krzycki's wife's maiden name, Kadau, was German in origin. Stanley Budny recalled that his uncles had belonged to the Socialist party in Prussian Poland. There, Poles and Germans had worked together in opposing the policies of Chancellor Otto von Bismarck.[38] Polish socialists tended to view themselves as "free thinkers" who were intellectually independent of clerical influence. Several old socialists recalled how their fathers continued to subscribe to the *Kuryer Polski* even after the paper was condemned by the archbishop under threat of excommunication. Polakowski recounted how, as a fourteen-year-old at confession, he had disputed his priest's command that he no longer read the newspaper. The priest had quickly retreated from his stand.[39]

The Polish socialists were of course a minority within Milwaukee's *Polonia,* and they were to be found almost exclusively on the city's South Side. Their numbers were kept small by the extremely hostile stand taken against socialism by the Catholic Church, a factor which deterred many Polish voters who cast socialist ballots from participating openly in the Socialist party. In 1902, Archbishop Sebastian G. Messmer of Milwaukee had issued an edict forbidding Catholics to join the party or even to vote for socialists under pain of excommunication.[40] This order was reinforced by Polish clergymen, who sometimes expressed their Democratic party preferences publicly. As one declared, "A good Catholic is a good Democrat." Even that stormy petrel of Polish Milwaukee, the Reverend Wenceslaus Kruszka, dismissed socialism's appeals as "the seduction of a serpent."[41]

However, a useful index of the popularity of socialists and socialist ideas among the Polish voters of Milwaukee's South Side is the party affiliation of successful candidates for public office from *Polonia.* From 1890 to about 1910, a Democratic party affiliation seems to have been a prerequisite for election to the state legislature. During the next two decades, however, socialists and progressive Republicans enjoyed far more success than they had earlier; in fact, between 1920 and 1930 only one Democrat of Polish extraction, Mrs. Mary Kryszak, was elected to the Wisconsin Assembly. Of thirty-one Polish politicians who were elected to the assembly between 1890 and 1942, twelve were either socialists or progressive Republicans; of nine state senators elected during the same fifty-two-year span, five were socialists or progressive Republicans.

A similar situation prevailed in the city's common council. Between 1910 and 1940, twenty-three Poles were elected as aldermen, seven of whom were socialists. It was not until the spring election of 1936 that the last Polish socialists were swept from local office, buried in landslides won by five antisocialist Polish candidates.[42]

This general trend from a traditional Democratic base toward a more liberal outlook—embracing both socialism and La Follette progressivism—reflected broader developments in both municipal and state politics, and indicates that Milwaukee's Poles were increasingly influenced by forces outside the ethnic community. Predictably, when the Democratic party underwent its New Deal renaissance during the Great Depression, both Republican and Socialist party candidates were overwhelmed by a revivified Democratic machine in Polish Milwaukee. Since 1938, for example, not a single Polish-American has been elected to the Wisconsin legislature except as an avowed Democrat. But between 1910 and 1930 the socialists did attain the status of a major party on the South Side. As one Polish-American grudgingly remarked, in a 1946 retrospective on the politics of *Polonia* in Milwaukee: "The Democratic party for many years has been considered the workingman's party, although for a period, some twenty-five years ago, the socialists, with such men as Seidel, Berger, and Hoan pointing the way, made a serious incursion into the Polish-American Democratic ranks with their claims of standing for the rights of the common man."[43]

Yet the trend in party politics in favor of socialist and progressive Republican principles could never have become as pronounced within *Polonia* during the period between 1900 and 1930 had it not been for the serious conflict over religious ideas that developed among the community's leaders at the same time. Religion, like politics, underwent a profound change, as many Catholics were called upon to question the traditional leadership of the church hierarchy and to adopt a more critical, intellectually independent attitude toward the Roman Catholic Church. The rise in this new, more critical spirit must be attributed largely to Michael Kruszka, founder, editor, and publisher of the Polish-language daily *Kuryer Polski* from 1888 to his death in 1918. Together with his half brother, the Catholic priest Wenceslaus Kruszka, Michael Kruszka devoted himself unstintingly to the cause of the Polish immigrant, stimulating a growing self-awareness among his countrymen, questioning the guidance of traditional clerical leaders, and supporting ideas which challenged the prevailing values of *Polonia*.[44] The *Kuryer Polski* often took editorial positions which were fiercely nationalistic, somewhat anticlerical, and politically liberal. Predictably, Michael Kruszka's views continually clashed with those of the Reverend Boleslaus Goral, editor of the city's other Polish-language daily, *Nowiny Polskie*, which was less nationalistic, more orthodoxly Catholic, and decidedly Democratic in its political leanings. But the ongoing feud between the two newspapers represented more than personal, religious, or party differences; it signified that *Polonia* was not merely heterogeneous in values and priorities but that profound antagonisms threatened at times to tear the Polish community apart.

The principal agent of change was Michael Kruszka, the immigrant journalist from the town of Slabomierz in German Poland. Energetic and politically ambitious, he had established the *Kuryer Polski* after several earlier unsuccessful ventures into the newspaper business. Financially sound, the *Kuryer Polski* was to become the first long-lived Polish-language daily in America, with its owner claiming as many as 35,000 readers by 1893. By 1915, readership was estimated to have reached the more plausible figure of 40,000, making the *Kuryer Polski* one of the most widely circulated Polish newspapers in the country.[45]

Kruszka's *Kuryer* achieved success by catering to immigrant readers' hunger for news about political and economic developments in the German-ruled regions from which most of them had come. Kruszka was also interested in disseminating cultural information broadly. Extensive literary sections could be found in the *Kuryer*, and the work of many popular novelists and essayists was serialized, particularly when it extolled Poland's past greatness and future promise.

In its coverage of domestic affairs the *Kuryer Polski* was stridently nationalistic. It proclaimed the virtues of Milwaukee's Poles and criticized any real or perceived slight the Poles experienced in dealing with others in the city. Intensely conscious of the low social status of the Milwaukee Poles, Kruszka continually strove to agitate the Polish population to fight for its own betterment. For example, in one editorial, "To Our Women Readers," he urged that women shop at Polish-operated stores whenever possible, rather than at stores run by persons of other nationalities. "And when this is necessary," the editorial went on, "always speak to them in Polish. Otherwise, they will not feel any need to hire Polish-speaking clerks, our people won't be hired and everyone will be worse off!"[46] Another editorial concerned an issue touched off by Kruszka: the teaching of Polish in Milwaukee's public schools. Unceasingly, Kruszka asked why instruction in German was offered in German neighborhoods, while Polish was not available in Polish neighborhood schools. (This struggle was finally won in 1907, when the Milwaukee Board of Education ruled in Kruszka's favor.)[47]

As for local politics, basically Kruszka agreed with the Polish clergymen and their allies that Poles should vote as a bloc in order to win recognition as a serious force in the city. However, he differed with other *Polonia* leaders about the wisdom of a permanent Polish marriage with the Democrats, for he believed that political parties were merely vehicles for gaining appointments and influence, not ends in themselves. Kruszka therefore recommended in his editorials that the Poles support that party which best met their needs. Initially, the *Kuryer* supported the party that promised the Poles the most and nominated Polish candidates for political office over non-Poles. Later, in the 1920s and 1930s, the paper refined its position and supported politically progressive Poles over conservative Polish office-seekers.[48] Kruszka's and the *Kuryer's* independent political position naturally antagonized Democratic party regulars and supporters of the traditional clerical leadership in *Polonia*. Kruszka himself had been a Democrat; but following the 1886 strike at the Bay View rolling mills, he backed the new People's party. Then, as a Democrat, he was elected in 1890 to the assembly and in 1892 to the state senate, but he lost in his try for re-election in 1896 as a self-proclaimed Bryan Democrat. In 1898 Kruszka and the *Kuryer* supported the mayoral candidacy of the Democrat, David Rose, but only on condition that Rose appoint a number of worthy Poles to the city administration—a promise that Rose made and promptly broke once he was elected.[49] In 1900, Kruszka broke permanently with the Democrats, this time in favor of Robert La Follette's progressive Republican gubernatorial campaign. He justified his action by arguing that the Rose Democrats were dominated by special interests, a condition not afflicting La Follette's progressives.[50]

Notwithstanding Kruszka's own erratic political position and his newspaper's readiness to criticize church leaders, the *Kuryer Polski* became a popular and commercial success. This achievement, moreover, was not unique. As one early observer of the Polish press in America noted, a number of Polish dailies which promoted liberal and/or anticlerical editorial positions enjoyed more popularity than their conservative competitors. In Buffalo and Detroit, as in Milwaukee, the more liberal paper enjoyed twice the circulation of its conservative rival. Before 1920, the most widely read Polish-language paper in America was the anticlerical and politically radical *Ameryka Echo*, originating in Toledo, Ohio, and claiming a weekly circulation of more than 80,000.[51]

Political disagreements, however, took second place in the intense debate between the Polish clergy and the *Kuryer* over the limits of clerical authority in community as well as parish life. It was Michael Kruszka's position that priests overstepped their bounds when they dictated the political views of their parishioners. His free-thinking orientation led him to criticize the churchmen, sometimes reasonably, often intemperately. Why, he asked, must Polish parishioners pay the heavy expenses of their churches' construction and maintenance when they had no voice in making parish decisions? He was especially critical of the enormous costs incurred by the Reverend William Grutza in building St. Josaphat's church between 1897 and 1901. Kruszka estimated that the project had burdened St. Josaphat's parishioners with a debt of at least $250,000, and he blamed the archdiocese for not exercising greater control over the project.[52]

The clergy and the archbishop responded to such charges by working against Kruszka's campaign to establish Polish in the Milwaukee public schools. They argued that he was really interested only in undermining the private parish schools, where Polish and the faith were taught, as well as the three Rs. They supported the creation of rival newspapers, first the unsuccessful *Slowo* (The Word), then in 1899 the *Dziennik Milwaucki* (Milwaukee's Daily). When this paper also went bankrupt, its backers lost over $60,000. Finally, in 1906, they sponsored the *Nowiny Polskie* under the editorship of the Reverend Boleslaus Goral. At first a weekly, the *Nowiny* became a daily competitor of Kruszka in 1907. It remained under its original ownership until 1928, when it was sold to conservative Polish business interests. Never, however, did the *Nowiny* succeed in besting its rival, either in terms of mass circulation or influence within the Polish community.[53]

Michael Kruszka's attacks gained momentum because they capitalized on a rising nationwide tide of Polish immigrant demands for greater Polish priestly advancement within the hierarchy of the Roman Catholic Church, which was widely believed to be in the tight grasp of the Irish. During the 1890s, breaks between "independent" Polish parishes and the Roman Catholic Church were not uncommon, particularly in Chicago. In 1899, added fuel was poured on when Francis Hodur, a Polish priest working near Scranton, Pennsylvania, was expelled from his pastoral post after a bitter quarrel with his bishop about the extent of episcopal authority over his Polish parishes. Hodur then established his own Polish National Catholic Church, an institution which came to hold several theological positions at odds with the Roman Catholics and also gave great power to a lay board representing the parish community.[54]

Moreover, it was at this time that Michael Kruszka's younger brother, the priest Wenceslaus Kruszka, entered the debate. Working from a relatively obscure parish in Ripon, Wisconsin, from 1895 to 1909, he became a vigorous polemicist. In 1906 he published the first attempt at a historical overview of the Polish people in America, and he took excellent advantage of the opportunity to express his thoughts in the family-owned newspaper. In publications and lectures, this charismatic priest mounted powerful arguments for nominating Poles to episcopal posts, and he achieved a certain amount of national attention. Since the Poles represented one-fifth of the Catholic population in America, he argued, they deserved to have their own Polish priests considered for promotion in roughly the same proportion. Wenceslaus Kruszka's outspoken and persuasive arguments in favor of naming a Polish bishop were nowhere more evident than at a 1903 convention of Polish priests in Buffalo. There his position was strongly endorsed, and he was dispatched to Rome to argue its merits before the Pope himself. His thirteen-month European trip had no immediate result, however. Pope Leo XIII was near death and long months passed with no opportunity to discuss the issue with responsible papal representatives. When Kruszka did gain an audience with Leo's successor, Pius X, the new pontiff would make no firm commitment, telling Kruszka, "It will be decided as soon as possible, and it will be made according to your wishes." A Pole, Paul Rhode, was named an auxiliary bishop of Chicago in 1908, to be followed by another, Edward Kozlowski, for Milwaukee in 1914; but this proved to be the sum and substance of the papal response to Kruszka's proposals.[55]

In Milwaukee, Father Kruszka's views tended to be rejected as an expression of "Cahenslyism," that is, the idea that each ethnic group within the Catholic church should have its own representative in the hierarchy. The American church had long perceived this to be at odds with its own self-image as a miniature melting pot, and the idea had been rejected as early as 1884 at its plenary council at Baltimore.[56] Archbishop Sebastian Messmer clearly interpreted the meaning of

Kruszka's thinking in these terms, declaring, in a letter he wrote to Archbishop James Gibbons of Baltimore: "The longer I think it over the more it seems to me a dangerous experiment at this stage to give the Polish people a bishop, for the very reason that he would be considered the bishop for all the Poles of the United States. I know it. Wherever a bishop would have any difficulty with a Polish parish, *their bishop* would be appealed to. The Polish are not yet American enough and keep aloof too much from the rest of us."[57]

That Messmer—himself a German Swiss and not an Irishman—could make this observation was illuminating, because the Milwaukee diocese was one of the few in the United States that had been headed by German bishops. That achievement itself was owing only to a long-running fight by German Catholics over the issue of recognition in a church dominated by an Irish-American hierarchy. In this light, the Poles' quest for recognition clearly demonstrated the plurality of conflicts challenging a Catholic church which incorporated a variety of increasingly restive ethnic groups.[58] Yet, given their anti-German nationalist rhetoric, the Kruszkas were unable to close ranks with German Catholics who might have sympathized with their demand for ethnic recognition.

The conflict between supporters of each side became increasingly heated. Within various *Polonia* organizations, individuals were identified either as Kruszka (and *Kuryer*) or as anti-Kruszka (and *Nowiny*) partisans. Wenceslaus Kruszka, who in 1909 had been named pastor of Milwaukee's St. Adalbert's parish, had already been ordered by Archbishop Messmer not to contribute articles to the *Kuryer Polski*. Though in 1895 Michael Kruszka had helped to found a Milwaukee-based fraternal, the Society of Poles in America, he and his associates in that group's leadership were abruptly ousted from its board of directors by opponents favoring Messmer.[59] In response, Kruszka's supporters created the Federation of Polish Catholic Laymen, which stridently repeated the *Kuryer's* message at parish meetings, particularly its proposals calling for Polish bishops and increased lay involvement in parish decision-making.[60] Then, on February 11, 1912, Messmer, together with seven other bishops, issued an edict forbidding the reading of the *Kuryer* and nine other anticlerical Polish publications. Disobedience of this edict constituted grounds for excommunication.[61]

This final blow, however, did not end the quarrel, which by then was attracting considerable notice among non-Poles. Kruszka's Laymen's Federation organized several mass protests against the edict in

Milwaukee, Detroit, and elsewhere. One taking place on June 12, 1912, was termed the "largest demonstration of Poles ever held in Milwaukee" by the sympathetic socialist *Leader* and consisted of a parade of approximately 25,000 persons culminating in speeches denouncing the bishops' action.[62] Michael Kruszka attempted to sue the bishops who had forbidden parishioners to read the *Kuryer*, arguing that their action abridged freedom of the press. Although his suit ultimately lost, appeals of the decision dragged on for years.[63] In September, 1912, Kruszka organized a new fraternal insurance society to rival the existing organizations which had opposed him. This group, based on the Laymen's Federation, was called the Federation of Poles in America; it remains active to this day as Federation Life Insurance of America, with headquarters in Milwaukee.[64] Ultimately, such divisions with *Polonia* led some Polish parishioners to break away from the church and to establish, in 1914, the first Polish National Catholic parish in Milwaukee. In time, three schismatic national parishes were organized, and land for a Polish cemetery free from diocesan control was also purchased.[65]

The outbreak of World War I and the hopes that the war raised for Polish independence had a marked effect upon the quarrels which had troubled Milwaukee's *Polonia*. For the Poles, optimism that victory over the Central Powers would lead to a restored independent Polish state prompted many young men to join General Jozef Haller's Polish Legion in France early in the war.[66] Woodrow Wilson's support of an independent Poland in his Fourteen Points electrified Polish-Americans and made American entry into the conflict in 1918 a patriotic call on behalf of not one but two fatherlands. More than 108,000 Poles had already volunteered for duty in Haller's army by 1917, and it is estimated that approximately forty thousand of the first hundred thousand Americans to volunteer for American military duty were Poles.[67]

In Milwaukee, a citizens' committee in behalf of Poland was organized representing a broad cross-section of *Polonia*.[68] In contrast to similar patriotic committees in other cities, the Milwaukee group suffered from few internal divisions brought about by rivalries among competing factions that sought to dominate postwar Poland. Both Kruszka and Goral emphasized Polish patriotic support for the effort and heaped contumely upon the city's socialist administration for its pacifist stand on the war issue. The failure of the Milwaukee socialists to recognize the force of nationalistic sentiments among the Polish population in turn weakened the socialists' appeal. Thus, the zenith of Hoan's popularity was to remain his 1916 success in the Polish precincts; never again did he win a majority of the Polish vote from those districts, although in the assembly and in aldermanic contests Polish socialists continued to enjoy increasing success throughout the following decade.

Michael Kruszka's death in 1918 coincided with the end of the war and Poland's rebirth.[69] With these events, the anticlerical era came to an end. Although the *Kuryer Polski* remained steadfast to the goals of promoting greater Polish political representation in government, greater Polish clerical visibility in the church, and the promotion of Polish national consciousness, its relationship with its old clerical opponents eased. Too, despite Archbishop Messmer's misgivings about the dangers to Catholic unity posed by a Polish bishop, Msgr. Edward Kozlowski was appointed an auxiliary bishop of the Milwaukee archdiocese in 1914, the second Pole in the United States to be elevated to such a post.

At the parish level, ordinary Polish workmen and housewives could hardly remain unaffected by the debates, although a number of facts indicate that the issues may have been more important to priests, intellectuals, and journalists than they were to the mass of men and women in *Polonia*. Only a relatively few persons actually left the Roman Catholic Church during the height of the controversy, and the circulation of the *Kuryer Polski* actually rose slightly after the announcement of the excommunication edict. Nonetheless, many must have wondered whether the bishops' interdict was not too extreme, an overreaction to what, at worst, were annoying complaints. As ordinary Poles continued to read the *Kuryer*, they must have asked themselves often what real harm was being done by the local newspaper. At the same time, the evidence that a growing number of Polish voters was willing to cast ballots for the socialist political candidates scorned by their pastors clearly indicates that they were no longer willing to obey the once-unchallenged leaders of *Polonia* in all matters.

During the first third of the twentieth century, then, the Poles of Milwaukee had passed through several crises which sent tremors through the traditional pillars of *Polonia*—the Roman Catholic Church and the Democratic party. The *Kuryer Polski*, widely read and presumably influential, had ceaselessly agitated against the clerical hierarchy; and clergymen themselves had in turn agitated for greater Polish representation in the ruling circle of the church. The Democratic party had gone into eclipse at all levels of government (the presidency of Woodrow Wilson being the single exception); and simultaneously there had arisen a broadly based political movement which, under the banners of either socialism or La Follette Republicanism, made substantial inroads among working-class Poles. In short, between the turn of the century and the Great Depression, the very foundations of religion and politics in Polish Milwaukee were shaken by events and ideas from within and without.

Ironically, in spite of this, practically no remnant of the progressive era survives in Milwaukee's Polish enclaves. (The three Polish National churches and the fraternal organization are the rather modest exceptions.) How is one to explain such a phenomenon: a period of social and political ferment whose vestiges are so scanty as to lead one to wonder whether it ever existed?

Politically, of course, the fate of the Polish progressives and socialists depended upon the fortunes of the statewide La Follette movement and the Milwaukee-based Socialist party. Both suffered a severe blow with the election of Franklin Roosevelt in 1932 and the revival of the Wisconsin Democratic party which began about the same time. Among the Poles the Progressive party of Philip La Follette won very few adherents after 1934. In Milwaukee, the demise of the Polish socialists can be explained in much the same terms as the collapse of the party citywide: lacking a base of mass support and chronically beset by financial difficulties, the socialists were unable to become an enduring force in local affairs. At its height, prior to World War I, Milwaukee's Socialist party had no more than four to five thousand members; by 1934, countywide membership had fallen to 2,339. The decline in the Socialist party nationally by the late 1920s severely dampened optimism about its possibilities. In Milwaukee as well as in its Polish community, the socialist movement seems to have been a one-generation phenomenon. Few new Bergers, Krzyckis, or Polakowskis arrived on the scene to take over where the early socialists had left off.[70]

A crucial factor explaining the demise of socialism in Polish Milwaukee was the depth of the Poles' commitment to the Roman Catholic Church. Despite their misgivings about many church leaders and about the wisdom of some of their actions, the great majority of Poles remained loyal to their local parishes and priests. To them, Polish nationality and Catholicism were two sides of the same coin. They agreed, after all was said and done, with the solemn admonition of Boleslaus Goral: "Woe to those who would ever dare to conspire against this most sacred heritage of ours."[71] The main institution of *Polonia* continued to be the church, and even the secular fraternal organizations gradually became increasingly dependent on parish members for most of their support, although clergymen no longer monopolized the leadership of *Polonia* as had once been the case.

By the mid-1930s Milwaukee's Poles had overwhelmingly opted to support Roosevelt's New Deal. In 1932, 1936, and 1940, Roosevelt won 67, 78, and 64 percent of the vote, respectively, in Milwaukee as a whole. In the same elections, the nine Polish wards gave him 75, 84, and 76 percent of their vote.[72] In the four gubernatorial campaigns between 1934 and 1940, the level of voter support in the Polish wards for Progressive party candidates was practically indistinguishable from citywide totals.

Events in Europe also helped to push the experience of the progressive era far back in the consciousness of the Milwaukee Poles. The state of Poland, for whose independence so much had been sacrificed during the First World War, fell under Nazi and then Communist rule, suffering in the process not only the destruction of millions of human lives but also a significant break in its historic ties with Americans of Polish descent.[73]

Yet a strong ethnic consciousness and a knowledge of how to use their political muscle had taken root among the Poles of Milwaukee— just as the brothers Kruszka and their rivals had hoped. On the eve of American entry into World War II, five of Milwaukee's twenty-seven aldermen were Poles, a Polish-American from Milwaukee sat in the House of Representatives, and another served on the Milwaukee bench. Symbolic of the new role played by Polish Milwaukee was the way in which the enemies of *Polonia* could be dealt with in election years. In 1900, for example, Michael Kruszka had urged his Polish countrymen to vote against Mayor David Rose, who had appointed only one Polish-American—not the promised fifteen—during his first two-year term. But even without the *Kuryer's* support, Rose had been re-elected with great majorities from the Polish districts of Milwaukee to four additional terms as mayor.

By way of contrast, in 1937 Mayor Hoan replaced a deceased Polish police captain, John Wesolowski, with a non-Pole. This caused a furor, not only in Wesolowski's fourth police district but throughout *Polonia*. A host of Polish organizational leaders asked the mayor to reconsider his decision, but Hoan remained adamant. Letters flooded in. Finally, Hoan produced a detailed list of all appointments he had made during his tenure in office, a list which included a host of Polish names. Hoan then reaffirmed his policy: "All must be treated equally."

Polonia's reaction to the mayor's avowed policy was swift and bluntly phrased. The secretary of the Casimir Pulaski Council (a political-action federation of Polish community organizations formed in 1929), himself a leader in Kruszka's old Laymen's federation, wrote back: "When the proper time arrives, we will know how to deal with matters." Daniel Hoan was ousted at the very next election.[74]

APPENDIX

MILWAUKEE POLES IN POLITICAL OFFICE IN THE PROGRESSIVE ERA, 1890–1940

POLES ELECTED TO THE STATE ASSEMBLY, WITH PARTY AFFILIATION, YEARS IN OFFICE, AND DISTRICT REPRESENTED IN PARENTHESES

Michael Kruszka (Dem; 1890–92; Wards 12, 14)
Michael Blenski (Dem; 1892–94; Ward 12)
Andrew Boncel (Dem; 1894–96; Ward 14)
August Gawin (Dem; 1896–1902; Ward 14)
Albert Wojciechowski (Dem; 1898; Wards 5, 12)
Jozef Rechlicz (Dem; 1898–1900; Wards 5, 12)
Frank Hassa (Dem; 1902–4; Wards 5, 12)
John Szymarek (Dem; 1902–4; Ward 14)
Joseph Domachowski (Dem; 1906–10; Ward 14)
Michael Katzban (Soc; 1910–12; Ward 14)
Martin Gorecki (Soc; 1912–14; Wards 14, 24)
Frank Kubatzki (Dem; 1914–20; Ward 8)
Thomas Szewczykowski (Dem; 1916–18; Wards 14, 24)
George Czerwinski (Dem; 1918–20; Ward 12)
John Masiakowski (Soc; 1918–20; Ward 14)
Walter Polakowski (Soc; 1920–22; Ward 8)
Stefan Stolowski (Soc; 1920–22; Wards 14, 24)
John Polakowski (Soc; 1922–24; Wards 8, 14)
Frank Cieszynski (Soc; 1924–26; Wards 8, 14)
Louis Polewczynski (Rep; 1926–28; Wards 8, 14)
Alex Chmurski (Rep; 1928–30; Wards 11, 24)
Mary Kryszak (Dem; 1928–30; Wards 8, 14; 1932–38, 1940–44; Wards 5, 8)
Joseph Przybylski (Rep; 1928–30; Wards 5, 12)
Ben Wicinski (Rep; 1930–32; Wards 8, 14)
Martin Franzkowiak (Dem; 1932–38; Wards 11, 24)
Max Galasinski (Dem; 1932–34; Wards 12, 24)
Clemens Michalski (Liberal Dem; 1934–36; Wards 12, 14)
Peter Pyszczynski (Dem; 1936–47; Wards 12, 14)
Clement Stachowiak (Progressive; 1938–40; Wards 11, 24)
William Nawrocki (Dem; 1940–44; Wards 13, 21)*
Ervin Ryczek (Dem; 1940–60; Wards 11, 24)

ELECTED TO THE STATE SENATE
Michael Kruszka (Dem; 1892–96; 8th District)
John Kleczka (Rep; 1908–12; 8th District)
Louis Fons (Rep; 1918–20; 8th District)
George Czerwinski (Rep; 1920–24; 8th District)
Walter Polakowski (Soc; 1922–34; 3rd District)
Leonard Fons (Rep; 1930–34; 7th District)
Max Galasinski (Dem; 1934–38; 7th District)
Arthur Zimmy (Dem; 1934–42; 3rd District)
Anthony Gawronski (Dem; 1938–49; 7th District)

ELECTED TO CITY COMPTROLLER
Roman Czerwinski (Dem; 1890–94)
Peter Pawinski (Dem; 1902–6)
August Gawin (Dem; 1908–10)
Louis Kotecki (1912–33)

ELECTED TO U.S. CONGRESS
John Kleczka (Rep; 1918–22; 4th District)
Thaddeus Wasielewski (Dem; 1940–46; 4th District)

ELECTED TO ALDERMAN, 1908–40
Max Kantak (Dem; 1908–10; Ward 14)
Frank Hopp (Dem; 1908–10; at-large)
Martin Gorecki (Soc; 1910–12; at-large)
Anthony Szczerbinski (Dem; 1910–12; Ward 14)
Thomas Szewczykowski (1912–16; Ward 24)
Leo Krzycki (Soc; 1912–16; Ward 14)
Anton Lukaszewicz (1916–20; Ward 14)
Martin Gedlinski (1918–20; Ward 12)
Casimir Kowalski (Soc; 1918–22; at-large)
John Baranowski (1918–20; Ward 8)
John Suminski (1918–23; Ward 1)*
Albert Janicki (allied with Socialists; 1920–28; 1932–36; Ward 14)
Joseph Drzezdzon (1920–28; Ward 12)
Robert Landowski (1920–28; 1932–36; Ward 13)*
Anthony Singer (1928–32; Ward 21)*
Frank Maciolek (Soc; 1928–32; Ward 24)
Max Galasinski (1928–32; Ward 14)
Edward Smukowski (1928–32; Ward 12)
Frank Boncel (Soc; 1932–36; Ward 12)
Felix Lassa (1932–36; Ward 24)
John Kalupa (1936–48; Ward 14)
Clemens Michalski (1936–52; Ward 13)
Bernard Kroenke (1936–64; Ward 18)*

John Schultz (1936-48; Ward 11)
Stanley Cybulski (1936-48; Ward 24)

Aldermen were elected as nonpartisans after 1912 unless otherwise noted. Asterisk (*) denotes that the office holder represented a North Side *Polonia* constituency; all others were from the South Side.

NOTES

1. Thaddeus Borun and John Jakusz-Gostomski, eds., *We, the Milwaukee Poles* (Milwaukee: Nowiny Publishing Co., 1946); Bayrd Still, *Milwaukee: The History of a City* (Madison: State Historical Society of Wisconsin, 1948); Wenceslaus Kruszka, *Historya Polska w Ameryce* (Milwaukee: Drukiem Spolki Wydawniczej Kuryera, 1906), pts. 3, 7; Robert Carroon, "Foundations of Milwaukee's Polish Community," *Historical Messenger of the Milwaukee County Historical Society* 26 (September 1970): 88-95.
2. Kruszka, *Historya Polska*, pt. 7, p. 137. In 1900 the Poles of Wisconsin numbered 31,882 and ranked as the third largest immigrant group in the state, after the Germans (242,777) and the Norwegians (61,575). By 1930 the Poles had advanced to second position with 42,537, following the Germans (128,269 foreign-born) and ranking ahead of the Norwegians (34,359 foreign-born). Because of serious limitations in the census methods used in enumerating peoples without independent states, such as the Poles, these figures ought to be viewed as giving a low estimate of the actual Polish population at the time. See U.S. Bureau of the Census, *Abstract of the Twelfth Census of the United States, 1900* (Washington: Government Printing Office, 1902); U.S. Bureau of the Census, *Fifteenth Census of the United States, 1930* (Washington: Government Printing Office, 1932); and Bernard Fuller, "Voting Patterns in Milwaukee, 1896-1920" (M.A. thesis, University of Wisconsin-Milwaukee, 1973), pp. 41-61.
3. In 1905, 12,482 (80.5 percent) of the estimated 15,500 foreign-born Poles of Milwaukee had emigrated from German-ruled territories, compared to 2,479 (16 percent) from "Russian" Poland and 599 (3.5 percent) from Austrian "Galicia." Wisconsin Department of State, *Tabular Statements of the State of Wisconsin Census* (Madison: Democratic Printing Company, 1906), pp. 170ff.
4. Borun, *We, the Milwaukee Poles*, esp. pp. 242-44; Adolph G. Korman, "A Social History of Industrial Growth and Immigrants: A Study with Particular Reference to Milwaukee, 1880-1920" (Ph.D. diss., University of Wisconsin-Madison, 1959), pp. 113-21. Korman's dissertation was published as *Industrialization, Immigrants, and Americanizers: The View from Milwaukee, 1866-1921* (Madison: State Historical Society of Wisconsin, 1967). See also Henryk Dzulikowski, *Milwaukee Poznanskie Miasto* (Chicago: Book-Druk, Publishers, 1945).

5 Boleslaus Goral, "The Poles in Milwaukee," in Jerome Watrous, ed., *Memoirs of Milwaukee County*, 2 vols. (Madison: Western Historical Association, 1909), 1:613–31; Still, *Milwaukee*, pp. 268–73; Borun, *We, the Milwaukee Poles*, pp. 3–50, 167–222. The Society of Poles in America (Stowarzyszenie Polakow w Ameryce) was established in 1895 by Milwaukee Poles who were dissatisfied with the Chicago-based leadership of the Polish Roman Catholic Union and set up their own locally based fraternal. See Kruszka, *Historya Polska*, pt. 4, pp. 44–48; Mieczyslaw Haiman, *Zjednoczenie Polskie Rzymsko-Katolickie w Ameryce, 1873–1948* (Chicago: Polish Roman Catholic Union in America, 1948), pp. 152ff.; Frank Renkiewicz, "An Economy of Self-Help: Fraternal Capitalism and the Evolution of Polish America," in Philip Shashko, Donald Pienkos, and Charles Ward, eds., *Aspects of the East European Ethnic Experience in America* (New York: Columbia University Press, 1980). A second fraternal society, the Federation of Poles in America (today Federation Life Insurance of America) was established in Milwaukee in 1913. See Angela Pienkos, *A Brief History of Federation Life Insurance of America, 1913–1976* (Milwaukee: Haertlein Graphics for Federation Life Insurance of America, 1976). In size the Milwaukee *Polonia* was nearly one-third as large as the Chicago Polish community in 1900, equal in numbers to the one found in Buffalo, and larger than the Polish group living in Detroit. However, the continuing influx of Poles into the other cities left Milwaukee far behind. By 1940, the Milwaukee *Polonia* was only 13 percent as large as Chicago's, 30 percent of Detroit's, and 74 percent of Buffalo's.

6 Joseph Wytrwal, *America's Polish Heritage* (Detroit: Endurance Press, 1961), pp. 159–67.

7 Borun, *We, the Milwaukee Poles*, p. 47–49; Goral, "Poles in Milwaukee," pp. 614–19. Gulski's role is also discussed by Anthony Kuzniewski, "Faith and Fatherland: An Intellectual History of the Polish Immigrant Community in Wisconsin, 1838–1918" (Ph.D. diss., Harvard University, 1973), pp. 162–67. Other leading Milwaukee Polish clergymen included a Franciscan, Felix Baran, and Bronislaus Celichowski. For their biographies, see *Dictionary of Wisconsin Biography* (Madison: State Historical Society of Wisconsin, 1960), pp. 25, 73.

8 *Wisconsin Census*, pp. 446–50; Roger Wyman, "Voting Behavior in the Progressive Era: Wisconsin as a Case Study" (Ph.D. diss., University of Wisconsin–Madison, 1970), p. 719. According to the 1905 state census, over 70 percent of the Polish heads of households listed their occupations as "laborer" or "unskilled laborer." Another 21 percent were identified as "artisans," and 9 percent were either businessmen or professional people. Poles were most commonly employed in tanneries (11 percent), as molders (7 percent), carpenters (5 percent), ironworkers (5 percent), butchers, saloonkeepers, machinists, blacksmiths, stonemasons (2 percent each), firemen, grocers, and shoemakers (1 percent), with 37 percent classified as "laborers." In 1880, 71 percent had fallen in that category, underscoring the Poles' upward occupational movement over time. Laura Sutherland,

"The Immigrant Family: Milwaukee's Poles: 1880–1905" (M.A. thesis, University of Wisconsin–Milwaukee, 1974), pp. 52, 88, 89. According to Korman ("Social History," pp. 42ff.), Polish workers enjoyed a reputation nearly as favorable as that of the Germans or Swedes and were believed to be much more industrious than the Greeks, Italians, and Hungarians. Nonetheless, they were also often limited to unskilled, "dirty" jobs.

9 My analysis of the biographies of eighty-three prominent Polish-American community leaders in comparison with a randomly sampled group of 121 non-Polish community figures drawn from Watrous' 1909 work showed the following: 15.7 percent of the Polish leaders were clergymen, to 3.3 percent of the non-Poles. While 31.4 percent of the non-Poles were professionally educated, this was true for only 13.3 percent of the Poles. Among the non-Poles 19 percent owned large companies, while 23 percent of the Poles were proprietors of small businesses. Nearly half of them (42 percent) were foreign-born and three-quarters (75.3 percent) were under forty years of age; the comparable figures for the non-Poles were 26 and 38 percent respectively. Three-fifths of the Poles listing their political orientations were Democrats, to fewer than 30 percent of the non-Poles. Only 19 percent of the non-Poles were identified as Catholics, to 93 percent of the Poles. See also Wyman, "Voting Behavior," pp. 20–21; Paul Kleppner, *The Cross of Culture* (New York: Free Press, 1970), pp. 22–67; Victor Greene, *For God and Country: The Rise of Polish and Lithuanian Ethnic Consciousness in America, 1860–1910* (Madison: State Historical Society of Wisconsin, 1975), chs. 4, 6; Walter Borowiec, "Politics and Buffalo's Polish-Americans," in Angela Pienkos, ed., *Ethnic Politics in Urban America: The Polish Experience in Four Cities* (Chicago: Polish American Historical Association, 1978), pp. 16–19.

10 Thomas Gavett, *Development of the Labor Movement in Milwaukee* (Madison and Milwaukee: University of Wisconsin Press, 1965), pp. 115ff.; Korman, "Social History," pp. 9–10; Borun, *We, the Milwaukee Poles*, p. 111; Frederick I. Olson, "The Milwaukee Socialists, 1897–1941" (Ph.D. diss., Harvard University, 1952), pp. 160–85; Wytrwal, *America's Polish Heritage*, pp. 181ff.; Kuzniewski, "Faith and Fatherland," pp. 149–222.

11 Frank Miller, "The Polanders in Wisconsin," in *Parkman Club Papers* (Milwaukee: n.p., 1896), pp. 239–46; Jerry Cooper, "The Wisconsin National Guard in the Milwaukee Riots of 1886," *Wisconsin Magazine of History* 55 (Autumn 1971): 31–48; and Borun, *We, the Milwaukee Poles*, pp. 123–25. In this last piece, members of Company K recalled that no shots had been fired by Polish guardsmen in their efforts to disperse the rioters. See also Roger D. Simon, "The Bay View Incident and the People's Party in Milwaukee," a paper in the files of the Research Division, State Historical Society of Wisconsin.

12 Still, *Milwaukee*, pp. 296–97; Roger Wyman, "Wisconsin Ethnic Groups and the Election of 1890," *Wisconsin Magazine of History* 51 (Summer 1968): 269–93.

13 Quoted in Still, *Milwaukee*, p. 298n.

14 Ibid., pp. 271–72, 297–99, 308–9.
15 Kruszka, *Historya Polska*, part 3, p. 133; Wyman, "Voting Behavior," p. 732.
16 Goral, "Poles in Milwaukee," p. 625; Borun, *We, the Milwaukee Poles*, pp. 77, 154–58, 163. Data for Polish-Americans elected to the state legislature were gathered from biennial volumes of *The Wisconsin Blue Book*.
17 Elected city comptroller in 1912, Kotecki had previously been identified as a Democrat. He met a tragic end when he committed suicide in 1933 at the age of fifty-three, following his indictment on charges of having failed to audit carefully the accounts of the city treasurer. In the forty-seven years since Kotecki's death, only one other Polish-American, John Kalupa, has been able to win election to the comptroller's office. See *Milwaukee Journal*, July 11, 12, 1933.
18 Still, *Milwaukee*, p. 468; Korman, "Social History," p. 24.
19 David Shannon, *The Socialist Party of America: A History* (New York: Macmillan, 1955), p. 23.
20 In the four-cornered race, Debs took 38 percent of the vote to 34 percent for the Democrat, Woodrow Wilson, 21 percent for the Republican incumbent, William Howard Taft, and 7 percent for progressive Republican Theodore Roosevelt. Ward data are from Sarah Ettenheim, *How Milwaukee Voted, 1848–1968* (Milwaukee: Institute of Governmental Affairs, University of Wisconsin–Milwaukee, 1970), and the *Milwaukee Sentinel*. The "Polish wards" were the twelfth and fourteenth (between 1900 and 1911), the eighth, twelfth, fourteenth, and twenty-fourth (1912–31), and the first, thirteenth, twenty-first, eighth, eleventh, twelfth, fourteenth, seventeenth, and twenty-fourth (1932–40).
21 Wyman, "Voting Behavior," p. 393; Fuller, "Voting Patterns," pp. 128, 135, 192.
22 The *Kuryer Polski* was founded in 1888 and continued to operate until 1963. The *Nowiny Polskie* was established in 1906 as a weekly, became a daily in 1907, and ceased publication in 1949. The entire run of the *Kuryer* can be found on microfilm in the Milwaukee Public Library. Sections of the *Nowiny* are in the Center for Research Libraries (Chicago). The Milwaukee Public Library's run has been lost.

The author conducted interviews of one to two hours each with the following persons in 1974 and 1975: Frank Zeidler, Socialist party activist and mayor of Milwaukee between 1948 and 1960; Szymon Deptula, formerly the chairman of the Slavic Languages Department of the University of Wisconsin–Milwaukee; John Polakowski, a socialist politician and Wisconsin assemblyman (1922–24); Clemens Michalski, long-time Democratic party politician and government official; Francis X. Swietlik, Polish ethnic leader and former circuit court judge; Alfred Sokolnicki, dean of the Marquette University school of speech; Anthony Szymczak, a reporter for the *Kuryer Polski*; Stanley Budny, a socialist politician in Milwaukee; Edmund Choinski, a former Milwaukee alderman; reserve court judge Thaddeus

Pruss; former city comptroller John Kalupa; and Mrs. Janet Dziadulewicz Branden.

Works treating the Milwaukee Poles but relying upon English- or German-language sources include Frederick I. Olson's dissertation; and Marvin Wachman, "History of the Social Democratic Party of Wisconsin, 1897–1910" (Ph.D. diss., University of Illinois, 1945). I much appreciated the opportunity to interview Professor Sally Miller and to read the paper she delivered on April 3, 1974, entitled "Milwaukee Retrospective: A Profile of Reform" and sponsored by the Department of History and the Center for Twentieth-Century Studies of the University of Wisconsin–Milwaukee.

23 Particularly the works of Roger Wyman and Paul Kleppner.

24 My thanks to Burt Hardinger, director of the City of Milwaukee Bureau of Records, for his assistance in my gathering of these data. See also Edward Kantowicz, "The Emergence of the Polish Democratic Vote in Chicago," *Polish American Studies* 29 (1972): 67–80.

25 Sutherland, "The Immigrant Family," pp. 84, 68–69.

26 See Helena Lopata, *The Polish-Americans: Status Competition in an Ethnic Community* (Englewood Cliffs, N.J.: Prentice-Hall, 1976), p. 84.

27 No single explanation for this phenomenon exists. Certainly, in an era before mass automobile transportation and the development of the freeway system, the North Side was quite isolated from the larger *Polonia* to the south. Organizational life was also less intense and extensive in a community with a smaller membership upon which to build. This meant that the Polish clergy's role in North Side affairs was less likely to be challenged by socialist-leaning workers' clubs, which do not seem to have appeared in that district.

28 The socialists' failure to respond to Polish patriotic feelings is evident from a reading of the resolutions the party convention approved at its 1918 meeting in Milwaukee. There, a resolution was approved condemning American and Japanese intervention against the new Bolshevik regime and calling for immediate United States recognition of the Soviet government. There was no mention of Polish independence. See Socialist party archives, Milwaukee County Historical Society.

29 Olson, "Milwaukee Socialists," p. 176; *The Wisconsin Blue Book* (Madison: Wisconsin Legislative Reference Library, 1913), p. 675; *Kuryer Polski*, December 20, 1928, p. 10.

30 *Milwaukee Leader*, December 28, 1911, p. 4; Olson, "Milwaukee Socialists," pp. 176, 316. In the late 1920s and through the 1930s Kowalski became active in the largest Polish fraternal, the Polish National Alliance, which had its headquarters in Chicago. Between 1928 and 1931 he held the position of general secretary in that organization. Adam Olszewski, *Historia Swiazku Narodowego Polskiego, 1905–1949*, 5 vols. (Chicago: Wydane Nakladem Zwiazku Narodowego, 1957), 4:157–458.

31 *Milwaukee Journal*, July 3, 1962.

32 Brief biographies of Krzycki are found in Gary M. Fink, ed., *Biographical*

Dictionary of American Labor Leaders (Westport, Conn.: Greenwood Press, 1974), p. 194; *Wielka Encyklopedia Powszechna* [*Great Polish Encyclopedia*], 13 vols. (Warsaw: Panstowy Wydawnictwo Nauk, 1971), 13:243. See also Eugene Miller, "Leo Krzycki—Polish American Labor Leader," *Polish American Studies* 33 (Autumn 1976): 52–64.

33 Report of the Wisconsin Socialist Party State Convention, 1934, in the Socialist party archives, Milwaukee County Historical Society. Opinions about Krzycki varied sharply. One interviewee described him as a "brilliant man of the labor movement," another as a "deep thinker and an effective speaker," and a third as "an out and out socialist—maybe even a communist." Two studies that touch on his later activities include Louis Gerson, *The Hyphenate in Recent Politics and Diplomacy* (Lawrence, Kans.: University of Kansas Press, 1964), pp. 164–67; and Edward Kerstein, *Red Star Over Poland* (Appleton, Wis.: C. C. Nelson Publishing Co., 1947), pp. 50–63. After World War II, Krzycki was awarded Poland's highest civilian honor, the Cross of Restored Poland, by the Communist party leader Boleslaus Bierut. See Bogdan Grzelonski, "Leon Krzycki," *Krajowa Agencja Informacyjna* (Warsaw), June 9–15, 1976, p. 6.

34 *Milwaukee Journal*, May 31, 1963; *Milwaukee Sentinel*, November 16, 1966. Polakowski's successful 1922 state senate campaign was endorsed by Senator Robert M. La Follette. See C. H. Backstrom, "The Progressive Party of Wisconsin, 1934–1946" (Ph.D. diss., University of Wisconsin–Madison, 1957), p. 324.

35 See Francis Bolek, ed., *Who's Who in Polish America* (New York: Harbinger House, 1943), p. 228; Angela Pienkos, *Federation Life Insurance*, pp. 1–10.

36 Gavett, *Labor Movement*, pp. 157–58.

37 Conversation with Victor Krzycki, May 2, 1976.

38 Tadeusz Daniszewski et al., *Historia Polskiego Ruchu Robotniczego, 1864–1964*, 2 vols. (Warsaw: Ksiazka i Wiedza, 1967), 1:30–115; M. K. Dziewanowski, *The Communist Party of Poland: An Outline of History* (Cambridge, Mass.: Harvard University Press, 1959), pp. 18–21.

39 In later years several old socialists mended fences with the Church. For example, Walter Polakowski and Cyborowski were buried with religious services, and a priest spoke at Krzycki's interment. Socialism, however, was not the sole avenue available to free thinkers. One of those interviewed recalled that his family had joined the newly established Polish National Catholic parish in the neighborhood after his father had been ordered in confession to "throw away that rag" (the *Kuryer Polski*) as a condition for absolution. See also Korman, "Social History," p. 25.

40 Wyman, "Voting Behavior," p. 545.

41 Ibid., p. 724; *Kuryer Polski*, April 2, 12, 1900; Wenceslaus Kruszka, *Siedm Siedmioleci* [*Seven Times Seven*], 2 vols. (Poznan, Poland: Nakladem Autora, Czcionkami Drukarni Sw. Wojciecha w Poznaniu, 1924), 2:690–92. See also Archbishop John Ireland's "Views on Socialism," in John T. Ellis, ed., *Documents of American Catholic History* (Milwaukee: Bruce Publishing Co., 1962), pp. 485–90; and *Silver Jubilee Album of St. Josaphat's Parish* (Milwaukee: Nowiny Publishing Co., 1913).

42 In 1932, socialist aldermanic candidates in the five most heavily Polish wards won four of the seats and 52 percent of the combined vote. Three of the four Poles elected to the common council were prosocialist. In 1936, however, all five winners were antisocialist Poles whose combined vote amounted to 62 percent of the total. John Banachowicz, Kotecki's Polish socialist opponent, narrowly lost the comptroller's contest in winning a majority in the Polish wards and 49.3 percent of the total vote. In 1936, the Polish socialist candidate Albert Janicki was crushed in the election, receiving only 35 percent of the vote.

Mary Kryszak, the one successful Polish Democrat in the 1920s and 1930s, had an unusually interesting career in politics and in the Polish fraternals. Like numerous other little-remembered Polish feminists of that era, she was active in the work of the Polish Women's Alliance, the third largest Polish American fraternal insurance organization and one of the earliest examples of female mass involvement in public affairs in America.

43 Borun, *We, the Milwaukee Poles*, p. 289.

44 Biographical data on the Kruszka brothers are in Borun, *We, the Milwaukee Poles*, pp. 50, 54; Edmund Olszyk, *The Polish Press in America* (Milwaukee: Marquette University Press, 1940), pp. 20ff.; *Dictionary of Wisconsin Biography*, pp. 214-15; Bolek, *Who's Who*, p. 73; *Great Polish Encyclopedia*, 6:212-13; and the fortieth anniversary issue of the *Kuryer Polski*, June 23, 1928. An invaluable insight into Wenceslaus Kruszka's thinking is found in his 1924 autobiography, which deserves translation. Additional information is provided by Kuzniewski, "Faith and Fatherland," and by Alexander Syski, "Reverend Waclaw Kruszka: The Nestor of Polish Historians in America," *Polish American Studies* 1 (1944): 62-70.

45 Korman, "Social History," p. 34n.; Wytrwal, *America's Polish Heritage*, p. 328; Kuzniewski, "Faith and Fatherland," p. 247. In 1942 the *Kuryer Polski* was recorded as having 26,073 daily and 28,822 Sunday subscriptions; 12,500 daily papers went to Milwaukee readers, 6,000 were delivered to persons in the surrounding Milwaukee suburbs, and 1,240 went to others in Wisconsin. A total of 927 subscriptions went to Pennsylvania, the birthplace of the Polish National Church, 825 to Illinois, and 702 to Michigan; 1,240 were sent to Canadian readers. See *Protocols of the Kuryer Polski*, vol. 2, and Still, *Milwaukee*, pp. 270-72.

46 *Kuryer Polski*, January 18, 1900.

47 Ibid., June 23, 1918. In a *Kuryer* editorial of March 14, 1912, Polish communities in other cities were urged to follow Milwaukee's example. In 1896 Kruszka had founded the Polish Educational Society to realize this goal.

48 Ibid., March 28, 1900; March 29, September 29, 1912; April 4, 1918; and November 5, 6, 1922; all contain but a few examples of such thinking. See Korman, "Social History," pp. 26-27, for one explanation of this view. One interviewee remembered the words of Chester Dziadulewicz, a successor to Kruszka at the paper, commenting about an aldermanic election pitting a Democrat named Smukowski against the socialist Boncel: "I don't care anything whether a candidate's socialist or not, so long as he's Polish."

49 *Kuryer Polski*, March 29, April 5, 1900.
50 Ibid., March 17, October 13, 1900; Kuzniewski, "Faith and Fatherland," pp. 193-94.
51 Paul Fox, *The Poles in America* (New York: George H. Doran Co., 1922), pp. 98-99.
52 Kruszka, *Historya*, pt. 8, pp. 10ff.; Kuzniewski, "Faith and Fatherland," pp. 202-7.
53 Olszyk, *The Polish Press*, pp. 56ff.; Kuzniewski, "Faith and Fatherland," pp. 315-16. Needless to say, Kruszka possessed excellent business instincts. For example, one achievement when he served as a state legislator was to win the contract to publish all state documents in Polish for the *Kuryer* company. In 1913 it was Kruszka who convinced the members of the Polish laymen's movement to reorganize into a fraternal insurance society to put it on a sound financial footing. See Angela Pienkos, *Federation Life Insurance*, p. 13.
54 Greene, *For God and Country*, ch. 6; Paul Fox, *The Polish National Church in America* (Scranton: School of Christian Living, [1961]); Hieronym Kubiak, *Polski Narodowy Kosciol Katolicki w Stanach Zjednoczonych, 1897-1965* (Warsaw: Zaklad Narodowy Imienia Ossolinskich Wydawnictwo, 1970). A succinct statement of Michael Kruszka's thinking appeared in a *Kuryer* article of May 13, 1911. In his words, "The most sensitive Polish question in America has for many years concerned the Church, particularly Church finances. . . . Poles in America have contributed over 200 million dollars for Church property. But this property does not belong to the Poles because ownership has passed into the hands of non-Polish bishops who obtain title under false pretense and who . . . treat the Polish nation with contempt. Therefore, the struggle of the *Kuryer* against foreign bishops is a struggle over the return of 200 million dollars worth of property to the Polish clergy and people. . . . [We, however,] do not criticize matters of faith and we respect membership in the Church."
55 Kuzniewski, "Faith and Fatherland," pp. 211-88; Kruszka, *Siedm* . . . , 1:803-6. Greene tends simultaneously to minimize Kruszka's part in the eventual decision to appoint a Polish bishop and to exaggerate the significance of this token action (*For God and Country*, pp. 141-42).
56 Kuzniewski, "Faith and Fatherland," pp. 61-64, 240ff.; Colman Barry, *The Catholic Church and the German Americans* (Milwaukee: Bruce Publishing Co., 1953); Thomas McAvoy, *A History of the Catholic Church in the United States* (Notre Dame, Ind.: University of Notre Dame Press, 1969), pp. 245-95; Daniel Buczek, "Polish-Americans and the Roman Catholic Church," *The Polish Review* 21 (Fall 1976): 39-55. Both Kuzniewski and Buczek argue that Kruszka was originally attracted to the Cahensly idea of Polish bishops ministering exclusively to Poles but in the face of fierce criticism modified his view to one supporting Polish representation in the hierarchy. See also Greene, *For God and Country*, pp. 132-35; Kruszka, *Historya Polska*, pp. 390ff.
57 Thomas Monzell, "The Catholic Church and the Americanization of the Polish Immigrant," *Polish American Studies* 26 (1969): 4; Kuzniewski, "Faith

and Fatherland," p. 264; Korman, "Social History," pp. 49–50. According to Greene, Bishop Rhode indeed behaved much as Messmer had predicted. See *For God and Country*, ch. 9; Buczek, "Polish Americans," p. 54.
58 Barry, *The Catholic Church*, pp. 44–50, 128–30, and, for a summary of Messmer's thinking, pp. 165ff. McAvoy asserts that domination by the Irish was one of the two major problems confronting the Catholic Church in its dealings with Protestants. At the Baltimore plenary council forty-six of seventy-two bishops in attendance were either Irish or of Irish heritage, and some of the latter were militantly "American" in national consciousness. See McAvoy, *History of the Catholic Church*, pp. 267, 296.
59 *Kuryer Polski*, August 10, 12, 13, September 12, 13, 1912.
60 The Federation's program can be found in Angela Pienkos, *Federation Life Insurance*, p. 4.
61 The text of the pastoral letter of February 11, 1912, is in Kuzniewski, "Faith and Fatherland," pp. 492–97.
62 *Milwaukee Leader*, June 8, 10, 1912; *Kuryer Polski*, June 10, 12, 1912. Goral's *Nowiny* estimated that only a thousand persons were in attendance.
63 Olszyk, *The Polish Press*, pp. 25–27.
64 At the group's 1912 convention, 50,000 persons, mostly from Wisconsin, were said to have joined. In 1913 the Federation claimed 100,000 members. Kuzniewski, "Faith and Fatherland," p. 382, estimates 10,000 to 15,000.
65 Gavett, *Labor Movement*, p. 115; Borun, *We, the Milwaukee Poles*, p. 234; Angela Pienkos, *Federation Life Insurance*, p. 8.
66 One interviewee recalled that Milwaukee was the first city where a "Polish legion" of volunteers was organized to fight under General Haller in France; another remembers Wenceslaus Kruszka's speech on the corner of Eighth and Mitchell streets urging support for Haller. A third man told of how "sixty fellows from one block enlisted" when the United States entered the war in 1917. See also Buczek, "Polish Americans," pp. 55–56; Borun, *We, the Milwaukee Poles*, pp. 205–11, 213.
67 Eugene Kusielewicz, "Woodrow Wilson and the Rebirth of Poland," *Polish American Studies* 12 (1955): 1–15; William Galush, "American Poles and the New Poland," *Ethnicity* 1 (October 1974): 209–21.
68 *Kuryer Polski*, April 15, 1918.
69 Mayor Hoan ordered the flags of the city flown at half-staff at his funeral. The rival *Nowiny* acknowledged that Kruszka's *Kuryer* had always been "extremely liberal and progressive . . . and at the same time anti-Catholic." See *Nowiny Polskie*, December 10, 1918.
70 Miller, "Milwaukee Retrospective . . . ," pp. 7–9. The 1934 party membership list is in the Socialist party archives in the Milwaukee Public Library.
71 Goral, "Poles in Milwaukee," p. 613. Several of the socialists who were interviewed stressed the impact that unceasing clerical criticism of their party and its program had on the Polish population.
72 In the old socialist stronghold, the fourteenth ward, Roosevelt received 91, 93, and 94 percent of the vote in 1932, 1936, and 1940, respectively.
73 Concern for Poland peaked in *Polonia* during the war. A nationwide fund-

raising campaign in behalf of Polish victims of the conflict raised $170,000 in Milwaukee alone. See Komitet Ratunkowy Polonii w Milwaukee, *Wisconsin American Relief for Poland* (Milwaukee: Nowiny Publishing Co., 1946), p. 12. The nature of *Polonia*'s concern was defined as early as 1934, when the American delegation to a world congress of *Polonia* groups in Warsaw asserted the limits of their identification with the ancestral homeland. That group, under the leadership of Milwaukee's Francis Swietlik, refused to swear allegiance to Poland and emphasized that Polish-Americans were an "inseparable, harmonious part of the American nation, however tied to Poland by feeling, tradition and culture." Haiman, *Zjednoczenie . . .*, pp. 422–34.

74 Letter from Leon Kazmierczak, in the Daniel Hoan Papers, Milwaukee County Historical Society. According to Olson, "Milwaukee Socialists," p. 566, the heavy Polish vote against Hoan was instrumental in causing his loss in 1940 to Carl Zeidler. For Hoan's own view, see Edward Kerstein, *Milwaukee's All-American Mayor: A Portrait of Daniel Webster Hoan* (Englewood Cliffs, N.J.: Prentice-Hall, 1966), pp. 167–85.

BIBLIOGRAPHY

MILWAUKEE NEWSPAPERS
Kuryer Polski (The Polish Courier), 1888–1963.
Milwaukee Leader, 1911–40.
Nowiny Polski (Polish News), 1906–49.
Milwaukee Journal, 1900–1970.
Milwaukee Sentinel, 1900–1970.

ARCHIVAL SOURCES
Milwaukee. Bureau of Records. Precinct Voting Registration Lists for the Years 1904, 1914, 1924.
Milwaukee. Milwaukee County Historical Society. Daniel Hoan Papers.
Milwaukee. Milwaukee County Historical Society. Wisconsin Socialist Party Records, 1900–1936.
Milwaukee. Public Library Local History Collection. Milwaukee Socialist Party Records.

OTHER SOURCES
Backstrom, C. H. "The Progressive Party of Wisconsin, 1934–1946." Ph.D. dissertation, University of Wisconsin–Madison, 1957.
Barry, Colman. *The Catholic Church and German Americans*. Milwaukee: Bruce Publishing Company, 1953.
Bolek, Francis, ed. *Who's Who in Polish America*. New York: Harbinger House, 1943.
Borowiec, Walter. "Politics and Buffalo's Polish Americans." In *Ethnic Politics*

in Urban America: The Polish Experience in Four Cities, edited by Angela Pienkos. Chicago: Polish American Historical Association, 1978.

Borun, Thaddeus, and John Jakusz-Gostomski, eds. *We, the Milwaukee Poles*. Milwaukee: Nowiny Publishing Company, 1946.

Brozek, Andrzej. *Polonia Amerykanska 1854–1939* [*The American Polonia, 1854–1939*]. Warsaw: Interpress Publishers, 1977.

Buczek, Daniel. "Polish-Americans and the Roman Catholic Church." *Polish Review* 21 (Fall 1976):39–55.

Carroon, Robert. "Foundations of Milwaukee's Polish Community." *Historical Messenger of the Milwaukee County Historical Society* 26 (September 1970):88–95.

Cooper, Jerry. "The Wisconsin National Guard in the Milwaukee Riots of 1886." *Wisconsin Magazine of History* 55 (Autumn 1971):31–48.

Daniszewski, Tadeusz, et al. *Historia Polskiego Ruchu Robotniczego, 1864–1964* [*History of the Polish Workers' Movement, 1864–1964*]. 2 vols. Warsaw: Ksiazka i Wiedza, 1967.

Dictionary of Wisconsin Biography. Madison: State Historical Society of Wisconsin, 1960.

Dziewanowski, M. K. *The Communist Party of Poland: An Outline of History*. Cambridge: Harvard University Press, 1959.

Dzulikowski, Henryk. *Milwaukee Poznanskie Miasto* [*Milwaukee-America's Poznan*]. Chicago: Book-Druk, Publishers, 1945.

Ettenheim, Sarah. *How Milwaukee Voted, 1848–1968*. Milwaukee: Institute of Governmental Affairs, University of Wisconsin–Milwaukee, 1970.

Fink, Gary M., ed. *Biographical Dictionary of American Labor Leaders*. Westport, Conn.: Greenwood Press, 1974.

Fox, Paul. *The Poles in America*. New York: George H. Doran Company, 1922.

Fox, Paul. *The Polish National Church in America*. Scranton: School of Christian Living, [1961].

Fuller, Bernard. "Voting Patterns in Milwaukee, 1896–1920." M.A. thesis, University of Wisconsin–Milwaukee, 1973.

Galush, William. "American Poles and the New Poland." *Ethnicity* 1 (October 1974):209–21.

Gavett, Thomas. *Development of the Labor Movement in Milwaukee*. Madison and Milwaukee: University of Wisconsin Press, 1965.

Gerson, Louis. *The Hyphenate in Recent Politics and Diplomacy*. Lawrence, Kans.: University of Kansas Press, 1964.

Goral, Boleslaus. "The Poles in Milwaukee." In *Memoirs of Milwaukee County*, edited by Jerome Watrous. 2 vols. Madison: Western Historical Association, 1909.

Greene, Victor. *For God and Country: The Rise of Polish and Lithuanian Ethnic Consciousness in America, 1860–1910*. Madison: State Historical Society of Wisconsin, 1975.

Groniowski, Krzysztof. "Socjalistyczna Emigracja Polska w Stanach Zjednoczonych (1883–1940)" ["The Polish Socialist Emigration in the United States (1883–1940)"]. *Z Pola Walki* 19 (Spring, 1977):3–33.

Grzelonski, Bogdan. "Leon Krzycki." *Krajowa Agencja Informacyjna* [*Polish Information Agency*] (Warsaw), June 9–15, 1976, p. 6.

Haiman, Mieczyslaw. *Zjednoczenie Polskie Rzymsko-Katolickie w Ameryce, 1873–1948* [*The Polish Roman Catholic Union in America, 1873–1948*]. Chicago: Polish Roman Catholic Union in America, 1948.

Ireland, Archbishop John. "Views on Socialism." In *Documents of American Catholic History*, edited by John T. Ellis. Milwaukee: Bruce Publishing Company, 1962.

Kantowicz, Edward. "The Emergence of the Polish Democratic Vote in Chicago." *Polish American Studies* 29 (1972): 67–80.

Kantowicz, Edward. *Polish American Politics in Chicago, 1888–1940*. Chicago: University of Chicago Press, 1975.

Kerstein, Edward. *Milwaukee's All-American Mayor: A Portrait of Daniel Webster Hoan*. Englewood Cliffs, N.J.: Prentice-Hall, 1966.

Kerstein, Edward. *Red Star Over Poland*. Appleton, Wisc.: C. C. Nelson Publishing Company, 1947.

Kleppner, Paul. *The Cross of Culture*. New York: Free Press, 1970.

Komitet Ratunkowy Polonii w Milwaukee. *Wisconsin American Relief for Poland*. Milwaukee: Nowiny Publishing Company, 1946.

Korman, Adolph G. *Industrialization, Immigrants, and Americanizers: The View from Milwaukee, 1866–1921*. Madison: State Historical Society of Wisconsin, 1967.

Korman, Adolph G. "A Social History of Industrial Growth and Immigrants: A Study with Particular Reference to Milwaukee, 1880–1920." Ph.D. dissertation, University of Wisconsin–Madison, 1959.

Kruszka, Wenceslaus. *Historya Polska w Ameryce* [*The History of the Polish People in America*]. 13 parts. Milwaukee: Drukiem Spolki Wydawniczej Kuryera, 1905–8.

Kruszka, Wenceslaus. *Siedm Siedmioleci* [*Seven Times Seven*]. 2 vols. Poznan-Milwaukee: Nakladem Autora, Czcionkami Drukarni Sw. Wojciecha w Poznaniu, 1924.

Kubiak, Hieronym. *Polski Narodowy Kosciol Katolicki w Stanach Zjednoczonych, 1897–1965* [*The Polish National Catholic Church in the U.S., 1897–1965*]. Warsaw: Zaklad Narodowy Imienia Ossolinskich Wydawnictwo, 1970.

Kusielewicz, Eugene. "Woodrow Wilson and the Rebirth of Poland." *Polish American Studies* 12 (1955):1–15.

Kuzniewski, Anthony. "Milwaukee's Poles, 1866–1918: The Rise and Fall of a Model Community." *Milwaukee History: The Magazine of the Milwaukee County Historical Society* 36 (Spring and Summer, 1978):13–24.

Kuzniewski, Anthony. "Faith and Fatherland: An Intellectual History of the Polish Immigrant Community in Wisconsin, 1838–1918." Ph.D. dissertation, Harvard University, 1973.

Lopata, Helena. *The Polish-Americans: Status Competition in an Ethnic Community*. Englewood Cliffs, N.J.: Prentice-Hall, 1976.

McAvoy, Thomas. *A History of the Catholic Church in the United States*. Notre Dame, Ind.: University of Notre Dame Press, 1969.

Miller, Eugene. "Leo Krzycki—Polish American Labor Leader." *Polish American Studies* 33 (Autumn 1976):52–64.

Miller, Frank. "The Polanders in Wisconsin." In *Parkman Club Papers*. Milwaukee: n.p., 1896.

Miller, Sally. "Milwaukee Retrospective: A Profile of Reform." Paper read at a meeting on Milwaukee history sponsored by the Department of History and the Center for Twentieth-Century Studies, University of Wisconsin–Milwaukee, April 3, 1974.

Monzell, Thomas. "The Catholic Church and the Americanization of the Polish Immigrant." *Polish American Studies* 26 (1969):1–15.

Osada, Stanislaw. *Historia Związku Narodowego Polskiego, 1880–1905* [*The History of the Polish National Alliance, 1880–1905*]. 1905. Reprint. Chicago: Wydane Nakładem Związku Narodowego Polskiego, 1957.

Olson, Frederick I. "The Milwaukee Socialists, 1897–1941." Ph.D. dissertation, Harvard University, 1953.

Olszewski, Adam. *Historia Związku Narodowego Polskiego, 1905–1949* [*The History of the Polish National Alliance, 1905–1949*]. 5 vols. Chicago: Wydane Nakładem Związku Narodowego, 1957.

Olszyk, Edward. *The Polish Press in America*. Milwaukee: Marquette University Press, 1940.

Pienkos, Angela. *A Brief History of Federation Life Insurance of America, 1913–1976*. Milwaukee: Haertlein Graphics for Federation Life Insurance of America, 1976.

Pienkos, Donald. "The Polish Americans in Milwaukee Politics." In *Ethnic Politics in Urban America: The Polish Experience in Four Cities*, edited by Angela Pienkos. Chicago: Polish American Historical Association, 1978.

Renkiewicz, Frank. "An Economy of Self-Help: Fraternal Capitalism and the Evolution of Polish America." In *Aspects of the East European Ethnic Experience in America*, edited by Philip Shashko, Donald Pienkos, and Charles Ward. New York: Columbia University Press, 1980.

Shannon, David. *The Socialist Party of America: A History*. New York: Macmillan, 1955.

Silver Jubilee Album of St. Josaphat's Parish. Milwaukee: Nowiny Publishing Company, 1913.

Simon, Roger D. "The Bay View Incident and the People's Party in Milwaukee." Unpublished paper in the files of the Research Division, State Historical Society of Wisconsin.

Still, Bayrd. *Milwaukee: The History of a City*. Madison: State Historical Society of Wisconsin, 1948.

Sutherland, Laura. "The Immigrant Family: Milwaukee's Poles: 1880–1905." M.A. thesis, University of Wisconsin–Milwaukee, 1974.

Syski, Alexander. "Reverend Waclaw Kruszka: The Nestor of Polish Historians in America." *Polish American Studies* 1 (1944):62–70.

U.S. Bureau of the Census. *Fifteenth Census of the United States*. Washington: Government Printing Office, 1932.

U.S. Bureau of the Census. *Abstract of the Twelfth Census of the United States,*

1900. Washington: Government Printing Office, 1902.
Wachman, Marvin. "History of the Social Democratic Party of Wisconsin, 1897–1910." Ph.D. dissertation, University of Illinois, 1945.
Wielka Encyklopedia Powszechna [*Great Polish Encyclopedia*]. 13 vols. Warsaw: Panstowe Wydawnictwo Naukowe, 1971.
Wisconsin. Department of State. *Tabular Statements of the State of Wisconsin Census*. 3 vols. in 2. Madison: Democratic Printing Company, 1906.
Wisconsin. Legislative Reference Bureau. *The Wisconsin Blue Book*. Madison, Wisc., 1862–.
Wyman, Roger. "Voting Behavior in the Progressive Era: Wisconsin as a Case Study." Ph.D. dissertation, University of Wisconsin–Madison, 1970.
Wyman, Roger. "Wisconsin Ethnic Groups and the Election of 1890." *Wisconsin Magazine of History* 51 (Summer 1968):269–93.
Wytrwal, Joseph. *America's Polish Heritage*. Detroit: Endurance Press, 1961.

**SIXTH ANNUAL
MORRIS FROMKIN MEMORIAL LECTURE**

The University & the Social Gospel

THE INTELLECTUAL ORIGINS OF THE WISCONSIN IDEA

J. David Hoeveler, Jr.

ASSISTANT PROFESSOR OF HISTORY
THE UNIVERSITY OF WISCONSIN—MILWAUKEE
Recipient of the 1975 Fromkin Research Grant

John Bascom
Richard T. Ely
John R. Commons
Charles R. Van Hise

**3:30 p.m.
Thursday, November 6, 1975
East Wing, first floor, UWM Library**

The public is cordially invited to attend.
Sponsored by the Fromkin Memorial Collection of the UWM Library.
Reception follows.

The University and the Social Gospel: The Intellectual Origins of the "Wisconsin Idea"

J. DAVID HOEVELER, JR.

A notable fact of American life in the late nineteenth century was the remarkable transformation of the American college and its emergence as the new university. As usually described, this metamorphosis derived from three major factors: a new concern for practicality and utility in the colleges' curricular program; a democratic effort to extend the benefits of education to a wider portion of the community and to repay the public by servicing its needs; and a new academic interest in research—that is, the advancement of knowledge instead of the mere passing-on of an acquired cultural tradition.[1] These three components were mutually reinforcing, and, as integrated aspects of the social role of the American university, they found their most famous statement in the "Wisconsin Idea," which received its fullest summarization during the administration of Charles R. Van Hise in the early twentieth century. The Wisconsin Idea pledged the University of Wisconsin to serve the state by applying its research to the solution of public problems, by training experts in the physical and social sciences and joining their academic efforts to the public, administrative functions of the state, and by extending the work of the University, through its personnel and facilities, to the boundaries of the state.[2]

Particularly with respect to the social sciences, the University of

---

J. David Hoeveler, Jr., who received his doctorate from the University of Illinois, is the author of *The New Humanism: A Critique of Modern America, 1900–1940* (University of Virginia Press). A specialist in social and intellectual history, he is now preparing a study of the origins and development of the "Wisconsin Idea." This essay, which originally appeared in the *Wisconsin Magazine of History* 59 (Summer 1976), is reprinted by permission.

Wisconsin truly did pioneer in merging the higher learning with public life. But the concept, and indeed the rhetoric, of service to the state was at this time becoming the norm of the state universities everywhere in America, and outside Wisconsin was often more starkly utilitarian in its operations. Nonetheless, Wisconsin became the focus of national interest because it gave dramatic and concrete illustration to a new concept. Historians, like the public itself, have long been interested in the Wisconsin Idea, and particularly in its reputation as a new experiment in politics associated with the governorship of Robert M. La Follette and in its network of affiliations with "the other end of State Street"—the University—in Madison. To this extent, however, they have neglected the origins of the Wisconsin Idea as it emerged within the changing intellectual milieu of nineteenth-century America. Those origins deserve emphasis, because a study of them suggests especially that the University of Wisconsin's special contribution was the conceptual as well as the practical elucidation of ideas generated by several individuals who served the institution in a critical period.

My subject, then, is in part the intellectual history of an institution; but I also endeavor to relate that history to the context of reform thought in the late nineteenth century. I wish especially to emphasize the elements of continuity between the reform impulse of evangelical Protestantism in the antebellum period and the later Social Gospel movement. Specifically, I will endeavor to show that the three persons who best articulated the Wisconsin Idea—John Bascom, Richard T. Ely, and John R. Commons—each found in the new role of the University the logical and critical vehicle of their ideals: the perfection of the Christian state.

Because the elements of continuity loom so large in the intellectual origins of the Wisconsin Idea, it is important to keep in perspective the major characteristics, the religious and social objectives of evangelical Protestantism. As Perry Miller once suggested, evangelical Protestantism was the central cultural force in the United States in the half-century before the Civil War; it in fact provided the fullest expression of America's quest for a national identity.[3] In a nation of diverse ethnic and religious groups, evangelical Protestantism looked beyond the institutional churches, the national established churches that typified the Old World, for a common religious substance, a core of spirituality that would cement the nation. The principal vehicle for evangelical Protestantism, and the answer to its quest for religious unity, was the revival. Bypassing church creeds and sectarian divisions, the revival, through the principles of divine grace and saving personal conversion, pursued a kind of "pure Christianity," one largely indifferent to the institutional church but obsessed with the notion that personal and public morality would serve as the foundation of a religious nation. This foundation was judged critical for the defense of the nation against its greatest enemies, the spirit of Mammon and the spirit of infidelity.[4]

There were important corollaries to this consensus in the realms of politics and social reform. Because America had forsaken the idea of a national church and its ties to a national government, and because it located its quest for a pure religion outside the institutional churches, the concept of the voluntary principle became important to it. A great variety of voluntary organizations emerged in nineteenth-century Protestant America: the American Education Society, the American Bible Society, the American Sunday-School Union, the American Tract Society, the American Home Mission Society, the Society for the Promotion of Collegiate and Theological Education in the West. Their united concern was the conversion and salvation of the country. These organizations, interdenominational in membership, had their counterparts in a host of others concerned with specific social causes—temperance and prohibition, Sabbatarianism, education, and antislavery most prominent among them. The voluntary organization was a kind of surrogate for church and state, but it was not exclusively so. When large moral issues loomed, the evangelicals quite willingly called upon the state. But whatever the situation, it was to the revival that evangelicals looked for the generating of a social energy that would ignite the community's moral resolve. Theirs was the pursuit of an energizing power that could convert a nation floundering in materialism and moral laxity. Nothing could more certainly save the drunkard than the revival's conversion of his soul. Lyman Beecher's call for "a disciplined moral militia" to confront America's spiritual and social ills was the quintessential expression of a key aspect of the evangelical mind.[5] But the concept of social and moral energy was also important to the formulators of the Wisconsin Idea.

The antebellum college (the "old-time college" as we call it now) was a critical part of the evangelical goal of a Protestant America. The nine colleges founded in the colonial period were supplemented by hundreds more in the early nineteenth century, most of them sponsored by one of the various Protestant denominations. The old-time college has not had a good press. Undoubtedly its heavily classical curriculum was narrow and its classroom life dull, often even anti-intellectual. A strict paternalism governed student life, and the college atmosphere was restrictive and inhibiting. But in ways often unappreciated, the old-time college tried to be relevant to the society it served. Revivals were common occurrences on campuses, a fact that attains special significance when seen in relation to the pattern of moral reform activities that revivals often generated.[6] Indeed, the old-time college's moral pattern related the school directly to the community outside. The spirit of collegiate reform efforts drew partly from the extracurricular life of the schools, especially the literary societies in which students debated important contemporary events, and the special student organizations to promote abolitionism, temperance, and other causes. Not surprisingly, therefore, at Oberlin College, the institution where revivalism and other evangelical ideals were most pronounced, antislavery sentiment and abolitionist activity among the faculty and students also were more pronounced than in any other American college.[7] Then, too, the moral force of the old-time college grew directly from the academic life of the college. Indeed, perhaps the oldest academic tradition in America was the one which required the college president to instruct all seniors in moral and mental philosophy. In these courses, the president outlined the doctrines of a moral universe and of innate moral ideas in the human mind. Usually a full year of instruction was devoted to this system of moral law and its applications to society. For moral philosophy—perhaps the unique aspect of higher education in the United States—was not a mere exercise in philosophical abstractions. One need only examine the index to Francis Wayland's *The Elements of Moral Science*, America's first domestic, academic best-seller, to appreciate the wide penumbra of "practical ethics" embraced by this subject. They included the Sabbath, personal property, oaths, marriage, chastity, the duties of parents, the rights and obligations of children, the nature of just government, charity and poor laws, war, and the treatment of animals.[8]

John Bascom was heir to this tradition when he came to the University of Wisconsin as its fifth president in 1874. Measured against the pattern of the American university then, Wisconsin had few distinctive traits. Like most state universities, it was still little different from the old-time college. Its curriculum was largely prescribed; its moral regimentation, denoted by such requirements as attendance at chapel services, was well intact; and its statutory pledges to promote agricultural and technical training were largely unfulfilled. Nor was there anything untypical about Bascom's background. Like so many college presidents of his day, he was born in a family of New Englanders who had removed by the time of his birth in 1827 to western New York. He was only one of a remarkable number of college presidents who grew up in the "burned-over" district, so called because of the flames of revivalism which between about 1800 and 1850 frequently swept this most intensely evangelical area in the nation. Bascom was a graduate of Williams College who had pursued studies at Auburn and Andover theological seminaries. He had returned to Williams to teach rhetoric, an unsuitable academic calling; the appointment at Wisconsin gave him opportunities both for administrative leadership and for bringing the full scope of his ideas personally to a growing student body.

But, as his work at Wisconsin soon proved, John Bascom was unique among the academic moral philosophers of his day. In many ways he set the future course of the institution, and one of his students, Robert M. La Follette, credits Bascom as the true originator of the Wisconsin Idea. Determining the truth of La Follette's assertion requires a close examination of Bascom's thoughts. Here it can be said that Bascom pioneered intellectually in three directions. He was one of the first religious thinkers in America to accept the main outline of evolutionary science and to establish upon it an entirely new theology, what he himself labeled the "New Theology." Secondly, he took moral philosophy, a course he taught to every individual student in the University, in important new directions. His own moral philosophy textbook, written while he was at Wisconsin and used by Bascom in his classes,[9] accorded 117 pages, significantly more than any other similar text, to the problems of government and politics and the need for expanded public authority.[10] And he pushed moral philosophy still farther by writing the first academic sociology text, a moral treatise more than a scientific one, but embracing the causes of temperance, women's rights, and the right of labor to organize. Thirdly, Bascom used his influence at Wisconsin to outline a new philosophy of state for America, a doctrine of enhanced moral powers for government and public institutions, including the state university. He worked carefully at this philosophical labor, preserving the essential objectives of the evangelical ideology in which he believed, but reconstructing that ideology to accommodate the public sphere. John Bascom was one of the first exponents of the Social Gospel in America; his unwavering quest was for the "Kingdom of Heaven."

Undoubtedly, Bascom was one of the most difficult and complex of America's philosophers, a fact that may explain a general neglect of his work. Influenced greatly by many of the liberal religious thinkers of the nineteenth century, including Ralph Waldo Emerson, Horace Bushnell, and, in philosophy, Laurens P. Hickok, Bascom combined their influences with evolutionary ideas to become one of the leading theological liberals. *The New Theology* grew out of his teaching at Wisconsin, as did *Evolution and Religion*, published after his departure. These two works carefully articulated new means to realizing the older ends of the Christian society desired by the evangelical philosophers. Bascom certainly did make important revisions in the evangelical theology, but the pervasive themes of moral advancements and social reform remained equally prominent. Essentially, Bascom perceived that evolution gave a whole new sense to the concept of the Kingdom of God and a new means of realizing it. Rejecting Herbert Spencer and William Graham Sumner's depiction of evolution as generated by powerful material and perhaps blind physical forces, Bascom painted the evolution concept in strokes of broad cosmic dimensions. Evolution demonstrated the oneness of life, the organic unity in all things; and, more important, it illustrated the spiritual powers at work in the world. Divine plan, as evolution showed, called for progressive improvement in the physical qualities of all the species; and it also incorporated, in the case of the human race, the unfolding of the rational, moral, and spiritual powers. Quite properly, in fact, evolution blurred the boundaries of the natural and the supernatural, and demonstrated an immanent God whose activity in the world assured the progressive realization of the Kingdom of Heaven on earth.[11]

From this perspective, Bascom drew implications for his entire educational and social philosophy. Evolution gave a whole new scope to the human intellect. The mind, Bascom said, was the correlative of the universe, and its constant expansion alone assured human grasp of God's progressive manifestation to the world, His revelation of Himself in the evolutionary scheme of things. Evolution also sounded the death knell of stale creeds, rituals, and religious formulations of divine truth. The revelation of God was not a completed fact or past event, but an indication of expanding spiritual powers in the world. Thus, Bascom wrote, "What we may call the movement of evolution is also the movement of reason. . . . The world is thus laid open to us as a dynamic, living spiritual product." Moreover, religious truth was not united with secular truth; it could no longer be compartmentalized as sacred dogma or the special prerogative of a priestly class. Truth was revealed not only by the spiritual insight of the human mind as it advanced through evolution, but by the expanded powers of the intellect in science. Science then was but one aspect of "the thought of God . . . the omnipresence of his wisdom."[12] Bascom here was elaborating one of the key ideas behind the emergence of the modern university—the concept of the dynamic, plastic nature of truth. That concept played a catalytic role in transforming the old-time college's ideal of preserving a specific intellectual heritage into the new university's objective of the open-ended pursuit of new knowledge.

Bascom thus saw the world, as the evangelicals had described it, in terms of its pervasive moral and spiritual character. But there was an important alteration in the perspective he took. The evangelical might have the model Christian society as his foremost objective, but he continued to see the world in terms of individual sin. Always, the path to social salvation lay along the lines of the special and separate conversion of individual souls. But as evolution illuminated the oneness of things, as it merged the spiritual and physical, and as it demonstrated the complicated matrix in which all things were imbedded, it greatly enlarged the whole sphere in which the moral sense must operate. It was necessary to view the world in terms of the "ever-growing tissue of moral relations" that embraced it. In short, the moral reformer could no longer rely upon the isolated individual as the vehicle for the perfection of the community; he needed instead to be master of all the social laws affecting society. Bascom thus wrote that "a theology which seeks the regeneration of society in ignorance of social laws is doomed to failure."[13]

Bascom continued to employ the language of the evangelicals, and gave much attention to his own new doctrine of "conversion." Not only did conversion now have an emphatic social meaning; it also described, not a sudden and convulsive change, but slow, constant improvement wrought in the social material of the world. Conversion in this sense required not so much the skill of the gospel preacher as the expertise of the social scientist, for as the race advanced, intellectual and rational powers would continually supplant emotional ones as the critical vehicles of human progress. Bascom used the terms "reason" and "spiritual power" interchangeably, and used both as surrogates for the evangelicals' "grace." They supplied for him the source of social energy and power that the evangelicals found in the revival, and Bascom even asserted that the full application of intellectual power to the unfolding spiritual laws of the universe was the certain means for the "redemption" of the world. "We are brought by these universal facts of law, unfolding themselves progressively in evolution, in contact with the world in a new way. It is not only capable of redemption, it is being redeemed."[14] Bascom, furthermore, employed the evangelical motif of pure Christianity in his new theology. Spiritual power dispensed with ritual and creeds, and had as its business the moral improvement of the world. Moral reason, in fact, was the purest expression of the religious sentiment, and of the religious nature of man.[15] And all these ideas fit nicely into the concept of the Kingdom of Heaven. "The Kingdom of Heaven," Bascom wrote, "is a physical, intellectual, social, and spiritual product. It adjusts all things and persons to each other."[16]

John Bascom brought together many of the ideas he had developed at Wisconsin, and he published them during his last year at Madison in his work, *Sociology*. This discipline was just emerging from moral philosophy as an independent academic subject in the American university,[17] and in fact Bascom made it a direct extension of moral philosophy. It was a key transitional work, though not a sociological treatise in the modern sense. Bascom defined sociology as the study of social, civic, economic, religious, and ethical forces in their various operations. But the last aspect, the ethical, was the most important. For with the evolutionary advance of the race, ethical forces emerge in more pronounced forms. Thus, not only is sociology itself a quest for the just society, but also it must rely on the spiritual as well as the empirical faculties as its tools of analysis and perception.[18] How may society discover and use spiritual power most fully? That question summarized for Bascom the central concern of the new science he now explored. "The widest and most inclusive diffusion of power, issuing in the largest aggregate of power, is the aim of society."[19]

These reflections led Bascom to one of his most important ideas, the doctrine of state power, which he developed and impressed forcefully upon the minds of the students at Wisconsin. Bascom was literally obsessed with the problem of organizing social power as outlined in *Sociology*. Bascom described for his students an age he judged to be destructive in its use of power, a ruthlessly competitive society with aggregated power in the hands of a few individuals. Such an arrangement of forces was unethical and un-Christian in nature, and ultimately debilitating to society as a whole. When Bascom therefore called for "harmonious power" as the truest expression of "beneficent power," he turned directly to the state, the agency of public power, for its exercise. The state, Bascom wrote in *Sociology*, must create social power, surpassing the work of isolated individuals.[20] Furthermore, the state must give power to the weaker elements in its midst, a concern that suffused most of the reform measures that Bascom endorsed.[21] Bascom was in fact making an important modification of the evangelical format: he now turned to the state as a surrogate for churches and voluntary societies. Modern America could no longer rely on these institutions for the perfection of the nation (Bascom even felt they had become too much the voice of entrenched private factions) and must instead look directly to the state for moral leadership and action.[22]

These views had important implications for Bascom's ideas about the role of the university in modern society, but it is important to bear in mind that the university question itself was only one part of the reform ideology that he and others brought to Wisconsin. On three other specific issues, Bascom was outspoken, and he examined each through the same social perspective that anticipated the Wisconsin Idea. One of these issues, prohibition, particularly shows the continuity between the older evangelical program and Bascom's sociology. Bascom was one of the most prominent members of the national Prohibition party in Wisconsin, a fact that was not a little responsible for the political embroilments that plagued his administration in Madison. He paid much attention to this problem in his sociology text, and in a pamphlet he wrote for public distribution entitled *The Philosophy of Prohibition*. Prohibition above all shows how easily the transition could be made from evangelicalism to the later reform efforts. Indeed, prohibition was the catalyst in the change from an emphasis on voluntary societies to an emphasis on government controls. Here was a large moral issue, and one that affected the whole power of society—it was by definition therefore a matter for the state. Nothing, Bascom believed, more seriously blighted the spiritual powers of contemporary America than the destructive abuses of drink. In fact, Bascom wrote, "the entire moral strength of the race must be brought to the task of lifting off this burden before mankind can resume its march." Indeed the same fallacious ideology that made individual rights sacred in economics threatened to deprive the public of its own rights in defending against the evils of liquor. But the right of the state, the public good, must prevail against these. Said Bascom: "To affirm the personal rights of an individual in a case like this is to enable him to stand across the path of public progress, to check the organic movement of society. . . . Society is under no obligation to subject . . . its own high fortunes to those morally ignorant and repellent." It must "overrule unreason with reason, unrighteousness with righteousness."[23]

Bascom's *Sociology* announced that no social issue was more critical to the theory he expounded than the rights of women.[24] Nor was this a theoretical issue for him, for, as in the case of prohibition, Bascom was active in the cause. He supported co-education at the University, and before the public and to a generation that was still skeptical he advocated woman's suffrage and other feminist causes. Bascom's stance derived directly from his New Theology. He did not pose the issue in terms of natural rights, but in terms of spiritual powers in the evolution of society. Rights merely loom larger as the world progresses and moves toward full spiritual integration. Women now must be admitted, in full standing Bascom believed, to the ongoing spiritual and social progress of the world. And in this matter, too, because it was one of great moral consequence, the state must assume an active role. It must provide the proper conditions "to make ready for the free exercise of [the] intelligence and virtue" of women. Bascom defended this issue even by calling for an end to certain sacred social customs. Old habits of chivalry, he believed, simply concealed a contempt for women and conspired against their exercising their strength.[25]

Finally on the issue of the rights of labor and unionization, John Bascom took a stand uncommon for the usual college president of his day. Indeed he was one of the first to break the stranglehold of laissez-faire doctrine on academic economics in the nineteenth century. He spoke for labor organizations because they too were vehicles of power that could redress the unfair balance in an age of industrial corporations. The greatest danger to any society was precisely this imbalance, and the consequent spiritual and physical deprivation by oppression of great numbers of the population. Here again organized spiritual force was the saving factor in an age that dangerously threatened to render much of society powerless and without influence.[26]

Bascom was a spiritual optimist who never doubted that the improvement of the world was the ordained order of things. But he could not rest content with society's present state. Ideals, he knew, outran realities, but those who were spiritually in advance of the day must fight for the perfection of the world. It is unlikely that any other college president so bluntly and so directly attacked the corrupting spirit, the individual pursuit of wealth and power, in modern America. Bascom's last baccalaureate address at Wisconsin, entitled "A Christian State," pulled no punches. Spiritually, he said, America was far from the Christian state. "We are in the full swing of individual assertion. Unbridled enterprise is our controlling temper."[27] The same year he wrote: "The money-power vigorously asserts itself, and it easily overawes the moral and social forces which should work with it. . . ."[28] Bascom's address became an urgent plea for public control of the economic forces that operated against the public interest, for "we are in danger of falling under a new economic tyranny." The collective society must assert its own rights, and, in the same way that it must protect itself against the debilitating influence of liquor, it must be equally vigilant toward the abuses of money. Bascom's religious and social thought merged at this juncture. If society was still "The Seat of Sin" (his 1876 baccalaureate address), the state must be the seat of righteousness. "The state like the individual has the duty to be righteous. It has the right and the duty to push to completion its own organization; to do all it can for its own highest attainments in itself and its citizens."[29]

As Bascom looked to the enlarged influence of the state for the promotion of moral power in modern society, he assigned increasing prominence to the place and function of the state university more than to any other public institution. This view directly extended his efforts to achieve evangelical objectives by new methods. As the volunteer principle yielded to the doctrine of state initiative, so also, in Bascom's mind, did the new state universities assume an importance greater than the small sectarian schools—the old-time colleges. But the same quest for greater spiritual and moral power still governed his thinking. In a baccalaureate address in 1877, Bascom explained that the small colleges, because of their wide diffusion and divided purposes and efforts, deprived the state—especially a state like Wisconsin—of the unified public purpose it needed. Religious and ethnic diversity was harmful if it dispersed efforts for moral improvement and left society to depend on "a rambling halting voluntaryism."[30] Not only was it imperative that intellectual and moral power become a concern of the state; the state university itself must also be the institutional epitome of that power. Bascom, like many other university leaders in his time, looked for the extension of public education to every corner of the state; and he believed that such an educational system naturally would culminate in academic preparation of the state's students for its university. To the people of Wisconsin, Bascom held up the example of Michigan, with its large, successful university and relatively few denominational schools. Ohio, by contrast, had small schools in profusion, and not one among them nationally recognized. Wisconsin resembled too much the latter state, he said, and the result was a tragic loss of public power within its own boundaries.[31]

Bascom thus moved significantly close to the modern conception of the state university; but his views were still governed largely by a nineteenth-century religious perspective, though one clearly more secularized than the older evangelical one. Bascom's views on the state university coincided directly with his theological and philosophical ideas. They expressed, in other words, Bascom's obsession with the spiritual and moral advancement of mankind. Quite simply, public education, and the state university as its highest expression, must strengthen society's "spiritually progressive resources." For "That system of education is alone good which builds society together under spiritual law." Bascom used the language of the old-time college president in declaring that education's most important quality was the moral. Indeed, insofar as ethical law was the underlying unity, the common denominator of all religion, then the state university itself was a surrogate for the churches. Furthermore, moral power in this age must have access to large public institutions. Moral education through the vehicle of the state university provides the means by which to make all acquired powers subservient to the interests of society.[32]

The language was familiar, to be sure, but Bascom was in fact widening its application. Because his theology so thoroughly merged the natural and the supernatural, when he spoke of moral law, and joined that to the objectives of the state university, he intended no mere abstractions. Bascom, who presided over a noticeable expansion of the curriculum at Wisconsin, saw this growth as one means of increased moral power in public life. For it was precisely the new academic concerns of the modern university—and Bascom named political science, economics, constitutional law, sociology, and others—that would best unite the university's social and academic missions. These new disciplines gave the most profound social expression to ethical law. "Here," said Bascom in his 1880 baccalaureate, "moral truths have their seat." The highest expressions of religion and spiritual force enter social life by these doors. In this way, Bascom critically reconstructed the evangelical program while actually extending it. All the new learning that was the creation and concern of the new university was now available for the redemption of the world. "We seem to see the Kingdom of Heaven coming along these very lines of union between scientific research and religious insight."[33] Here, perhaps, John Bascom most completely joined his social philosophy to the academic revolution of the late nineteenth century.

His philosophical argument that brought him to this point leads directly to the message he impressed most indelibly upon the students of the University of Wisconsin. He believed that evolutionary progress dictated the spiritual and moral improvement of the race,

quired more of "divine grace" than the conduct of the business and commercial life of the nation. America in the late nineteenth century faced a spiritual crisis denoted by the selfish and egotistical worship of Mammon. In 1889, shortly before coming to Wisconsin, Ely had written *Social Aspects of Christianity*, one of the major works of the Social Gospel movement. He called then for "a profound revival of religion, not in any narrow or technical sense . . . but a great religious awakening which shall shake things, going down into the depths of men's lives and modifying their character." Ely employed all the force and style of evangelical rhetoric, but he crucially shifted the focus of religious outreach. "This religious reform," he said, "must infuse a religious spirit into every department of political life."[41] Like Bascom, Ely shifted attention to the state and made it the critical vehicle of social improvement and moral power. This, in fact, was the first article in the creed of the New Economics: "We regard the state as an educational and ethical agency whose positive aid is an indispensable condition of human progress."[42] A year after his appointment at Wisconsin, Ely, with John R. Commons and others, organized the American Institute for Christian Sociology.[43]

Ely came to Madison because he foresaw a great opportunity there to put into action his ideas of social reform. Particularly at the University of Wisconsin would he and his associates have access to the state capital, the courts, the legislature, and the state's administrative bureaus. The state university in fact now loomed large in Ely's mind as a factor in both the religious and the social aspects of his concerns. For although the "theological seminaries" might help us fulfill the commandment to love God, the new social sciences will help us fulfill the commandment to love our neighbor. Ely then proposed that the religious denominations center their activity around the state universities of the country; they should form Christian associations, guild houses with libraries and dormitories. This was a significant way of joining the religious life to the public life of the country, and far more useful—for Ely too was obsessed with the phenomenon of moral power—than promoting separate denominational colleges. In fact a major advantage of this approach, as Bascom had recognized, was its aiding the "unity of Christendom." Sectarianism had been ruinous to that ideal.[44] Religious perspectives probably played a lesser role in Ely's later work at Wisconsin, yielding to more strictly political and academic matters. He supported the reforms of La Follette and, as an occasional consultant, helped make the University conspicuous in the political life of the state. But his own version of the Social Gospel was important to Ely's contribution to the Wisconsin Idea.[45]

Even more active in the actual reform programs of the Wisconsin progressive movement was John R. Commons, professor of economics in Ely's new school. The Social Gospel acted as a catalyst also in Commons' life, resulting in his political and academic activity. Commons leaves no doubt that the major early influence on his life was his mother, "the strictest of Presbyterian Puritans," who raised him on Foxe's *Book of Martyrs*. She herself represented the spirit of antebellum Oberlin College, that outstanding expression of revivalism and reform, from which she had graduated in 1853. Active then in the institution's antislavery cause, she continued her reformist work afterwards in the movement for temperance and woman's rights. Commons himself spent his undergraduate years at Oberlin. There, joined by his mother, he established an antisaloon league, the beginnings of the Ohio Anti-Saloon League, later one of the most powerful in the country. In 1884 Commons cast his first ballot, for John P. St. John, Prohibitionist candidate for President of the United States.[46] The temperance campaign was probably the major factor in widening Commons' social perspectives and propelling him into leadership, with Ely and others, in the New Economics. A series of essays, written by Commons and collected into an 1894 publication entitled *Social Reform and the Church*, illuminates his views as they emerged in the years before he came to Wisconsin.

Commons' essay called "Temperance Reform" in this volume wholly endorses complete prohibition of the liquor traffic. Like much of the old evangelical literature, it cites the social damage charged to the abuses of drink, even the harm done to unborn children. But Commons, who had recently completed studies with Ely at Johns Hopkins, treated intemperance as a symptom as well as a cause of social evils. It was now the duty of government, in fact, to remove the causes of intemperance. Specifically, government must enforce shorter hours for labor, preserve the Sabbath (Commons now simply said "Sunday") as protection for labor from forced work, write new factory laws for women and children, abolish sweatshops, and require better wages and greater security of employment. "When all these reforms are carried out," said Commons, "it will be possible to have universal prohibition." Temperance, therefore, still remained an end in itself, but the issue carried Commons directly from evangelicalism to progressivism.[47] And for Commons, progressivism meant the union of Christian ideals with the social sciences. Sociology, by Commons' definition, "co-ordinates all the special social sciences, such as ethics, politics and religion." Commons, who had just helped establish the American Institute for Christian Sociology, still believed that "Christianity is the only solution for social problems," but he added that sociology is "one half of religion."[48] Probably more than any other individual, Commons personified the Wisconsin Idea, for his academic work at Madison was often indistinguishable from his public reform efforts. He was a major figure behind the La Follette reforms, drafting the Civil Service Law of 1905, the Public Utility Act of 1907, and the Industrial Commission Law, among others.[49]

Bascom, Ely, and Commons each brought to the University of Wisconsin perspectives on the educational function of the university that were shaped by their own efforts to define a Social Gospel program for America. But the Wisconsin Idea was not in any strict sense a religious concept. And that it was perfectly possible to accept the social content without the gospel content of the program is quite clearly indicated by the ideas of La Follette and Van Hise. La Follette left no doubt that Bascom greatly influenced him. This was true probably in a large rather than in a specific sense. One suggestion is that Bascom's moralism was most influential,[50] and La Follette himself seems to have corroborated that idea.[51] The ethical sense of life of course bore directly on La Follette's political work, but he saw the University of Wisconsin as a partner in that work. La Follette as governor occasionally sought Bascom's counsel, and particularly when he told the state legislature that the University must justify itself to the state either by its material contributions or as "an ethical force," he employed the language of his former teacher.[52]

Charles R. Van Hise, also a student of Bascom, a classmate of La Follette, and president of the University of Wisconsin after 1902, best illustrates the secularization of the evangelical and Social Gospel ideals and their reformulation as the Wisconsin Idea. Van Hise's background was almost entirely in the sciences; he was one of the foremost geologists of his time.[53] Religious concerns were not prominent in his thought, but emphasis on the moral and social responsibilities of the scholar to the public interest loomed very large and, it is probable, owed much to the influence of Bascom.[54] Van Hise supported the causes of prohibition and woman's rights as his former teacher had, and his own work, *Concentration and Control*, was a significant contribution to the literature of progressivism.[55] But Van Hise's version of the Wisconsin Idea was the most materialistic in content, transforming Bascom's sense of spiritual power into a doctrine of economic growth. This dogma then defined the state university's research activity, for new knowledge must be applied directly to the improvement of the lives of the people. The service ideal meant especially the invigoration of extension—the new "missionary" work of the university to use the evangelical vocabulary—so that virtually every home or business in the state, from machine shops to model dairy farms, would feel the long outreach of the state university. But this too was a doctrine of power, one that stated in stark, secular form the essential outline of Van Hise's former teacher's philosophy. It was a new kind of gospel and a new program for social redemption, indeed a new calling for America's institutions of higher learning.

NOTES

1 The best general account of these trends is in Lawrence R. Veysey, *The Emergence of the American University* (Chicago: University of Chicago Press, 1965), pp. 57–179.
2 Ibid., pp. 107–9.
3 Perry Miller, *The Life of the Mind in America: From the Revolution to the Civil War* (New York: Harcourt, Brace and World, 1965), p. 6.
4 Ibid., pp. 8–13; Robert T. Handy, *A Christian America: Protestant Hopes and Historical Realities* (London: Oxford University Press, 1971), pp. 30–31, 35.
5 Miller, *Life of the Mind*, pp. 36–42, 47, 83; Handy, *A Christian America*, pp. 42–43, 48–51 (Beecher quotation, p. 45); Sydney Ahlstrom, *A Religious History of the American People* (New Haven: Yale University Press, 1972), pp. 637–47; Timothy L. Smith, *Revivalism and Social Reform: American Protestantism on the Eve of the Civil War* (New York: Abingdon Press, 1957), passim. Some of the most valuable recent scholarship on American society in the nineteenth century has demonstrated two broad divisions, with stark political contrasts and allegiances, based on religious affiliation. Three works in particular confirm the existence, before and after the Civil War, of a broad evangelical (pietistic) party united on a series of political issues, such as those outlined above. They are: Paul Kleppner, *The Cross of Culture: A Social Analysis of Midwestern Politics, 1850–1900* (New York: Free Press, 1970); Richard Jensen, *The Winning of the Midwest: Social and Political Conflict, 1888–1896* (Chicago: University of Chicago Press, 1971); and Ronald P. Formisano, *The Birth of Mass Political Parties: Michigan, 1827–1861* (Princeton: Princeton University Press, 1971).
6 See David Robert Huehner, "Reform and the Pre–Civil War American College" (Ph.D. diss., University of Illinois, Urbana-Champaign, 1972), pp. 50–51.
7 Ibid., pp. 87–136, 148–98, 202–50, 262–311.
8 See Francis Wayland, *The Elements of Moral Science*, ed. Joseph L. Blau (Cambridge, Mass.: Belknap Press of Harvard University Press, 1963).
9 University of Wisconsin, *Catalogue*, 1879–80.
10 See John Bascom, *Ethics: Or Science of Duty* (New York: G. P. Putnam's Sons, 1879), pp. 208–324.

11 John Bascom, *Evolution and Religion: Or Faith as a Part of a Complete Cosmic System* (New York, 1897), pp. 53, 103; John Bascom, *The New Theology* (New York: G. P. Putnam's Sons, 1892), pp. 13, 49; John Bascom, "The Gains and Losses from Faith in Science," *Journal of Christian Philosophy* 1 (July 1882): 8–13.
12 Bascom, *Evolution and Religion*, pp. 6, 72–73 (first quotation), 134; Bascom, *New Theology*, pp. 17–18, 54, 61; Bascom, "Gains and Losses," pp. 5–16 (second quotation).
13 Bascom, *Evolution and Religion*, pp. 8–9; Bascom, *New Theology*, p. 118. To this extent also Bascom felt that science "gives solidity and breadth to moral questions." See "Gains and Losses," p. 4. In an address at Madison, Bascom employed the evangelical rhetoric, saying, "If we use words as broadly as we ought, the evangelization of the world is strictly a scientific movement." *Truth and Truthfulness* (Milwaukee: Cramer, Aikens, & Cramer, 1881), pp. 18–19 (baccalaureate address).
14 Bascom, *Evolution and Religion*, pp. 80–81, 84–85, 99; Bascom, *New Theology*, p. 171; Bascom, "Gains and Losses," p. 6 (quotation).
15 Bascom, *New Theology*, p. 51. This is the sense in which Bascom sought to bring evangelical inspiration into modified and wider use. "The movement which we designate as the New Theology owes much of its vigor to a renewed effort to unite the pietism of religion and the virtue of morality to a higher, wider, deeper spiritualism, which shall have the mastery of ideas in their practical development." Ibid., pp. 8–9. Later, "Pietism must break camp, dismiss its camp followers, and carry the glad tidings of a salvation that waits to sweep through every kingdom, physical, economic, social." Ibid., p. 181.
16 Bascom, *Evolution and Religion*, p. 139.
17 See Gladys Bryson, "The Comparable Interests of the Old Moral Philosophy and the Modern Social Sciences," *Social Forces* 11 (1932): 19–27; Gladys Bryson, "Sociology Considered as Moral Philosophy," *Sociological Review* 24 (1932): 26–36.
18 John Bascom, *Sociology* (New York: G. P. Putnam's Sons, 1887), pp. 4–5. For a more detailed summary of this idea in Bascom's sociology, see Robert A. Jones, "John Bascom, 1827–1911: Anti-Positivism and Intuitionism in American Sociology," *American Quarterly* 24 (October 1972): 501–22.
19 Bascom, *Sociology*, p. 48.
20 Ibid., pp. 34, 41. "Government," Bascom wrote, "is . . . always passing beyond the office of protection, securing the conditions of industry, and laying, in various ways, the foundations of enterprise, intelligence and virtue. This great function of government by which it combines the power of all, and makes it immediately and universally available, is as natural and spontaneous a function as that of protection, and can not be dispensed with." See his pamphlet, *The Philosophy of Prohibition* (New York: National Temperance Society & Publishing House, 1884), p. 4.
21 Bascom, *Sociology*, p. 45.
22 Ibid., p. 162; John Bascom, *The Freedom of Faith* (Madison: Atwood & Cul-

ver, 1874), pp. 11–12 (baccalaureate address).
23 Bascom, *Philosophy of Prohibition*, pp. 3–9; Bascom, *Sociology*, pp. 197–98 (quotation); see also John Bascom, "What Do the Members of a State University Owe to the State?" *The University Review* 1 (December 1884): 96. Bascom felt this point urgently, so concerned was he with the doctrine of moral improvement in society. Elaborating on the need for prohibition, he wrote: "The majority are compelled to endure the expense, the moral exposure, the physical and social deterioration of all sorts incident to the vice, debauchery and animalism of the intemperate, simply that the intemperate may have easy access to intoxicants. In order that the minority may spend their money for their pleasure, the majority are compelled to spend their means on what they loathe—the correction of crime, the support of pauperism, the treatment of idiots, the sustenance of the insane." See his *Sociology*, p. 198.
24 Bascom, *Sociology*, p. 184; and see the ensuing discussion, pp. 184–94.
25 John Bascom, *Woman Suffrage* (n.p.: n.d.), pp. 3–6 (quotation, p. 3). Bascom's prominence in the women's rights movement won him the special recognition and gratitude of feminist Susan B. Anthony. See Merle Curti and Vernon Carstensen, *The University of Wisconsin: A History, 1848–1925*, 2 vols. (Madison: University of Wisconsin Press, 1949), 1:291.
26 Bascom, *Sociology*, pp. 229–31; John Bascom, *Sermons and Addresses* (New York: G. P. Putnam's Sons, 1913), pp. 142–43.
27 John Bascom, *A Christian State* (Milwaukee: Cramer, Aikens, & Cramer, 1887), p. 10. No one more blatantly exemplified this wanton danger, in Bascom's mind, than John D. Rockefeller, who more than once was the object of the moralist's wrath. Wrote Bascom of Rockefeller: "He has turned business into unceasing and unflinching warfare.... He has done this with an open profession of Christian faith.... Herein lies the guilt of this man, and of others of the same ilk, and of all who put themselves in fellowship with them, that they confound ethical distinctions and make the world one medley of wrong-doing." *Sermons and Addresses*, pp. 144–45.
28 Bascom, *Sociology*, p. 211.
29 Bascom, *A Christian State*, pp. 16, 25; see also John Bascom, *The Seat of Sin* ([Madison]: Democrat Printing, 1876), *passim* (baccalaureate address).
30 John Bascom, *Education and the State* ([Madison]: n.p., 1877), pp. 8–13.
31 Ibid., pp. 14–15; John Bascom, *The Common School* (Madison: D. Atwood, 1878), p. 13 (baccalaureate address).
32 John Bascom, *Tests of a School System* (Milwaukee: Cramer, Aikens, & Cramer, 1880), pp. 10–11, 18–22 (quotation, p. 18). To this extent Bascom wholly accepted the fact that state universities could not legally teach a specific religious doctrine. "Only the more strongly and clearly may their attention be turned to a beautiful and fruitful ethical life—the culmination of religion." See "What Do the Members of a State University Owe to the State?" p. 100.
33 Bascom, *Tests of a School System*, p. 23; John Bascom, *The New Theology*

(Milwaukee: 1884), p. 22 (baccalaureate address). By no means did Bascom slight the humanities in the university curriculum. He defended philosophy as the most important study and believed that "the entire ethical and spiritual world is open to us in the humanities." See *Sermons and Addresses*, p. 196.

34 Robert M. La Follette, *La Follette's Autobiography: A Personal Narrative of Political Experiences* (Madison: University of Wisconsin Press, 1960), p. 13.
35 Bascom, "What Do the Members of a State University Owe to the State?" pp. 94–96.
36 Bascom, *Truth and Truthfulness*, p. 9.
37 Bascom, *Education and the State*, p. 17.
38 Curti and Carstensen, *University of Wisconsin*, 1:631–33; 2:88.
39 Benjamin G. Rader, *The Academic Mind and Reform: The Influence of Richard T. Ely in American Life* (Lexington: University of Kentucky Press, 1966), pp. 4–5, 46–48; Richard T. Ely, *Ground Under Our Feet: An Autobiography* (New York: Macmillan Company, 1938), pp. 1–5, 14–16 (quotation, p. 16), 41–47.
40 Ely, *Ground Under Our Feet*, p. 77; Rader, *The Academic Mind*, p. 36 (quoting Ely).
41 Richard T. Ely, *Social Aspects of Christianity* (New York: T. Y. Crowell, 1889), pp. 147–48.
42 Quoted by Ely from the "Platform" of the American Economic Association in *Ground Under Our Feet*, p. 136.
43 Rader, *The Academic Mind*, p. 121.
44 Ely, *Ground Under Our Feet*, p. 74; Richard T. Ely, "The Universities and the Churches," 31st University Convocation (Albany: University of the State of New York, 1893), pp. 351–56 (an address).
45 If Ely's own story may be believed, La Follette was highly influenced by Ely's writings and once told him, "You have been my teacher!" See *Ground Under Our Feet*, p. 216.
46 John R. Commons, *Myself* (Madison: University of Wisconsin Press, 1963), pp. 7–8, 21, 48.
47 John R. Commons, *Social Reform and the Church* (New York: A. M. Kelley Publishers, 1967), pp. 107–14. As in Ely's case, the discovery of the New Economics and his commitment to its application allowed Commons to channel a religious concern of the old evangelical variety into modern social reform. He wrote in his autobiography that this commitment "was my tribute to [my mother's] longing that I should become a minister of the Gospel." See *Myself*, p. 44.
48 See his essay "The Christian Minister and Sociology," *Social Reform and the Church*, pp. 3–19 (quotations on pp. 3, 13, and 19).
49 Lafayette G. Harder, Jr., *John R. Commons: His Assault on Laissez-Faire* (Corvallis: Oregon State University Press, 1962), pp. 69–86; Curti and Carstensen, *University of Wisconsin* 2:551–52; Belle Case La Follette and Fola La Follette, *Robert M. La Follette*, 2 vols. (New York: Macmillan Company, 1953), 1:157, 164, 190. For a corresponding statement of the theme outlined in this essay, see Jean B. Quandt, "Religion and Social Thought: The

Secularization of Postmillennialism," *American Quarterly* 30 (October 1973): 390–409.
50 David Paul Thelen, *The Early Life of Robert M. La Follette, 1855–1884* (Chicago: Loyola University Press, 1966), p. 50.
51 La Follette, *Autobiography*, p. 13.
52 La Follette, *Robert M. La Follette*, 1:38–39, 145–46; Curti and Carstensen, *University of Wisconsin*, 1:607.
53 Maurice M. Vance, *Charles Richard Van Hise: Scientist Progressive* (Madison: State Historical Society of Wisconsin, 1960), pp. 8–75.
54 Ibid., pp. 79–82; Curti and Carstensen, *University of Wisconsin*, 2:18–19.
55 Vance, *Van Hise*, p. 81; Curti and Carstensen, *University of Wisconsin*, 2:23–24.

BIBLIOGRAPHY

Ahlstrom, Sydney. *A Religious History of the American People*. New Haven: Yale University Press, 1972.
Bascom, John. *A Christian State*. Milwaukee: Cramer, Aikens, & Cramer, 1887.
Bascom, John. *The Common School*. Madison, Wisc.: D. Atwood, 1878.
Bascom, John. *Ethics: Or Science of Duty*. New York: G. P. Putnam's Sons, 1879.
Bascom, John. *Evolution and Religion: Or Faith as a Part of a Complete Cosmic System*. New York: G. P. Putnam's Sons, 1897.
Bascom, John. *The Freedom of Faith*. Madison, Wisc.: Atwood & Culver, 1874.
Bascom, John. "The Gains and Losses from Faith in Science." *Journal of Christian Philosophy* 1 (July 1882):8–13.
Bascom, John. *The New Theology*. New York: G. P. Putnam's Sons, 1892.
Bascom, John. *The Philosophy of Prohibition*. New York: National Temperance Society & Publishing House, 1884.
Bascom, John. *The Seat of Sin*. [Madison, Wisc.]: Democrat Printing, 1876.
Bascom, John. *Sermons and Addresses*. New York: G. P. Putnam's Sons, 1913.
Bascom, John. *Sociology*. New York: G. P. Putnam's Sons, 1887.
Bascom, John. *Tests of a School System*. Milwaukee: Cramer, Aikens, & Cramer, 1880.
Bascom, John. *Truth and Truthfulness*. Milwaukee: Cramer, Aikens, & Cramer, 1881.
Bascom, John. "What Do the Members of a State University Owe to the State?" *The University Review* 1 (December 1884):89–101.
Bascom, John. *Woman Suffrage*. [Madison, Wisc.: n.p., 188–?]
Bryson, Gladys. "The Comparable Interests of the Old Moral Philosophy and the Modern Social Sciences." *Social Forces* 11 (1932):19–27.
Bryson, Gladys. "Sociology Considered as Moral Philosophy." *Sociological Review* 24 (1932):26–36.
Commons, John R. *Myself*. Madison: University of Wisconsin Press, 1963.

Commons, John R. *Social Reform and the Church*. New York: A. M. Kelley Publishers, 1967.
Curti, Merle, and Vernon Carstensen. *The University of Wisconsin: A History, 1848–1925*. 2 vols. Madison: University of Wisconsin Press, 1949.
Ely, Richard T. *Ground Under Our Feet: An Autobiography*. New York: Macmillan Company, 1938.
Ely, Richard T. *Social Aspects of Christianity*. New York: T. Y. Crowell, 1889.
Ely, Richard T. "The Universities and the Churches, an Address Delivered at the 31st University Convocation, Senate Chamber, Albany, New York, July 5, 1893." Albany: University of the State of New York, 1893.
Formisano, Ronald P. *The Birth of Mass Political Parties: Michigan, 1827–1861*. Princeton: Princeton University Press, 1971.
Handy, Robert T. *A Christian America: Protestant Hopes and Historical Realities*. London: Oxford University Press, 1971.
Harder, Lafayette G., Jr. *John R. Commons: His Assault on Laissez-Faire*. Corvallis: Oregon State University Press, 1962.
Huehner, David Robert. "Reform and the Pre–Civil War American College." Ph.D. dissertation, University of Illinois–Urbana-Champaign, 1972.
Jensen, Richard. *The Winning of the Midwest: Social and Political Conflict, 1888–1896*. Chicago: University of Chicago Press, 1971.
Jones, Robert A. "John Bascom, 1827–1911: Anti-Positivism and Intuitionism in America." *American Quarterly* 24 (October 1972):501–22.
Kleppner, Paul. *The Cross of Culture: A Social Analysis of Midwestern Politics, 1850–1900*. New York: Free Press, 1970.
La Follette, Belle Case, and Fola La Follette. *Robert M. La Follette*. 2 vols. New York: Macmillan Company, 1953.
La Follette, Robert M. *La Follette's Autobiography: A Personal Narrative of Political Experiences*. Madison: University of Wisconsin Press, 1960.
Miller, Perry. *The Life of the Mind in America: From the Revolution to the Civil War*. New York: Harcourt, Brace & World, 1965.
Quandt, Jean B. "Religion and Social Thought: The Secularization of Postmillenialism." *American Quarterly* 30 (October 1973):390–409.
Rader, Benjamin G. *The Academic Mind and Reform: The Influence of Richard T. Ely in American Life*. Lexington: University of Kentucky Press, 1966.
Smith, Timothy L. *Revivalism and Social Reform: American Protestantism on the Eve of the Civil War*. New York: Abingdon Press, 1957.
Thelen, David Paul. *The Early Life of Robert M. La Follette*. Chicago: Loyola University Press, 1966.
University of Wisconsin. *Catalogue*. 1879–80.
Vance, Maurice M. *Charles Richard Van Hise: Scientific Progressive*. Madison: State Historical Society of Wisconsin, 1960.
Veysey, Lawrence R. *The Emergence of the American University*. Chicago: University of Chicago Press, 1965.
Wayland, Francis. *The Elements of Moral Science*. Edited by Joseph L. Blau. Cambridge: Belknap Press of Harvard University Press, 1963.

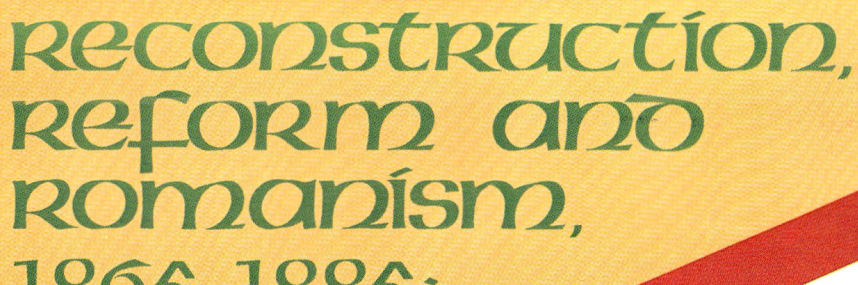

Reconstruction, Reform and Romanism, 1865-1885:

America as Seen by an Irish-American and his Irish MP Cousin

Seventh Annual Morris Fromkin Memorial Lecture

JANET E. DUNLEAVY
GARETH W. DUNLEAVY
Professors of English
THE UNIVERSITY OF WISCONSIN—MILWAUKEE
Recipients of the 1976 Fromkin Research Grant

3:30 p.m.
Thursday, November 4, 1976
East Wing, first floor, UWM Library

The public is cordially invited to attend. Reception follows.

Sponsored by the Fromkin Memorial Collection of the UWM Library.

Reconstruction, Reform, and Romanism, 1865–1885: America as Seen by an Irish-American and His Irish M.P. Cousin[1]

JANET EGLESON DUNLEAVY *and* GARETH W. DUNLEAVY

IN the 1860s, 1870s, and 1880s, as the United States approached, celebrated, and then looked back on its centennial, the issues that troubled the popular mind were, in many instances, not very different from those that concern Americans today. From 1861 to 1865, the nation had suffered an unpopular and divisive war, leading to such questions in the next decade as how to restore national unity; how to learn from what had been, for the entire country, a very painful experience; how to focus anew national attention on the future. In the early seventies, the nation had been rocked by revelations that almost the entire administration of its largest and most influential city had been engaged in widespread corruption. Rumor that, were the net thrown wide, it would catch other public figures as well—some, perhaps, with ties in the nation's capital—continued to be heard during the presidential election year of 1876.[2] Tammany Hall was the nineteenth century's Watergate; in its aftermath the power of government officials, the multiplicity of government offices, were ques-

---

Janet Egleson Dunleavy, who studied at Hunter College and New York University, is a specialist in English and Irish literature of the nineteenth and twentieth centuries. She has written on George Moore, Mary Lavin, and Douglas Hyde and is co-editor of *The O'Conor Papers: A Descriptive Catalogue and Surname Register of the Materials at Clonalis House* (University of Wisconsin Press).

Gareth W. Dunleavy, who received degrees from Clark, Brown, and Northwestern Universities, has done research on the Irish at Lindisfarne, Douglas Hyde, and various topics in medieval English and Irish literature and history. He is co-editor of *The O'Conor Papers*.

tioned. Respectable, educated, even conservative Americans called for radical reforms. Their concerns focused not only on corruption and inefficiency in government but also on the problems of assuring equal treatment under the law to those guaranteed equal treatment by the law in a climate in which, despite claims of support for democratic principles, prejudice and discrimination flourished. Public statements by an outspoken few reflected the private attitudes of many and identified those Americans for whom, because of prejudice and discrimination, opportunities to participate in democratic government were limited. For Irish-Americans in the years 1865–85, the message was especially clear. The diary of a prominent New York attorney noted that "England is right about the lower class of Irish. They are brutal, base, cruel, cowards, and as insolent as base. . . . St. Patrick's campaign against the snakes is a Popish delusion. They perished of biting the Irish people."[3] The Chicago *Post*, September 9, 1868, opined: "The Irish fill our prisons, our poor houses. . . . Scratch a convict or a pauper, and the chances are that you tickle the skin of an Irish Catholic." The Presbyterian minister Samuel Burchard publicly stated to presidential candidate James G. Blaine on October 29, 1884, that "We . . . don't propose to leave our party and identify ourselves with the party whose antecedents have been RUM, ROMANISM, and REBELLION."[4]

Reconstruction, reform, romanism: these were the issues of the years 1865 to 1885. In the middle of this period, just over one hundred years ago, Carolan O'B. Bryant, editor of a pamphlet published during the presidential campaign of 1876, called for reassessment of national priorities: "All the various complex calamities entailed by the . . . war have combined to engage the public mind to the exclusion of that vital subject—the great experiment of developing the Democratic principle in government," and continued: "Now that the centennial epoch is made the occasion of a general retrospect and review, it would seem above all other things expedient to examine our progress in the application of this idea."[5] And in the same year Charles O'Conor, an eminent Irish-American legal scholar, published *Democracy*, a monograph in which he expanded ideas concerning the structure of democratic government which he previously had expounded in letters, speeches, and essays: "The Federal government was designed as an organ of limited powers, yet it has exhibited ample capacity to crush or modify at will not only State institutions, but the States themselves." "A court of ultimate appeal, as well from the States as from the Federal tribunals, composed of judges selected by the States, and neither subject to official interference nor possessing coercive machinery of its own, might preserve . . . unity of jurisprudence throughout the whole country, and might also defend the autonomy of the States." However, "a long quarrantine [sic] should be required between exercising military command and accession to the chief magistracy."[6]

In an open letter of August 31, 1872,[7] to a Democratic convention in Louisville, Kentucky, Charles O'Conor had charged that "Governmental intermeddling with those concerns of society which, under judicious laws, might beneficially be left to individual action, is the only real evil actually developed in our system. . . . Four-fifths of the governmental intervention now practiced in carrying on the affairs of society should be dispensed with."[8] Four years later, however, in *Democracy*, he warned of another evil: "Through the ordinary revolutions of the political lottery . . . contestants divide between themselves, and alternately enjoy all that can be wrung from the multitude. . . . Those who enact the laws and administer them will . . . promote their private interests at the public cost if vested with sufficient power."[9] In *Peculation Triumphant*, his account of Tammany Hall and the Tweed Ring trials, O'Conor declared: "The State plainly *owes* to its tax-payers, present and future, protection . . . from the frauds of its own agents."[10] But in *Democracy*, he cautioned: "Appointing one set of official persons to watch another is a bootless contrivance. The remedy really aggravates the disease; it fosters the private evil of government—a multiplication of public agents. The watcher and the watched soon learn to co-operate for joint benefit."[11] Privately, in letters to an Irish kinsman, Charles Owen O'Conor, Don, M.P., who from his seat in the English Parliament across the Atlantic watched with interest American attempts to solve American problems, Charles O'Conor of New York complained of still another evil: "I have before advised you of the social and political ban which covertly exists . . . against Roman Catholics. . . ." "Though there is no legal disqualification, Catholics rarely attain to official honors in this country."[12]

Reconstruction, reform, romanism: these were the issues that led Charles O'Conor to question the forms of government that had been established by the "new American experiment" in democracy; to suggest reforms; and to devote his feared and admired legal abilities to questions of social and political justice.

Who was this fiery Irish-American pamphleteer? Charles O'Conor of New York was born in the United States in 1804, the first member of the O'Conors of Connacht, a family that traced its history back ten centuries and more through two of Ireland's last high kings and the traditional kings of ancient Connacht, to hold American citizenship.[13] Born in Ireland in 1770, Charles O'Conor's father, Thomas O'Connor, had, at the age of twenty-one, taken the oath of allegiance of the Society of United Irishmen, the revolutionary group whose espousal of French Jacobin ideas led to the ill-fated Irish rebellion of 1798.[14] Compelled to flee Ireland, following the defeat of French and rebel forces and the enactment of the Act of Union uniting Great Britain and Ireland, Thomas O'Connor found success elusive in the United States, even though he had been educated in the best European tradition by his grandfather, Charles O'Conor of Belanagare, the eminent eighteenth-century Gaelic scholar and historian. In succession Thomas O'Connor tried his hand at land colonization schemes for fellow Irish immigrants, a seed business, and finally the editorship of a series of weekly Irish-American newspapers published in New York City. In the columns of his own and other newspapers—among them, *The Shamrock*, *The Truth Teller*, and *The Hibernian Chronicle*—O'Connor worked to mobilize Irish-American sentiment for Catholic freedom in Ireland, explained doctrines of Catholicism to suspicious Anglo-Americans, argued for a share of public school funds for Catholics, fought to free Catholic children from the obligation of reading Protestant-oriented religious books in public schools, and supported the American publication and distribution of histories of Ireland. In addition to his journalistic campaigns, Thomas O'Connor worked steadily to help newly arrived Irish immigrants find employment as teachers, as customs house clerks, and as trade apprentices. Fiercely loyal to the country of his adoption, he also entered politics, rose to the position of Sachem of Tammany Hall before it became, after his death, a symbol of political corruption, and was nominated several times to political office including, in 1842, the office of Mayor of New York City. Although his work never had earned financial rewards and he had been dependent upon his son, Charles, for support during the last thirty years of his life, at his death in 1855 Thomas O'Connor was widely recognized as the "soul and voice of the New York Catholic Irish lay community."[15]

Thomas O'Connor's devotion to Irish and American liberty, to the principles of Jefferson and Jackson, and to the doctrines of the Catholic Church strongly influenced his only son, Charles, although the younger O'Conor also endured poverty, bigotry, and disappointment in the land of his birth. One of Charles O'Conor's early jobs was with a maker of lampblack, who hired him because, as a poor, young Irish-American unable to command higher wages, he could be underpaid. When O'Conor's demand for equitable pay was refused, he quit. The experience reinforced his father's arguments that poor Irish Catholics needed their own legal advocates if they were to secure the benefits of American justice and democracy.[16]

Charles O'Conor was educated at home, by his father, in the tradition of his ancestors, from whom he derived his strong, traditionally Irish belief in self-education. Thus, although poor, O'Conor found the means of preparing himself for a career in law through a series of apprenticeships in various New York City law offices. In these offices, from 1816 to 1823, he learned not only from observing his employers but also from early morning and late night study in their law libraries. Blackstone he read as a duty—twice. His prodigious memory, trained in the Irish tradition, enabled him to memorize much of Comyn's *Digest of English Common Law*. He developed a particular interest in precedent-setting cases from Irish law. Among those who assisted the solemn, industrious, although gaunt and ragged young man during these years was Joseph D. Fay, a practicing attorney who took O'Conor into his office and home because he "saw the signs of genius in him." Fay's son, Theodore Fay, later secretary of the United States legation in Berlin and United States minister to Switzerland, used to describe himself and O'Conor as "fellow students." "That is," Fay used to explain, "I was the fellow, he was the student."[17]

In 1824, at the age of twenty, O'Conor was admitted as an attorney to the Court of Common Pleas, where he was designated counselor after only three months despite a rule that specified two years' service as an attorney before the title, with its greater privileges and responsibilities, could be conferred. In the next three years he quickly built a successful practice in New York's Irish Sixth Ward, gaining admission to the Supreme Court as both attorney and counselor on the same day in 1827—again despite regulations that ordinarily specified a longer probationary period for admission to the more prestigious rank. Thereafter, O'Conor rose rapidly to preeminence in the New York Bar, achieving a respected reputation not only as a practicing attorney but also as a legal scholar. Contemporary accounts all mention his unusual memory. He was noted also for superb preparation—based on research of every relevant precedent in American, English, and Irish law—of each case he undertook, for eloquence, for cutting irony, and for sarcasm. When a decision went against him, he frequently used his considerable talents against the unfortunate judge, often resorting to letters to the newspaper to deride and destroy contrary opinion.[18]

In 1846 Charles O'Conor was nominated by all political parties to the convention to revise the New York State Constitution. Although one of a minority of six voting against adoption of the revised document—in O'Conor's opinion it did not go far enough in establishing those reform measures which he considered necessary—he did succeed in arguing for the reorganization of the courts that led to the establishment of the New York State Court of Appeals.[19] Within the next ten years his reputation as a "lawyer's lawyer" became so firmly established that his name was put forth several times for appointment to the office of attorney general of the United States, a position that O'Conor consistently declined. In 1864, when General George McClellan accepted the Democratic nomination for the presidency of the United States but refused to be bound by the peace proposals in the party platform, the *Freeman's Journal* called for the nomination of O'Conor, a "*new* and *true* standard bearer of the democracy, . . . the great and spotless man that the occasion demands."[20] At the end of the Civil War, O'Conor served as counsel to Jefferson Davis, former president of the Confederacy.[21] In 1869 O'Conor became president of the New York Law Institute, a post he held until 1878. In 1872 he was nominated for the presidency of the United States, with John Quincy Adams as his running mate, by a splinter group of the Democratic party meeting in Louisville. Despite the fact that O'Conor openly and publicly declined the nomination, it was repeated by a second splinter group meeting in Philadelphia, and election results showed that he polled a substantial number of votes in the contest that pitted Horace Greeley against Ulysses S. Grant as the major candidates.[22]

The major event of American politics of the seventies was the trial of the so-called Tweed Ring in New York City. In 1871 the mayor of New York, Abraham Oakey Hall, the comptroller, Richard B. Connolly, the commissioner of public works, William M. Tweed, and the president of public parks, a Mr. Sweeney, were implicated in a scandal in which the city of New York was bilked of more than $6,000,000. Tweed ("Boss" Tweed of Tammany Hall) was said to be the leader of the quartet; he was not only a powerful figure in the New York Democratic party and member of the city administration but also president of the Board of Supervisors and a state senator. Concerned citizens appealed to the governor of New York State for official action. The governor established a branch of the attorney general's office in New York City, headed by Charles O'Conor and three other New York City lawyers, with instructions to initiate proceedings against the conspirators. O'Conor's role in the successful prosecution, which took years and involved all the legal defensive tactics the Tweed lawyers could devise, is well-known; the story of the trial itself is often retold in print.[23] An eyewitness who attended the last court trial, in February, 1876, described the scene in which Charles O'Conor, special prosecutor for the people of the state of New York, coolly and methodically destroyed the Tweed defense, rising from his sick bed to administer the *coup de grâce:* "I saw the tall form of Charles O'Conor, pale, emaciated and feeble looking, with the collar of his greatcoat raised about his neck, slowly and painfully walking toward the bench. Almost every man in the Court Room rose to his feet, but maintained a respectful silence."[24]

O'Conor's last appearance on the national scene came in the aftermath of the disputed presidential election of 1876, when his longtime friend, the Democratic candidate Samuel J. Tilden, apparently defeated the Republican candidate, Rutherford B. Hayes, by a popular majority of over 200,000 votes, only to have his term as the nineteenth president of the United States denied him in February by an electoral commission. The climax of over two months of behind-the-scenes maneuvering and trading for the presidency of the United States provided Gore Vidal with materials for the concluding pages of his novel, *1876*: in chapter 13, Charles O'Conor is described on the floor of Congress on February 1, 1877, a respected elder statesman and Tilden's representative before the electoral commission.[25]

Charles O'Conor left New York in 1881, moving his 18,000-volume law library, including his comprehensive collection of Irish law books, into a specially constructed building near his new house on Nantucket Island. There he lived quietly the remaining eight years of his life, occasionally visiting New York in connection with some case in which his opinion had been requested. After his death on May 12, 1884, the people of Nantucket discovered that he had been the mysterious benefactor who had paid off the entire sum owed by the township, with the admonition that its townspeople never again burden themselves with what he considered to be that root of all evil, public debt.[26] In a memorial meeting of the bar of the court of the state of New York, May 23, 1884, and in essays later published by Chief Justice Charles P. Daly and John Bigelow, Charles O'Conor's contemporaries acknowledged that, despite his achievements, O'Conor's Irish Catholicism had been "a most serious political, social, and professional disadvantage" that had prevented his accomplishing even more of the goals he set for himself and his country.[27]

For Charles O'Conor of New York, reconstruction, reform, and romanism were related issues, symptomatic of "defects" in that "glorious though unfinished work," the American democratic system, that had been initiated by the founding fathers. The Constitution was, he believed, the best document that they could have devised at the time, when "history furnished no precise parallels" of "human experience under just systems of government." Reconstruction offered the opportunity to "detect and remedy . . . defects" that permitted the growth of special interest groups, concentrating power in what O'Conor described as a new kind of aristocracy. These he identified as political parties and officeholders, who maintained control over government institutions and enjoyed the benefits of privilege as, under European systems of government, control over government institutions and the benefits of privilege had been enjoyed by members of an inherited aristocracy.[28]

Special interest groups had obtained undemocratic power in the United States, according to O'Conor, because the founding fathers had made the mistake of incorporating aspects of European systems (by this, he clearly meant the British example) into their "glorious experiment" for want of a different and better model. Thus he challenged the effectiveness of checks and balances in the American system, based on principles of social and political equality, while acknowledging their usefulness in the English system in which he perceived each of the three estates as representing an interest group antagonistic to the others and therefore less likely to cooperate with the others against the general welfare.[29] He criticized the machinery of primogeniture that, in England and Ireland, had enabled the few to rule for centuries over the many, warning that inherited wealth is as effective in creating an aristocracy as inherited office. He asserted that a large military, naval, and civil service is inimical to the best interests of democracy, for it provides a means by which those who are in power provide employment and other benefits for those who support them in power at the cost of the multitude.[30] Thus, as he knew, did England maintain itself in Ireland by rewarding, through employment and legal privileges, members of what became known as "the Ascendancy." He declared that a legislative body with discretionary power to govern by special act—therefore the power to reward through legal privileges—is and always will be "an instrument in the hands of organized faction" that "operates for personal ends," wringing from the multitude "the fruits of their industry and the just acquisitions of lawful individual effort."[31] Such acts were familiar to him from his study of English and Irish law. "The framers of American institutions should drink charily at the fountains of European experience," O'Conor wrote; "they should accept no seeming analogies without first adapting . . . variations to our more beneficent and lofty career."[32]

Romanism, the pejorative term used to accuse Catholics of loyalty to a foreign power and, by implication, disloyalty to the United States, was, to O'Conor, simply evidence that—although the American system was based on the principle that all men were created equal, and although religious freedom, implicit in the Constitution, was guaranteed by the Bill of Rights—special interest groups, if not checked, could use their power to discriminate against adherents of a religion other than their own.[33] Prejudice and bigotry, therefore, were to him not separate problems but problems directly related to the fact that, in the Reconstruction period, the United States had reached the point at which a "second stage of democratic reform" was necessary.[34] Against those who would avoid Yankee prejudices by moving south—where, he acknowledged, Irish Catholicism was less of a social and economic disadvantage—he maintained that geography offered no permanent solutions. If Irish Catholics of the eighteenth and early nineteenth century had moved from Ireland to America to escape religious discrimination institutionalized in the Penal Laws, could they find the refuge they sought by moving again, this time from the Anglo-Protestant East Coast to another part of the North American continent?[35]

Charles O'Conor's opposition to the Civil War—shared by many other Irish-Americans, including those who fought on either side of the conflict—was rooted in his conviction that the United States was a union in which no one part could be allowed to coerce, oppress, or exercise dominion over any other, no matter what the conflict. He believed that this also was the conviction of the founding fathers—that it was through inexperience and oversight that they had left loopholes in the Constitution through which office holders were able to form the new kind of aristocracy with "all the evils incident to hereditary rule" that O'Conor perceived in nineteenth-century America. The worst of these powers, he declared, was the power of borrowing money on the public credit, which made possible the raising of armies and the waging of war, including civil war, and the protection of special interest groups in office.[36]

O'Conor's recommendations for legislative reform were radical, tempting, even Swiftian in the nature of the solutions to social and political problems they proposed: "Regulation by general laws would . . . reduce the volume of statute law, simplify its form, . . . diminish litigation and restrain corrupt practices. . . . Laws might become few, simple, and easily understood. We should not behold . . . a legislative body sitting for four months of each year, surrounded by a hired lobby, and engaged in confounding the courts and the people with two thousand pages of additional legislation, most of it hurriedly passed during the last week of the session in . . . confusion and disorder. . . ."[37] As for the executive branch of government, O'Conor suggested that "very controlling arguments might be offered to prove that in . . . extinguishing the great office of President, no sound public policy would be violated, nor any blight thrown upon the seemingly praiseworthy ambition of the demigods who from time to time arise among us, and captivated by the far-off prize, spend their lives in prodigious displays of ability for the purpose of establishing their claim to it. . . . The evils produced are an unavoidable consequence of placing such a prize in the arena of competition." No great leaders would thus be lost, according to O'Conor, for: "If we may judge the future by much of the past, no man inspired by a laudable ambition should regret the removal of this glittering bauble from his sight. . . . Those to whom natural gifts and laborious effort attracted just admiration have not been permitted to attain this exalted office. . . . The manipulators of the convention or of the ballot-box invariably set them aside and award the seat to persons little distinguished." Nor were O'Conor's arguments based on sour grapes: several times in his long and distinguished career, as noted above, he had refused public office, including nomination to the presidency of the United States. In place of a president, O'Conor suggested—perhaps the most Swiftian of his suggestions—a chief executive selected by lot once a month from among the national legislators.[38]

In 1839–40 Charles O'Conor visited Ireland, encouraged by his father's correspondence with his kinsmen of Connacht and by their cordial responses to requests for books written by Irish members of the family and for portraits of illustrious ancestors. Thereafter, correspondence continued between the American and Irish branches of the family, often accompanied by newspaper and journal articles, and in the years that followed, O'Conors of Ireland often visited Charles O'Conor in the United States. Thus during a period of major changes in both countries, the O'Conors exchanged information and views across the Atlantic.

Among the Irish relatives who corresponded frequently with Charles O'Conor of New York during the period of 1865–85 was Charles Owen O'Conor Don, M. P. It was to Charles Owen O'Conor Don, in the early years of the Reconstruction period, that Charles O'Conor of New York complained of the difficulties of instituting reforms or even rousing interest in reform among American officeholders: "There is scarcely any such thing as political philosophy or political morals. The party exigencies of the hour determine for every representative the necessary line of action and he cannot deviate from it." To O'Conor Don's acceptance of the English system, as adequate to the establishment of a republic, he put but two questions: "Why is Ireland poor and the other island prosperous? Does the Imperial Parliament discriminate against Ireland?" To those who believed the Constitution to be a perfect document, beyond improvement, O'Conor offered the example of the Civil War that had threatened to destroy the Union. The purpose of the Constitution was, he declared, to preserve republican institutions. These very nearly had perished "when the first calls for troops to coerce the South were responded to."[39]

Charles Owen O'Conor Don, M. P., was born in Ireland in 1838 of the same stock as Charles O'Conor of New York.[40] He too was a direct descendant of two of Ireland's last high kings and the traditional kings of ancient Connacht; Charles O'Conor of Belanagare, the eighteenth-century Gaelic scholar and historian, was his great-great-grandfather. Between 1800, the year in which Thomas O'Connor, the American O'Conor's father, fled Ireland, and 1859, the year in which Charles Owen O'Conor Don had taken his seat in Parliament, much had occurred in Ireland: in 1829 Catholic Emancipation permitted the election of Catholics to Parliament; in 1832 the enactment of the Poor Laws relieved in some measure the distress of the desperately poor; in 1846–48 the Famine, for which no relief measures were adequate, struck down nearly half the population.

Throughout these years, among the O'Conors who had remained in Connacht, traditions of scholarship, public service, defense of Gaelic Ireland, and struggle for Catholic Ireland continued to run strong. Denis, the eighteenth-century scholar's eldest son, who perceived education and financial security as important weapons in the war on anti-Catholicism, had devoted his life to improving and expanding family holdings, providing his many children with sufficient means to live with dignity if not in affluence, and maintaining pressure on the English government for relief for the Irish from the last of the eighteenth-century anti-Catholic Penal Laws. His eldest son, Owen, close friend of Daniel O'Connell, "The Liberator," and Thomas O'Connor's first cousin, had taken a leading role in the struggle for Catholic Emancipation. When Catholics were admitted to full civil rights in 1829, Owen was among the first elected to represent Ireland in the British Parliament. Owen's brother, Dr. Charles O'Conor, was librarian to the Duke of Buckingham at Stowe, a distinguished scholar like his grandfather and a controversial figure in

Catholic Church history who proposed 150 years too soon reforms similar to those adopted by Vatican II. Another brother, Mathew, a successful lawyer, also achieved recognition as an author and scholar. Owen's eldest son, Denis—Charles Owen O'Conor's father—was educated in fashionable English Catholic schools and traveled widely on the Continent before being elected to his father's place in Parliament. His distinguished career in Parliament included appointment as a Lord of the Treasury.

Poverty and the Rising of 1798, important influences on Charles O'Conor of New York through his father, were but stories out of family history to Charles Owen, in mid-nineteenth-century Ireland. Closer to his own childhood world were discussions of the tenant organizations that threatened the financial and physical security of the Irish landlord class into which he had been born; extension of suffrage; commitment on the part of affluent Catholics to education of the Catholic poor; the Famine of 1846-48, during which Charles Owen helped his aunts distribute food to the poor while his father tried to rouse the English bureaucracy to relief action; the Young Ireland movement; and aborted plans for a revolution in 1848. Orphaned by his father's death in 1847, when he was but nine years old—at which time he inherited the title "Don," designating him head of the O'Conors of Connacht—Charles Owen was tutored by his guardians in the necessity of carrying on family tradition. Educated in England, he was groomed for Parliament, where he assumed an elected seat in Commons, in accordance with family expectations, as soon as he became of age. Like his father before him, he traveled extensively on the Continent before settling down to family and parliamentary responsibilities. Throughout his life he continued to travel, recording in letters and journals his perceptive observations, satisfying his keen curiosity about what he saw through reading and talking with others, and using the world view he thus acquired to gain new perspectives on the social and economic problems with which he wrestled as a member and often as chairman of important parliamentary commissions. At home in Ireland, he worked to preserve Irish antiquities; strongly supported the Society for the Preservation of the Irish Language; published a one-volume history of the O'Conors of Connacht, completing research begun by John O'Donovan; and numbered among his friends such men as Martin Blake, a barrister and well-known antiquarian, and Douglas Hyde, scholar, author, and folklorist, a founding member of the Gaelic League and later first president of the Republic of Ireland.

In 1865-66 Charles Owen O'Conor Don traveled extensively

through the United States and Canada. He attended political rallies; visited prominent political figures; studied educational and penal institutions; talked with Irish-Americans and Irish-Canadians, Catholic and Protestant, from all walks of life; observed the Reconstruction Congress in session; met President Johnson and Civil War generals from both sides of the recent conflict; and listened to his traveling companion, formerly the Catholic chaplain at Andersonville, talk about the war. His journal of his 1865-66 tour of North America fills two notebooks; another journal, of a second trip in 1872, also contains detailed observations; his letters reflect not only what he learned from personal experience but also what he gleaned from reading and from correspondence and conversations with his American cousin. These reflections appear also in his drafts of speeches and reports for Parliament and in such essays as "Abolition of the Viceroyalty," "National Education," and "Representative Government," preserved in manuscript among the O'Conor Papers in Ireland.[41]

The differences as well as the similarities that mark the lives of Charles Owen O'Conor Don and Charles O'Conor of New York are significant.

The fact that both O'Conors viewed the Constitution as an interim draft for an experiment in progress was consistent with attitudes toward the American system expressed by Catholic Irishmen of the eighteenth and early nineteenth centuries. During the American Revolution, Charles O'Conor of Belanagare and his correspondents had exchanged news of the progress of the war and had speculated on its outcome. If the Americans were successful, they thought, Irish Catholics could determine the sincerity of promises of religious freedom: "Catholics of affluence" from County Kilkenny were prepared to emigrate as soon as hostilities ceased if guaranteed full civil rights by the new government. If the British were successful, Irish Catholics could petition King and Parliament for a regrant of the Maryland charter, thus establishing a colony in which Catholics would not be subject to anti-Catholic penal laws. In either case the New World would offer Catholics a new society in which their views might be considered and their voices might be heard.[42]

Organization of the Society for United Irishmen and plans for a French-supported rebellion increased Irish interest in the United States in the last decade of the eighteenth century. If the rebellion succeeded, participants would be safe in Ireland. If it failed, they would need a refuge. In 1791 an O'Conor—most likely Charles O'Conor's father, Thomas—briefly visited the United States, traveling along the eastern seaboard.[43] Correspondence of this period preserved in the O'Conor Papers in Ireland contains references to descriptions by others of Maryland and Pennsylvania, indicating the extent of interest in the new nation.[44] Letters written by Thomas O'Connor following his emigration to the United States confirmed that many "men of '98" had settled in New York. These letters also note the problems that beset new arrivals, the advantages of United States citizenship, and the opportunities for entering politics and thereby having a voice in the development of American society in its formative years.[45]

For men like Charles Owen O'Conor Don, however, the recommendations offered by Charles O'Conor of New York for reform of the American system must have sounded like anarchy. O'Conor Don's views of reconstruction, reform, and romanism in the United States between 1865 and 1885 were quite different. Party was the strength of the English system in which, in the nineteenth century, Ireland at least had gained a voice, however small. To him, party discipline was what stabilized a government that otherwise might be turned out of office over every issue, with consequent changes also in the ministry and therefore in the executive as well as the legislative branch. An inherited aristocracy also was a stabilizing force, although on the one hand the Irish experience made clear the necessity to maintain checks upon it; on the other hand, without support from peers beyond popular control, would Catholic Emancipation have been achieved? In the absence of an inherited aristocracy, a corps of professional office holders seemed to O'Conor Don a reasonable alternative.[46]

Reconstruction, therefore, to O'Conor Don, was a period that called for not reform or rewriting of the Constitution but for a realignment of factions. That factions themselves should exist and compete for power was, to him, natural; it indicated no such fundamental defect in the American system as that perceived by his American kinsman. Rather, the American scene in the years immediately following the Civil War fascinated him, for the war had fragmented old alliances and multiplied the potential for new combinations. His chief interest during his tour of North America in 1865–66, as indicated by his diaries, seems to have been the identification of factions, the assessment of their political strength, and the determination of the place old leaders might find in the new scheme of things. Among those factions in which O'Conor Don was most interested were the Irish, the Catholics, and the supporters of the Confederacy.[47]

In the Reconstruction period, as Charles Owen O'Conor Don observed, Irish-Americans assumed a new position in American society. Thousands had received training in the use of arms during the Civil War. These men, actively recruited into the Fenian Brotherhood, formed a political and military organization dedicated to freeing Ireland. In order to achieve their goal, they worked to incite revolution in Ireland and Canada, planned a military invasion of Canada, and were willing to risk even war between England and the United States. While funds for the organization were raised openly in monster rallies in the United States, Civil War veterans returned to Ireland to assume posts as military leaders of a rebel army. At the same time the political arm of the Fenian organization, meeting in Philadelphia in 1865, drafted an American-style constitution providing for a president and a congress and sought the support of major political parties in the United States. Aware that behind the Fenians was a sympathetic and populous Irish-American community, the Johnson administration in 1865 was reluctant, as O'Conor Don observed, to take public notice of their obviously illegal activities, even when they elected a secretary of war and openly revealed their plans. Johnson moved against them only to prevent a Maine-based Fenian assault on Canada in April 1866 and he was promptly criticized by politicians seeking Irish-American votes. Wooing the Irish-Americans in 1868, Grant's Republican supporters went even further, incorporating into the Republican platform a plank sympathizing with oppressed people "struggling for their rights."[48]

On November 3, 1865, Charles Owen O'Conor Don arrived in Jersey City, following a thirteen-day crossing of the Atlantic. It was election eve: in New York's Tammany Hall he heard speeches pledging that England would be made to pay its "just debts" and free Ireland. From New York, O'Conor Don traveled northward, stopping at West Point and discussing with General Michel in Montreal the latter's plan for the defense of Canada against a possible Fenian invasion. Crossing Canada, O'Conor Don discussed Fenianism and the possibility of an American invasion with Protestant and Catholic Irish-Canadians, comparing their attitudes with those of Irish-Americans. Moving south to Chicago, he continued his discussions with Irish-Americans, noting the connections between their religion, their party politics, and their support of Fenianism. From Chicago, he traveled down the Mississippi to St. Louis and New Orleans, observing the attitudes of voters toward Irishmen, Catholics, and blacks, then headed east and north, toward Washington, D.C., through the Old South.

What O'Conor Don took back with him when he returned to Ireland and England in 1866 was a careful assessment of the strength of Fenianism in the United States, its influence on American politics and politicians of the Reconstruction period, and its implications for Irish immigrants in America. Among his notes also there were passages scribbled out of the Declaration of Independence, the Constitution of the United States, and the Constitution of the State of Massachusetts, in which the words "free" and "independent" were heavily underlined.[49] Had O'Conor Don examined these documents only as a Member of Parliament, with an academic interest in the workings of the American system? Had he taken notes merely for use in his discussions with his reform-oriented American cousin? Or did he feel that, since the political arm of the Fenians called for establishing an American-style government in a free Ireland, with a president and congress, he ought to understand the workings of the American system? Among the letters with which he returned were some from Irish-Americans, hailing him as king of Ireland, and pledging their support should ever there come a time when Ireland free could once again set an Irish monarch upon an Irish throne.[50]

As for reform, for the most part O'Conor Don's interests were specific. In Ireland, he was deeply involved in the problems of bringing education to the Catholic poor at reasonable expense. How was the new American nation able to provide public schools for its children? In Parliament, he had been charged with responsibility for recommending reforms in the prison system. How did the several states, with their different criminal laws and separately administered penal institutions, treat its felons? The idea that England might learn how to institute necessary reforms in these areas from its former American colonies through an Irishman must have been irresistible to him; the prospect of increased bureaucracy and the proliferation of government offices did not trouble him. As for problems of political corruption, he noted them dutifully, repeating in his diaries what his American cousin told him of their extent and nature. But his nineteenth-century Irish background, his training in Parliament, and his conviction that progress was best achieved in a climate of social and political stability made him wary of American-style radical reform. He preferred the English method of appointing investigatory commissions.

Thus these two O'Conors—the one dedicated to the American system, suspicious of England, and shaped by an Irish ethnic background; the other shaped by English influences, dedicated to Ireland, and wary of the American system—discussed America and debated the issues that engaged the public mind in the years 1865–85. Both, like their contemporary, the poet Walt Whitman, heard America singing—even if each wished for changes in both the timing and the tune. Both surely would have agreed with Whitman—Charles O'Conor of New York with enthusiasm for and yet impatience with the "glorious experiment," O'Conor Don with fascination and a certain scepticism—that

> These States are the amplest poem,
> Here is not merely a nation but
> a teeming Nation of nations.

NOTES

1 This essay, originally published in *Éire-Ireland*, vol. 15, no. 3 (Fall 1980), is reprinted by permission of the Irish American Cultural Institute. It has been expanded and developed from the Seventh Annual Morris Fromkin Memorial Lecture of the same title presented by the authors, recipients of the 1976 Fromkin Research Grant, at the University of Wisconsin–Milwaukee, November 4, 1976.

2 Cf. Leo Hershkowitz, *Tweed's New York: Another Look* (New York: Doubleday and Company, 1976). In an interview reported in *The New York Times*, October 17, 1976, pp. 1, 58, Professor Hershkowitz asserted that "William M. (Boss) Tweed, for a century the leading symbol of urban corruption, did not rule New York City government; was the victim of illegal procedures at his trial; made important contributions to the city's growth, often showing more vision than the reformers; was persecuted to divert attention from much greater Republican corruption in Washington because he was a champion of immigrants; and may have been the victim of greedy contractors who looted the city treasury, rather than their master." Professor Hershkowitz's assertions concerning Tweed himself are not consistent with the contemporary account of the Tweed Ring trials, *Peculation Triumphant, Being the Record of a Four Years' Campaign against Official Malversation in the City of New York, A.D. 1871 to 1875* (New York: John Polhemus, Printer, 1875), written by Charles O'Conor; they are consistent, however, with O'Conor's later writings which make clear his perception, too, that corruption was not confined to Tammany Hall, or even New York City. As noted later in the text, O'Conor served as special prosecutor in the Tweed trials; his opinions concerning Tweed were based, therefore, on the evidence he had before him.

3 *The Diary of George Templeton Strong*, ed. Allan Nevins and Milton Halsey Thomas (New York: Macmillan and Company, 1952), 3:342–43. Cf. "the recurring chorus of praise and abuse" quoted by Edward Wakin, *Enter the Irish-American* (New York: Thomas Y. Crowell Company, 1976), pp. 4–5, and Lawrence J. McCaffrey's examination of the nineteenth-century social,

economic, and political climate, *The Irish Diaspora in America* (Bloomington: Indiana University Press, 1976).

4 For a fuller description of the incident and its aftermath, widely reported in contemporary newspapers, see Wakin, *Enter the Irish-American,* pp. 105–7, and Florence E. Gibson, *The Attitudes of the New York Irish toward State and National Affairs, 1848–1892* (New York: Columbia University Press, 1951), p. 390.

5 Published as an introduction to *Democracy* by Charles O'Conor. Sunny Side Tracts—first series, no. 1 (Scarborough, New York: The Sunny Side Printing Company, 1876), p. 3

6 Ibid., pp. 34, 35.

7 In 1876, published as a preface (pp. 5–8) to *Democracy.*

8 O'Conor, *Democracy,* p. 6.

9 Ibid., pp. 20–21.

10 Ibid., p. 21.

11 Ibid., p. 21.

12 Unpublished letters, Charles O'Conor to Charles Owen O'Conor Don, M. P., March 8, 1864, and October 5, 1863, preserved among the O'Conor Papers, Clonalis House, Castlerea, Co. Roscommon, Ireland. Cf. Gareth W. Dunleavy and Janet E. Dunleavy, *The O'Conor Papers: A Descriptive Catalogue and Surname Register of the Materials at Clonalis House* (Madison: University of Wisconsin Press, 1977), 9.3.HS.262. The authors gratefully acknowledge permission from the Trustees of the Estate of O'Conor Don to consult and quote from these and other letters, diaries, and notebooks identified as among the O'Conor Papers.

13 The following accounts of the careers of Charles O'Conor of New York and his father, Thomas O'Connor, have been drawn for the most part from materials among the O'Conor Papers at Clonalis House (see n. 12 above) and from the Thomas O'Connor Papers on loan from Mrs. Robert Hufstader to the American Irish Historical Society, New York City. The authors wish to acknowledge permission from Mrs. Hufstader to consult and quote from the Thomas O'Connor Papers and to thank the American Irish Historical Society for its cooperation in making them available to us.

14 Throughout his life Thomas O'Connor used the double-*n* spelling of his surname, although following a trip to Ireland in 1839–40 his son, Charles O'Conor, adopted the traditional single-*n* spelling used by his Irish relatives and his ancestors. Cf. summaries of documents that contain discussions of the spelling of the O'Conor family name in Dunleavy and Dunleavy, *The O'Conor Papers,* 9.2.HS.298, 9.3.SH.335, 9.4.HO.041, 9.4.HL.137.

15 George Potter, *To the Golden Door: The Story of the Irish in Ireland and America* (Boston: Little, Brown, 1960), p. 182.

16 Joseph C. Walsh, "Charles O'Conor," *The Journal of the American Irish Historical Society* 27 (1928): 291.

17 Charles P. Daly, "Charles O'Conor: His Professional Life and Character," *Magazine of American History* 13:6 (June 1885):517.

18 Ibid., pp. 525-26.

19 Ibid., p. 529.
20 Quoted by Gibson, *The Attitudes of the New York Irish*, pp. 166–67.
21 Walsh, "Charles O'Conor," p. 298. For more than two years O'Conor worked to free Davis from jail and from federal indictment. His efforts on behalf of Davis, who was released in May, 1867, under the terms of the General Amnesty, as the result of an agreement between O'Conor and the prosecution, usually are cited as the reason why O'Conor was not asked finally to undertake the defense of President Andrew Johnson in Johnson's 1868 trial for impeachment, although O'Conor's name frequently was mentioned by Johnson's supporters: public sentiment against anyone perceived to be pro-South at that time would have made O'Conor more a political liability than an asset.
22 Ibid., p. 300.
23 The first account was Charles O'Conor's *Peculation Triumphant* (1875); the most recent was Leo Hershkowitz's *Tweed's New York* (1976). An extensive bibliography measures the years between them.
24 Matthew P. Breen, *Thirty Years of New York Politics* (New York: The Author, 1899), p. 546.
25 Hershkowitz, *Tweed's New York*, pp. 335–37.
26 Walsh, "Charles O'Conor," p. 301.
27 *Report of A Meeting of the Bar Association of the Court of the State of New York and of the United States for the Second Circuit Held in the City of New York on Friday, May 23, 1884*; Daly, "Charles O'Conor," pp. 513-35; John Bigelow, "Some Recollections of Charles O'Conor," *Century Magazine* 7 (March 1885):725–36. Cf. also Walsh, "Charles O'Conor," p. 303.
28 Open letter to Democratic Convention, Louisville, Kentucky, August 31, 1872, reprinted in *Democracy*, pp. 5–6; *Democracy*, p. 14.
29 Open letter to Democratic Convention, Louisville, Kentucky, August 31, 1872, reprinted in *Democracy*, p. 5.
30 Charles O'Conor, *The Constitutions* (New York: Randolph and Company, 1877), pp. 23–24.
31 Ibid., p. 27.
32 Ibid., p. 18.
33 Open letter to Democratic Convention, Louisville, Kentucky, August 31, 1872, reprinted in *Democracy*, p. 5; *Democracy*, p. 17.
34 Open letter to Democratic Convention, Louisville, Kentucky, August 31, 1872, reprinted in *Democracy*, p. 6.
35 Unpublished letter, Charles O'Conor of New York to Charles Owen O'Conor Don, March 8, 1864; Dunleavy and Dunleavy, *The O'Conor Papers*, 9.3.HS.262.
36 Open letter to Democratic Convention, Louisville, Kentucky, August 31, 1872, reprinted in *Democracy*, pp. 6–7; *Democracy*, p. 13.
37 Ibid., p. 26.
38 O'Conor, *The Constitutions*, pp. 34–37.
39 Unpublished letters, Charles O'Conor of New York to Charles Owen O'Conor Don, May 19, July 23, September 6, 1867; Dunleavy and Dun-

leavy, *The O'Conor Papers*, 9.3.HS.332.
40 The following accounts of the careers of Charles Owen O'Conor Don, M. P., and his forebears have been drawn from materials among the O'Conor Papers at Clonalis House (see. n. 12 above); see also Dunleavy and Dunleavy, *The O'Conor Papers*, pp. ix–xxiv.
41 Cf. Dunleavy and Dunleavy, *The O'Conor Papers*, 9.3.HN.117, 9.3.HS.200, 9.3.HS.249, 9.3.SE.290, 9.3.SH.306, 9.3.HL.308, 9.3.HS.337, 9.4.HL.156.
42 Cf. ibid., 8.4.HS.143.
43 Cf. ibid., 8.4.SH.126.
44 Cf. ibid., 8.4.SH.126, 8.4.HS.143.
45 Unpublished letter, Thomas O'Connor to Eliza MacDermot, June 23, 1842, cf. Dunleavy and Dunleavy, *The O'Conor Papers*, 9.2.SH.131; unpublished letters, Thomas O'Connor Papers, undated (2), April 30, 1839, December 12, 1842, March 27, 1843, October 4, 1846, June 5, 1849.
46 Cf. manuscript essay, "Representative Government," O'Conor Papers, Dunleavy and Dunleavy, *The O'Conor Papers*, 9.3.HL.308.
47 Cf. ibid., 9.3.HS.249.
48 T. W. Moody, "Fenianism, Home Rule, and the Land War," *The Course of Irish History*, ed. T. W. Moody and F. X. Martin (New York: Weybright and Talley, 1967), pp. 278–79; Rembert W. Patrick, *The Reconstruction of the Nation* (New York: Oxford University Press, 1967), pp. 137, 197–98; Wakin, *Enter the Irish-American*, pp. 140–43.
49 Cf. Dunleavy and Dunleavy, *The O'Conor Papers*, 9.3.SH.133.
50 Cf. ibid., 9.3.SH.133, 9.3.SH.170, 9.3.HS.200, 9.4.HL.156.

BIBLIOGRAPHY

Bigelow, John. "Some Recollections of Charles O'Conor." *Century Magazine* 7 (March 1885):725–36.

Breen, Matthew P. *Thirty Years of New York Politics*. New York: The Author, 1899.

Daly, Charles P. "Charles O'Conor: His Professional Life and Character." *Magazine of American History* 13 (June 1885): 513-35.

Dunleavy, Gareth W., and Dunleavy, Janet E. *The O'Conor Papers: A Descriptive Catalogue and Surname Register of the Materials at Clonalis House*. Madison: University of Wisconsin Press, 1977.

Gibson, Florence E. *The Attitudes of the New York Irish toward State and National Affairs, 1848–1892*. New York: Columbia University Press, 1951.

Hershkowitz, Leo. *Tweed's New York: Another Look*. New York: Doubleday and Company, 1976.

McCaffrey, Lawrence J. *The Irish Diaspora in America*. Bloomington: Indiana University Press, 1976.

Moody, T. W. "Fenianism, Home Rule, and the Land War." In *The Course of Irish History*, edited by T. W. Moody and F. X. Martin. New York: Weybright and Talley, 1967.

New York Times, October 17, 1976.

O'Conor, Charles. *The Constitutions.* New York: Randolph and Company, 1877.

O'Conor, Charles. *Democracy.* Sunny Side Tracts—first series, no. 1. Scarborough, New York: The Sunny Side Printing Company, 1876.

O'Conor, Charles. *Peculation Triumphant, Being the Record of a Four Years' Campaign against Malversation in the City of New York, A.D. 1871–1875.* New York: John Polhemus, Printer, 1875.

Patrick, Rembert W. *The Reconstruction of the Nation.* New York: Oxford University Press, 1967.

Potter, George W. *To the Golden Door: The Story of the Irish in Ireland and America.* Boston: Little, Brown, 1960.

Report of a Meeting of the Bar Association of the Court of the State of New York and of the United States for the Second Circuit Held in the City of New York on Friday, May 23, 1884.

Strong, George Templeton. *The Diary of George Templeton Strong.* Edited by Allan Nevins and Milton Halsey Thomas. 4 vols. New York: Macmillan and Company, 1952.

Wakin, Edward. *Enter the Irish American.* New York: Thomas Y. Crowell Company, 1976.

Walsh, Joseph C. "Charles O'Conor." *Journal of the American Irish Historical Society* 27 (1928):285–313.

Eighth Annual Morris Fromkin Memorial Lecture

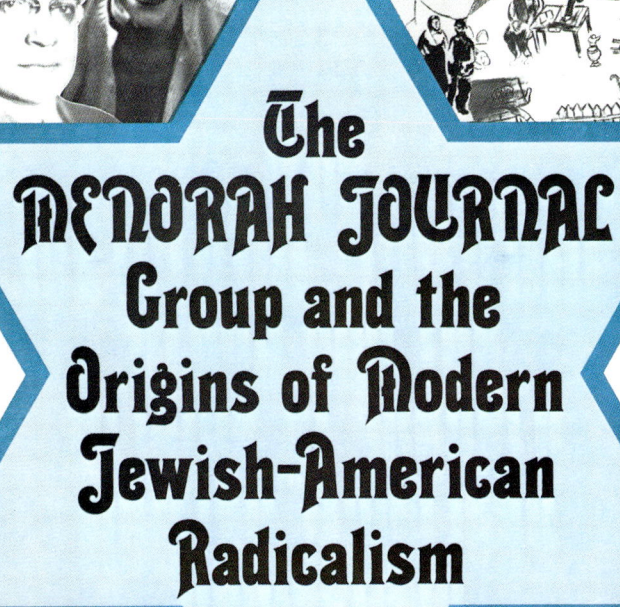

The MENORAH JOURNAL Group and the Origins of Modern Jewish-American Radicalism

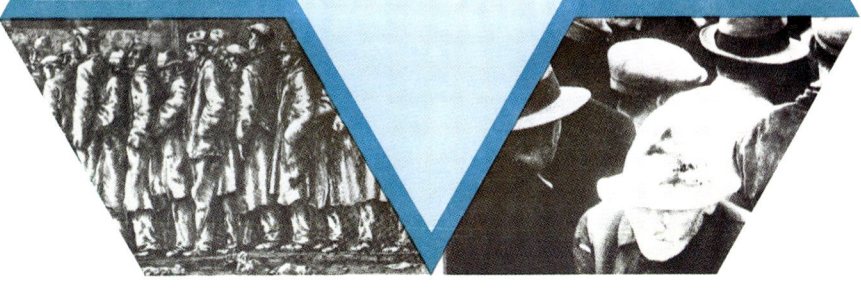

MARK L. KRUPNICK
Associate Professor of English
THE UNIVERSITY OF WISCONSIN—MILWAUKEE
Recipient of the
1977 Fromkin Research Grant

October 19, 1977
Wednesday
3:30 p.m.

The public is cordially invited to attend.
Reception follows.

UWM Library
East Wing,
First Floor

SPONSORED BY THE FROMKIN MEMORIAL COLLECTION OF THE UWM LIBRARY.

The Menorah Journal *Group* and the Origins of Modern Jewish-American Radicalism

MARK L. KRUPNICK

JEWISH-American intellectuals flocked to the radical movement of the 1930s. In this essay I want to consider the specifically Jewish aspect of Jewish-American radicalism by suggesting the continuities between the cultural radicalism of Jewish critics of the organized Jewish community in the late twenties and their political radicalism as communists in the early thirties. My emphasis is on the seedtime—the late twenties at the *Menorah Journal*—rather than on this group's political history in the next decade.[1]

The *Menorah Journal* group were founders, the first generation of a great dynasty which established itself during the Depression and which lingers on today, however moribund. There are still Jewish intellectuals, but no longer a coherent Jewish intelligentsia. This, at least, is the verdict of Irving Howe, who wrote the death notice in 1968 in an essay called "The New York Intellectuals."[2] In an autobiography published at about the same time, Norman Podhoretz spoke of this same intelligentsia as "the family."[3] He, too, agreed that the family was breaking up. In the late twenties at the *Menorah Journal* it was just getting started. Lionel Trilling and Elliot Cohen and Herbert Solow[4] had no consciousness of themselves as patriarchs. They were just young men writing for a Jewish magazine and satirizing the culture and institutions of their Jewish elders. They were preoccupied

---

Mark Krupnick, a graduate of Harvard College and Brandeis University, is editor of *Displacement: Literary Theory After Structuralism* (University of Illinois Press) and is preparing separate critical studies of Lionel Trilling and of the New York Intellectuals. From 1970 to 1972 Dr. Krupnick was associate editor of *Modern Occasions,* a journal edited by Philip Rahv.

with Jewish identity, Jewish writing, Jewish communal life. If they had not abandoned Jewish particularism for more universalist concerns in the crisis that followed 1929, we would not be talking about them today. But their early phase of Jewish self-consciousness deserves to be remembered. It imparted to their later writing, and to the writing of later waves of the New York intellectuals, something of its characteristic style and subject matter.

Who were the Jewish intellectuals? What got started at the *Menorah Journal* in the later twenties? "The family" may best be seen as a regional grouping united by a shared social history and a common intellectual concern summed up in their great debate, now over fifty years old, about Marxism. Building on the work of the founders, they created in New York during the Depression years this country's first European-style intelligentsia, such as we associate with the Paris of Sartre or St. Petersburg in Dostoevsky's time. The influence of the group on American cultural and moral opinion during the past thirty years has been immense. As a kind of shorthand, I might mention a few of the periodicals that have spread that influence—*Partisan Review* (started 1934), *Commentary* (started 1945), *The New York Review of Books* (started 1963), and *The Public Interest* (started 1965). Also, I might mention some of the better-known writers and intellectuals who have been part of this intelligentsia. Others besides Trilling, Cohen, and Solow in the first generation of "the family" were Sidney Hook (b. 1902), Harold Rosenberg (1906–78), Paul Goodman (1911–72), Clement Greenberg (b. 1909), and Lionel Abel (b. 1910). Many of them were communists in the early thirties and had become anti-Stalinist radicals by the end of the decade. A later wave, which made its appearance in the early forties, included Delmore Schwartz (1913–66), Saul Bellow (b. 1915), Isaac Rosenfeld (1918–56), and Alfred Kazin (b. 1915). They were succeeded in turn by a third wave, which included Leslie Fiedler (b. 1917), Irving Howe (b. 1920), Daniel Bell (b. 1919), Nathan Glazer (b. 1923), and Irving Kristol (b. 1920). Norman Podhoretz (b. 1930), the current editor of *Commentary* magazine, was himself a central figure in a succeeding generation which appeared on the scene in the fifties. Apart from this last wave, which came of age in the era of Cold War, almost all of the Jewish intellectuals started out as radicals and in almost every case moved at least a few notches to the right as they grew older.

The New York intellectuals were for the most part not religious. Their Jewishness was wholly secular, a quality of self-consciousness rather than a doctrine. It was a matter of Jewishness, not Judaism. It is difficult to define the content of that Jewishness in most cases, because few of the Jewish intellectuals wrote about it explicitly. The

Menorah Journal group, the first generation of "the family," was atypical in this respect, and hence valuable for my purpose. They had started out explicitly espousing an ideology of Jewish culture and Jewish identity.

But what was the *Menorah Journal*? In 1925, when Elliot Cohen took over as managing editor, the magazine had been in existence for ten years, publishing articles on the Jewish past and on the current scene in America and the world over and also publishing new creative work by Jewish poets and storytellers. The editor was Henry Hurwitz,[5] a Lithuanian immigrant who was forty years old in 1925 and in all respects a man of an earlier generation than that of the Cohen circle, all of whom were in their twenties, and almost all American-born and American in outlook. Hurwitz was himself less an intellectual than the promoter of a Jewish cultural movement. The *Menorah Journal* was the creature of the Menorah movement, which had begun with Hurwitz's founding of the first Menorah Society at Harvard in 1906 and which by the twenties embraced a hundred or so Menorah Societies at colleges and universities all over America. The idea was to promote Jewish ideals and learning among Jewish college students so as to offset the negative effects of American anti-Semitism. By demonstrating the interest and dignity of the Jewish past, the Menorah movement encouraged its members to accept and identify themselves as Jews. The hope was that the damage to Jewish self-esteem caused by anti-Semitism might be repaired by the Jew's accepting his difference and finding strength in it. A quotation from an essay in the *Menorah Journal* in 1927, on "The Jew as Radical," suggests the purpose of the magazine and the movement. As the writer, Maurice Hindus, put it: "The Jew must remain a torment to himself, and an annoyance if not a nuisance to others, so long as he fails to make it part of his ethical consciousness that he has as much right to indulge in the expression of his own nature—without the constant fear of the disapprobation of other peoples—as has the Frenchman or the Englishman." The purpose, then, was to normalize the American Jew's sense of himself.

The journal was the voice of the Menorah movement, but it was always something more than a house organ. By 1925 it was one of the better literary quarterlies in the country, with a national circulation and prestige that drew to it such established Jewish writers as Ludwig Lewisohn (1882–1955), Maurice Samuel (1895–1972), Mordecai Kaplan (b. 1881), Waldo Frank (1889–1967), Harry Wolfson (1887–1974), and Israel Zangwill (1864–1926). Its non-Jewish contributors included Lewis Mumford (b. 1895), Mark Van Doren (1894–1972), and Charles Beard (1874–1948).

The kind of articles the journal published may be suggested by some representative titles: Lewis Mumford on "Herzl's Utopia," Horace Kallen asking "Can Judaism Survive in the United States?," Waldo Frank's "Toward an Analysis of the Problem of the Jew," Ludwig Lewisohn's "The Fallacies of Assimilation," and Mordecai Kaplan's "Toward a Reconstruction of Judaism." Add plays, poems, and stories by writers like Charles Reznikoff, Babette Deutsch, and Meyer Levin, and it added up to a very mixed bag. Scholarly articles such as that on "Economic Conditions of Palestine in the Time of Jesus of Nazareth" jostled work of contemporary sensibility such as an excerpt in 1930 from Mike Gold's proletarian novel *Jews Without Money*.[6] The eclectic character of the journal was intensified by its freedom from any specific denominational tie. In all the years of its operation, up to its demise shortly after Henry Hurwitz's death in 1961, the journal never had regular support from any wing of religious Jews or from any agency of Jewish philanthropy.

In 1925 the *Menorah Journal* was widely respected but also a little staid. It needed a firmer hand, a grand design, to make it more lively and pertinent. This Elliot Cohen arrived to provide. Cohen, the son of a Jewish general store merchant in Mobile, Alabama, had studied English and philosophy at Yale and graduated in 1917. He spent a few years in graduate school and at desultory jobs before joining the journal in 1923, when he was twenty-four years old. From then until 1931, when he resigned from the journal, Cohen introduced a new tone and approach and a whole new group of contributors, his "family," as he called them. Almost all of them had been born in 1904 or 1905, and many had been at Columbia College in the early twenties.

These young writers, whom I am referring to as the *Menorah Journal* group, included Lionel Trilling, who became in later years an internationally renowned literary critic; Clifton Fadiman (b. 1904), who later became a judge for the Book-of-the-Month Club; Herbert Solow, a radical journalist who later turned against radicalism and became a valued writer for *Fortune* magazine; Anita Brenner (1905–74), who studied anthropology at Columbia and wrote a number of works about Mexico; Tess Slesinger,[7] an author of short stories and of a novel, *The Unpossessed*, which satirized the group; Albert Halper (b. 1904), who became well known in the thirties for his novel *Union Square*; Felix Morrow, a journalist and later a political activist on the left; and Henry Rosenthal (1906–77), who was studying for the rabbinate in the late twenties and later became a professor of philosophy at Hunter College.

What the group had in common, besides the apprenticeship at Columbia which bound some of them, was a powerfully negative attitude toward American middle-class society, which became especially negative when it directed itself against that aspect of society it knew best: the institutions and ideology of the organized Jewish community. Most of the *Menorah Journal* group were middle class in background and many had as fathers well-off businessmen. Perhaps because they knew it so well, they bent their formidable satiric talents against the staid respectability of their elders. So long as their criticism confined itself to questions of Jewish culture, the Jewish community tolerated their criticism as a form of naughtiness. But when, after the stock market crash of 1929, the cultural criticism of the *Menorah Journal* group modulated into a fundamental political attack, they were cast out.

For a time, however, the journal provided a spiritual home for this group and a way of thinking about society and personal identity. Lionel Trilling's example is typical. Trilling's very first publication appeared in the journal in 1925, when he was twenty years old and a senior at Columbia. Between then and 1931 Trilling published a translation, four more short stories, and eighteen reviews in the journal.[8] Almost every piece touched on the problem of Jewishness in one way or another.

A short story of 1927, when Trilling was only twenty-two, dramatizes the ideal of Jewish self-realization he had adopted through his association with the journal. The story was published soon after Trilling returned from the University of Wisconsin at Madison, where he had taught for a year after completing his M.A. at Columbia. The story, given the ironic title "Funeral at the Club, with Lunch," concerns a new instructor, a Jew in an otherwise Gentile department, and his anxiety at the funeral of an English Department colleague. What the instructor fears is a unity in grief among the surviving colleagues that will make him feel his own separateness and difference as an outsider and a newcomer. For the first time the instructor is brought face to face with the chief element in his sense of difference—his Jewishness. He is also brought face to face with his previously unacknowledged wish to transcend that difference. Why should he be branded because of the noisiness, vulgarity, and pushiness which others and sometimes he himself attribute to his race? He confronts his deep wish to ally himself with what he takes to be Christian refinement as against what he regards as Jewish crudity. Thinking on his bland, mild-mannered departmental colleagues, he remembers: "He had wanted this sort of society, cultivated men living pleasantly, well-mannered, civilized, among whom he could be one. . . ." (p. 386).

These value terms—"cultivated," "well-mannered," "civilized"—

are recognizably the positives of the Trilling who in later years would make himself over into the American Matthew Arnold. But in 1927 Trilling was testing the limits of genteel assimilationism, rather than affirming it, as he later did. The story is set up this way to underline the instructor's reversal, his repudiation of Gentile civility in favor of a specifically Jewish solution more in keeping with the Menorah ideal. The instructor finds that his colleagues are not unified in grief. They have not cared at all about the dead professor. The fact is they are incapable of getting excited about anything, and in their blandly tolerant way they show themselves willing enough to accept the stranger. But now the Jewish instructor is not ready to accept them. Noting their passionless response to death, he repudiates them for what he takes to be their spiritual emptiness, their lack of moral energy. Their very tolerance damns them in the newcomer's eyes. From here on, he decides, he will insist on his difference, dedicate himself to aloneness. His Jewishness will be a "liberating fetter" (p. 387), as he says.

The story affirms a specifically Jewish tradition of rebellion, which Hannah Arendt has called the tradition of the conscious pariah.[9] This had been the mode of rebellion popularized in the generation before Trilling's by the Jewish novelist and critic Ludwig Lewisohn,[10] and the solitude of the self-chosen pariah became one implication of the Menorah ideal of positive Jewishness.

After Trilling's break with the journal in 1931, he never again affirmed this uncomfortable and unsociable ideal. Indeed he hardly ever referred again to his Jewishness. In 1944 he interrupted his silence on the Jewish question to lash out against "the impasse of sterility" to which the American Jewish community had been reduced. His harshest words were for the Menorah ideal he had once espoused. That ideal, of a specifically Jewish self-realization, Trilling wrote, had fostered a false "'adjustment' on a wholly neurotic basis. It fostered," he said, "a willingness to accept exclusion and even to intensify it, a willingness to be provincial and parochial."[11] Trilling's later attitude toward the *Menorah Journal*'s ideology of positive Jewishness can be said to represent the working attitude of most of the other members of his group following their traumatic break with the journal in 1931. Most would also have seconded Trilling's damning judgment that "As the Jewish community now exists it can give no sustenance to the American artist or intellectual who is born a Jew" (p. 17). It may be illuminating now to trace the course which led Trilling and his friends at the *Menorah Journal* first to affirm their Jewishness as the central fact of their being and later to reject, if not

Jewishness, at least Jewishness as defined by the journal and by the dominant institutions in the American Jewish community.

The central fact about their situation was pervasive American anti-Semitism which excluded Jews from certain areas of the general life. Anti-Semitism was increasing in the twenties because the Jews themselves were bettering their status so rapidly, their social and cultural as well as their economic status. The recently arrived immigrants and their children were knocking at the gates, seeking the full privileges and opportunities of middle-class society. Making a lot of money but remaining within the Jewish ghetto was not for the immigrants' children an acceptable solution. The Jewish enrollment at the great universities now ballooned, so that in the early twenties, when the core members of the *Menorah Journal* group were undergraduates, nearly 40 percent of the students at Columbia College were Jewish. A great expansion also occurred at Harvard, where the president, Abbott Lawrence Lowell, publicly expressed dismay.[12] Fearful that they would turn into the Ivy League equivalents of City College of New York, Columbia and Harvard now instituted quotas.[13] And even if Jewish enrollments could not be restricted, presumably for financial reasons, as at New York University, the proportion of Jewish instructors could be limited. Felix Morrow, one of the *Menorah Journal* group, reported in the magazine in 1930 that out of 7,000 students in the liberal arts division of New York University 93 percent were Jewish, but the percentage of Jewish instructors was less than 1 percent.[14]

The most important effect of anti-Semitism was its impact on Jewish self-consciousness, what we would call the Jew's self-image. It made them apologize for themselves. Apology took different forms. One form was the anxious warning of German Jews to the more recently arrived East European Jews not to make a spectacle of themselves, not to act too Jewish. The Jewishness of Walter Lippmann, political writer and a third-generation American of German-Jewish descent, reduced to warning less decorous, newly arrived Jews that they were becoming an embarrassment. Lippmann, the totally assimilated *New Republic* liberal, worried that Jewish ostentation would undermine what he regarded as the natural liberalism of the host culture. Obviously, for Lippmann, Jews expressing their own nature was no solution if being natural meant being pretentious and vulgar. He wrote in 1922 in a Jewish periodical: "I waste no time worrying about the injustices of anti-Semitism. There is too much injustice in the world for any particular concern about summer hotels and college fraternities. . . . I worry about the Jewish smart-set in New York. . . . They can in one minute unmake more respect and decent human kindliness than Einstein and Brandeis and Mack and Paul Warburg can build up in a year. . . ."[15]

Walter Lippmann's comments suggest the worries of assimilated Central European Jews that they would be despised along with their greenhorn brethren. Apology took other forms as well. Jewish insecurity and self-doubt were expressed not only by Jews outside the organized Jewish community but also by Jews within. If Lippmann chastised the parvenu Jews for indecorous conduct, the rabbis and community spokesmen, in contrast, laid down a more affirmative line. Be proud of your Jewishness, the lodge-orators intoned. But instead of offering good reasons for pride, they offered only a blend of racial self-congratulation and Rotarianism as empty of positive content as Walter Lippmann's assimilationism.

Self-effacement on the one hand, a compensatory self-adulation on the other: assimilation or chauvinism. These opposing but complementary themes define the apologetic structure of Jewish communal ideology in the American 1920s. It was the chauvinism that Elliot Cohen attacked. He took it as his mission at the *Menorah Journal* to purge American Judaism of its puerile spirit of brag and bluster. In Cohen's view the bumptiousness of official Jewish spokesmen was a sign not of confidence but of a cultural inferiority complex.

When he took over at the *Menorah Journal* in the mid-twenties, Cohen initiated his grand design of a wholesale reconstruction of Jewish communal life. The conservative Henry Hurwitz remained nominally the editor, but Cohen moved quickly to recruit a group of younger writers who shared his disdain for the Jewish Establishment. Cohen's long 1925 article "The Age of Brass"[16] became the manifesto of the *Menorah Journal* group and inaugurated in its pages a golden age of satire. Cohen's article called for a transformation of Jewish-American values away from the philosophy of apology to the making of a culture with real intellectual content. But what was the real intellectual content? The positive aspect of Cohen's essay was vague—he was always vague and half-hearted when it came to positives—but his attack on the Jewish community was precise and vivid. Three years before, when he was not yet working for the magazine, Cohen had offered Henry Hurwitz an outline for an article he wanted to write on the American Reform Rabbinate in which he promised to be "intemperate, malicious, violent and altogether impolite and inconsiderate." In "The Age of Brass" and during the years that followed at the *Menorah Journal,* Cohen made good on that promise.

Commenting in his essay on Jewish communal life, Cohen wrote: "We are a people who have come a long way and are at last lost" (p.

427). Citing examples from the speeches and articles of rabbis and Jewish journalists and philanthropists, Cohen attacked what he called the "blatant, self-praising, vainglorious" voice of American-Jewish chauvinism (p. 433). He argued that beneath what he saw as "this constant posturing, [the] continual playing to the Gentile gallery" (p. 433) was "a restlessness, a confusion, an inner sense of instability about our communal existence" (p. 427). He went on to say that "the first thing needful in American Jewry is to realize how perniciously destructive both to our inner strength and to the strength of our position in the world is the shoddy and sterile spirit that pervades our life; American Jewry must be made to see that a life of apology is a shameful apology for life. . . ." (p. 445).

"The Age of Brass" was one of Cohen's very few full-length essays in the journal. His own original contribution was a regular *Menorah Journal* feature under the heading "Notes for a Modern History of the Jews,"[17] which was a collage of statements and news items from the Jewish press adding up to a panoramic overview of what, after H. L. Mencken, Cohen might have called the Jewish booboisie. It was a technique ideally suited to Cohen's knack for ironic observation and his preference for marginal comment on others' work as against speaking in his own voice. He adapted the method of collage also in another *Menorah Journal* feature which he compiled regularly and signed "An Elder of Zion."[18] But Cohen's genius expressed itself more characteristically in the achievements which he inspired: Tess Slesinger's short stories, "Mother to Dinner" and "The Friedman's Annie," which suggest a cross between Mary McCarthy and Grace Paley; Clifton Fadiman's marvelous send-up of the social-climbing, Yiddish-speaking Jewish family who pretend that they are white-Russian emigrés; Henry Rosenthal's satire on the assimilating young Jewish academic circa 1925; and Herbert Solow's cutting reviews of rampantly sentimental new books on Jewish history.[19]

But why should Cohen and the others have minded so much? Why should they have been so intent on puncturing pretension and showing the Jews as they really are, in their unheroic normalcy? The answer has to do with the group's longing to be at one with the Jewish community and their inability to find a spiritual home there or see their own images and aspirations reflected in the propaganda of that community. Felix Morrow, one of the group, summed it up only a few years ago when he said: "I think Herbert, Lionel, and I, and Anita Brenner, were all examples of American Jews who remain all their lives alienated from the synagogue but who would have functioned in some other (secular) institution in Jewish life if such an institution was possible and really viable."[20] For the *Menorah Journal* group there was no such institution outside the journal itself, and when the group stepped up its criticism of Jewish life after 1929 Henry Hurwitz and the Menorah Board decided they had no use for them either. Expelled from the journal on account of his growing radicalism, Morrow sought out an alternative spiritual home as a Trotskyist activist. Morrow's convictions cost him a term in jail in the forties as a Communist under the provisions of the Smith Act. He had come a long way from the *Menorah Journal*.

Herbert Solow was the most important member of the group in pushing it leftward from the cultural radicalism of Cohen and Trilling to Marxist revolutionism. Solow propelled himself directly into current Jewish controversies as Cohen had never done, and his jabs at the Jewish leadership threatened it as Trilling's critical reviews of new Jewish novels never had. One of Solow's main subjects around the end of the decade was the strategy of such Jewish defense agencies as the American Jewish Committee. To Solow's consternation, wherever there was a wrong against Jews to be righted or an abridgment of civil rights to be protested, such Jewish leaders as Louis Marshall would rely on private, secret appeals to Gentiles in power. These, in the eyes of Solow, were the tactics of servility, and he was among the first to argue that Jewish and other minority rights should be pursued openly and directly. As the historian Oscar Handlin has put it, behind-the-scenes intercession on behalf of Jewish interests was "simply the extension of the traditional means by which, for centuries, the Jews had courted the good will or capitalized upon the cupidity of princes to secure the privilege of existence."[21] For Solow it was shameful. This pattern of caution and begging, of deference to the established order, had made Jewish communal life what it was: correct, well behaved, respectable, oppressively middle class in outlook, and conformist in relation to the overall social order.

For Solow the problem of Jewish communal life was a problem not of cultural style but of economics and politics. He promoted the Marxist idea of class struggle in his circle and convinced others in the group that class differences among Jews made it impossible to speak in general terms about the "Jewish question." The most important and controversial issue to which he applied the Marxist point of view in 1930 and 1931 was the politics of Zionism.[22] Solow argued in the *Menorah Journal* that Zionism ought to have been a movement of social protest, an alliance of Arab peasants and Jewish workers. Instead, Zionist policy was being made by European and American Jewish capitalists who relied on the support of English imperialists and Arab feudal landlords, the groups which in Solow's view were responsible for the problems of the Jewish settlers in the first place. According to Solow's analysis of the situation in Palestine, the English and Arab ruling classes were united in a drive to crush any possibility of either a Jewish national home or an Arab peasant uprising, for the sake of perpetuating a feudal Palestine under the sway of the British Empire. Solow's move to the left was clear. "The Jewish problem" he wrote, "is a function of capitalism and imperialism, just like all the major problems which bedevil the human race today" (p. 124).

Solow's anti-Zionist articles created a storm. They revealed as nothing had before just where the *Menorah Journal* group was heading. Solow himself was not yet a Communist, but his criticisms of Zionist policy were essentially those of the Communist Party. Henry Hurwitz, the journal's editor, now found himself under intense pressure from his financial backers to repudiate Solow's position. The same financial backers had also stopped writing checks as a consequence of the stock market crash in 1929. Faced with the possible collapse of his magazine and of the entire Menorah movement, Hurwitz wrote to his managing editor Cohen in August 1931, not exactly to fire him but clearly offering him an opportunity to resign.

Cohen replied in a coldly bitter four-page open letter dated September 17, which he circulated to the members of his group. The letter, stored with the rest of the *Menorah Journal* files in the American Jewish Archives in Cincinnati, states clearly Cohen's grand design for the magazine in the twenties and his conviction that Hurwitz, in bowing to his Board, had betrayed the journal's mission. That mission, on which Cohen and Hurwitz had once agreed, was to pursue "an unsparing analysis of all current ideals and 'values' offered by the various established sects, parties, movements and groups in Jewish life." Hurwitz replied to object once again to what he called "the excessive jibing and sniping" that Cohen and his protégés had introduced into the journal, and he announced that from here on his magazine would avoid controversy and publish no more articles likely to make enemies. There would be an end to radicalism and satire. In general, discussion of contemporary social problems would be sacrificed in favor of purely "cultural" essays. Hurwitz himself was going to resume control of the journal after five years of Cohen's direction. He tried to justify the changes by telling Cohen, "My present mood is less in tune with First Isaiah (You rotten people!) and more in the spirit of Second Isaiah (Comfort ye, comfort ye, my people)."[23]

Censorious as Elliot Cohen had been in his accusation that Hurwitz was selling out the magazine, Herbert Solow in a letter the following month to the Menorah Board of Directors[24] was even more bitter. Solow, always more political than Cohen, argued that Hurwitz's retreat revealed a truckling to capitalist influence. The *Menorah Journal*, once devoted to creating a rejuvenated Jewish culture, would now satisfy itself pandering to the interest of one particular class. As Solow saw it, Hurwitz's renewed impulse to comfort and console and to look on the bright side had less to do with Isaiah I and II than with capitulation to the wealthy and influential Board of Directors. Addressing this same Board, Solow quoted to them Hurwitz's own theory of the social classes. He quoted Hurwitz as saying to him that

> there are in Jewry three classes: that of bankers and magnates; that of suffering masses (especially East European); and that typified by himself, many Menorah Governors and Directors, and certain friends of his in Westchester County—small manufacturers, tradesmen, professionals and executives with comfortable but "modest" incomes. He said that for each class the Jewish problem is different; for the magnates it is how to be elected to an exclusive club and marry Gentile aristocrats; for the masses how to keep alive despite anti-Semitic persecution; for Weschesterites how to find a nice summer place, get the kiddies into college, and repair the spiritual disintegration of their lives. He said that the antagonism between the classes is deeper than any bonds of union. Henceforth the Journal will represent the interests and voice the views only of Westchesterites and their fellows, and offer them a constructive program of Jewish education. . . .

In the crisis of the *Menorah Journal* and in the crisis of American capitalism, Hurwitz opted to comfort the unhappy and disoriented Jewish bourgeoisie. This decision was in effect a rejection of the young writers who had found a spiritual home at the *Journal*. In actuality Hurwitz did not fire Trilling, Morrow, Halper, Berg, and the others, but they all walked out on him in a demonstration of solidarity with Cohen and Solow. For almost every one of them, the walkout represented the effective end of their relationship with the Jewish community. As Elliot Cohen summed up the damage in his letter of resignation to Hurwitz, the young writers would "wonder, as I do, how you could bring yourself to so great a betrayal of everything decent and good that the Journal has been or has become—so complete and callous a dissipation of the store of intellectual and emotional energy and achievement brought to the Journal through many years by men who saw in it a fit—and trustworthy—repository for the best they had to give to Jewish life."[25]

In retrospect the young Jewish intellectuals of the *Menorah Journal* group may appear to have been naive. Could they not see that the *Menorah Journal* was itself part of the organized Jewish community and that it would not forever tolerate attacks on itself from within? These same intellectuals would not have been so naive twenty years later, after their stormy experience in the left-wing movement. But in the late twenties they were still young. Disillusionment with communism and, for some of them, with politics altogether was reserved for a later part of their lives.

It is pleasant to remember the New York intellectuals in the days of their innocence, when they were aspiring, brilliant, ironic, and totally out of things. For who could have been more out of it than a cultural avant-garde in the America of Herbert Hoover? Here was a group of young people who were at war with the respectable Jewish community and their parents because they were radicals; who were unable to get university jobs because they were Jews; and who found themselves distrusted by the Communists because they were middle-class intellectuals. They were caught between Jewishness and Americanness, between the right and the left. Essentially they belonged to no class, and their contributions to the *Menorah Journal* convey the pathos of their striving to create a social identity and a place for themselves.

It is especially pleasant to consider the members of "the family" in the days of their youth because nowadays these same writers have lost most of their one-time radical élan. There is in their writing these days a sense of exhaustion, of having reached the end of the line. The melancholia of mature insiders has its own charm, but it is not to be compared with the proud irreverence of young outsiders struggling to make their way.

NOTES

1 Almost none of the intellectuals I discuss actually joined the Communist Party in the thirties. Most remained independent intellectuals sympathetic to the Party's goals without being bound by its program. I indicate this independent status by using the lower case ("communist"). Wherever the Communist Party is involved, Communist is capitalized.

  I am grateful to the staff of the American Jewish Archives at the Hebrew Union College–Jewish Institute of Religion in Cincinnati, Ohio. The Archives supplied me with microfilm copy of material from its files of the *Menorah Journal*. These files, covering the forty-seven years of the *Journal's* history, are extremely rich and might well provide the basis of an interpretative study of the complicated relations between Jewish intellectuals and the official Jewish community in America in this century.

I have been aided also by Alan M. Wald's monograph, "The Menorah Group Moves Left," *Jewish Social Studies* 38 (Summer-Fall 1976): 289–320, as well as by his biographical essay, "Herbert Solow: Portrait of a New York Intellectual," *Prospects* 3 (1977): 419–60. Professor Wald's paper on the Menorah group is primarily concerned with that group in the early thirties, after they had broken with the magazine and had become a radical political vanguard. My own essay is centrally concerned with cultural issues and with these young writers' relation to their Jewishness in the twenties rather than with their relation to the communist movement in the thirties.

This essay has been revised and expanded for the present volume. I wish to thank Professor Ralph Aderman, the volume's editor, for valuable suggestions. A shorter version appeared in *Modern Jewish Studies Annual* for 1977. I thank the editors for permission to reprint.

2 "The New York Intellectuals: A Chronicle and a Critique," *Commentary* 46 (October 1968): 29–51. It is reprinted in Irving Howe, *The Decline of the New* (New York: Harcourt, Brace and World, 1970).

3 Norman Podhoretz, *Making It* (New York: Random House, 1967).

4 Lionel Trilling (1905–75) taught in the English Department at Columbia from 1932 until his death in 1975. In his last years he was also Eastman Professor at Oxford and a fellow of All Souls College. Of his many books, perhaps the best known are *The Liberal Imagination* (1950) and *Sincerity and Authenticity* (1973). Trilling's collected works have recently been reissued in a twelve-volume Uniform Edition by Harcourt Brace Jovanovich (1978–80).

Elliot Cohen (1899–1959) joined the staff of the *Menorah Journal* after graduation from Yale College and a few years of graduate study at Yale. He became the magazine's guiding spirit and its managing editor from 1925 until his resignation in 1931. After leaving the *Journal,* Cohen was involved briefly in propaganda activity as executive secretary of a Communist party "front" organization, the National Committee for the Defense of Political Prisoners. Like most of his "family" at the *Journal,* many of whom followed him into the NCDPP, Cohen soon became disillusioned with the party and cut his ties. During the thirties and the early forties Cohen supported himself as director of public information for the Federation of Jewish Philanthropies. In 1945 he reemerged on the cultural scene as founding editor of *Commentary,* which he edited until his death in 1959.

Herbert Solow (1903–64) was the most politically conscious of the *Menorah Journal* writers. Like others in the group, Solow was briefly a communist in the early thirties. By the end of the decade, however, he had turned against the party and was writing articles exposing Communist Party underground activity in the United States. It was to Solow that Whittaker Chambers came for aid when in 1938 Chambers decided to discontinue his underground spying for the party and was fearful of reprisal. Solow joined the staff of *Fortune* magazine in 1945.

5 Henry Hurwitz (1886–1961) graduated in 1908 from Harvard College, where he studied with William James and George Santayana. He attended Harvard Law School but soon turned to Jewish organizational work. Hurwitz directed the fortunes of the *Menorah Journal* until his death in 1961. The magazine discontinued publishing the next year. His extensive correspondence with prominent figures in the Jewish community is contained in the *Menorah Journal* files of the American Jewish Archives in Cincinnati.

6 Mumford, "Herzl's Utopia," 9 (August 1923): 155–69; Kallen, "Can Judaism Survive in the United States?" 11 (April 1925): 101–13; 11 (December 1925): 544–59; Frank, "Toward an Analysis of the Problem of the Jew," 12 (June-July 1926): 225–34; Lewisohn, "The Fallacies of Assimilation," 11 (October 1925): 462–72; Kaplan, "Toward A Reconstruction of Judaism," 13 (April 1927): 113–30; Charles Reznikoff, "Uriel Acosta," 11 (February 1925): 35–42; "Hebrew," 14 (May 1928): 434; "Nudnik," 17 (November 1929): 184–86; "Salesman," 17 (December 1929): 279–80; "A Dialogue: Padua 1727," 18 (March 1930):220; "By the Waters of Manhattan: 1930," 18 (May 1930): 417–21; "Passage at Arms," 19 (October 1930): 63–66; "In the Country," 19 (November-December 1930): 185–88; Deutsch, "A Meeting of Jacob and Joseph," 11 (August 1925): 369–70; "Sun Bath," 15 (October 1928): 341–42; "Saffron Flower," 16 (June 1929): 532, Levin, "Maurie Finds His Medium," 15 (August 1928): 175–81; "Reb Feivel Read the Holy Books," 18 (February 1930): 129–35; "The Commune," 19 (March 1931): 297–304; Joseph Klausner, "The Economic Conditions of Palestine in the Time of Jesus of Nazareth," 11 (February 1925): 43–58; Gold, "Portrait of My Mother," 18 (January 1930): 59–70.

7 Tess Slesinger (1905–45) became part of the *Menorah Journal* "family" through Herbert Solow, whom she married in 1928, divorced in 1932, and satirized in 1934 in *The Unpossessed*, her witty *roman à clef* about New York radical intellectuals in the early Depression years. Following upon the success of her novel, Slesinger moved to Hollywood, where she wrote the screen versions of Pearl Buck's *The Good Earth* and Lillian Smith's *A Tree Grows in Brooklyn*. She died of cancer at the age of thirty-nine.

8 "Impediments," 11 (June 1925): 286–90 [first publication]; *translation:* "Napoleon, the Jews, and the Modern Man," 18 (March 1930): 211–19; *short stories:* "Chapter for a Fashionable Jewish Novel," 12 (June-July 1926): 275–82; "Funeral at the Club, with Lunch," 13 (August 1927): 380–90; "A Light to the Nations," 14 (April 1928): 402–8; "Notes on a Departure," 16 (May 1929): 421–34; *reviews:* "What Price Jewry" [rev. of Hugo Bettauer, *The City Without Jews*], 13 (April 1927): 218–19; "Competent, But—" [rev. of Lester Cohen, *The Great Bear*], 13 (November 1927): 522–24; "Of Sophistication" [rev. of Ludwig Lewisohn, *Roman Summer*], 14 (January 1928): 106–9; "Our Colonial Forefathers" [rev. of Hannah R. London, *Portraits of Jews by Gilbert Stuart and Other Early American Artists*], 14 (February 1928): 217–20; "Mr. Untermeyer as Poet" [rev. of Lewis Untermeyer, *Burning Bush*], 14 (June 1928): 604–8; "Whether to Laugh" [rev. of David Pinski, *Arnold Lev-*

enberg, Man of Peace], 15 (September 1928): 290-92; "Burning Doorbells" [rev. of Paul Rosenfeld, The Boy in the Sun], 15 (November 1928): 483-86; "Obsession" [rev. of L. Steni, Prelude to a Rope for Myer], 16 (January 1929): 84-85; "Another Jewish Problem Novel" [rev. of Milton Waldman, The Disinherited], 16 (April 1929): 376-79; "Despair Apotheosized" [rev. of Gertrude Diamant, Labyrinth], 17 (October 1929): 91-94; "A Too Simple Simplicity" [rev. of Robert Nathan, There is Another Heaven], 17 (December 1929): 292-94; "The Necessary Morals of Art" [rev. of Jean-Richard Bloch, ——— & Co.], 18 (February 1930): 182-86; "Publisher's Classic" [rev. of Manuel Komroff, Coronet], 18 (March 1930): 282-85; "Flawed Instruments" [rev. of Ludwig Lewisohn, Adam; and Ludwig Lewisohn, Stephen Escott], 18 (April 1930): 380-84; "The Promise of Realism" [rev. of Edward Dahlberg, Bottom Dogs; Nathan Asch, Pay Day; and Meyer Levin, Frankie and Johnnie], 18 (May 1930): 480-84; "Genuine Writing" [rev. of Charles Reznikov, By the Waters of Manhattan], 19 (October 1930): 88-92; "The Latest Matriarch" [rev. of G. B. Stern, Mosaic], 19 (November-December 1930): 206-8; "Art and Justice" [rev. of Lion Feuchtwanger, Success], 19 (June 1931): 470-72; articles: "A Friend of Byron," 12 (August-September 1926): 371-73; and "The Changing Myth of the Jew," an essay on the image of the Jew in English literature from Chaucer to George Eliot, which was written for publication in the Menorah Journal in 1929. It never appeared, however, and was published only in 1978 in Commentary 66 (August 1978): 24-34, after it was discovered in the Menorah Journal files.

9 Hannah Arendt, "The Jew as Pariah," Jewish Social Studies 6 (1944): 99-122.

10 Lewisohn (1882-1955) was the most influential spokesman for "positive Judaism" in the generation before Trilling. His creed and how he arrived at it are explained in his autobiographical memoir, Up Stream: An American Chronicle (New York: Boni and Liveright, 1922).

11 Trilling's contribution to "Under Forty: A Symposium on American Literature and the Younger Generation of American Jews," Contemporary Jewish Record 7 (February 1944): 15-17.

12 John Higham, Send These to Me: Jews and Other Immigrants in Urban America (New York: Atheneum, 1975), pp. 160-61. Higham writes of the Jews in America: "Their experience . . . was different. Whereas other European groups generally gained respect as assimilation improved their status, the Jews reaped more and more dislike as they bettered themselves. The more avidly they reached out for acceptance and participation in American life, the more their reputation seemed to suffer" (p. 166).

13 An illuminating account of the social situation of Jewish students at Columbia is provided by M. G. Torch, "The Spirit of Morningside: Some Notes on Columbia University," Menorah Journal 18 (March 1930): 253-61.

14 Felix Morrow, "Higher Learning on Washington Square: Some Notes on New York University," 18 (April 1930): 346-56.

15 Walter Lippmann, "Public Opinion and the American Jew," American Hebrew 110 (April 14, 1922): 575, cited in John Murray Cuddihy, The Ordeal of Civility: Freud, Marx, Lévi-Strauss, and the Jewish Struggle with Modernity (New York: Delta Books, 1974), p. 143.

16 Volume 11 (October 1925): 425–47.
17 Volume 11 (April 1925): 178–81; 11 (June 1925): 283–85; 11 (August 1925): 393–95; 11 (October 1925): 502–5; 11 (December 1925): 617–19; 12 (February 1926): 79–81; 12 (April-May 1926): 192–94; 12 (June-July 1926): 306–8; 12 (August-September 1926): 413–14; 12 (December 1926): 633–34; 13 (February 1927): 77–78; 13 (April 1927): 203–4; 13 (June 1927): 307–9; 13 (August 1927): 417–18; 13 (November 1927): 508–11.
18 "Marginal Annotations" by An Elder of Zion, 17 (November 1929): 190–98; 17 (December 1929): 281–89; 18 (January 1930): 73–80; 18 (February 1930): 170–81; 18 (March 1930): 271–79; 18 (April 1930): 369–76; 18 (May 1930): 466–76; 19 (October 1930): 75–83; 19 (November-December 1930): 189–98; 19 (March 1931): 308–18; 19 (June 1931): 455–64.
19 Tess Slesinger, "Mother to Dinner," 18 (March 1930): 221–34; "The Friedman's Annie," 19 (March 1931): 242–59; Clifton Fadiman, "A la Russe," 12 (June-July 1926): 313–16; Henry Rosenthal, "Emancipated Jew: Faculty Model," 11 (April 1925): 182–84; Herbert Solow, "Wanted: A New Kind of Jewish Writing" [rev. of Ismar Elbogen, *History of the Jews*], 13 (June 1927): 320–24; "A Liberal-Reform Jewish History" [rev. of Abram Leon Sachar, *A History of the Jews*], 18 (May 1930): 477–80.
20 Quoted in Alan M. Wald, "The Menorah Group Moves Left," *Jewish Social Studies* 38 (Summer-Fall, 1976): 293.
21 Oscar Handlin, *Adventure in Freedom: Three Hundred Years of Jewish Life in America* (New York: McGraw-Hill, 1954), p. 212.
22 "The Realities of Zionism," 19 (November-December 1930): 97–127; "Camouflaging Zionist Realities," 19 (March 1931): 223–41; "Rebuttal" [to reactions to the above articles], 19 (June 1931): 410–15.
23 November 2, 1931. Letter in the *Menorah Journal* file of the American Jewish Archives.
24 October 12, 1931. Letter in the *Menorah Journal* file of the American Jewish Archives.
25 September 17, 1931. Letter in the *Menorah Journal* file of the American Jewish Archives.

9th Annual Morris Fromkin Memorial Lecture

BOOKS FOR NEW CITIZENS

Public Libraries and Americanization Programs, 1905-1925

ELAINE FAIN

Assistant Professor of Library Science, The University of Wisconsin—Milwaukee
Recipient of the 1978 Fromkin Research Grant

PHOTO: CLEVELAND PUBLIC LIBRARY

Wednesday, November 1, 1978
3:30 P.M.

East Wing, first floor, UWM Library

The public is cordially invited to attend.
Reception follows.

Sponsored by the Fromkin Memorial Collection of the UWM Library

Books For New Citizens: Public Libraries and Americanization Programs, 1900–1925

ELAINE FAIN

PUBLIC libraries are rarely mentioned in American history books; public schools, settlement houses, and even the Chautauqua movement have excited more attention. The standard image of the public librarian has remained the rather grim female in flat shoes and severe hairdo who demands silence and hides the sex books. A *New York Times* writer recently characterized the librarians of his Michigan childhood as "agelessly fusty." "From behind a variety of spectacles, they kept watch with moist, vigilant eyes. Their skirts always fell inches longer than the current style. If, stretching on tiptoe to remove a volume from some top shelf, one of the ladies inadvertently exposed calf or knee, the skin gleamed pale as bleached book paper."[1] Yet, ironically, the public library movement was linked from its inception to ideas of social reform, and many librarians thought of themselves as vigorous educators, reformers, and progressives.

The splendid downtown library buildings constructed in cities all over the country during the 1870s, '80s, and '90s were frequently referred to as "people's universities," places where scholarly and useful materials might be consulted by ambitious, sober adults both for their own uplift and the general social betterment. Reform-minded business men, such as Enoch Pratt and Andrew Carnegie, favored public libraries as a particularly safe means of social improvement. In their zeal to make certain that every citizen had access to a public

---

The late Elaine Fain, who received her doctorate from the University of Wisconsin–Madison, was assistant professor in the School of Library Science of the University of Wisconsin–Milwaukee. Her long-standing interests in immigrant history and in public libraries as educational agencies are combined in this essay.

library, both supported the establishment of neighborhood library branches. Between 1886 and 1919, Carnegie supplied hundreds of communities with library buildings, most of which were either branches of big city systems or main libraries for small towns.

Bolstered by these donations as well as by tax funds, turn-of-the-century library boards and administrators tried to keep pace with the explosive growth of American cities. In the wake of new streetcar, railroad, and subway lines, and the residential areas which bloomed along them, libraries followed with branch buildings and deposit stations. During these decades of rapid growth, the basic conception of public library service began to change, mostly in response to changing conditions in American cities. The self-help theme was still heavily stressed; many librarians continued to cling to the idealized image of the sober, decent workingman spending his leisure hours at the public library instead of the tavern. Now, however, there began to be an increasing awareness of the growing problems connected with urban life: sanitation, public health, crime, juvenile delinquency. Librarians, like other middle-class Americans, responded with alarm to the muckrakers' accounts of the slums and the slum dwellers. Librarians were educators, after all; they ought to do more than sit behind their desks and wait for earnest adults to enter. A tremendous agitation began to take hold in the newly organized library profession for the provision of services to children, especially to children in urban, industrial areas. "Must we wait," asked Minerva Sanders in 1887 (she was librarian in Pawtucket, Rhode Island, a manufacturing town), "until our children . . . are fourteen years of age or upwards before we begin to teach them the first principles of right living, of mental growth, of love to their neighbor?"[2] The question was rhetorical; the answer to "Must we wait?" was a resounding "No." Children's services and the specialists to run them spread across the public libraries of the land during the 1890s.

Many of the boys and girls who flocked to the new children's rooms were immigrants or the children of immigrants. It could not be otherwise, for the foreign population in American cities was becoming tremendous as a result of terrible economic and political conditions in Europe and the promise of opportunity in the industrializing United States. "Nothing so forcibly impressed commentators upon early twentieth-century America," the historian Maldwyn A. Jones has written, "as the increasing prominence of the immigrant. In all the larger American cities, and in scores of smaller ones too, there were great masses of immigrants speaking strange languages, following strange customs, and, with their children, outnumbering the native population by as much as two to one."[3] Boston, Cleveland, Chicago, New York, Pittsburgh, Buffalo, Detroit, Baltimore, and other industrialized cities had ethnic ghettos, many with dreadful living conditions. Urban growth and urban problems were inextricably intertwined with immigration.

Adjustment to American life was extraordinarily difficult for immigrants, faced as they were with the immediate problems of making a living, finding housing, dealing with a strange culture. Mostly the immigrants had to fend for themselves, relying on fellow countrymen who had arrived earlier and knew the ropes. Until the 1880s and the large immigration from southern and eastern Europe, most native-born Americans more or less assumed that immigrants would adjust to the United States one way or another. Despite a long and ugly history of anti-Catholicism, directed especially against the Irish, and various antiforeign movements of the Know-Nothing variety, the general attitude toward immigrants seemed to be one of complacency. Beginning in the 1880s, however, as the historian John Higham has noted, another point of view began to be heard. " . . . [A] growing company of reformers sounded alarms at the polarization of American society. Protestant advocates of a Social Gospel, a new generation of German-trained economists, and a host of municipal reformers charged immigration with increasing the rift of classes, complicating the slum problem, causing boss-rule, and straining the old moralities."[4] For some, the answer to America's urban problems was to stop immigration, especially the undesirable "new" immigration from southern and eastern Europe. For others, the solutions lay in government aid to immigrants and, above all, in programs designed for the education and assimilation of immigrants.

The role of the public schools in assimilating the children of immigrants is well known; compulsory education laws passed in state after state insured that all immigrant children (except those who attended parochial schools or who managed to escape the truant officer's net) would spend at least a few years learning the three Rs in English, saluting the flag, singing patriotic anthems, and becoming acquainted with George Washington and other national heroes. Public libraries, unlike the schools, could not compel anyone to enter their doors; they had to make their facilities and services readily available and appealing. With children, as it turned out, they had little problem; if anything, libraries were overwhelmed by the numbers of boys and girls who begged for books and literally wore out the pages. Adults were another matter. The number of native-born adults who wished to read the classics and serious literature proved to be disappointingly small; high-minded librarians were forced to resort to "bait" in the form of light novels and magazines. For immigrant adults, who could not read English well and who were in any case overwhelmed by everyday problems, the public library was hardly an essential institution.

How could the situation be changed? What *ought* the public libraries to be doing for adult immigrants? Or doing to them, for that matter? These questions were discussed in the nineties in articles with titles like "Why Public Libraries Should Supply Books in Foreign Languages." I am going to examine the sentiments in such pieces. I am also going to look at everyday branch library work in immigrant neighborhoods (especially Brooklyn, New York, and Cleveland), at the attempts by reformers to involve public libraries in the great mission of assimilating immigrants, and at the steadily increasing emphasis in public libraries on Americanization efforts. My source materials are library records, newspaper stories, magazine articles, and the papers and correspondence of a gentleman named John Foster Carr. Educator, municipal reformer, founder and sole director of an organization called The Immigrant Publication Society, Carr was the impresario of library Americanization projects. He played a large role in shaping the attitudes of public librarians toward work with immigrants.

This library Americanization work, on which I shall concentrate, is of course only a small part of the history of connections between public libraries and immigrants. Prosperous immigrants were involved in the formation of many libraries (Carnegie, it must be remembered, came from Scotland). In many instances, book collections put together by immigrants were incorporated into public libraries. Some of the librarians working in the big public libraries were immigrants who had been educated at European universities. My major concern here, however, is with deliberate attempts by public librarians to assimilate immigrants, and with—to use a contemporary term—the consciousness-raising which took place among public librarians on the subject of immigrants.

In two decades, roughly from 1890 to 1910, American public libraries in the larger cities developed most of the systems and services we take for granted today: branch libraries, children's rooms, reference services. Further, public librarians during those two decades undertook special projects in conjunction with schools, settlement houses, charity organizations, playground and neighborhood groups, and a variety of persons interested in social betterment and urban reform.

This astonishing growth and expansion of library services matched the tremendous expansion of American cities and the huge increases in urban populations.

The Carnegie Library of Pittsburgh, for example, had one central building in 1895; by 1909, there were seven branches and 227 distributing stations. To reach the foreign-born and their children, who in 1900 comprised two-thirds of the city's population, considerable effort was put into what today would be called outreach services. Books were placed in mills, factories, fire stations, stores, schools (public, private, parochial, and Sunday), settlements, churches, synagogues, playgrounds, and homes.

The Cleveland Public Library organized branches and deposit stations in the 1890s, established a children's department in 1894, and built several Carnegie branches between 1902 and 1907. In 1908, Cleveland opened the first branch in the United States designed for children only—Perkins House, located in a crowded immigrant area and sponsored jointly by a day nursery association, a settlement, and the library. The new branch was ringed by factories, foundries, and a good many saloons; by way of contrast, there were reproductions inside of Michelangelo's *Moses* and Turner's *Grand Canal*. Over the fireplace, a Robert Louis Stevenson couplet was inscribed: "Where the roads on either hand / Lead onward into fairy land."[5] Cleveland also had thirty-two home libraries for children. A home library was a box of forty or fifty books sent to a private house. Each week, a volunteer visitor (a young man or woman interested in social betterment) would conduct a children's meeting in the house. The visitor read or told a story, played a game, gave each child a book to take home, and in general exerted a "social influence" which was "very strong."[6]

New York Public Library's Circulation Department, founded in 1901, incorporated several settlement house libraries directly into its system, among them the Aguilar (part of the famous Educational Alliance), the University Settlement, and the Webster. Each branch was allowed to acquire foreign language materials suitable for its clientele. The Webster was a center for Czech books and gatherings; the Seward Park Branch on the Lower East Side had Russian and Hebrew books; Rivington and Chatham Square had Yiddish, Rumanian, Polish, and Italian; 125th Street had Scandinavian; and so on. By 1913 over one-tenth of the circulation department's books were in foreign languages—99,609 volumes representing 32,311 titles in twenty-five languages.[7] Anne Carroll Moore, who became the New York Public Library's supervisor of children's services in 1906, encouraged the celebration of foreign holidays, the reading of folk tales, exhibits of folk art, and even the appearance of well-known foreign literary figures and artists.

Brooklyn's public library system, which remained separate from New York's consisted solely of branches for many years. The borough's immigrant population, already substantial when Brooklyn joined New York City in 1898, increased dramatically after the Williamsburg Bridge opened in 1903. "This community," the librarian of the Brownsville Branch commented in 1908,

> is not the result of a slow, steady growth, but rather has grown up over night and is in all essentials new. New, in that six or seven years ago, before the opening of the Williamsburg Bridge permitted the teeming ghetto of Manhattan to pour some of its overflow into Brooklyn, Brownsville was but a barren suburb part of the sparsely settled East New York. And new, in that its inhabitants have been in America but a short time varying from a month to fifteen years.

"With hardly another cultural institution in the district," he continued, "the possibilities and responsibilities of the library's position are enormous."[8] From the first day of opening, circulation was brisk. Library rules and regulations were typed in Yiddish as well as English, and a Yiddish newspaper clippings file was maintained with information about naturalization, American marriage customs, etc.[9]

Many similar public library histories could be recited: Boston, St. Louis, Minneapolis. The details are different, but the lines of development are similar. In his well-known book *Streetcar Suburbs,* the historian Sam Bass Warner, Jr. said of Boston that, although the city suffered severe ethnic tensions during the period of large scale immigration,

> . . . its public agencies pursued a policy of service without regard to ethnic background. Just as the streetcar companies undertook to serve all the villages and quarters of the metropolitan region, so the schools and libraries undertook to serve all the children and adults within the municipality. . . . By providing equal service to all citizens, by extending service as rapidly as possible to the whole geographic jurisdiction, Boston's public agencies hoped to give the greatest scope to the workings of individual capitalists. Education, health, transportation, and plentiful land were tools to encourage individuals to work effectively as profit makers.[10]

In a brief period of about twenty years' time, then, extensive public library systems developed as part of a network of urban services for rapidly growing industrial cities. The expansion of urban library services inevitably entailed services to immigrants and their children simply because they were the ones who formed the bulk of large city populations at the time. Some idea of how rapidly all this took place can be gathered from the somewhat bewildered comments in 1894 of the conservative editor of the prestigious *Library Journal*. He deplored what he referred to as "the rather recent tendency to consider the supplying of books in foreign languages as one of the functions of a public library." He had no quarrel with the purchase of the best literature for serious study purposes, but supplying works to foreign-speaking readers in little-known tongues was another matter. His diatribe was inspired by the proposed publication of a list of Swedish books for suggested library purchase; the argument for the list's publication was that the Swedish population in many American cities had become substantial. "The same argument," he acidly observed,

would apply . . . not only to Swedes, but to Germans, French, Italians, Hebrews, Hungarians, and Poles, not to mention Chinese. Carrying out the idea, then, we would have a polyglot public library issuing polyglot literature to the denizens of the various foreign "colonies" . . . This is certainly not conducive to good citizenship, and the promotion of good citizenship is, we take it, one of the functions of a public library. . . .[11]

Axel Josephson, a Swedish-American bibliographer who had supplied the list in the first place, responded with annoyance. He had hardly expected, he said, to find the ghost of Know-Nothingism in the organ of "such a progressive body as the American Library Association." Public libraries were supplying trash fiction to readers in the hope that this would eventually lead them to good literature; how could there be any objection to using foreign language books as a drawing card for immigrants? Josephson's position was substantially the one taken by public librarians in the 1900–1910 decade. They favored lending books to immigrants, just as they favored lending books to all social classes and, indeed, to all citizens.

This simple story of public library expansion into immigrant neighborhoods is complicated by several factors, however. To begin with, very few branch librarians knew much about immigrants, immigrant culture, or even foreign culture. There were some exceptions, of course. Certain librarians, like Leon Solis-Cohen of Brooklyn Public, had worked originally for private ethnic organization libraries and had been kept on when those libraries became part of a public system. Others were themselves immigrants or the children of immigrants; this situation became common only after World War I, though, when enough time had elapsed for the children of the new immigration to acquire some higher education. Finally, a few public librarians took their work with immigrants seriously enough that they tried to learn the relevant foreign languages. Eleanor Ledbetter of Cleveland studied both Polish and Czech. Another Cleveland librarian, May Sweet, studied Italian; her daughter, also a librarian, not only studied Italian but married an Italian immigrant. Staff members at some of the New York Public branches took classes in Yiddish and Russian literature.

On the whole, however, public librarians spoke only English and relied on foreign booksellers, interpreters, organizations like John Foster Carr's Immigrant Publication Society, and the immigrants themselves to help them out. In children's rooms, the language barriers didn't matter much, for work was carried on almost entirely in English, but with immigrant adults, it was different. As those librarians who were more or less plunged into branches in immigrant neighborhoods began to gain experience, they passed on tips to others. Here is J. Maud Campbell, for example, a public librarian in Passaic, New Jersey, in 1907, explaining earnestly how she became involved in "catering to immigrants." (She later, in fact, became known as something of an expert and headed the Division for Work with Foreigners of the Massachusetts Department of Education.) Foreigners, she said, were like death and taxes—there was no evading them. And talking of taxes, foreigners paid them too. So why, she asked equably, should they not have library materials in their own languages? Passaic sensibly subscribed to some foreign language newspapers and found that these attracted immediate interest among immigrants. When people discovered that the library would consider buying books for them in their own languages, they were delighted. As for information about what to buy and where, Miss Campbell found that the greatest assistance came from the people themselves.

> I have been surprised at the lists of books that have been put into my hands by apparently illiterate working people. They take pride in showing you what good books there really are in their literature. To satisfy myself that such things really exist, before we bought any books, I read with care the articles on the literature of the different nationalities to be found under the headings of the countries in the *Encyclopaedia Britannica*.[12]

Whenever an immigrant child produced a signed application for a library card, the Passaic staff would ask if the parents had cards and would tell the child they hoped his or her parents would come to the library. If a parent, usually a father, did appear, Miss Campbell would speak to him, using the child as an interpreter. "The quickest way to the heart of the foreigner," she confided, "is to ask his native town and then show him that place on a map and follow the course of his trip over here. He will show you the spot with as much pride as if it were a ducal palace. . . ."[13]

Naiveté, sentimentality, and provincialism permeated library circles, where there was a strong atmosphere of cultural gentility and moral purity. Public librarians of the pre–World War I era believed without question that they knew which authors were best, which books were of enduring value, which poems were ennobling. They were not alone in this realm of genteel arts and letters, to be sure. A terrible priggishness surrounded what most middle-class Americans called "culture." The typical American, Van Wyck Brooks stated in 1915, grew up in "a sort of orgy of lofty examples, moralized poems, national anthems and baccalaureate sermons. . . ."[14]

Gentility flourished in both the settlement houses and the libraries. When Jane Addams and Ellen Starr founded Hull House in 1889, one of their first enterprises was a reading circle for young working girls at which Miss Starr read aloud from George Eliot's *Romola*. On the walls of Hull House, the two founders hung photographs and reproductions of works of art, including several colored prints of Fra Angelico's angels. These could be borrowed. "There is something pathetic," two historians recently commented, "about little immigrant girls hanging copies of Fra Angelico angels on the dreary walls of their tenement rooms, and about Miss Addams' conviction that the youngsters gained a heroic and historic impulse from viewing art reproductions."[15] Motivated in much the same way as Jane Addams, the reformer Jacob Riis organized a drive in 1888 to bring hundreds of wild flower bouquets into the New York slums. An armful of daisies, he wrote, could keep the peace of a block better than the patrolman's club. The slum, Riis observed, hungered for the beautiful.[16] Similar sentiments were very evident among public librarians, especially children's librarians. Through literature, pretty pictures, and quiet surroundings, they hoped to compensate for the crowdedness and ugliness of the slums. "No one can observe city life closely," said the children's librarian of Cleveland in 1898,

without seeing something of the evil which comes to the children who are shut up within its walls; the larger the city the greater is the evil, the more effectually are the little ones deprived of the pure air, the sweet freedom of the fields and woods. . . . For these the library must to some extent take the place of Mother Nature, for under present conditions it is through books alone that some of them can ever come to know her. . . .[17]

Over the years at Hull House, the genteel atmosphere of the early culture projects began to disappear. Cultural activities remained important, but Hull House residents increasingly became involved in direct social and political action: the formation of labor unions, the passage of child labor laws, health and safety regulations for factories, immigrant protective legislation. In the public libraries of 1890–1910, on the other hand, the work pretty much stayed in the area of genteel culture and bringing civilized influences to bear upon the unwashed. "Clean hearts, clean hands, clean books" was the apt motto of the Cleveland Public Library League, a children's club founded in 1897. Librarians sometimes became active in political causes, but not as an integral part of their jobs. The ready acceptance by librarians of tainted Carnegie money alienated political radicals and labor union leaders from the public library movement as a whole. Even the more moderate progressives at times became exasperated with the rather simple-minded public library credo that good books made for a good society. Herbert Croly, editor of the *New Republic*, spoke in 1909 of "the credulity of the good American in proposing to evangelize the individual by the reading of books."[18] The economist E. A. Ross insisted in 1914 that petty betterment schemes only diverted people from fundamentals. Those who started innocent charities got support, he said, while "those who promoted movements that lessen somebody's profits or dividends or rentals get the cold shoulder and fail. So that the promoters of social service learn the lesson: 'Ask for reading rooms, or fresh air, or teddy bears; don't ask for less risk, or less hours, or for more pay, or more rights.'"[19]

Library adherence to the commonly-accepted literary standards of the refined middle class naturally resulted in carefully screened collections and a considerable amount of what would now be called censorship. Librarians kept their eyes peeled for coarseness, vulgarity, and low morality; they tended to disapprove of the new realism in literature. Leon Solis-Cohen reported in 1908 that the Russian-Jewish immigrants at the Brownsville Branch could not comprehend why American libraries occasionally saw fit to withhold certain volumes of Tolstoi, Zola, or Shaw. The immigrants became quite indignant, he said.[20] Peter Roberts, secretary of the YMCA, expressed pleasure in 1911 at the "quiet, refining influences of the library . . . upon the alien."[21]

Another striking aspect of the librarian-immigrant relationship in the early part of the century was the eagerness with which librarians stereotyped the various national groups. They were not alone; everybody at the time, including immigrants, seemed to play the National Stereotype Game. Public librarians often set up favorable stereotypes for groups they thought receptive to library offerings, and they would pass these judgments along to newspaper reporters. "The Jewish child has more than an eagerness for mental food; it is an intellectual mania," the *New York Evening Post* reported in a 1903 story headlined "Jew Babes at the Library." A 1904 *New York Evening Sun* story disclosed that "Irish babies are more literary in taste than their parents."

Our turn-of-the-century setting, then, is of public library systems expanding quickly in growing industrial cities with large immigrant populations and of genteel librarians beginning to discover the rougher world of the slums and the strange customs of the foreign born. To this must be added the growing conviction among Americans, especially the progressives, that something had to be done about the terrible problems of the cities, a conviction which encompassed the notion that something had to be done about the immigrants. The children were not such a problem if they could be gotten into the public schools, but the assimilation of immigrant adults was another matter. They didn't speak English; they continued to live in ghettos; they remained obstinately foreign; they voted for machine politicians; they were woefully ignorant of the American democratic heritage. It was imperative that all educational institutions be harnessed to the assimilation task. The really militant, vicious Americanization programs weren't fully unleashed until America's entry into World War I, but a great many projects to assimilate the foreign-born got under way in the fifteen years or so before that. The Daughters and Sons of the American Revolution, for example, began their enthusiastic patriotism crusades around 1900. They promoted the use of English, reverence toward the Constitution and the founding fathers, and respect for law and order. A Sons of the American Revolution leaflet called "Information for Immigrants" had a last paragraph which began "This is a great country" and ended with "May you be worthy of it."[22] As Gerd Korman put it in his excellent study of Americanization programs in Milwaukee, such groups "proposed to replace the melting pot with a pressure cooker."[23] Settlement house workers, on the other hand, spoke of adding love and understanding to the melting pot ingredients. Immigrant customs and traditions enriched America, they argued; immigrants should be welcomed and helped. They should be permitted to see American idealism in action instead of vicious commercialism.

Regardless of their political beliefs, those who promoted any variety of assimilation or Americanization began to see public libraries as possible vehicles for their work. Library branches contained meeting rooms in convenient neighborhood locations. Libraries had the mechanisms for distributing literature; librarians were in the business of adult education and already in contact with immigrants; the children who used libraries were conduits to immigrant adults. True, libraries could only invite immigrants to enter their doors (the door of Cleveland's Broadway Branch said "Free Public Library" in five different languages), but they could accomplish valuable educational work with those who accepted the initial invitation. So rapidly did all this come together that, by 1912, the Massachusetts Library Association formed a Committee on Work with Foreigners, and the American Library Association published a pamphlet which announced that the assimilation of the immigrant was the gravest national problem before the American public. The public library, the authors noted sternly, had "an important duty to perform."[24]

John Foster Carr was the most active of the Americanizers in enlisting the help of public librarians. Born in 1869, Carr attended Yale and Oxford, then traveled extensively on the continent. Upon his return to the United States, he settled in New York City and helped found the Citizens Union, which was devoted to "the political education and the uplifting of the Italian element in the city of New York." As an admirer of Italian culture, Carr was distressed by the generally low esteem accorded Italians in the United States. In a 1904 article on Italian-Americans, Carr expressed the theme which was to underlie his work—that harshness toward immigrants only made them more anxious than ever to remain in their own colonies and seriously impeded assimilation. He called for understanding, patience, and appreciation of the fact that most Italian immigrants were ambitious and industrious.[25]

Carr's first extensive contacts with public libraries came about through the Dante Alighieri Society, a cultural group which had embarked on a project to provide Italian books to immigrants. Carr raised funds for the enterprise, selected and purchased the books, and became involved in their distribution. He discovered that DAR chapters, already active in Americanization work, were willing to contact local public libraries as potential deposit stations. In attempting to fill the book boxes, Carr found that there was a lack of simply written texts in Italian about America and American life. He undertook to remedy the situation and wrote a pamphlet of which the translated title was *Guide for the Immigrant Italian in the United States of America*. It was published in 1911. The following sentences appeared in the last section: "An Italian, like any other foreigner, is appreciated when he lives the American social life. Until then he counts for nothing. Join American clubs; read American papers. Try to adapt yourself to the manners, and customs, and habits of the American people. . . . Speak in a low voice. Try not to gesticulate, and do not get excited in your discussions."[26] In 1911, Carr wrote to a friend: "Privately, I may tell you, that on the part of some Italians there is a certain jealousy as to our work. They feel that we are too anxious to turn Italians into Americans. My own eagerness for this I never attempt to conceal in the slightest degree, and though it may be painful to some Italians, I try to temper the pain by letting them see how very cordially I do appreciate Italy."[27] Speaking before the Connecticut DAR in 1913, Carr mentioned difficulties he had encountered earlier in securing the interest of librarians in his work with foreigners. All that had changed, he was happy to report.

The Guide was the first book not in English placed in the recommended list of the American Library Association Booklist. And following the efficient example of the Massachusetts Free Public Library Commission libraries all over the country are industriously using the Guide and opening their doors more hospitably to our foreign born.

For a first result, librarians, East and West and North are taking up the new work, asking advice of us, and help of many kinds, demanding the Guide in twenty-four additional languages.[28]

(It did appear in two more languages: Polish and Yiddish.)

Carr spoke regularly before library groups. He formed an Immigrant Education Society; under its imprint and that of the American Library Association, he published a pamphlet in 1914 called *Immigrant and Library: Italian Helps with Lists of Selected Books*. The "Italian helps" were phrases useful in library situations; the book lists were based on the boxes Carr had compiled for the Dante Alighieri Society. Carr urged that librarians bring the best side of American civilization to Italian immigrants, who so often saw the worst. Public libraries were warm and friendly places, he wrote, and they were open at night. The library, better than any other agency, "could destroy the impression of heartless commercialism, that many of our immigrants, in their colonies, continually assert is the main characteristic of our civilization." Carr was aware that public library work with immigrants was not a wholly new thing. "It dates back many years," he said, "but it is new in the extent of its present enterprise and interest."[29]

Among many pages of advice on how to attract immigrants to a library, Carr included a set of "Library Notices, Rules and Friendly Helps" in Italian which were pasted on the covers of all Italian books at the Mount Vernon, New York, Public Library. "Friend Reader!" it said, "Treat this book as thou wouldst a dear friend. Do not rumple it; do not soil it; do not tear it; do not mark it with a pencil or pen; do not moisten your fingers to turn its pages. . . . Respect this book for the good name and for the advantage of Italians."[30] Clearly librarians remained librarians even as they evolved into Americanizers.

Carr formed the Immigrant Publication Society in 1914. It had a distinguished advisory council which included social workers, educators, church people, and reformers, along with the director of the New York Public Library. Despite an impressive letterhead, the Society remained pretty much a one-man operation, with Carr often searching rather frantically for funds. One hundred sixty-five public libraries belonged to the Immigrant Publication Society, and Carr not only sold his pamphlets to libraries in bulk but continued to write articles and booklets especially for librarians. Over and over he proclaimed the value of a gentle assimilation program. " . . . [R]igorous and 'Prussian' methods of Americanization," he wrote in the *Library Journal* in 1919, "accomplished nothing but bitterness, stirring incredible resentment and antagonism among our foreign-born. They directly nourish the Bolshevism that we fear."[31]

Though not a librarian, Carr was named the first chairman of the American Library Association's Committee for Work with the Foreign Born, established in 1917. Its official purposes were : (1) to extend the knowledge and use of libraries among the foreign born, especially the unassimilated foreign born, and (2) to assemble a body of information and practice relating to work in this field. Among the early members of the Committee were Eleanor Ledbetter of Cleveland and Ernestine Rose and Mary Frank of the New York Public Library. Each wrote a pamphlet on library work with immigrants which Carr's Immigrant Publication Society then published. Mrs. Ledbetter noted ruefully in her pamphlet, *Winning Friends and Citizens for America; Work With Poles, Bohemians, and Others*, that although the butcher in her neighborhood could converse with immigrant customers in different languages, she could speak only one.

Eleanor Ledbetter had come to the Cleveland Public Library's Broadway Branch as a young widow in 1909. Within a year, she reported that 600 to 700 children were at the branch each day, that she was supplying book reviews to ethnic newspapers, and that "In a foreign neighborhood, each new friend is the beginning of a geometrical progression."[32] She diligently made the rounds of parochial schools, ethnic newspaper offices, churches, shops, and homes. An all-English speaking area would be monotonous, she stated; she did not find her library neighborhood foreign, but cosmopolitan. In 1918, she worked briefly for the Cleveland Americanization Committee but resigned because she thought their approach to immigrants was patronizing and offensive. "I have long ceased to think of any one at all as a 'foreigner,'" she said.[33]

Ideas similar to those of Carr and Mrs. Ledbetter were expressed by Ernestine Rose of the New York Public Library. The Seward Park Branch where she worked was in the very heart of the Jewish ghetto.

> The population in the ten blocks immediately surrounding the library is between 16,000 and 17,000. . . . The inner life of the older folk, mostly newcomers, is intensely foreign. To talk of "foreign work" as a phase or department in such a neighborhood is surely folly. All the work of the library must be foreign, if it is to be effective. Yet the library is and must remain an aggressively American institution.[34]

Rose recommended the extensive use of foreign assistants, home visits, good foreign collections, folk art exhibits, story hours in foreign languages, and the throwing open of the building for clubs, forums, and discussions. "We do not urge war or even patriotism," she wrote in 1917, "but we show, if we can, what patriotism really is, what our nation stands for, and what it demands from patriots in order that the ideals of America may be realized." She was intensely proud of having been told by a Jewish patron: "You have the Jewish spirit in this room. We feel it we Jews! And yet, you are Christians."[35]

Carr and the other ALA Committee members genuinely believed in the ideology of the melting pot. Immigrants and natives together could build America into the greatest nation in the world. "It is our duty," Carr told the ALA in 1916, "to reveal the ideal America, to prove that the sacred things of our past, and the great ideals of our fathers . . . can still be found in the America of today. This is the remedy for the divided allegiance that some fear."[36] Carr and the others were fighting a losing battle, however. Nativist groups had been gaining in strength since the 1880s and pushing steadily for restrictive legislation. They played upon a number of fears which were widespread in the country: that America was ceasing to be Protestant, that immigrants were importing radicalism, that a process of racial degeneration was taking place. The outbreak of World War I inspired the belief in many Americans that immigrants could not be trusted because they would remain loyal to their ancestral countries. General fears of foreign ideologies and loyalties coalesced with labor union complaints that there must be immigration restriction if American economic and social problems were ever to be solved.

All these things affected libraries and librarians. In a 1919 booklet for the Immigration Publication Society, Mary Frank of the New York Public Library denounced crude Americanization efforts but devoted her last few pages to the magnificent naturalizing effects of World War I on New York's East Side immigrant community. These immigrants, Frank said, had been pacifist by tradition. Then the draft had come and the boys had gone off to army camps. "To untold thousands of them," she said, "the training camp was not only teaching English, but also providing a liberal education in some of the essentials of Americanism." Describing a stirring parade of East Side school children for a Liberty Loan campaign, Frank commented: "One with us at last, the East Side was devotedly responding to the call of the President, rallying in love for the defense of their country."[37] The Juvenile Department Supervisor at the Los Angeles Public Library, carried away by the home guard task of "bringing out of the strange medley of nations in our midst united loyal Americans," asked her fellow librarians: "Have you ever seen an almond-eyed Cinderella or a Japanese Miles Standish in Puritan costume? There is a novelty and piquancy about the sight you will not forget."[38]

Carr and the other Committee members continued their efforts after the war; a definitely new note began to appear, however, in Carr's letters, articles, and speeches. He more and more frequently cautioned librarians to choose their foreign books carefully. The librarian who depended on the chance and irresponsible adviser, he warned, would soon have shelves "crowded with books of radical socialism, anarchism, bartenders' guides, books of religious propaganda, trash."[39] "In one short list of Yiddish books," he wrote in 1923, "we discovered 17 revolutionary books—all issued from one small shop on the East Side."[40]

The Quota Acts of 1921 and the Immigration Restriction Act of 1924 drastically reduced the number of new immigrants, particularly from southern and eastern Europe. By the 1930s, those who had been twenty and thirty years old during the decades of mass immigration were in their sixties or seventies. The next twenty years, therefore, brought a rapid decline in the numbers of Americans whose mother tongues were languages other than English. The "immigrant problem," in the sense in which the urban reformers of the pre–World War I period had perceived it, was over. The Committee for Work with Foreign Born had little with which to occupy itself. Those refugees from Nazism who did arrive were well educated; they helped shape our educational institutions rather than the other way around. Committee members talked of moving into different kinds of activities. An attempt in 1935 to set up a "Section for Inter-Racial Service" was denied by the ALA Council because a majority feared that the word "inter-racial" might be offensive in some parts of the country.[41] Early in 1941, there was talk among committee members of the inroads of Fascist propaganda among Italian-Americans, and they wondered if anything could be done to counter this. Long defunct in practice, the Committee on Work with the Foreign Born finally dissolved in 1948.

In the first quarter of this century, then, public librarians expanded their facilities into immigrant neighborhoods, consciously attempted some foreign language services as an opening wedge to assimilating immigrants, and cooperated with groups involved in citizenship programs. Their activities along these lines were cautious and modest. Certainly they did not grapple with the great economic, social, and political problems of the day but were engaged instead in what E. A. Ross so witheringly termed "petty betterment schemes." Compared to the powerful acculturation forces at work in American society, the overall public library impact on the assimilation of immigrants must have been slight.

Nonetheless, it is undeniably true that for certain individuals, the public library was crucial—not, I think, because of its special programs for immigrants or because of the social reform views of its employees, but because it was the major source of influential books which transmitted powerful ideas and changed lives. If there is irony in the fact that painfully genteel and conservative librarians thought of themselves as vigorous reformers, there is equal irony in the fact that these genteel custodians assembled library collections which supplied the intellectual children of poor immigrants with the keys to further education. Those library branches, despite their meager reproductions and their goody-two-shoes ambience, were linked—more than the public schools—to the great traditions of Western culture.

The cultural impact of the Brooklyn Public Library—in fact, the impact of that very branch in Brownsville described by Solis-Cohen—has been powerfully attested to by the Nobel prize physicist, I. I. Rabi. Rabi's family, orthodox Jews from Galicia, moved to Brownsville in 1908, and he discovered the public library branch soon after. "I saw some kid in class who had a book that was clearly not a schoolbook," Rabi recounts.

I asked him where he got it, and he told me about the library. . . . I read all the fairy stories and other stories in the children's section of the library. . . . Then I came to the end of *those* shelves, and there was a science shelf. So I started with astronomy. That was what determined my later life more than anything else—reading a little book on astronomy. That's where I first heard of the Copernican system. . . . Ours was such a fundamentalist family that my parents hadn't heard of the Copernican system, and for me it was a tremendous revelation. I was so impressed—the beauty of it all, and the simplicity.[42]

Another child of immigrants, the literary critic Alfred Kazin, has expressed beautifully what the Brooklyn Public Library meant to him. His autobiography, *A Walker in the City,* has a chapter called "The Block and Beyond." The block was the poor, crowded immigrant area of Brownsville in which Kazin's family lived. *"Beyond,"* he writes,

was anything old and American. . . . It was the Children's Library on Stone Avenue, because they had an awning over the front door; in the long peaceful reading room there were storybook tiles over the fireplace and covered deep wooden benches on either side of it where I read my way year after year from every story of Alfred the Great to *Twenty Thousand Leagues under the Sea.*[43]

Later, as a boy of sixteen, Kazin walked every night to an adult branch to get fresh books. In a single summer, from that single Brooklyn branch, Kazin obtained the plays of Eugene O'Neill, Turgenev's *Fathers and Sons,* Mann's *Death in Venice, The Education of Henry Adams,* biographies of Keats and Blake and Beethoven, *The Forsyte Saga,* histories, and dozens of other books.

[T]here was such ease at the long tables under the plants lining the windowsills, the same books of American history lay so undisturbed on the shelves, the wizened, faintly smiling little old lady who accepted my presence without question or suggestions or reproach was so delightful as she quietly, smilingly stamped my card and took back a batch of new books every evening, that whenever I entered the library I would walk up and down trembling in front of the shelves. For each new book I took away, there seemed to be ten more of which I was depriving myself.[44]

For these two, and for hundreds of other children of immigrants, public library branches supplied the spark which propelled them not just into America, but into wider worlds.

NOTES

1 James Harkness, "Growth Stock," *New York Times,* June 28, 1978, p. 31.
2 Minerva Sanders, "The Possibilities of Public Libraries in Manufacturing Communities," *Library Journal* 12 (1887): 398.
3 Maldwyn A. Jones, *American Immigration* (Chicago: University of Chicago Press, 1960), p. 207.

4 John Higham, *Send These to Me: Jews and Other Immigrants in Urban America* (New York: Atheneum, 1975), p. 37.
5 C. H. Cramer, *Open Shelves and Open Minds: A History of the Cleveland Public Library* (Cleveland and London: Press of Case Western Reserve University, 1972), p. 69.
6 Cleveland Public Library, *The Work of the Cleveland Public Library with the Children and the Means Used to Reach Them* (June, 1908), p. 34.
7 Phyllis Dain, *The New York Public Library: A History of Its Founding and Early Years* (New York: New York Public Library, 1972), p. 293.
8 Leon M. Solis-Cohen, "Library Work in the Brooklyn Ghetto," *Library Journal* 33 (1908): 485.
9 Margaret B. Freeman, "The Brownsville Children's Branch of the Brooklyn Public Library, Its Origin and Development" (unpublished M.A. thesis, Brooklyn Public Library, 1940), p. 23.
10 Sam Bass Warner, Jr., *Streetcar Suburbs: The Process of Growth in Boston, 1870–1900* (Cambridge: Harvard University Press, 1962), p. 32.
11 Editorial in *Library Journal* 19 (1894): 328.
12 J. Maud Campbell, "The Public Library and the Immigrant," *New York Libraries* 1 (1908): 105.
13 Ibid.
14 Van Wyck Brooks, *America's Coming of Age* (New York: Huebsch, 1915). Quoted in Henry May, *The Discontent of the Intellectuals: A Problem of the Twenties* (Chicago: Rand McNally, 1963), p. 7.
15 Allen F. Davis and Mary Lynn McCree, *Eighty Years at Hull House* (Chicago: Quadrangle Books, 1969), p. 50.
16 Jacob A. Riis, *The Making of an American* (New York: Macmillan, 1964), pp. 185–86.
17 Linda A. Eastman, "The Library and the Children . . . ," *Library Journal* 23 (1898): 143–44.
18 Herbert A. Croly, *The Promise of American Life* (New York: Macmillan, 1909), p. 400.
19 *NEA Proceedings*, 1914, p. 106.
20 Solis-Cohen, "Library Work," p. 487.
21 Peter Roberts, "The Library and the Foreign Speaking Man," *Library Journal* 36 (1911): 497.
22 U.S. Immigration Service, *Report*, vol. 41 (1911), pp. 9–10.
23 Gerd Korman, *Industrialization, Immigrants and Americanizers* (Madison, Wis.: State Historical Society, 1967), p. 138.
24 Marguerite Reid and John G. Moulton, *Aids in Library Work with Foreigners* (Chicago: American Library Association, 1912), p. 1.
25 John Foster Carr, "The Italians in the United States," *World's Work* 8 (1904): 5393.
26 John Foster Carr, *Guide to the United States for the Immigrant Italian* (Garden City, N.Y.: Doubleday, Page and Company, 1911), p. 71.
27 Letter, June 28, 1911, John Foster Carr Collection, Manuscripts and Archives Division, New York Public Library, Astor, Lenox and Tilden Foun-

dations.
28 "Our Work for Foreigners" (manuscript of speech delivered at the 21st anniversary of the Connecticut DAR, Nov. 11, 1913), John Foster Carr collection, Manuscripts and Archives Division, New York Public Library, Astor, Lenox and Tilden Foundations.
29 John Foster Carr, *Immigrant and Library* (New York: Immigrant Educational Society, 1914), p. 8.
30 Ibid., p. 89.
31 John Foster Carr, "Books in Foreign Languages and Americanization," *Library Journal* 44 (1919): 246.
32 Cleveland Public Library, *Annual Report 1910,*, p. 60.
33 Eleanor Ledbetter, *Winning Friends and Citizens for America: Work with Poles, Bohemians and Others* (New York: Immigrant Publication Society, 1918), p. 32.
34 Ernestine Rose, *Bridging the Gulf: Work with the Russian Jews and Other Newcomers* (New York: Immigrant Publication Society, 1917), p. 19.
35 Ibid., p. 23.
36 John Foster Carr, "Some of the People We Work For," *ALA Proceedings* 38 (1916): 154.
37 Mary Frank, *Exploring a Neighborhood: Our Jewish People from Eastern Europe and the Orient* (New York: Immigrant Publication Society, 1919), p. 37.
38 Jasmine Britton, "The Library's Share in Americanization," *Library Journal* 43 (1918): 723.
39 Carr, "Books in Foreign Languages and Americanization," p. 246.
40 Letter to Mary B. Bristol, Sept. 22, 1923. Immigrant Publication Society Papers, Manuscripts and Archives Division, New York Public Library, Astor, Lenox and Tilden Foundations.
41 *American Library Association Proceedings*, 1935, p. 732.
42 Jeremy Bernstein, *Experiencing Science* (New York: Basic Books, 1978), pp. 44–45.
43 Alfred Kazin, *A Walker in the City* (New York: Harcourt Brace Jovanovich, 1971), pp. 90–91.
44 Ibid., p. 170.

BIBLIOGRAPHY

Bernstein, Jeremy. *Experiencing Science*. New York: Basic Books, 1978.
Britton, Jasmine. "The Library's Share in Americanization." *Library Journal* 43 (1918):723–27.
Campbell, J. Maud. "The Public Library and the Immigrant." *New York Libraries* 1 (1908):105.
Carr, John Foster. "Books in Foreign Languages and Americanization." *Library Journal* 44 (1919):245–46.
Carr, John Foster. *Guide to the United States for the Italian Immigrant*. Garden

City, N.Y.: Doubleday, Page & Company, 1911.

Carr, John Foster. *Immigrant and Library.* New York: Immigrant Educational Society, 1914.

Carr, John Foster. "The Italians in the United States." *World's Work* 8 (1904):5393–5404.

Carr, John Foster. "Some of the People We Work For." In *ALA Proceedings* 38 (1916):149–54.

Cleveland Public Library. *Annual Report 1910.*

Cleveland Public Library. *The Work of the Cleveland Public Library with the Children and the Means Used to Reach Them.* 1908.

Cramer, Clarence H. *Open Shelves and Open Minds: A History of the Cleveland Public Library.* Cleveland: Press of Case Western Reserve University, 1972.

Croly, Herbert A. *The Promise of American Life.* New York: Macmillan, 1909.

Dain, Phyllis. *The New York Public Library: A History of Its Founding and Early Years.* New York: New York Public Library, 1972.

Davis, Allen F., and Mary Lynn McCree. *Eighty Years at Hull House.* Chicago: Quadrangle Books, 1969.

Eastman, Linda A. "The Library and the Children: An Account of the Children's Work in the Cleveland Public Library." *Library Journal* 23 (1898):142–44.

"Foreign Books in American Libraries" (editorial). *Library Journal* 19 (1894):328.

Frank, Mary. *Exploring a Neighborhood: Our Jewish People from Eastern Europe and the Orient.* New York. Immigrant Publication Society, 1919.

Freeman, Margaret B. "The Brownsville Children's Branch of the Brooklyn Public Library, Its Origin and Development." Master's thesis, Brooklyn Public Library, 1940.

Harkness, James. "Growth Stock." *New York Times,* June 28, 1978.

Higham, John. *Send These to Me: Jews and Other Immigrants in Urban America.* New York: Atheneum, 1975.

Jones, Maldwyn A. *American Immigration.* Chicago: University of Chicago Press, 1960.

Kazin, Alfred. *A Walker in the City.* New York: Harcourt Brace Jovanovich, 1971.

Korman, Gerd. *Industrialization, Immigrants, and Americanizers: The View from Milwaukee, 1866–1921.* Madison: State Historical Society of Wisconsin, 1967.

Ledbetter, Eleanor. *Winning Friends and Citizens for America: Work with Poles, Bohemians and Others.* New York: Immigrant Publication Society, 1918.

May, Henry. *The Discontent of the Intellectuals: A Problem of the Twenties.* Chicago: Rand McNally, 1963.

New York. New York Public Library. Manuscripts and Archives Division. Immigrant Publication Society papers.

New York. New York Public Library. Manuscripts and Archives Division. John Foster Carr collection.

Peterson, Mildred Othmer. "Work with the Foreign Born Committee Round Table." In American Library Association, *Proceedings* 57 (1935):731–33.

Reid, Marguerite, and John G. Moulton. *Aids in Library Work with Foreigners.* Chicago: American Library Association, 1912.

Riis, Jacob A. *The Making of an American.* New York: Macmillan, 1964.

Roberts, Peter. "The Library and the Foreign-Speaking Man." *Library Journal* 36 (1911):496–99.

Rose, Ernestine. *Bridging the Gulf: Work with the Russian Jews and Other Newcomers.* New York: Immigrant Publication Society, 1917.

Ross, Edward A. "Education for Social Service." In *NEA Proceedings* 52 (1914):103–6.

Sanders, Minerva. "The Possibilities of Public Libraries in Manufacturing Communities." *Library Journal* 12 (1887):395–400.

Solis-Cohen, Leon M. "Library Work in the Brooklyn Ghetto." *Library Journal* 33 (1908):485–88.

U.S. Immigration Service, *Report,* vol. 41 (1911).

Warner, Sam Bass, Jr. *Streetcar Suburbs: The Process of Growth in Boston, 1870–1900.* Cambridge: Harvard University Press, 1962.

TENTH ANNUAL MORRIS FROMKIN MEMORIAL LECTURE

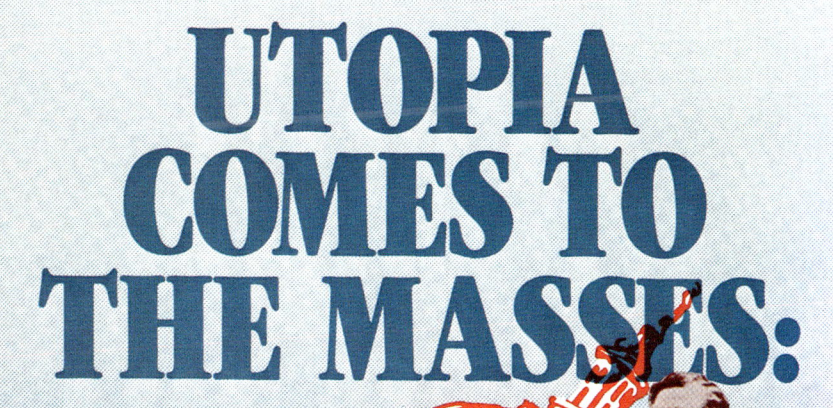

UTOPIA COMES TO THE MASSES:

Huey P. Long's Share-Our-Wealth Society

GLEN JEANSONNE
Assistant Professor of History
THE UNIVERSITY OF WISCONSIN—MILWAUKEE
Recipient of the 1979 Fromkin Research Grant

Thursday, November 15, 1979
3:30 PM

East Wing, First Floor
The Golda Meir Library

THE PUBLIC IS CORDIALLY INVITED TO ATTEND.
RECEPTION FOLLOWS.
SPONSORED BY THE FROMKIN MEMORIAL COLLECTION OF THE GOLDA MEIR LIBRARY, THE UNIVERSITY OF WISCONSIN—MILWAUKEE

Utopia Comes to the Masses: Huey P. Long's Share-Our-Wealth Society[1]

GLEN S. JEANSONNE

ALTHOUGH his career spanned only a decade and a half, Huey P. Long, popularly known as the Kingfish, is widely acknowledged as the most important politician the state of Louisiana ever produced. However, there is no consensus about Long's legacy. Former governor Sam Jones writes: "More bunkum has been written about Huey Long and his place in history than any man in this region I know of."[2] One historian hails him as the first southerner since Calhoun to have an original idea, but others condemn him as a man obsessed with personal power. John Kingston Fineran, who entitled his book about Long *The Career of a Tinpot Napoleon,* terms him "that most extraordinary mountebank, that most mendacious liar, that eminent blackguard and distinguished sneak-thief, Huey P. Long."[3] On the other hand, the late Professor T. Harry Williams claims that Long was a genuine champion of the people, excusing the excesses of his rule on the grounds that "the politician who wishes to do good may have to do some evil to achieve his goal."[4] A contemporary summed up Huey's impact when he said that Long did more good, and more evil, than anyone in Louisiana's history.[5]

Long's high intelligence is unchallenged, however misdirected it may have been. James A. Farley said that the Louisianian had the best mind that he had ever witnessed, but had squandered it. Long

---

Glen S. Jeansonne, who studied at the University of Southwestern Louisiana and Florida State University, has written on Louisiana politics and gubernatorial elections and on Leander Perez. He is now at work on a biography of Gerald L. K. Smith, a close associate of Huey Long.

himself boasted, "There may be smarter men than me, but they ain't in Louisiana."[6]

The Kingfish's brilliance certainly was not the result of his sporadic formal education. Expelled from one high school, he later graduated from another, but never received a college degree. His indiscriminate reading consisted of romantic novels, biographies, and history and philosophy books he only partly understood. Part of Long's appeal sprang from his limitations; his simple, direct approach to alleviating poverty would have been impossible if he had viewed the world in all its complexity.

In Long's time Louisiana provided a tempting opportunity for a charismatic leader. It was perhaps the most backward state in the union—impoverished, illiterate, and with a tradition of boss rule. Long later exaggerated his own family's poverty because it was good politics, but it is true that he could not afford a college education. Instead he became an itinerant salesman peddling books, cooking lard, and Lydia E. Pinkham's patent medicine. At nineteen he married one of his customers. Then he daringly borrowed money, enrolled in the Tulane University Law school, crammed three years of study into one, and passed a special bar examination.

His political career began in 1918 when, at the age of twenty-five, he was elected to the commission that regulated railways, public utilities, and pipelines. He was so proud of his first political office that he suggested to the other commissioners that they all wear gold badges. By opposing the Standard Oil corporation's monopoly of pipelines, Public Service Commissioner Long achieved a statewide reputation as an enemy of corporate power and a champion of the underdog. In 1923 he lost a race for governor, but in 1927 he ran again and won. On the night of his victory, Long told his followers: "Stick by me. . . . I'm going to be President some day."[7]

Governor Long fulfilled enough of his promises to make credible his claim as champion of the poor, launching a grandiose public works program unmatched in the South. The audacious young governor provided free schoolbooks, expanded adult education, and made Louisiana State University a showcase of his administration. But in doing so, he thoroughly politicized the university, sheltering mediocrities and making personal loyalty the chief criterion of employment. In both public works and education, Long was more concerned with publicity than with substance. His activities at LSU centered on the football team and the band more than on mundane academics. He made the band the largest in the nation. He bought players and coaches and gave state jobs to football heroes—he even appointed one halfback to the state legislature. When editors of the student newspaper condemned this childish display, he had them expelled. After LSU lost one game 7–6, Long had a follower introduce a bill outlawing the point after touchdown.[8]

Those opposed to Long found little humor in such episodes. Through an electrifying display of raw power, Long constructed a state political machine unparalleled in America for subservience to a single individual. Stalking the floor of the legislature, he told senators and representatives how to vote and bullied committees. On one occasion his rubber-stamp legislature passed forty-four administration bills in twenty-two minutes, without even reading them. He was candid about his methods: He said of one obedient legislator, "We bought him like a sack of potatoes"; of another, "We got that guy so cheap we thought we stole him." When an opponent charged that Huey was flouting the state constitution, the Kingfish replied, "I'm the Constitution around here now."[9]

Long was never satisfied. While holding one office, he dreamed of a higher one. In 1930, two years before his term as governor ended, he ran for the United States Senate. He defeated the incumbent by 40,000 votes but did not take his seat until his term as governor expired because he distrusted his lieutenant governor. After 1932 he continued to control Louisiana through an amiable puppet, O. K. Allen, a Winnfield friend whom he rewarded with the governorship for having loaned Huey $500 in his first political campaign. He made no secret about his presidential aspirations. When ex-president Coolidge and his wife visited Louisiana and were photographed with the Kingfish, Long suggested a caption: "It's a picture of past and future Presidents." He asked the Coolidges if the Hoovers were good housekeepers because, he said, he planned to move into the White House.[10]

Long's path to the White House was to be prepared by a stroke of inspiration—the Share-Our-Wealth Society. Long, who had never read economics and was proud of it, gleaned figures from government reports and popular magazines to demonstrate that 65 to 70 percent of the wealth of the United States was owned by only 2 percent of the people. He had first theorized about the consequences of such a concentration of wealth in a letter to the *New Orleans Item* in 1918. Although at the time he proposed no solution, even Long's critics had to admit that he had directed attention to a festering problem which was all too real and painful.

Long borrowed some of his ideas, although not the specific Share-Our-Wealth plan, from state senator S. J. Harper, a Winnfield radical who had demanded conscription of wealth during World War I. In 1934, still citing the same figures he had used in 1918, Long proposed an ingenious remedy for the unequal distribution of wealth which he and Harper had pointed out almost two decades earlier: Put the entire burden of taxation upon millionaires! No one would pay a single cent until he had earned at least $1,000,000. Taxes would start at 1 percent on the first million and double with each additional million until the levy reached 100 percent on the seventh million. Inheritances and total personal wealth would be strictly limited.[11]

The middle and lower classes would not only pay no taxes, but would have their material comforts provided by the federal government. Long promised that he would provide each family with:

1. A home, a car, and a radio worth $5,000 in all.
2. A guaranteed annual income of at least $2,500. (He sometimes promised as much as $5,000.)
3. A free college education for all youths who qualified by I.Q. tests.
4. A temporary moratorium on debts.
5. Old-age pensions and veterans' bonuses.
6. A $10,000,000,000 reclamation project to control floods and convert the dust bowl into fertile farms.
7. Free medical care and a "war on disease" directed by the Mayo brothers.[12]

The appeal of the plan was dramatic. Within a month of its founding in January, 1934, the Share-Our-Wealth Society boasted 200,000 members; within a year 3,000,000. By the beginning of 1935 there were 7,500,000 on the roles. Huey's mail increased enormously. He received more than the president and as much as all the other senators and representatives combined, requiring a special truck to deliver his mail alone. His national organizer, Gerald L. K. Smith, claimed that in 1934 the public spent half a million dollars on postage to write Huey.[13]

The strength of Huey's grass roots support lay in the simplicity of his program. There were no dues and no fund raising, but every member received a copy of Long's autobiography, *Every Man a King*, broadsides, buttons, and copies of Huey's speeches—all mailed under the senator's franking privilege. In writing as well as speeches, Long reduced economic theory to the idiom of the masses and presented his case in an unvarnished, entertaining style. But he had little respect for the intellect of the average American. The Kingfish told a secretary that the secret of his success as a propagandist was to "always write everything so a six-year-old child can understand it."[14] Nonetheless, he promoted his program by citing support of wealth sharing from such famous Americans as Daniel Webster, Abraham Lincoln, and Theodore Roosevelt and such eminent world figures as Plato, Pope Pius XI, and the poet John Milton.[15]

Although contemporary journalists identified Long as a radical or at least an extreme liberal, the Kingfish himself denied that such labels were meaningful. In his fantasy account of a mythical Long administration, entitled *My First Days in the White House*, he writes, "Other politicians had promised to re-make America: I had promised to sustain it."[16] His utopia is predominantly a middle-class America. It springs to life not by revolution but by the electoral process—election of a president committed to the Share-Our-Wealth Plan. In fact, Long's new economic order depended on nothing more potent than his own powers of persuasion. In *My First Days in the White House*, every obstacle to wealth sharing crumbles with Long's election as president: unemployment is abolished simultaneously with the introduction of labor-saving machinery; schools, colleges, and adult education flourish. Most millionaires surrender to Long with no more than a whimper. John D. Rockefeller signs away his entire fortune; Andrew Mellon praises Long for relieving him of a fortune he considered a burden.

As his little fantasy book indicates, Long fully intended to run for president. His pretense for breaking with Roosevelt was that something more effective than the New Deal was needed to end the depression. But more important than differences in ideology was the fact that Roosevelt stood in the way of Long's quest for national power. By mid-1935 Long had discussed a third party with such potential allies as Father Coughlin, Georgia governor Eugene Talmadge, and Minnesota governor Floyd Olson. He sent Gerald Smith to talk with Republican leaders. Smith reported that the Republicans would help finance Long's candidacy and that the Kingfish would help name the Republican nominee.

Long based his strategy on three possible scenarios. The most likely plan would be to cause a Republican victory in 1936. By 1940 the nation would be exasperated with an ineffectual Republican administration. Then Long would hold the Democrats hostage to another third-party threat, extort the nomination, and win easily. This scenario, which Long believed most likely, is indicative of his priorities. He was willing to force upon the nation four bleak years of suffering before he personally would lead them to prosperity.

Another possibility was a three-cornered contest where no candidate received a majority, thereby relegating the decision to the House, which, because Long controlled a bloc of voters from Louisiana and other southern states, would make him a president. Finally, there was the remote possibility that Huey could engineer an incredible upset. In one of his expansive moods, he told Arthur Krock of the *New York Times:* "I can take this Roosevelt. He's scared of me. I can out promise him, and he knows it."[17]

President Roosevelt, who termed Long "one of the two most dangerous men in the country," was so concerned that he commissioned a poll to determine Huey's electoral potential. The results were disturbing. Huey would receive almost 8 percent of the popular vote, splitting the Democratic electorate and producing Republican pluralities in five key states, including New York and California.[18]

Long's potential candidacy and reputation as a utopian reformer did not go unchallenged. Walter Lippmann suggested discrediting the Kingfish with his own handiwork: Let him frame a bill and introduce it in Congress, which would then prove it ridiculous in committee hearings. Upton Sinclair, who advocated his own socialist panacea, condemned Long for exploitation of suffering by raising hopes that could never be fulfilled. He pointed out that Long himself had estimated that it would require $100 billion to raise twenty million indigent families out of poverty at a time when the book value of capital wealth in the entire country was somewhere between $70 billion and $90 billion. Much of this book value would disappear if Long's plan were adopted because there would be no potential buyers. Others pointed out that Long had underestimated the number of poor families who would be eligible for his grants—there were thirty million, not twenty million such families.[19]

Long's tax plan was equally impractical. By 1933 only forty-six individuals in the United States earned more than $1 million yearly. Long's tax on this handful of millionaires would yield only about $1.50 for each of his twenty million indigent families. Long could not redistribute more than there was, and total business income had fallen from $9.13 billion in 1929 to $1.96 billion in 1930. By 1932 there was a deficit of $4.60 billion. Huey's premise that no man can consume more than his physical requirements ignored other uses for capital, such as industrial investment, which were necessary to prevent a total collapse of production.[20]

Overestimation of the wealth available was not the only economic flaw in Long's plan. He had no means of liquidating tangible wealth such as factories, ships, and mines into a form that could be distributed equally. The only things that could be distributed were profits, and these represented only a small fraction of the total value of any great fortune. How could the Ford Motor Company's assets be converted to provide homes, radios, and college educations? A family might find itself the owner of two gears from an assembly line, a car door, a two-ton cornerstone from an office building, or the mast of a millionaire's yacht.

Long's critics did not hesitate to point out these absurdities. The *New York Journal* challenged Long to "put up or shut up." Such criticism was not limited to conservatives or to millionaires who were in danger of losing their fortunes. The Communist party, Upton Sinclair, Walter Lippmann, and the old Populist economist, William H. "Coin" Harvey, ridiculed the plan. The *New Republic* posed a series of questions which Long could not, or at least did not answer: what were the sources of his statistics; what would be done to the economic system in order that everyone have enough; did he favor public ownership; how would he induce capitalists to accept his plan; with what industries would he begin; and what would prevent his movement from turning into facism? The *New Republic* questioned Long's candor and then concluded: "But even if Long were sincere, his economic ignorance, his total lack of understanding of or appreciation for the labor movement, would make it almost certain that he would fail." Certainly Long could not convince his colleagues in Congress. He introduced his Senate bill several times and once proposed it as an alternative to social security, but it never polled more than fourteen votes.[21]

There is nothing in Long's background to indicate that he could be trusted with the power to reorder society. Huey showed little concern for poverty in his own parish (county) or even in his own family. He made no charitable contributions, nor did he manifest any personal charity in human relationships that was not accompanied by exploitation. For example, Long did not practice in Louisiana what he preached in Washington. Anyone who believed that Long's rhetoric was sincere need only have looked at Louisiana, where blacks were disenfranchised, women second-class citizens, labor unorganized, free speech repressed, and children exploited for long hours in fields and mills. When asked why he did not push for ratification of the Child Labor Amendment by his compliant state legislature, Long replied that it would be unpopular in Louisiana and added that "picking cotton is fun for the kids, anyway." When questioned by labor leaders about the absence of a minimum wage law in Louisiana, Long bristled. He told them that the minimum wage on state projects was as low as he could get men to work, adding that they should be happy to get work at any salary.[22]

Long's Louisiana was hardly a utopia. The standard of living there was 60 percent lower than in the northern states. After seven years of rule by the Long machine, Louisiana had no unemployment insurance. The state had no income tax at all until 1934, the year before Huey's death, and then it was one of the least graduated in the nation. In 1933, when Long's term as governor ended, Louisiana still ranked forty-seventh in the union in literacy and school attendance. The belief that Long brought improved social services to the state is a misconception. Huey did not introduce old-age pensions in Louisiana. In fact, he attacked such a program when advocated by a political opponent—on the grounds that one-third of the money would go to blacks.[23]

Professor T. Harry Williams argues in his biography of Long that there was no discrimination against blacks in Huey's economic program. But the programs that did help blacks, such as free textbooks, did so for purely bureaucratic reasons rather than from an absence of racial prejudice. Huey's financial aid to LSU was subsidization of a strictly Jim Crow school. There was no corresponding effort to improve black education or to equalize salaries of black and white teachers. Long's public works rewarded builders who refused to employ blacks. Every aspect of business, government, public services, and politics, including the Share-Our-Wealth Society, was racially segregated. Long had as lieutenants two men who later ranked among the most infamous racists in the nation, Leander Perez and Gerald L. K. Smith, both of whom prided themselves for their role in Long's organization. Smith, himself an accomplished demagogue, worshipped Long. A spellbinding orator steeped in fundamentalist rhetoric, Smith exhorted his listeners to "share, share, share" the wealth and urged them to "pull down these huge piles of gold until there shall be a real job, not a little old sow-belly, black-eyed pea job but a real spending money, beefsteak and gravy, Chevrolet, Ford in the garage, new suit, Thomas Jefferson, Jesus Christ, red, white and blue job for every man." Smith claimed that Wall Street would stop at nothing, including assassination, to silence Long and him. Once when a firecracker exploded while he was speaking, Smith blurted: "They've tried to shoot me before. But if they ever did and I went down in a pool of blood there would be a thousand men in this parish to rise up in my place."[24]

No one questions Long's or Smith's effectiveness as orators; what should be questioned, though, is their effect, if any, on institutional change. Some journalists and historians credit Long with forcing Roosevelt to veer left by enacting social security and a steeply graduated wealth tax in 1935. But Roosevelt was hardly converted to Long's view and in any case wanted the legislation passed before the 1936 election. There was nothing in any of his bills that President Roosevelt had not advocated previously, and social security had been in planning before Long broke with the president. Roosevelt's actions were an expedient response to conditions generally rather than to Long explicitly.

Many Louisianians believe that Long would have been elected president in 1936. Elmer Irey of the Internal Revenue Service disagrees. He contends that Long would have been convicted of income tax evasion, bribery, embezzlement, private use of state facilities, and mail fraud in the fall of 1935, and along with his chief assistants he would have sat out the election in a federal penitentiary. All of this is speculation, because Long was assassinated in Baton Rouge in September, 1935, by a lone gunman, Dr. Carl Austin Weiss. The coroner found one bullet in Huey and sixty-one bullet holes in Dr. Weiss, whose body was shredded by bullets from Long's bodyguards.[25]

As Long lay in Our Lady of the Lake Hospital, in the shadow of the thirty-four-story state capitol he had built, thousands prayed that he would live. Others prayed that he would die. After his body lay in state for the 200,000 who attended his funeral, he was buried on the capitol grounds, his grave bathed in light from a spotlight on the top of the skyscraper and protected by an armed guard. Most people thought the guard was hired to keep vandals out, but some wisecracked that it was really to keep Huey in.

With the publication in 1969 of T. Harry Williams's biography *Huey Long*, the scholarly community replaced an overly critical stereotype of Long with an excessively laudatory one. Vague on Long's vices, specific and detailed on his virtues, the work convinced many socially concerned historians who knew little firsthand about Long or Louisiana. It is time for a balanced evaluation, judging Long neither on his self-assessment nor on those of his enemies, but upon his place in the context of American history.

Although Long claimed he was unique, actually he was not as original as he liked to appear. Father Coughlin, Dr. Townsend, and Upton Sinclair had all proposed programs to increase the purchasing power of the poor. Advocates of an inflated national currency date back to the early days of the Republic. The Populists of the 1890s advocated inflationary "soft" or silver currency to end the imbalance between what impoverished farmers bought and sold. The muckrakers, advocates of the New Freedom, and Justice Louis D. Brandeis had inveighed against the concentration of wealth that Long deplored. So had common people: the corner grocer, the country doctor, and the hardscrabble farmer. Since the industrialization of America had accelerated in the decades after the Civil War, a segment of opinion equated big business with repression and exploitation; this opinion hardened into hatred when hard times set in. Long appealed to these legions of the deprived. But Huey did not want to go forward; rather, he wanted to go backward. He was in fact fighting a rear guard action against what America was becoming in the twentieth century. He was more a product of rural, fundamentalist orthodoxy than his critics realized or he was willing to admit. Consider his plans: simplify the tax structure by taxing only millioniares; streamline the government and eradicate the unproductive bureaucracy; and emphasize the verities of the Bible, the Puritan ethic, the morality of rural America, and the social uplift of nineteenth-century utopians.

Because he attacked the wealthy, Long is sometimes branded a socialist. But he always opposed government ownership of the means of production and thus had little connection with socialism except as a common enemy. Others describe Long as a fascist. There is indeed in Long's thought a resemblance to fascism, with his authoritarianism, anticommunism, and reorganization of the economy without public ownership. In his personal charisma and ability to electrify a crowd, he resembled fascist demagogues. But at heart Long was neither a socialist nor a fascist. Instead Long belongs to the tradition of economic tinkerers, of single interest advocates who hatched such ideas as the single tax, unbacked greenbacks, and the coining of silver—the tradition of Henry George, William Jennings Bryan, and "Coin" Harvey.

Long, like the American populists, combined economic radicalism with social prejudice. Long and the populist leaders were joined by a common prejudice against bankers, establishment politicians, and city people. They also shared a conspiratorial world view. This concept of conspiracy runs through Long's entire career: conspiracies of lumber barons in his birthplace, Winnfield; of Standard Oil; of the opponents who allegedly compelled him to "fight fire with fire"; of Wall Street, John D. Rockefeller, and Andrew Mellon. This conspiratorial paranoia, and Long's ability to exploit it, is a key element in understanding the Kingfish and his place in history.

Conspiratorial delusion has a long history in America in the fear of different races, economic groups, and religious or secular philosophies. Anti-Catholicism, anti-Semitism, the anti-Masonic movement, the Ku Klux Klan, and more recently the White Citizens' Council and the American Nazi Party all thrive on fear and resentment, though not necessarily fear of the same thing. But they appeal to the same types of individuals: the frustrated, the defeated, those seeking a scapegoat. Just as George Wallace's career would be inconceivable without racial tension or Joseph McCarthy's without communism, Huey could not have advanced so far so swiftly without his particular scapegoat—the millionaire.

Huey Long is still used as a yardstick by which other southern politicians are judged, and thus it is important that our perception of Long be accurate. In eulogizing Huey Long, Professor Williams does a disservice to sincere and honest public servants. The tragedy is that many have accepted Long himself and his chief biographer on their own words and thus have permitted corruption and demagoguery to go virtually unchallenged. At the state level Long and his partisans sanctified the notion that the cost of progress must inevitably be authoritarianism and fiscal corruption.

If Long jolted a backward state out of apathy, he did not bring lasting change. On the contrary, many Louisianians have become thoroughly disenchanted with politics, and today only one-third even read a daily newspaper. Only 13 percent receive a college education, and in 1979 almost 50 percent of the education graduates of state colleges failed the national teacher certification test. The state is forty-fifth in per capita income. Fully 22 percent of Louisiana families live below the government-established poverty line; among blacks the figure is 47 percent.[26]

On the national level, Long's legacy is moral enervation. Because he fought enemies who conspicuously opposed reform, sometimes he is mistakenly considered a reformer. But in his excesses and in the totalitarian nature of his regime in Louisiana, he retarded true reform. Labeling Long a reformer, as Professor Williams has done, dangerously links reform with despotism. Extremism in the pursuit of superficial reform is no virtue, particularly when one is interested mainly in the rhetoric of reform.

Even Long's motivations were vain, and the hate he stirred in others was not conducive to rational debate. Unlike responsible socialists and populists, Long did not actually draw up a national platform, run for office, and live to see his ideas either rejected or endorsed. His assassination prevented that. But we hope that his martyrdom will not lead us historians to be more generous to his memory than his character merits.

NOTES

1. I would like to thank Stephen A. Webre, Bruce Fetter, Margaret Dalrymple, Michael Beschloss, and Wendy Bousfield for their critical reading of the manuscript.
2. Harnett T. Kane, *Louisiana Hayride: The American Rehearsal for Dictatorship, 1928–1940*, 2nd ed. rev. (Gretna, La.: Pelican Publishing Company, 1971), p. vii.
3. John Kingston Fineran, *The Career of a Tinpot Napoleon: A Political Biography of Huey P. Long* (New Orleans: The Author, 1932), p. 172.
4. T. Harry Williams, *Huey Long* (New York: Alfred A. Knopf, 1969), p. x.
5. Kane, *Louisiana Hayride*, p. 141.
6. Stan Opotowsky, *The Longs of Louisiana* (New York: E. P. Dutton & Company, 1960), p. 96.
7. Kane, *Louisiana Hayride*, pp. 42, 47, 58; Opotowsky, *The Longs of Louisiana*, p. 39; Thomas Martin, *Dynasty: The Longs of Louisiana* (New York: G. P. Putnam's Sons, 1960), pp. 23–32.
8. Opotowsky, *The Longs of Louisiana*, pp. 93–94; Martin, *Dynasty*, pp. 90–92.
9. Kane, *Louisiana Hayride*, pp. 64–65.
10. Williams, *Huey Long*, pp. 429–30; Kane, *Louisiana Hayride*, p. 87; Martin, *Dynasty*, p. 84.
11. Huey P. Long, *Every Man a King* (Chicago: Quadrangle Books, 1964), pp. 295, 338–40; Williams, *Huey Long*, p. 693; *Oklahoma City Daily Oklahoman*, September 3, 1935; Huey Long Scrapbook no. 35, p. 39, Louisiana State University Archives, Baton Rouge, La. (hereafter cited as HLS).
12. Buel W. Patch, *National Wealth and National Income*, Editorial Research Reports, vol. 1, no. 15, April 20, 1935 (Washington, 1935), pp. 302–3; Vernon L. Parrington, Jr., *American Dreams: A Study of American Utopias* (Providence: Brown University Press, 1947), pp. 198–99; Huey P. Long, *My First Days in the White House* (Harrisburg, Pa.: Telegraph Press, 1935), pp. 45–46, 59–64, 109–15; Opotowsky, *The Longs of Louisiana*, p. 72; Arthur M. Schlesinger, Jr., *The Age of Roosevelt: The Politics of Upheaval* (Boston: Houghton Mifflin Company, 1960), pp. 62–63.
13. "Huey's Organizer Says He'll Share 15 Million Votes," unmarked clipping, HLS no. 28, p. 73; Carleton Beals, *The Story of Huey P. Long* (Philadelphia: J. B. Lippincott Company, 1935), p. 292.
14. Williams, *Huey Long*, p. 454.
15. Huey P. Long, *Share Our Wealth*, in HLS no. 28, p. 86.
16. Long, *My First Days in the White House*, p. 3.
17. Robert E. Snyder, "Huey Long and the Presidential Election of 1936," *Louisiana History* 16:2 (Spring 1975): 127–28.
18. Ibid., pp. 117, 131–34. The other "dangerous man" was General Douglas MacArthur (p. 117).
19. Max Knepper, "Share the Wealth Plan No Solution," *Upton Sinclair's National Epic News*, June 3, 1935, in HLS no. 26, p. 102; Beals, *The Story of Huey P. Long*, pp. 311–12; *New York Daily News*, March 8, 1935, in HLS no. 35, p. 39.

20 Beals, *The Story of Huey P. Long*, pp. 311–12; *Little Rock Arkansas Democrat*, quoting *St. Louis Post-Dispatch*, n.d., in HLS no. 28, p. 25; Warren J. Bishop, "Can We Make Everybody Rich?" *Nation's Business* 22 (October 1934): 81.
21 "Huey Proposes," *New Republic* 82 (March 20, 1935): 146–47; Williams, *Huey Long*, pp. 632–33.
22 January 12, 1935, in HLS no. 28, p. 80; Kane, *Louisiana Hayride*, p. 117; Opotowsky, *The Longs of Louisiana*, p. 86.
23 Beals, *The Story of Huey P. Long*, p. 340; Opotowsky, *The Longs of Louisiana*, p. 76; "Sharing the Wealth in Louisiana," *New York Post*, May 11, 1935; *New Orleans Times-Picayune*, January 13, 1979; Neal R. Pierce, *The Deep South States of America: People, Politics and Power in the Seven Deep South States* (New York: W. W. Norton & Company, 1974), pp. 77–79; Martin, *Dynasty*, p. 99.
24 Williams, *Huey Long*, p. 700; Lillian B. Miller et al., *If Elected . . . : Unsuccessful Candidates for the Presidency, 1796–1968* (Washington: Smithsonian Institution Press, 1972), p. 408; *Baton Rouge State Times*, May 28, 1934.
25 Kane, *Louisiana Hayride*, p. 135; Williams, *Huey Long*, pp. 864–65; Martin, *Dynasty*, pp. 144–45.
26 *New Orleans Times-Picayune*, January 13, 1979; Pierce, *The Deep South States of America*, pp. 77–79.

BIBLIOGRAPHY

NEWSPAPERS

American Progress (New Orleans), 1933–37.
Baton Rouge Morning Advocate, 1934–37.
Louisiana Progress (Hammond), 1930–32.
New Orleans Item, 1934–37.
New Orleans States, 1934–37.
New Orleans Times-Picayune, 1934–37.
New York Times, 1934–37.
Shreveport Journal, 1934–37.

ARCHIVAL SOURCES

Baton Rouge, Louisiana State University Archives. Huey P. Long papers.
Eureka Springs, Arkansas. Gerald L. K. Smith papers (in possession of family).
Hyde Park, New York. Franklin D. Roosevelt Library. Franklin D. Roosevelt papers.
Natchitoches, Louisiana. Huey P. Long Museum.
New Orleans. Tulane University Archives. Cecil Morgan papers.
Washington, D.C. Library of Congress. Franklin D. Roosevelt papers.

PRINTED SOURCES

Baldwin, Hanson W., and Shepard Stone, eds. *We Saw It Happen: The News Behind the News That's Fit to Print.* New York: Simon and Schuster, 1938.

Bass, Jack, and Walter DeVries. *The Transformation of Southern Politics.* New York: Basic Books, 1976.

Beals, Carleton. *The Inside Story of Huey P. Long.* Philadelphia: J. B. Lippincott Company, 1935.

Bennett, David H. *Demagogues in the Depression: American Radicals and the Union Party, 1932–1936.* New Brunswick, New Jersey: Rutgers University Press, 1969.

Billington, Monroe Lee. *The Political South in the Twentieth Century.* New York: Scribner's, 1975.

Blakey, Roy G., and Gladys C. Blakey. "Revenue Act of 1935—Share the Wealth." Ch. 15 in *The Federal Income Tax.* New York: Longmans, Green and Co., 1940.

Bliven, Bruce. "Huey in 1936?" *New Republic* 82 (March 13, 1935):126.

Bliven, Bruce. "Roosevelt and the Radicals." *New Republic* 75 (July 12, 1933):228–230.

Brinkley, Alan. "Huey Long, the Share-Our-Wealth Movement, and Political Insurgency in the Great Depression." Paper presented to a meeting of the Southern Historical Association, St. Louis, Missouri, November 10, 1978.

Bunche, Ralph J. "Restrictions on Voting in the South." In *The Political Status of the Negro in the Age of FDR,* edited by Dewey W. Granthan. Chicago: University of Chicago Press, 1973.

Burns, James MacGregor. *Roosevelt: The Lion and the Fox.* New York: Harcourt Brace and Company, 1956.

Calverton, V. F. "Our Future Dictator: Is It Huey Long?" *Scribner's Magazine* 97 (March 1935):171–75.

Carter, Franklin Hope. *American Messiahs.* New York: Simon and Schuster, 1935.

Carter, Hodding. "The Kingfish on His Way." *New Republic* 81 (November 21, 1934):40–42.

Carter, Hodding. "Louisiana Limelighter." *Review of Reviews* 91 (March 1935):23–28, 64.

"A Challenge to the New Deal." *Review of Reviews* 92 (October 1935):14–15.

Chase, Francis, Jr. *Sound and Fury.* New York: Harper and Brothers, 1942.

"Dangers of Demagogy." *Commonwealth* 19 (December 8, 1933):144.

Davis, Forrest. *Huey Long: A Candid Biography.* New York: Dodge Publishing Company, 1935.

"Demagogues: Johnson Lambastes Senator and Priest; Long Counters with Utopia; Coughlin Parries with Spirit of '76." *Newsweek* 5 (March 16, 1935):5–7.

Dethloff, Henry C., ed. *Huey P. Long: Southern Demagogue or American Democrat?* Lafayette: University of Southwestern Louisiana, 1976.

Dethloff, Henry C. "Huey Pierce Long: Interpretations." *Louisiana Studies* 3 (Summer 1964):219–27.

Dethloff, Henry C. "The Longs: Revolution or Populist Retrenchment?" *Louisiana History* 19 (Fall 1978):401–12.

Deutsch, Hermann B. *The Huey Long Murder Case.* Garden City, N.Y.: Doubleday, 1963.

Deutsch, Hermann B. "Huey Long: The Last Phase." *Saturday Evening Post* 208 (October 12, 1935):27, 82–91.
Dykeman, Wilma. "The Southern Demagogue." *Virginia Quarterly Review* 33 (Autumn 1957):558–68.
Ellis, Edward Robb. *A National in Torment: The Great American Depression, 1929–1939.* New York: Capricorn Books, 1971.
"Facts are Stubborn." *Saturday Evening Post* 207 (May 4, 1935):26.
Farley, James A. *Behind the Ballots: The Personal History of a Politician.* New York: Harcourt Brace and Company, 1938.
Farley, James A. *Jim Farley's Story.* New York: McGraw-Hill Book Company, 1948.
Fields, Harvey G. *A True History of the Life, Works, Assassination and Death of Huey Pierce Long.* [Farmerville, La.: Fields Publishing Agency], 1945.
Fineran, John Kingston. *The Career of a Tinpot Napoleon: A Political Biography of Huey P. Long.* New Orleans: The Author, [1932].
Fortier, James J. A., ed. *Huey Pierce Long, the Martyr of the Age.* New Orleans: Louisiana State Museum, 1937.
Freidel, Frank. *F. D. R. and the South.* Baton Rouge: Louisiana State University Press, 1965.
Freidel, Frank. *Franklin D. Roosevelt: Launching the New Deal.* Boston: Little, Brown and Company, 1973.
Graham, Hugh Davis, ed. *Huey Long.* Englewood Cliffs, N.J.: Prentice-Hall, 1970.
Green, Joe L. "The Educational Significance of Huey P. Long." *Louisiana Studies* 13 (Fall 1974):263–76.
Harris, Thomas O. *The Kingfish: Huey P. Long, Dictator.* New Orleans: Pelican Publishing Company, 1938.
"How Come Huey Long?" Pt. 1, "Bogeyman," by Hodding Carter, Pt. 2, "Or Superman?" by Gerald L. K. Smith. *New Republic* 82 (February 13, 1935):11–15.
Howard, Perry H. *Political Tendencies in Louisiana.* Baton Rouge: Louisiana State University Press, 1971.
"Huey Proposes." *New Republic* 82 (March 20, 1935):146–47.
"Huey's S.O.W." Letter by Huey P. Long. *Review of Reviews* 91 (April 1935):38.
Irey, Elmer, and William J. Slocum. "The Gentleman from Louisiana: Huey Pierce Long." Ch. 4 in *The Tax Dodgers.* New York: Fireside Press, 1949.
"Is President Roosevelt in Any Danger of Losing the National Election?" *New Republic* 82 (March 6, 1935):87.
Johnson, Gerald W. "Live Demagogue or Dead Gentleman?" *Virginia Quarterly Review* 12 (January 1936):1–14.
Johnson, Hugh S. "Pied Pipers." *Vital Speeches* 1 (March 11, 1935):359.
Kane, Harnett T. *Louisiana Hayride: The American Rehearsal for Dictatorship, 1928–1940.* Gretna, La.: Pelican Publishing Company, 1971.
Kendrick, Alexander. "Huey Long's 'Revolution.'" *Nation* 139 (August 22, 1934):207–9.
Key, V. O., Jr. *Southern Politics in State and Nation.* New York: Vintage Books, 1949.

King, Peter. "Huey Long: The Louisiana Kingfish." *History Today* 14 (March 1964):151–60.
"Kingfish: Square Dealers Attack Huey; Huey Attacks Millionaires; Colleague Asks to Be Butler." *Newsweek* 5 (January 26, 1935):7.
Leighton, Isabel, ed. *The Aspirin Age, 1919–1941.* New York: Simon and Schuster, 1968.
Leslie, J. Paul, Jr. "Louisiana Hayride Revisited." *Louisiana Studies* 11 (Winter 1972):282–94.
Leuchtenberg, William E. *Franklin D. Roosevelt and the New Deal.* New York: Harper & Row, 1963.
Long, Huey P. *Every Man a King.* Chicago: Quadrangle Books, 1964.
Long, Huey P. *My First Days in the White House.* Harrisburg, Pa.: Telegraph Press, 1935.
Lovett, Robert Morss. "Huey Long Invades the Middle West." *New Republic* 83 (May 15, 1935):10–12.
Luthin, Reinhard H. *American Demagogues.* Boston: Beacon Press, 1954.
Luthin, Reinhard H. "Flowering of the Southern Demagogue." *The American Scholar* 20 (Spring 1951):185–95.
Luthin, Reinhard H. "Some Demagogues in American History." *American Historical Review* 57 (October 1951):22–46.
Martin, Thomas. *Dynasty: The Longs of Louisiana.* New York: G. P. Putnam's Sons, 1960.
McCoy, Donald R. *Angry Voices: Left of Center Politics in the New Deal Era.* Lawrence: University of Kansas Press, 1958.
McGriffin, Norton. "The Long Way to Atlantis." *North American Review* 240 (June 1935):106–18.
Michie, Alan A., and Frank Rhylick. *Dixie Demagogues.* New York: Vanguard Press, 1939.
Miller, Lillian B., et al. *If Elected . . . : Unsuccessful Candidates for the Presidency, 1796–1968.* Washington: Smithsonian Institution Press, 1972.
Moley, Raymond. *After Seven Years.* New York: Harper & Brothers, 1939.
Moley, Raymond. *Twenty-Seven Masters of Politics in a Personal Perspective.* New York: Funk & Wagnalls Company, 1949.
Moore, Harry Thornton. "Just Folks in Utopia." *New Republic* 85 (November 13, 1935):9–10.
Moreau, John Adam. "Huey Long and His Chroniclers." *Louisiana History* 6 (Spring 1965):121–39.
"NRA: Huey Long's Filibuster Fails." *Newsweek* 5 (June 22, 1935):7–8.
Opotowsky, Stan. *The Longs of Louisiana.* New York: E. P. Dutton & Company, 1960.
Parrington, Vernon L., Jr. *American Dreams: A Study of American Utopias.* Providence: Brown University, 1947.
Patch, Buel W. *National Wealth and National Income.* Editorial Research Reports. Vol. 1, no. 15, April 20, 1935. Washington, 1935.
Pierce, Neal R. *The Deep South States of America: People, Politics and Power in the Seven Deep South States.* New York: W. W. Norton & Company, 1974.

"Politician in Homespun." *Saturday Review of Literature* 12 (September 21, 1935):8.
"Rabble-Rouser." *Collier's* 35 (February 23, 1935):70.
Ratcliffe, S. K. "The New American Demagogues." *Fortnightly* 137 (June 1935):674–84.
Rausch, Basil. *The History of the New Deal*. New York: Capricorn Books, 1963.
Reeve, Joseph E. *Monetary Reform Movements: A Survey of Recent Plans and Panaceas*. Washington: American Council on Public Affairs, 1943.
Robison, Daniel M. "From Tillman to Long: Some Striking Leaders of the Rural South." *Journal of Southern History* 3 (August 1937):289–310.
Rodman, Selden. "The Insurgent Line-Up for 1936." *American Mercury* 35 (May 1935):77–83.
Rorty, James. "Callie Long's Boy Huey." *Forum* 94 (August 1935):74–79, 126–27.
Schlesinger, Arthur M., Jr. *The Age of Roosevelt: The Politics of Upheaval*. Boston: Houghton Mifflin Company, 1960.
Schott, Matthew J. "Class Conflict in Louisiana Voting Since 1877: Some New Perspectives." *Louisiana History* 12 (Spring 1971):149–65.
"Share-the-Wealth Wave." *Time* 25 (April 1, 1935):15–17.
Simon, Rita James, ed. *As We Saw the Thirties*. Urbana: University of Illinois Press, 1967.
Sindler, Allan P. *Huey Long's Louisiana: State Politics, 1920–1952*. Baltimore: John Hopkins Press, 1956.
Smith, Gerald L. K. *Huey P. Long: Summary of Greatness, Political Genius, American Martyr*. Eureka Springs, Ark.: Elna M. Smith Foundation, 1975.
Smith, Webster. *The Kingfish: A Biography of Huey P. Long*. New York: G. P. Putnam's Sons, 1933.
Snyder, Robert E. "The Concept of Demagoguery: Huey Long and His Literary Critics." *Louisiana Studies* 15 (Spring 1976):61–83.
Snyder, Robert E. "Huey Long and the Presidential Election of 1936." *Louisiana History* 16 (Spring 1975):117–43.
Sokolsky, George E. "Huey Long." *Atlantic Monthly* 156 (October 1935):523–33.
Steinberg, Alfred. *The Bosses*. New York: Macmillan Company, 1972.
Swing, Raymond Gram. "The Build-up of Long and Coughlin." *Nation* 140 (March 20, 1935):325–26.
Swing, Raymond Gram. *Forerunners of American Fascism*. New York: Julian Messner, 1935.
Swing, Raymond Gram. "The Menace of Huey Long." Pt. 3: "His Bid for National Power." *Nation* 140 (January 23, 1935):98–100.
Taylor, Joe Gray. *Louisiana: A Bicentennial History*. New York: W. W. Norton & Company, 1976.
Terkel, Studs. *Hard Times: An Oral History of the Great Depression*. New York: Avon Books, 1971.
"Third Party Threat." *Literary Digest* 121 (June 27, 1936):5–6.
Thomas, Norman. *After the New Deal*. New York: Macmillan Company, 1936.

T. R. B. "Doping the Presidential Derby." *New Republic* 83 (May 15, 1935):17.
T. R. B. "Third Party Chances." *New Republic* 84 (September 11, 1935):128.
Tugwell, Rexford G. *The Democratic Roosevelt*. Baltimore: Penguin Books, 1969.
Wecter, Dixon. *The Age of the Great Depression, 1929–1941*. New York: Macmillan Company, 1948.
Williams, T. Harry. "The Gentleman from Louisiana: Demagogue or Democrat?" *Journal of Southern History* 26 (1960):3–21. Reprinted in *Readings in Louisiana History*, edited by Conrad, Glenn, et al. New Orleans: Louisiana Historical Association, 1978, pp. 348–55.
Williams, T. Harry. *Huey Long*. New York: Alfred A. Knopf, 1969.
Williams, T. Harry. "The Politics of the Longs." Lecture 4 in *Romance and Realism in Southern Politics*. Athens: University of Georgia Press, 1960.
Wolfskill, George, and John A. Hudson. *All But the People: Franklin D. Roosevelt and His Critics, 1933–1939*. New York: Macmillan Company, 1969.

FDR WPA
and Wisconsin Art of the Depression

ELEVENTH ANNUAL MORRIS FROMKIN MEMORIAL LECTURE

Presented by
ROBERT BURKERT, Professor of Fine Arts
THE UNIVERSITY OF WISCONSIN—MILWAUKEE
Recipient of the 1980 Fromkin Research Grant

WED., NOVEMBER 12, 1980 – 3:30 P.M. – UWM UNION CINEMA

THE PUBLIC IS CORDIALLY INVITED TO ATTEND.
RECEPTION FOLLOWS.

SPONSORED BY THE FROMKIN MEMORIAL COLLECTION OF THE GOLDA MEIR LIBRARY
THE UNIVERSITY OF WISCONSIN—MILWAUKEE

F.D.R., WPA, and Wisconsin Art of the Depression

ROBERT BURKERT

In presenting the Fromkin Lecture I used a multimedia approach encompassing photographic slides and artistic works from the Great Depression, music from the thirties, taped interviews with artists who worked on government-sponsored art projects of the time, and a formal lecture presenting the details of my research in manuscript collections and libraries and of my firsthand inspection of murals and other works of art that have survived. Since the dimensions of that approach cannot be communicated solely by words and a few photographs, I have found it necessary to revise the material into a conventional essay. To suggest what the audience experienced on November 12, 1980, I have included in appendixes a list of the Wisconsin murals and sculptures and the musical selections which were heard at the same time. Before the start of the formal lecture, while the audience was assembling, folk songs and music of the Depression accompanied a series of slides culled from the photographic collections of the Farm Security Administration, the Archives of American Art, and the Partridge papers in the University of Wisconsin–Milwaukee Archives. Perhaps as he proceeds through the essay with the pictures and music in mind, the reader can re-create something of the breadth and diversity of the original presentation.

DECEMBER 1933 was the beginning of a very cold winter and the

---

Robert Burkert, who has bachelor's and master's degrees from the University of Wisconsin–Madison, is professor of art at the University of Wisconsin–Milwaukee. His paintings and prints can be found in the Tate Gallery, London; the Metropolitan Museum of Art; the Boston Museum of Fine Arts; the Philadelphia Museum of Art; the National Collection of Art; the Library of Congress; and the Golda Meir Library, as well as many other public and educational collections. He has exhibited at the Museum of Modern Art, New York; the Camden Arts Center, London; the Chicago Art Institute; the Pennsylvania Academy; the Tel Aviv Museum of Modern Art; the Library of Congress; and many other art centers and educational institutions throughout the country.

close of the worst year of the most severe depression the United States of America had faced. Some called it the "Great Depression"; others said it was "Hard Times." Fifteen million were out of work, almost one-quarter of the American work force. It was estimated that 10,000 artists were unemployed. There were bread lines and soup kitchens in cities throughout the country. Severe strikes gripped the nation with concurrent union organizing that fed violent demonstrations. "Hoovervilles" (tin and cardboard shanties) had sprung up on the fringes of cities; apples and shoe laces were sold on street corners to earn a few pennies; "Brother, Can You Spare a Dime?" was a hit tune. Some overwhelming change in our social welfare structure was needed! Franklin Delano Roosevelt had taken office in 1932 and had brought with him into his administration many who felt the nation's industry and work force must be heavily "pump primed" to get going again.

Among these individuals was George Biddle, an artist from a prominent Eastern family and a Groton classmate of F.D.R.'s. Biddle had studied in Mexico and had been very much impressed with the murals created during the revolution in the twenties by Diego Rivera, José Orozco, David Siqueiros, and others. He wrote a letter to Roosevelt, dated May 9, 1933, which stated:

> There is a matter which I have long considered and which someday might interest your administration. The Mexican artists have produced the greatest national school of mural painting since the Renaissance. Diego Rivera tells me that it was only possible because Obregon allowed Mexican artists to work at plumber's wages in order to express on the walls of the government buildings the social ideals of the Mexican Revolution. The younger artists of America are conscious, as they never have been, of the social revolution that our country and civilization are going through, and they would be very eager to express their ideas in a permanent form, if they were given the government's cooperation. They would be contributing to and expressing in living monuments the social ideals that you are struggling to achieve, and I am convinced that our mural art, with a little impetus, can soon result, for the first time in our history, in a vital national expression.[1]

F.D.R., who was genuinely interested but was mindful of recent scandal over Rivera's Rockefeller Center mural which was destroyed on orders from John D. Rockefeller, told Biddle "that he did not want a lot of young enthusiasts painting Lenin's head on the Justice Building."[2] However, F.D.R. passed Biddle's letter to the Treasury Department, where it soon found fertile ground, as Henry Morgenthau, Jr., secretary of the treasury, and his wife, Eleanor, were intensely involved in the arts.

In December of 1933 a meeting was held at the home of Edward Bruce, a college friend of F.D.R.'s, and from this six-hour discussion among top New Deal personnel the skeleton organization of the first Federal Arts program was formed. Edward Bruce's unique qualities were the elements that created and kept running the art programs throughout the nation and inside the federal bureaucracy.

Bruce graduated from Columbia University and practiced law in New York City and then in Manila, where he also went into newspaper work and published the *Manila Times*. Soon after, in China, he was president of the Pacific Development Company and engaged in banking activities and foreign trade throughout the Far East. During this time he continued painting and collecting oriental art. Before the crash of 1929 he left business, went to live and paint in France, and held several successful shows of his art in Paris and New York City. In the early thirties Bruce was back in Washington as a lawyer and international silver currency expert. Edward Bruce suffered from a crippling affliction of his legs, establishing another kinship to F.D.R. This blending of legal expertise, business executive organizational skills, newspaper experience, and sensitivity to the visual arts made Bruce the ideal chief officer of a program that through the years ahead had to circumnavigate the mine fields of Congress and federal bureaucratic red tape.

From its inception important figures in Washington watched over this foundling program. The Roosevelts, the Morgenthaus, Frederick Delano, Harry Hopkins, Frances Perkins (Secretary of Labor), Judge Frankfurter of the Supreme Court, and Bob and Belle La Follette of Wisconsin all contributed to seeing it develop in spite of congressional budget attacks that occurred from its birth to its burial during World War II.

On December 16, 1933, the first Public Works Art Project (PWAP) was launched, and in December artists were receiving their first checks. Since the initial program was set up on a stopgap basis, the funds were limited; no one thought the Depression would last so long. The funding closed on May 20, 1934, six months later. Within this period 3,749 artists, including Blacks and American Indians, were hired at a rate of $26.50 to $32.50 a week. Four hundred five mural designs were developed for federal buildings and 706 mural projects were undertaken in this short time. When the PWAP funds ran out, the artists were temporarily transferred to FERA, the Federal Emergency Relief Administration. This branch of public works was headed by Harry Hopkins, a social worker from New York City, who was a protégé of Eleanor Roosevelt's from the period when F.D.R. was governor of New York. He and diverse personalities from many regions of the United States were to converge in these "100 days" to create one of the largest official patronages of the arts since the Medicis, the Roman Catholic Church, and the Pharaohs. A rival branch of F.D.R.'s Medusa-headed bureaucracy was Harold Ickes' Public Works Administration (PWA). Hopkins and Ickes were vying for the power and ultimate control over the New Deal's public works programs. Hopkins was a loner in the government, well protected by Roosevelt, who thought quickly on his feet. He was very clever at squeezing every drop out of federal funds and cutting through government red tape. Ickes was serious, methodical, and effective in a plodding, bureaucratic fashion. F.D.R. said, "Ickes is a good administrator, but often too slow" and "Harry gets things done. I am going to give this job to Harry."[3] In two weeks Hopkins designed the Works Project Administration, and in October of 1934 the WPA was set up with the Fine Arts Project within it (the WPAFAP).

It is necessary to clarify the very confusing use of shortened titles, especially those that relate to the various relief and art programs, that someone labeled the "alphabet soup" of the New Deal.

1. Public Works of Art Project (PWAP)
   December 1933 until June 1934
   Directed by Edward Bruce

2. Works Project Administration Fine Arts Project (WPAFAP)
   Referred to as "The Project." Federal Project No. 1
   Directed by Holger Cahill

3. Treasury Section of Painting and Sculpture
   (This changed its name many times.)
   October 16, 1934 until 1943
   Directed by Edward Bruce

4. Treasury Relief Arts Project (TRAP)
   July 1935 until January 1938
   WPA relief money was used.
   TRAP was a subdivision of the Treasury Section under Edward Bruce

5. Farm Security Administration (FSA)
   1937 until 1943
   Photographic Section employed photographers.
   Under direction of Roy Stryker

6. Federal Emergency Relief Administration (FERA)
   Temporary Relief began in September 1931
   Under direction of Harry Hopkins
   Absorbed by WPAFAP in December 1935[4]

There were also the PWA, the TVA, the ERA, the AAA, the RA, the CCC, and many more agencies which sometimes used artists but do not pertain to this particular study.

I shall concentrate on the structure and philosophy of two of these programs—the WPA Fine Arts Project and its companion the Treasury Section of Painting and Sculpture. I shall refer to them as they were in their time, the *Project* and the *Section.*

Although Edward Bruce was asked to direct the Project as well as his Treasury Section, he refused because he did not believe in a government art program that did not maintain high professional standards. He was known to be not very sympathetic with the relief aspect of the Project.

After considerable search among various American museum directors, Holger Cahill was chosen to direct the WPA Fine Arts Project. Born in Iceland, Cahill changed his name when he came to the United States and grew up in St. Paul, Minnesota. Cahill, a disciple of Thorstein Veblen, followed the theories of John Dewey to art in action. American folk art, his passion, later manifested itself in one of his pet projects, the Index of American Design. Cahill was with the Museum of Modern Art and was a highly regarded curator of American arts when Harry Hopkins offered him the controversial directorship of the Project. At the time an important eastern museum director advised him not to take the job because "you'll get so many dead cats thrown at you that you'll never live it down."[5] Later in his career Cahill remarked he had heard the "whoosh" of many dead cats flying past him.

Cahill was an idealist who saw the Project as a context for an American cultural revolution. He wanted the nation to develop an indigenous American art form that did not ape the mannerisms of Europe. In the late twenties this idea had already found expression in the regionalism of Missouri's Thomas Hart Benton, John Steuart Curry's rural midwestern paintings, and Grant Wood's Iowa images. From the beginning, Cahill was much more concerned with putting the artist to work than with controlling the quality of his product. Cahill and others were also very much concerned with what they felt was the commercial stranglehold of the New York galleries on the visual culture of the United States.

In contrast, the Section, under Edward Bruce's direction, used professionally trained artists exclusively. He was very much concerned with professional competence because the Section's mural projects, housed mainly in federal buildings, especially in post offices, were subject to close public scrutiny.

The Project, headed by Cahill, was organized into sixteen regions supervised by regional directors. Many women held high administrative posts in the Project throughout the United States. Wisconsin was

Reprinted by permission from *TIME, The Weekly Newsmagazine;* Copyright Time Inc. 1938.

in Region 10 along with Illinois and Minnesota. Mrs. Increase Robinson of Chicago was the region's director, and each state had its own supervisor. For Wisconsin, Charlotte Partridge of Milwaukee, a friend of Holger Cahill and director of the Layton Art School and Gallery, accepted his request to serve as a "Dollar a Year" volunteer. Miss Partridge then appointed a local technical committee that selected artists, assessed their qualifications, and assigned them to projects which utilized their special skills.

There were four categories with different pay schedules. The pay per week varied from region to region, depending on the cost of living. The artists were paid from $103 a month in New York City to $39 a month in Alabama. The four categories were:

1. Professional and Technical. A standard of excellence. This was the largest category.
2. Skilled. Not quite as competent or experienced. Often supervised by A's if on a project.
3. Intermediate. Craftsmen that need guidance.
4. Unskilled. Gallery attendants, handymen, and office boys.[6]

The artists who applied to the Project and could qualify for relief either produced their easel paintings, sculptures, and drawings or were selected for mural projects after a design competition. Because 25 percent of the Project artists could have nonrelief status, the program was able to maintain a high degree of quality. In some districts the artist had to sign the Pauper's Oath, a requirement which created a great deal of resentment. This practice, and many other aspects of the Project, varied across the nation.

The bureaucratic supervision flourished, especially where the majority of the funds were disbursed. Bookkeepers would come to the studios of the artists to see if they were putting in their prescribed eight hours a day and not "leaning on their WPA shovels." Later the relief artists were asked to report in each work day at a clearing house in New York City. But after strong protests from the aggressive Artist's Union, these rules were dropped, and instead the artist brought his works, if portable, into the Project's offices where they were recorded (not too well), displayed for rental by state or federal institutions, or shipped to Washington to be exhibited in the many traveling WPA art exhibits across the United States.

The WPA Fine Arts Project was divided into four major units: art, music, theater, and writing. Each was fascinating, but here my concern will be with the visual arts. The statistics for the art unit are very confused and misleading, but I feel that we must look at them in order to grasp the complexity and magnitude of the Project. Over the years 40,000 artists were employed in the United States, a number representing much less than 2 percent of the total unemployed working under WPA through the decade of its activity. Unbelievably, approximately 2,550 murals were painted; 16,600 sculptures and 107,000 paintings were created; more than 240,000 prints were made from 12,581 original designs. Cahill's Index of American Design developed 23,000 watercolors and drawings by 500 artists.

A related area, the Farm Security Administration (FSA), produced over 300,000 photographs of the Depression period, one of the finest documents of a period any nation has ever attempted. Working under Roy Stryker, artists Ben Shahn, Walker Evans, Gordon Parks, Bernice Abbott, Dorothea Lange, and others were employed in assembling this unique record which Edward Steichen, the famous photographer from Wisconsin, said represented an achievement of high artistic merit.[7] Artists often crossed over from one WPA program to another.

After Holger Cahill toured throughout the United States overseeing the state art projects, he realized that truly to spread the American art philosophy, which he called "imaginative realism," the Project should have community art centers in areas bypassed by cultural activities. As a result, over 107 community art centers were begun, mainly in the South and Southwest. Interestingly, none were established in Wisconsin. Particular attention was given to Black communities, that had virtually nothing, with emphasis on children's classes, arts and crafts projects, exhibits, and visiting artists. These centers touched eight million lives, with over $800,000 contributed by many communities themselves.

Cahill's pet project was the Index of American Design. It was suggested to him by Ruth Reeves, a New York textile designer who became its national coordinator. Its purpose was "to make and preserve a record of our native arts and crafts."[8] Much of the work was done by commercial artists in the B category who worked mainly in watercolor and sometimes in pencil, rarely in photography, as color photography was not technically advanced in the mid-thirties. (Unfortunately, Indian and Black arts and crafts were not included.) Cahill wished to have the Index to American Design reproduced and distributed in folio form throughout the United States, but this dream was not realized. Since then a fragment of the collection, which is now housed in the National Gallery, has been published in a volume containing 3,000 illustrations of these historic arts and crafts. It is now fully recorded in color microfiche.

The Section, under Edward Bruce, accomplished much less, as it was a more selective art support program and was totally separated from relief. In its eight years 850 American artists worked on about 1,000 murals and sculptures in federal buildings under the jurisdiction of the Treasury Department. Most of these were in post offices thoroughout the country.

Bulletins were sent out announcing the competitions, and local technical juries ranked the artists' entries done in a mural sketch format. The final decisions were made in Washington, and most of the time they followed the local state's selections. If an artist did not win the competition but caught the eye of the two committees, he or she would be referred to the Project murals. The advantages of the Section murals came from the financing arrangements which were in two categories, grants over $5,000 and those under $5,000. The under-$5,000 grants were used to discover and encourage younger artists, and more prestige was attached to the winning of a Section competition. These awards were free from the on-again, off-again nature of the Project relief program. Disadvantages stemmed from the tendency to censor and create an official "Section" style of painting. Not one out-and-out abstraction was commissioned. Because of the budgetary framework of the Section, the commissioned artists had to pay for their own materials and cost of living on the site, and these limitations caused the artists to work in their studios and then to place their works on the site after completion, with a resulting lack of relationship to the immediate space. This problem was often criticized by consulting architects.

In Wisconsin in 1935 Charlotte Partridge—a native of Minneapolis who had taught at Milwaukee Downer College from 1914, then directed the Layton Art Gallery, and founded the Layton School of Art in 1920—was appointed the state director as "a Dollar a Year Man," as were so many volunteers in the initial stages of the Federal Arts Program. She soon drew a salary of $10 per diem and expenses for twenty days a month, or $200. At the height of the program, in 1936, she had 100 artists employed in Wisconsin. This number fluctuated with the financial vicissitudes of the project. Olin Dows said of Charlotte Partridge's professional direction of the Wisconsin WPA program: "She was able to accomplish so much through her hard work, good eye and enthusiasm."[9]

In 1934, during the initial six months of the PWAP, the works of eleven state artists were sent to Washington to the Corcoran Gallery, where an important exhibit was held. Edward Bruce and Forbes Watson, his publicist and technical advisor, saw to it that a great deal of

Charlotte Partridge (left), Director of the Wisconsin WPA art program, and Miriam Frink, her Assistant Director, at the Layton School of Art. *Milwaukee Journal Photo.*

propaganda was presented for the arts program. Schomer Lichtner's painting "Potato Planting" was selected from the exhibit by the Roosevelts to show in the White House. I understand the painting is now missing.

The quality of work from Wisconsin was high, as noted in this letter of Edward Bruce to Ms. Partridge:

My dear Miss Partridge: Certainly no state in the Union has produced a higher general class of work, especially in watercolor, than Wisconsin has.

Compared with the number of artists available for work it is quite amazing; and with the painting produced there and the watercolor these works rank with those produced in any other part of the United States.[10]

Throughout my research I repeatedly found notes about the quality of Wisconsin watercolorists. The Wisconsin artists on the project were mainly from Milwaukee with some from Madison and a few from out in the state. This imbalance produced criticism by artists not on the Project who said that Layton Art School controlled Project membership. However, the technical committee that Ms. Partridge appointed represented various art backgrounds, and she was able to successfully refute these charges of favoritism. Wisconsin art of the Project tended to represent midwestern pastoral regionalism, although there were some urban life paintings.

Very little subject matter was controversial, a pattern which was paralleled across the nation except for larger cities such as New York, Chicago, and Los Angeles. In these cities, there was more social realism reflecting the Mexican revolutionary style mixed with mild Marxist ideology. Arshile Gorky, one of the pioneers of abstract expressionism who was on the Project, called social realism "poor art for poor people." Another minor style little mentioned but definitely visible in New York City was social surrealism, a strange mix of history, Freudian psychology, and surreal imagery which appeared later in abstract expressionism.

Some of the young Wisconsin artists, such as Santos Zingale and Alfred Sessler, were politically involved both in their works and their lives. John Reed Clubs flourished at this time, and artists in the WPA Fine Arts Project identified with the workers and assisted their causes by making signs, posters, handbills, etc.

A letter to Ms. Partridge from Olin Dows, one of Cahill's assistant directors, stated that possibly Sessler (Alfred Sessler) should "cut down on the relief propaganda working paintings and do more objective worker paintings."[11]

Olin Dows, a painter himself, often sent very interesting letters commenting on the works, criticizing or praising them with pet words such as "awfully nice" and "swell." There was considerable correspondence over the nature of the works, giving the entire program a very intimate quality. For example, Roosevelt himself often wrote to Edward Bruce about various murals that he admired or disliked.

Edward Rowan, a top assistant in Edward Bruce's Section, told sculptor Homer St. Gaudens that ordinarily he did not believe in telling artists what they should execute. However, he continued, if an artist is willing to take pay from the federal government, he should also be willing to accept his employer's guidelines and restrictions. Painting nudes, in Rowan's view, was one area that government artists should avoid.

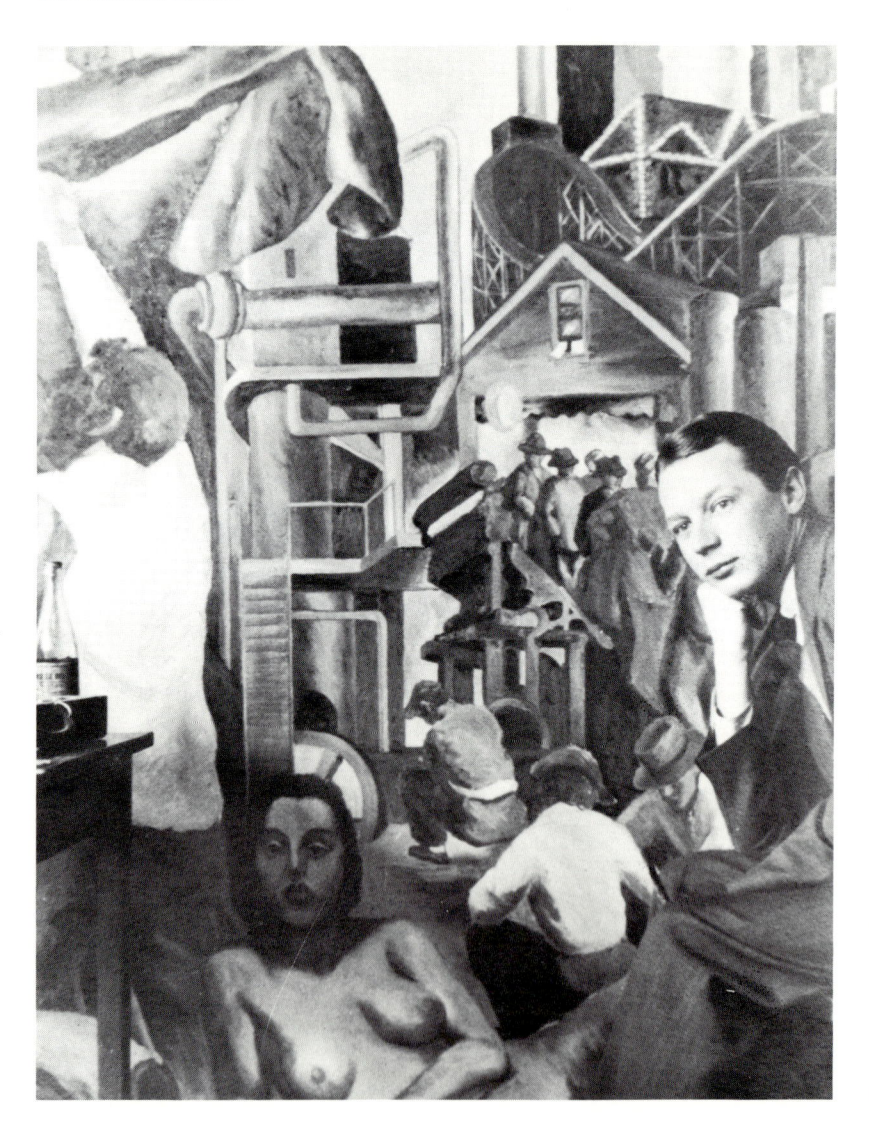

Robert Schellin seated next to his controversial mural commissioned by the Wisconsin WPA Art Project for the Milwaukee State Teachers College (now the University of Wisconsin–Milwaukee).

Robert Schellin won a mural commission for the Wisconsin State Teachers College (now the University of Wisconsin–Milwaukee) under the PWAP's initial six-month program. The mural not only presented Mexican-influenced social commentary, the exploited worker, and corrupt industrialism, but also managed to include the nudes which Mr. Rowan so opposed in Section art. Needless to say, it created quite a stir with the press. The president of the college, the Milwaukee Art Institute, and Joseph Padway, prominent labor lawyer, all entered the fray. The mural stayed up but with a screen to protect it from innocent eyes. I understand from Professor Schellin that this mural since has disappeared and was probably destroyed.

A little-known aspect of the WPA Art Project was the CCC camp program. Five Wisconsin artists were hired to record young men working in the fields, on the roads, lumbering, planting trees, etc. in Wisconsin. These artists—Ed Morton (who did the painting of "Bumming" on my poster for the Fromkin Lecture), Richard Jansen, Forrest Flower, Tom Rost, Ray Redell, and Victor Volk—were paid $1.50 a day and had to be robust and familiar with outdoor work.

As another dimension of these activities, I would now like to share with you some of the recollections of several artists who participated in these art programs during the Depression. From interviews with Robert Schellin, Schomer Lichtner, Ruth Grotenrath, and Santos Zingale I have excerpted comments which provide their assessments of the arts projects of the Depression.

About his experiences with the art programs of the thirties, Robert Schellin observes:

> If you had a job you couldn't apply in the art program. Originally it was quality as the most important thing, and the committee passed upon the quality of the work. In fact, anything you turned in to the Project had to be approved by that same committee. . . . All the way through it was a quality basis. I experienced no censorship. Although there may have been criticism, nobody said you can't paint this or you can't paint that. When the Project started, we worked in our own studios at that time and simply took our work over every so often and turned it in. It was either accepted or not accepted by that committee. You did whatever you felt like doing. The thing that I feel about the Project at the time was that it gave people in the arts the opportunity to be artists. . . . They produced art, they developed their art, and they were supported at a time when they probably would have had to do menial labor in order to make a living. When you look back, you'll see that these are the people who later on carried on the traditions in the arts. A lot of them taught, of course, in New York and became the professional artists of the 50s and 60s and even 70s. To be able to work as an artist during that period was the greatest incentive I could think of for the growth of the arts, and I think

maybe that was really the beginning of the period when the art capital more or less moved away from Paris and came to this country. Prior to that point, if you wanted to be an artist you assumed, more or less, that you would have to go to Europe, Munich or Paris, and study there. I recall maybe prior of course to the 30s, Benton came back and he had to paint American. He wanted to get rid of that Parisian influence, and so did Grant Wood and John Steuart Curry, who later came to Madison.

Schomer Lichtner and Ruth Grotenrath recount some of their experiences:

LICHTNER: All of a sudden out of the blue sky one day I received the following telegram: "Will you act as supervisor for Treasury Relief Art Project and execute murals in federal buildings with relief assistance? Pay $94.00 monthly. 98 hours work. Materials supplied. Wire me collect. Federal Warehouse. Washington. Olin Dows, Chief Treasury Relief Art Project."

GROTENRATH: And believe me that was out of the blue. I could remember how excited we were and thrilled when we got that telegram. We had this wonderful studio on Downer Avenue with a big skylight and a perfect place to paint murals and it was really quite a thrill.

This letter then followed the telegram: "I was very glad to get your telegram yesterday telling me that you were interested in the new project. I am enclosing the operating plan of this project which will explain its scope and purposes to you. After reading this sheet I hope you will be willing to accept a position under it as designer of certain mural decorations and as head of a group of artists whom you will select to work with you." That's always rather amusing—"We are glad to hear that you will accept"—because we were quite thrilled with the whole idea.

LICHTNER: Well, that was the beginning; I guess it was the beginning of the American scene. So it was in the air; everybody wanted to try to paint what was around them. We were also getting on to the idea of painting rural subject matter. Everybody seemed to be interested in getting out of the city at that time too and painting things in the country. Many of the artists even had studios, part-time studios, in the country. They would rent a cabin or cottage somewhere, and they painted out there. They were allowed to do that on the Project. And I remember I tried to paint many things regarding the farm, work around the farm. It was very stimulating.

GROTENRATH: We certainly always enjoyed going into the country. Of course, we still do. But I remember we used to go out a great deal, and we would follow the farmers around when they were haying and when they were cutting corn. Lots of times we would be invited to have dinner with them, and we got to know quite a few of the farmers. And the way they harvested their crops in those days, of course, was very picturesque, compared to how it is done now, and was very good subject matter. But I don't remember seeing murals done by very many other artists. I do remember Thwaites'; that's about all.

Santos Zingale's mural sketch for the Henry Mitchell Junior High School Library in Racine. The sketch won the WPA competition.

LICHTNER: Well, at one of those meetings, there were probably some of the supervisors from Washington there, and that was the occasion for having the dinner very likely.

GROTENRATH: It was quite a festive thing, I recall. I can still see the huge table and all the people sitting around it.

LICHTNER: And all of a sudden Miss Partridge got up and announced, "And now I want to introduce you to the WPA bride and groom." So Ruth and I had to stand up.

GROTENRATH: We have often wondered what our careers would have been like had we not been on the Project.

LICHTNER: It gave us a good start in painting. Trying to paint every day became a habit. I don't remember how long that project was.

GROTENRATH: Well, when did it start actually? In 1933, '34? Thirty-three I think, because we already knew about it before we were married. As I said, we had this beautiful studio, and, of course, we were intent on being artists. But there weren't many prospects for selling one's work then, and so we had to think about doing other things. In fact, we had a small framing business and so on. And then the Project developed, and it was marvelous to feel you were doing something which was being accepted and for which you were being paid.

Santos Zingale, another Milwaukee painter who began his work during the Depression, recounts some of his experiences:

Now first came the easel aspect of the Works Progress Administration. The easel aspect of WPA was later on. In fact, I did the big painting ("The Lynch Scene") that's at State Teacher's College. I was teaching at the time at Country Day School, and I was allowed to teach part time and work at the same time on this project. What we did was to hand in paintings, because there was never any very strict regimentation of work habits. Later on, under WPA, we had to be a little more disciplined in our work habits. In fact, WPA supervised our work at the Blatz building there on Broadway Street.

But Al Sessler, another Milwaukee artist, was doing stuff with social realism in it, and he had one pencil sketch that he called "Cops Will Be Cops." I knew the validity of what Al was doing, for we had firsthand experience with police intimidation. In 1935, I believe, the ambassador from Germany came to the States and visited Milwaukee for a dinner at the Milwaukee Athletic Club, which is right off of Wisconsin Avenue. Al and I were among the people that had congregated to protest the invasion, you might say, by this Nazi, because he was part of the Nazi Party. Well, what the police did in those days—and this is pretty well documented—was to have some provocateurs in the ranks. These provocateurs would be part of this working mass and would join these so-called protesters. They would pretend that they were part of the group, and then they would shove a worker against, or one of the protesters against a cop. The cop would then push back, and turmoil

Santos Zingale, on ladder, directing progress on his WPA mural in Racine's Henry Mitchell Junior High School. Assistant Alfred Sessler is on scaffold. The mural has now been destroyed.

was precipitated, you might say. And this poor fellow that got shoved into this group of cops had his hat torn off of his head some way or other, and at that instant we saw a billy club swing down on this man's bald head. And the guy died, absolutely! It just cracked his head. Let me tell you, that had quite an impression on me and Al, and I think Al did his sketch "Cops Will be Cops" from that incident.

The central panel of the mural entitled "The Landing of Captain Knapp at Racine" (since destroyed) by Santos Zingale, commissioned by the WPA art program in Wisconsin. Height 12 feet.

I think the very strong thing that federal support of art did was to allow a lot of top notch artists who eventually made it big to work through those years. They couldn't have sustained themselves otherwise when their work wasn't selling. All these fellows, with Ben Shahn leading the group there, had an oppportunity to work with the WPA. The same was true in Milwaukee, of course too, and Chicago. It kept us alive.

One can see the products of these artists who participated in the Project in many places in Wisconsin. Robert Schellin's paintings were on display at the State Historical Society of Wisconsin last year in a traveling exhibit entitled *Wisconsin's New Deal Art*. It was shown at the Milwaukee Public Museum from July 24 until September 1, 1981. In Hudson you can see Ruth Grotenrath's post office mural "Unloading a River Boat at Hudson," which was completed in 1943. Schomer Lichtner has a multipaneled mural closer to home at the post office in Sheboygan, painted in 1937. Santos Zingale's mural "Fruits of Sturgeon Bay," done in 1940, can be seen in that city. At least thirty other murals are to be found throughout the state in post offices and many more in other public buildings. My wife and I recently traveled

Schomer Lichtner inking a lithograph stone in preparation for printing an edition for the Wisconsin WPA Art Project.

through the state and photographed some of the murals painted during the Depression. Many of the Wisconsin easel works have been scattered through Washington, D. C., Wisconsin, and various other states. Now and then they may turn up in public buildings, attics, basements, and sometimes at auctions and galleries. Many thousands have disappeared and been destroyed. Years ago, early Jackson Pollocks and Mark Rothkos turned up in junk shops, selling for $5.

As the war clouds gathered in the late thirties, negative congressional pressures mounted on all of the WPA projects. The four art projects were favorite targets of the House Committee on Un-American Activities for "being the hotbed of Communists." The right-wing press was extremely hostile, and the conservative coalition in Congress managed to cut Project funding and turn control of the Project over to the participating states. Wages were reduced and artists with more than eighteen months of FAP employment were fired. The remainder had to sign a loyalty oath. This was the beginning of the end.

James Watrous' Park Falls, Wisconsin, post office mural, commissioned by the Federal Arts Project. Because the mural, which depicts a fight between two logging crews on the Flambeau River, was designed to accommodate features of the building, spaces were left (lower center) for the clock and (lower left) for the bulletin board and doorway.

Because of these disappointing events and other expanding duties, Charlotte Partridge resigned from her job as Art Project director in August of 1939, and her assistant, Mrs. Margaret Davis Clark, carried on. Funding was again cut, and to stay alive the project gradually shifted toward education, recreation, and hand crafts, and away from the fine arts. This also was the time of the excellent hand-craft project in Wisconsin under the creative guidance of Elsa Ulbricht of the Milwaukee State Teachers College. It was a rich, diverse program, one of the best in the nation. After Pearl Harbor, in order for the WPAFAP to remain functioning, project director Cahill again shifted the emphasis, this time to national defense projects such as posters, training manuals, camouflage, and some murals for warships, but the Project as I have described it was at an end.

In conclusion, what did this large infusion of funds do for the arts in America during the Depression? What did the Project achieve? Was it a failure? Was it merely a relief system to create jobs, to have workers "leaning on shovels," "raking leaves," or "painting pictures"? Was it just a "boondoggle"? And was it truly "a hotbed of

Schomer Lichtner working on an oil painting for the WPA Art Project.

Communism"? I believe it was a truly significant period for American art. In less than a decade many cultural goals were achieved, more than its founders expected or could foresee. Remember, this was not the Golden Age of Flanders, the Renaissance of the Medici, or the Medieval patronage of the Church. This was a period of the most severe depression in our history.

This program touched millions of American lives, affected thousands of cities and towns, and almost all of our states. Officially, the WPAFAP was "to provide employment to artists in need, to educate the public to a higher appreciation of art, and to encourage activities which lead to a greater use and enjoyment of the visual arts by the community at large."[12] These goals were met, never totally, but certainly positively. You have read the comments of four Wisconsin artists concerning the Project's effects on their lives. The abstract artist, Stuart Davis, said, "I was able to do whatever I damned pleased and nobody told me how to do it."[13] Robert Gwathmey, a favorite artist of mine, said, "If there were 500 artists who made it, 400 were on WPA. . . . The most important thing was the artist had a patron who made no aesthetic judgments; so artists for the first time had a pa-

Edmund Lewandowski, in his studio, painting a watercolor under the WPA Art Project.

tron, the Government. . . . "[14] Herman Rose, New York painter, observed, "I do not know if I could have even continued to be an artist if not for the WPA."[15] Although the artists were highly critical of the financial, technical, and bureaucratic aspects of both the Project and the Section, they were unanimously positive about how it affected their lives, their work, and their futures.

Staggering quantities of work were turned out by government-supported artists during the Depression: 2,550 murals, installed in federal buildings, post offices, libraries, schools, and hospitals; over 107,000 easel paintings in all media; 16,645 sculpture pieces; 239,000 original prints from 12,581 original designs; 2,000,000 posters from 35,000 original designs; and 23,000 watercolors and drawings, done for the Index of American Design.

Beyond these products, what of the technical, experimental, and expressive aspects of the Project and the Section? The 100 community art centers created in various states played an important role in educating and exposing art to the general public, in training the unskilled, and in sponsoring traveling exhibits and visiting artists. The

An oil wash painting of the Blatz Palm Gardens by Milwaukee artist Charles Thwaites dated May 8, 1937, and produced under the WPA Art Project.

artists thought of themselves as workers and, in their relationship to other WPA workers, were exposed to and learned techniques that allowed them to experiment with new media such as plastics. Project artists such as David Smith learned welding, cement casting, bronze casting, and new industrial techniques. The airbrush was introduced as a tool for the fine artist. Plastic paints, polymers, and acrylics were experimented with and used in the New York World's Fair murals. Under the Project, photo murals were produced. New York City had a unique Art and Industry Design Laboratory, as well as a paint research laboratory, financed by the Project. Artists were trained in the emerging silk-screen printing process, and in the Project the first color prints in serigraphy were produced. Color printing workshops utilized craftsmen who taught the fine artists and advanced the understanding of color lithography and color relief printing.

Other achievements should be noted. The Project developed America's first art therapy program in Bellevue Hospital. Many school art programs were created and expanded with the professional artists and art teachers who were sent to them. Major artists were sent into the hinterlands to teach, lecture, and exhibit their work through the community art centers. The artists often painted murals where the public could see the daily progress and become involved. When Reginald Marsh painted his large mural on the dome of New York City's Custom House, there was a great deal of antagonism from its staff who were shunted about by the huge scaffolding and annoyed by the general mess the painters created while working. Complaints were presented to the artists; but as the months went by, the staff saw the hard work and dedication of Marsh and his artisans. Upon completion of the mural, the Customs House employees threw a grand banquet for the artists. The mural is one of the truly outstanding works of this period. The craft heritage of the United States was permanently recorded and elevated by the American Index of Design.

Surrounding us, often totally unknown to us, are the visual remnants of this program. The Children's Zoo in Central Park, New York City, is a WPA Project. In Milwaukee survivors of this energetic era are the Parklawn Housing Project and its sculptures, the murals in the Courthouse and the Public Museum, and the carvings and decorations at Whitnall Park.

But it was not all positive. Much mediocre, incompetent work was produced. Many murals were poorly drawn, drab in color, and poor in technique. Cahill's comment on this was, "You don't often find mountains where there is no plateau."[16] Many murals were overblown easel paintings. The record keeping and conservation were slipshod. The artists rarely knew where their studio work went once it became government property. The works were sloppily warehoused, damaged, destroyed, given away, and in some places auctioned off by the pound. Colonel Brehan Somervell, the New York City WPA head administrator (and leading enemy of the Art Project), supervised the destruction of art work that he felt was "Communist inspired." The on-and-off financing of the WPA fostered an ever increasing anxiety among the artists. Bookkeepers and supervisors were openly hostile to the Project because many of them felt "to create pictures" was not actual work. Many congressmen felt the same way, and even today artistic activity is considered frivolous by many.

The most important aspect of the WPA Fine Arts Project and the Section was what it did for the American artists' awareness of their importance to their native culture: they could make contemporary visual statements expressive of this country and were not limited to stylistic derivations of past European cultures. These artists were allowed to work full time in their fledgling years, relatively free from financial pressures and the gallery and museum politics so prevalent today.

Sculptor Ruth Blackwell stone-carving "Climb-upon-Us" animals for the Parklawn play area in Milwaukee.

Jackson Pollock, Mark Rothko, Willem DeKooning, Arshile Gorky, Ad Reinhardt, Adolph Gottlieb, James Brooks, Louise Nevelson, Loren Maciver, Isamu Noguchi, Jack Levine, Ben Shahn, Yasuo Kuniyoshi, Jacob Lawrence, David Smith, and Wisconsin's Carl Holty and Karl Knaths are masters of the American art that burst forth after World War II, soon changed the direction of the world's art, and made the United States and specifically New York City the new art capital of the world. Not Paris, not London, not Rome, anymore. These changes occurred because the WPA nurtured in the thirties the growing art that flowered in the fifties.

Though its roots were in what Holger Cahill referred to as "Imaginative Realism," after World War II American art evolved in a different direction—into what art historians today call "action" painting or "abstract expressionism." This is the vital work that in its monumental breadth and inner depth soon made New York the modern art market of the world. This uniquely American style certainly was a partial realization of the dreams of Edward Bruce, Holger Cahill, Forbes Watson, Olin Dows, and Charlotte Partridge. But they might have had different ideas about the *paradox* that New York became the monetary and the political power in the marketplace of contemporary art. Even so, the vitality of the fine arts in the United States in the past thirty or forty years is deeply indebted to the opportunities and financial support provided by the federal arts programs of the Depression years.

APPENDIX A

MUSICAL SELECTIONS

Representative musical selections from the Depression period were played before the lecture and after it was concluded.

PRECEDING THE LECTURE
"Talking Union" by Pete Seeger
"The Preacher and the Slave" by Joe Glazer
"Death of the Blue Eagle"
"Jungle Love" by Teddy Wilson and Orchestra
"Bourgeois Blues" by Pete Seeger
"Gloomy Sunday" by Billie Holiday

FOLLOWING THE LECTURE
"Blue Night Blues" by LeRoy Carr
"God Bless the Child" by Billie Holiday
"If the Light Has Gone Out in Your Soul" by Ernest Phipps and His Holiness Singers
"It Had to Be You" by Eddie Duchin
"When You're Smiling" by Billie Holiday

APPENDIX B

WISCONSIN POST OFFICE MURALS AND SCULPTURES

Location	Artist	Title	Year
Berlin	Raymond Redell	"Gathering Cranberries"(mural)	1938
Black River Falls	Frank E. Buffmire	"Lumbering—Black River Mill"(mural)	1939

Chilton	Charles W. Thwaites	"Threshing Barley"(mural)	1940
Columbus	Arnold Blanch	"One Hundredth Anniversary"(mural)	1940
De Pere	Lester W. Bentley	*"Giving Thanks"(mural)	1942
		*"The Red Pieta"(mural)	1942
		*"Nicholas Parret"(mural)	1942
Edgerton	Vladimir Rousseff	"Tobacco Harvest"(mural)	1941
Elkhorn	Tom Rost	"Pioneer Postman"(mural)	1938
Fond du Lac	Boris Gilbertson	"Birds and Animals of the Northwest" (11 sculptures on the S., E., W. facades)	1937
Hartford	Ethel Spears	"Autumn Wisconsin Landscape"(mural)	1940
Hayward	Stella E. Harlos	"Land of Wood and Lakes"(mural)	1942
Hudson	Ruth Grotenrath	"Unloading a Riverboat at Hudson"(mural)	1943
Janesville	Boris Gilbertson	"Wild Ducks"(sculpture)	1940
Kaukauna	Vladimir Rousseff	"A Grignon Trading with the Indians"(mural)	1938
Kewaunee	Paul Faulkner	"Winter Sports"(mural)	1940
Ladysmith	Elsa Jemme	**"The Log Roller"(mural)	1938
Lake Geneva	George A. Dietrich	"Winter Landscape"(mural)	1940
Mayville	Peter Rotier	"Wisconsin Rural Scene"(mural)	1943
Milwaukee—West Allis Branch	Frances Foy	"Wisconsin Wild Flowers—Spring"(mural)	1943
		"Wisconsin Wild Flowers—Autumn"(mural)	1943
Neillsville	John Van Koert	"The Choosing of the County Seat"(mural)	1940
Oconomowoc	Edward Morton	*"Winter Sports"(mural)	1938
Park Falls	James Watrous	"Lumberjack Fight on the Flambeau River"(mural)	1938
Plymouth	Charles W. Thwaites	"Cheese"(mural)	1942
Prairie du Chien	Jefferson E. Greer	"Discovery of Northern Waters"(sculpture)	1938
Reedsburg	Richard Jansen	"Dairy Farm"(mural)	1940

Rice Lake	Forrest Flower	"Rural Delivery"(mural)	1938
Richland Center	Richard Brooks	"The Post Unites America"(mural)	1937
Shawano	Eugene Higgins	"The First Settlers"(mural)	1939
Sheboygan	Schomer Lichtner	"The Lake"(mural)	1937
		"The Pioneer"(mural)	1937
		"Present City"(mural)	1937
		"Indian Life"(mural)	1937
		"Agriculture"(mural)	1937
Stoughton	Edmund D. Lewandowski	"Air Mail Service"(mural)	1940
Sturgeon Bay	Santos Zingale	"Fruits of Sturgeon Bay"(mural)	1940
Viroqua	Forrest Flower	"War Party"(mural)	1942
Waupaca	Raymond Redell	"Wisconsin Countryside"(mural)	1940
Wausau—Federal Building	Gerrit Sinclair	"Lumbering"(mural)	1940
		"Rural Mail"(mural)	1940
City Hall	LeRoy F. Jonas	**"Wisconsin Loggers"(mural)	1934
West Bend	Peter Rotier	"The Rural Mail Carrier"(mural)	1937

*Since destroyed
**Since removed

NOTES

1 George Biddle, *An American Artist's Story* (Boston: Little, Brown and Company, 1939), p. 273.

2 Edward Bruce papers, Archives of American Art, Roll D91, Smithsonian Institution, Washington, D.C.

3 Arthur M. Schlesinger, Jr., *The Age of Roosevelt: The Politics of Upheaval* (Boston: Houghton Mifflin Company, 1960), p. 344.

4 Francis V. O'Connor, ed., *The New Deal Art Projects: An Anthology of Memoirs* (Washington, D.C.: Smithsonian Institution Press, 1972), p. 3.

5 "In the Business District," *Time Magazine* 32 (September 5, 1938): 35.

6 Charlotte Partridge papers, Golda Meir Library Archives, University of Wisconsin–Milwaukee.

7 F. Jack Hurley, *Portrait of a Decade: Roy Stryker and the Development of Documentary Photography in the Thirties* (New York: Da Capo Press, 1977), p. 132.

8 Francis V. O'Connor, ed., *Art for the Millions: Essays from the 1930s by Artists and Administrators of the W.P.A. Federal Art Project* (Boston: New York Graphic Society, 1975), p. 173.
9 Holger Cahill papers, Archives of American Art, Roll 1105, Smithsonian Institution, Washington, D.C.
10 Charlotte Partridge papers, Golda Meir Library Archives, University of Wisconsin–Milwaukee.
11 Holger Cahill papers, Archives of American Art, Roll 1106, Smithsonian Institution, Washington, D.C.
12 Holger Cahill papers, Archives of American Art, Roll 1105, Smithsonian Institution, Washington, D.C.
13 "WPA Dividends," *Newsweek* 58 (August 14, 1961): 52.
14 See Studs Terkel, *Hard Times: An Oral History of the Great Depression* (New York: Pantheon Books, 1970), p. 374.
15 O'Connor, *The New Deal Art Projects*, p. 130.
16 "In the Business District," *Time Magazine* 32 (September 5, 1938): 36.

BIBLIOGRAPHY

Agee, James, and Walker Evans. *Let Us Now Praise Famous Men*. 2d ed. Boston: Houghton Mifflin Company, 1960.

Baigell, Matthew. *The American Scene: American Painting of the 1930's*. New York: Praeger, 1974.

Biddle, George. *An American Artist's Story.* Boston: Little, Brown and Company, 1939.

Bruce, Edward, and Forbes Watson. *Mural Designs, 1934–36.* Art in Federal Buildings, vol. 1. Washington, D.C.: Art in Federal Buildings, 1936.

Cahill, Holger. *New Horizons in American Art*. New York: Museum of Modern Art, 1936.

Craig, Lois, and Staff of Federal Architecture Project. *The Federal Presence.* Cambridge, Mass.: MIT Press, 1980.

"50 Painters and Sculptors Turn Out Work for Permanent Loans." *Milwaukee Journal,* March 28, 1937.

Hurley, F. Jack. *Portrait of a Decade: Roy Stryker and the Development of Documentary Photography in the Thirties.* 1972. New York: Da Capo Press, 1977.

"In the Business District." *Time Magazine* 32 (September 5, 1938):35–38.

Key, Donald. "Milwaukee's Art of the Depression." *Historical Messenger of the Milwaukee County Historical Society* 31 (1975):38–49.

Mangione, Jerre. *The Dream and the Deal: The Federal Writer's Project, 1935–1943.* Boston: Little, Brown and Company, 1972.

Marlung, Karal Ann. "William A. Milliken and Federal Art Patronage of the Depression Decade." *Bulletin of the Cleveland Museum of Art* 61 (1974):360–70.

McKinzie, Richard D. *The New Deal of Artists.* Princeton: Princeton University Press, 1973.

O'Connor, Francis V., ed. *Art for the Millions: Essays from the 1930s by Artists and Administrators of the WPA Federal Art Project.* Greenwich, Conn.: New York Graphic Society, 1973.

O'Connor, Francis V. *Federal Support for the Visual Arts: The New Deal and Now.* Greenwich, Conn.: New York Graphic Society, 1969.

O'Connor, Francis V., ed. *The New Deal Art Projects: An Anthology of Memoirs.* Washington, D.C.: Smithsonian Institution Press, 1972.

Park, Marlene, and Gerald E. Markowetz. *New Deal for Art: The Government Art Projects of the 30's, with Examples from New York City and State.* Hamilton, N.Y.: Gallery Association of New York State, 1977.

Phillips, Bertrand. "The W.P.A. and the Black Artist." *New Art Examiner* 5 (May 1978):8.

Rubenstein, Erica B. "Tax Payer's Murals." Ph.D. dissertation, Radcliffe College, 1944.

Schlesinger, Arthur M., Jr. *The Age of Roosevelt: The Politics of Upheaval.* Boston: Houghton Mifflin Company, 1960.

Taylor, Joshua. *America as Art.* Washington, D.C.: published for National Collection of Fine Arts by Smithsonian Institution Press, 1976.

Terkel, Studs. *Hard Times: An Oral History of the Great Depression.* New York: Pantheon Books, 1970.

This Fabulous Century, vol. 4, *1930–1940.* New York: Time-Life Books, 1969–70.

Wisconsin's New Deal Art. Catalogue of Travelling Exhibit. Foreword by Karel Yasho. Introduction by Mary Michie. Wausau, Wis.: Leigh Yawkey Woodson Art Museum, 1980.

"WPA Dividends." *Newsweek* 58 (August 14, 1961):52.

APPENDIX

Appendix

Third Forces in American Politics: A Symposium

On November 22, 1970, the Fromkin Memorial Collection was officially opened with a day of activities which included a symposium in the afternoon and the inaugural Fromkin Lecture in the evening. The participants in the symposium were:

Thomas W. Evans, a partner in the law firm of Mudge, Rose, Guthrie, and Alexander and the national director of the United Citizens for Nixon-Agnew. The general counsel to the Republican national campaign in 1968, Mr. Evans is president of the Robert A. Taft Institute of Government.

W. H. Ferry, a consultant to foundations, colleges, and other nonprofit enterprises and former vice-president of the Fund for the Republic and the Center for the Study of Democratic Institutions. Among his books are *The Corporation and the Economy* (1959), *The Economy Under Law* (1961), *What Price Peace* (1963), *Farewell to Integration* (1967), and *The Unanswerable Questions*.

David L. Graven, a professor of law at the University of Minnesota from 1963 to 1974 and now a partner in the law firm of Holmes, Kircher, and Graven in Minneapolis. He has long been active in Democratic-Farmer-Labor politics in Minnesota. He was a member of the Metropolitan Council of the Twin Cities area from 1971 to 1974 and has served on its transportation advisory board since 1977.

The late Isabel Bacon La Follette, widow of former Wisconsin governor Philip F. La Follette and a dynamic supporter of women's participation in political and social activities. For eighteen years she wrote a column, "A Room of Our Own," in the *Progressive,* and she organized the Women's Service Exchange Committee of Madison.

Charles E. Rice, a professor of law at the University of Notre Dame and state vice-chairman of the New York Conservative Party from 1962 to 1969. He is the author of *Freedom of Association* (1962), *The Supreme Court and Public Prayer* (1964), *The Vanishing Right to Live* (1969), and *Authority and Rebellion* (1971).

Frank P. Zeidler, mayor of Milwaukee from 1948 to 1960 and an arbitrator and consultant on public administration. He has been national chairman of the Socialist Party U.S.A. and was its nominee for president in 1976. He served as director of the Milwaukee Public Schools from 1941 to 1948 and as director of the Wisconsin Department of Resource Development from 1963 to 1964.

Austin Ranney, the moderator of the symposium, now a resident scholar of the American Enterprise Institute, Washington, D.C., and formerly a professor of political science at the University of Wisconsin–Madison. His publications include *The Doctrine of Responsible Party Government, Its Origins and Present State* (1964), *Referendums: A Comparative Study of Practice and Theory* (edited with David Butler, 1978), *The Federalization of Presidential Primaries* (1978), and *The Past and Future of Presidential Debates* (1979). He is a member of the Democratic National Committee's Commission on the Role and Future of Presidential Primaries.

(Editor's note: The text of the symposium which is printed in the following pages is an edited version of the tape recording made at the meeting. Unfortunately, because of technical difficulties, the opening statement of Thomas W. Evans was not preserved. Similarly, certain portions of the proceedings were lost; however, in no case was the loss extensive. The places where the losses occurred are noted in the text. The editor has deleted irrelevancies, redundancies, and pointless digressions from the remarks of the moderator, the panelists, and the questioners from the audience. These omissions from the text are indicated by ellipsis points. In no case do the deletions alter the intention or meaning of the speaker. The editor has not attempted to update the biographical details exhaustively beyond the time of the Symposium.)

RANNEY: It is especially fitting that the Morris Fromkin Collection be housed at the University of Wisconsin–Milwaukee. The city of Milwaukee is famous all over the world as one of America's main centers of progressive thought and politics in the nineteenth and twentieth centuries. It has long been associated with the Progressive movement so splendidly led by the La Follette family; and the Socialist Party leaders, Dan Hoan, Victor L. Berger, and Frank Zeidler, have shown us all that progressive politics can make good government as well as ideological controversy.

It is also fitting that the ceremonies inaugurating the Fromkin Collection begin with this symposium on "Third Forces in American Politics." And since we are considering this topic in an academic setting, perhaps it will be well to begin with a definition of the key term. By "third forces" we will mean those nonestablishment political forces, both ideas and movements, that do not find satisfactory outlets and expressions in the established political framework of the American two-party system. Let us be clear that such forces can be of either the Left or the Right, and we have spokesmen from both ends of the ideological spectrum with us today. . . .

The central question of this symposium is: Do we need effective third forces in American politics today, or can the needed changes in our society be brought about through the major parties and the established political system? And a closely related question is: How does today's need—or lack of need—for third forces compare with the situation at other periods in our history, the periods covered so well by the Fromkin Collection?

[Mr. Thomas W. Evans spoke at this time, but owing to technical problems his remarks were not recorded.]

RANNEY: Our next speaker, W. H. Ferry, has had a long and varied career. Mr. Ferry has been a newspaperman, vice-president of the Fund for the Republic, a consultant to the Ford Foundation, and an executive at the Center for the Study of Democratic Institutions. Mr. Ferry has an extensive background in third-force activities, including his work as instigator of the Committee on the Triple Revolution. Mr. Ferry.

FERRY: The topic of this symposium, "Third Forces in American Politics," is shrewdly chosen. For it seems, at least to me, that social justice has almost always emerged not as the result of institutions but in spite of them; not because of political parties or governors but because third forces gave them no choice except to take the road of social justice. To be sure, there have been and are third forces of a less benevolent character at work in our midst, and I shall take note of them in a moment. . . .

Social justice has come about not as the result of logic or step-by-step historical development, but as the result of third forces working on the establishments of their time. This phenomenon—the relation of third forces to the progress of human welfare—admittedly is a difficult problem in historical interpretation. But the Fromkin program promises to bring this relationship into the light. We may hope that the work of scholars here will, on the one hand, dispel the hagiology surrounding the principal figures in the social justice account and, on the other, discover for us the truth about the ability of unusual men and women to change the course of their times.

My guess is that a major result of this program will be to add a novel moral dimension to American history. At every stage of our national career there has been a collision between practical politics and morality, between exponents of what can be done and exponents of what should be done. . . .

Never in my lifetime has the need for understanding the potential of third forces been greater. . . . Chicanos, blacks, young people, Indians are hated, restricted, cheated, brutalized. The sin of these people is to shout against social injustice, to question their elders, to try to break out of ghettos, reservations, and other colonial enclaves. Their sin is their preoccupation with social justice. They are a kind of third force the nation has seen before—but never in such baffling variety, never with so sweeping a bill of indictment. And like their courageous, idealistic, and despised predecessors, they are having as hard a time of it as a frightened and self-righteous establishment can bring down on them.

It is the apparent nature of things that third forces should be feared and harassed while present, revered when out of the way or dead. The wholesome additions of early-day Socialists to American political consciousness are today acknowledged, but in their time duly elected Socialist representatives were denied their seats. Eugene Debs went to prison, and the most famous picture of Norman Thomas is on a public platform with egg dripping from his forehead. Martin Luther King was a trouble-making, black scoundrel while he lived, but now, safe in his grave, he is honored.

All were prophets of social justice. All were third forces in themselves and captains of collective third forces. . . . committed to human dignity and betterment, to seeing men not as consumers, colonial subjects, or computer bits, but as human beings with inalienable rights.

There is, however, a different brand of third force in American politics, . . . never absent from our public life. These are individuals and groups basely motivated, whose objects are fear and suspicion and hate. These would include the Ku Klux Klan, the Birch Society, the Minute Men, the Hargis-McIntyre crypto-Christian gangs, and—not to neglect my audience— the late senator from this state, whose malign influence lingers on in laws and practices and institutions throughout the land, not the least in my own state of California.

Despite the importance of these spiritual and political desperadoes, I am glad that the Fromkin program is to concentrate on those singular men and women who have kept bright the beacon of social justice. For it is to such people, and to the collective efforts they inspire, that we must look, in Laertes' words, for "the sanity and health of the whole nation."

RANNEY: Thank you, Mr. Ferry.

Our next speaker teaches law at the University of Minnesota, but this is only David L. Graven's occupation. On the side—I think we can say this—he is a politician, with a long record of activity and service in the Democratic-Farmer-Labor Party of Minnesota. Most recently Mr. Graven was unsuccessful in his bid for his party's gubernatorial nomination; but, as you can see, he's still very young and energetic, and there will be other elections in the future. Now let's listen to what Mr. Graven has to say about third forces in American politics.

GRAVEN: On a program such as this I suppose a representative of a successful party like the Minnesota DFL has to start from a somewhat defensive position. . . . Its roots lie in the populist past of the third party Farmer-Laborites, but today it is basically the Democratic party in Minnesota. Starting from nowhere twenty-five years ago, it produced not one, but two presidential candidates in 1968. A small party from a small, midwestern state can indeed gain national and international influence.

Our topic today concerns the past and its influence on the present and future. One must, of course, concede immediately the impact of progressive, third-party forces on midwestern politics. The impact has obviously been considerable, and the legacy in a number of midwestern states, including Minnesota, is a vigorous two-party structure with increasing involvement of people. This involvement stems from a sense of frustration among increasingly articulate groups: minorities, blacks, students, tenants, wage earners, farmers, and police, for example. For those of us who care about the past and its lessons, as Morris Fromkin undoubtedly did, and for those who think that relevance is perhaps something more than "doing your thing," can we learn anything worth while from a look backward at the prairie populists' quest for social justice?

In some ways one can wonder, in 1970, why bother at all about the prairie populists? Is there really that much of their handiwork left? Some legislation, to be sure—much of it hopelessly outdated in a modern, urban society. And rhetoric, of course; in our state, as in others, the Democrats still run and win on the rhetoric of the big interests versus the little guy, a survival of the rhetoric which surrounded the so-called economic issues of the 1930s. This rhetoric lives on, . . . and the cutting edge of reform in Wisconsin, Minnesota, and the Dakotas is not in the established parties. It is in the neighborhood law offices, the tenant unions, the welfare organizations.

One wonders why the legacy of the prairie populists is not greater than it is. In thinking about this I came to one possible hypothesis: that the populist reform movements really owed their thrust and appeal and power to their leaders, who may be classified as charismatic county attorneys. . . . I say *charismatic* to emphasize the personally brilliant leadership and oratory these county attorney types provided. In many ways by their personal leadership they dominated the movements of which they were part. In Minnesota, when Floyd B. Olson died, the Farmer-Labor Party degenerated into a nest of factionalism and a sink of corruption. In Wisconsin, there were more La Follettes to carry on after Bob, Sr.'s, death, and Progressivism as a force continued, tied to the magical appeal of the family's name and leadership.

The second part of my phrase emphasizes that these men had something else in common: They were all county attorneys familiar with the rituals and ideas of courthouse politics. La Follette, Sr., and Phil, Floyd B. Olson and Harold Stassen (if he may be included) were all county attorneys when they got their start in politics. They started out and continued in higher offices to emphasize essentially local politics. They were the best the courthouse had to offer, but it was still the courthouse. They assumed high offices screaming for a cleanup of government. . . . It was reform they wanted. They believed that local regulations would take care of things if you could combine them with codes of ethics. Their approach was a county attorney's: legal answers to legal problems, codes of ethics, commissions, regulation. In Minnesota, Floyd B. Olson took office during the Depression denouncing the corruption and ineffectiveness of the state government. He wanted a cleanup, because only an honest government, he said, could grasp the rapidly deteriorating conditions and establish some control over an economy that was running out of hand. Probably the high point of his administration was the enactment of the mortgage moratorium laws; this was a legal response to the alarming rise in farm foreclosures and the inability of the government to stop the trend under existing laws. The mortgage moratorium laws saved a lot of farmers in our state.

In the field of regulation, Olson's achievements and, I might add, the achievements of his good-government-type predecessors, were neither big nor permanent. Olson thundered against bank holding companies, but his rhetoric sailed right past two of the country's largest, which are still thriving today in Minneapolis. The Railroad Warehouse Commission controlled the railroads and the grain, but it's been a long time since this Commission in

Minnesota or Wisconsin's Public Service Commission, which is supposed to do the same kind of regulating here, really served the public. It's always been a question of whose interests these Commissions would serve, and it seems that the public's interests have been shortchanged more often than not.

Olson's movement never swept the legislature. His time in the governorship was one essentially of personal executive government, and that's not the kind that moves worlds in a representative form of government.

Perhaps the greatest achievement of the prairie populists was the raising of the level of politics in some ways. In this century civil service for the most part has wiped out old-fashioned patronage politics and introduced a politics of citizen participation in which a lot of people work very hard but only a handful ever get any reward beyond personal satisfaction. . . .

This local and citizens' politics of the prairie populists . . . had a mixed record in handling local problems that could deal with regulation, codes of ethics, commissions, and laws. . . . But the local emphasis was totally inadequate for coping with the great foreign policy issues of the thirties. Midwestern third forces didn't understand the dangers of Nazi aggression, and their response was totally inadequate. And even while they were doing the best they could in domestic affairs, under Roosevelt's New Deal the national government became the great engine of social reform in the country, and it has been ever since.

But the dynamics of American politics are changing. Today we see a trend of getting back to the states and local governments to generate new ideas and new programs. Many of the problems . . . are technical problems, like some of the problems Olson solved during the Depression, and these problems must be solved with technical remedies. . . . We need answers to problems of getting control of our metropolitan areas through new governmental structures, . . . and we need answers to the questions of tax distribution, racial imbalance in the schools, and the roles and work of the various levels of government within a new federalism. Answers to these questions will have to be the kinds of legal and structural solutions which are the specialty of good-government-types. These are not the kinds of problems we will solve with slogans and talk about social justice; . . . they require the grind of working out highly technical tax distribution formulas and of establishing the responsibilities of the various levels of government. . . .

At the same time that good-government-types are at work on these problems within the established structure of politics, there is important work for third forces. The crusades which vault new and unpopular ideas and policies into the public forum can occur only outside the formal structure of major parties. The structure of an established party is really a barrier against innovation, regardless of what party people say. The emphasis in major parties is on winning elections, getting out the vote, and balancing interests—things members of political parties work at and things that move them to action long before they think about ideology. The almost inevitable stodginess of the major parties indicates to me not only that third forces have a place in American life today but also that they are absolutely essential if we are to survive.

The way third-force prairie populists handled the problems of the twenties and thirties has an important lesson for us today. The prairie populists encouraged the sense of citizen participation, the belief that the individual counts. This idea is tremendously important today. As I look at the political situation, at least in the Midwest, I see and hear people feeling swallowed up by the growing cities and suburbs; I see and hear the frustration of students; I see and hear people who feel left out of the society and deserted by politics. What people today really want is at least a *sense* of participation, if not participation itself. . . . Decentralization of government, and the citizen participation which, theoretically at least, will go with it, is no longer just a rallying cry for conservatives. It has become part of the new liberal ethic. Liberals and conservatives today can agree on at least one thing: Let's get government back into the hands of the people. On this subject the prairie populists and their leaders have something to say to us. . . .

RANNEY: Thank you, Professor Graven.

Professor Graven spoke eloquently of the charismatic leadership of third forces in American politics. We are honored today to have with us someone else who can speak with authority on this subject: Mrs. Philip La Follette. Mrs. La Follette is the widow of the three-term Progressive governor of Wisconsin, Philip Fox La Follette, and therefore the daughter-in-law of governor and senator Fighting Bob La Follette, who for many years was almost a third force in American politics all by himself. One of the truly great ladies of Wisconsin Progressivism and of progressive third-force politics everywhere, Mrs. La Follette.

LA FOLLETTE: Thank you very much.

I don't know how many of you are old enough to remember a book that appeared in the late twenties called *Life Begins at Forty* by Walter Pitkin. The only thing I remember about it is that he made a list of about ten of the most exhausting jobs in the world. At the top of the list was getting people to do things. That's what I think politics is. As far as the third-party movement in Wisconsin goes, I came late, and I'm not of the blood royal, as one of my brothers-in-law used to say.

I'm no scholar, but having lived in a university community all my adult life I'm not in awe of scholarship. But I do appreciate it, especially when it is applied to life. This was true of the La Follette family, beginning with the elder generation. In tackling the problems of politics as they saw them, . . . they naturally turned to the university for expert help of all kinds. During the administrations of both La Follettes, when the Wisconsin Idea was being born and then put to work, there was a close connection between the university and the capitol. With this background and help, plus their own originality, they developed a rare gift for putting complicated problems into understandable form. This is vital to constructive politics. And they also made their talks entertaining. In the days before TV or even radio, people would drive miles to hear them speak. There was no money to be made in our kind of politics. Both Bob, Sr., and Phil spent many hours keeping the wolf from the door by Chautauqua tours outside the state. People responded to what they had to say, and the so-called La Follette machine was nothing more than an army of volunteers. People outside Wisconsin thought we had a comfortably Progressive state. Those of us who were part of the Progressive movement knew that keeping it going was a day-to-day struggle.

When I came to the university from an actively Democratic Utah family in 1917, I had never heard of the La Follettes. I was active in undergraduate affairs, but not in politics. How I was in Madison and didn't know that Senator La Follette was being burned in effigy, I don't know. When I came to Madison I was interested in people, but I had not found my ultimate calling. My mother had told me I was a good executive, but I had replied that I couldn't just go out and execute. I majored in sociology and worked at it in Bayonne, New Jersey, for a year before I married. Bayonne was 85 percent foreign-born at that time, and I felt very awkward going into homes during a depression to urge women with big families to limit their families and otherwise conform to certain conditions in order to receive aid.

When I married into the La Follette family, I found the most complex and fascinating man I'd ever known. He was so full of enthusiasm, and whatever he touched was fun. But I didn't know I was marrying an institution. I never saw a family work the way they did. After Phil and I were married, Mrs. La Follette put me to work on *La Follette's Magazine*, writing, addressing envelopes, doing book reviews, and other jobs. We were not telling people what to do, but asking them to join us in a great cause. You must remember that we had just been through World War I "to make the world safe for democracy," and we were sure that all we had to do was to right what was wrong with the system, most of it economic. I enjoyed my apprenticeship. I was working hard, and I was learning. I had no idea of protesting. I just wanted to work.

Some years later, . . . after Phil was elected governor, people would come to me to see if I wouldn't prevail on Phil to do this or that. People liked to think that they could get at a man in office through his wife. . . . I soon found that it was easy to go to Phil with their problems, but it was not so easy to answer the question he always put to me: "What would you do about it?" To a conscientious person this is a sobering question. This all occurs to me when somebody asks, "What do you think of the women's liberation movement?" I tell them that I'm not a good person to ask that question, because I never felt any need to be liberated. There was so much work to do that I just put my shoulder to the wheel. In my younger days one of my friends, who never made a really satisfactory adjustment in life, used to say that if you didn't get paid for your work it wasn't appreciated. But Belle Case La Follette, who was a very wise woman, always said there was much valuable and satisfying work to be done; and if there was enough family income, the pay was not important. I went on that advice.

Of course, I will admit that in those days we had very good health and lots of help around the house. Madison is located in Dane County, which is a very rich farming area; and in those days farmers' daughters liked to come into town to work for a year or two before they went back and got married and settled down to be farmers' wives. We simply didn't have the housekeeping problems that working and professional women have today. There was always somebody to keep the house while I was out campaigning very vigorously and organizing and speaking. Today this is not as easy unless one is very rich.

Anyway, that's what I was doing. Of course, I was not a professional person. . . . I had never been president of an organization nor received an honorary degree. . . . I'd just been out there investigating and working. My work had been experimental and pioneering. In those days, the 1930s, too many women stayed home on election day. Mostly I organized and spoke to other women at home meetings in the countryside and in villages and in cities like Milwaukee. At one time Phil and I thought it would be fun to go out as a team, but we never got to do it. We always were forced to go separately, because as many people as possible wanted the La Follette name as a drawing card. . . .

Politics and campaigning were lots of fun in those days. I think they had it all over the TV approach of today. We got into cars and rode around the state, and we used shoe leather. We went into little villages and farm homes all over the state and worked here in Milwaukee, all to meet people. . . . There were problems, however. It was tough going trying to talk to Polish women absorbed in a church basement bingo game or to an Italian group in which no one really understood English. (Most of our meetings were held in homes. Everybody said, "Well, women won't go out to meetings." So I said, "Well, then we'll go to them.") . . . It was great fun, and I wonder how many experiences like this campaigners have today. I think this is very important today, to have some fun in politics. . . .

Now as for TV, I'm glad other speakers have brought that up. I hope the Congress will override President Nixon's veto of the bill on TV campaign expenditures. Ronald Reagan, who is an expert in this field, said . . . that he thought paid ads were frightfully costly and did no good at all. He thought the only really effective kind of TV appearance for a politican was the interview show.

I'm a great TV fan. I live alone, and I'm being educated by TV. The other night, when I heard that John Lindsay was going to be on the "Johnny Carson Show," I thought to myself, what's he up to now? (Shortly after he was first elected mayor, I heard Lindsay on one of the interview programs. When asked the question, "What kind of Republican are you?" he replied that he would *like* to be the kind of Republican like La Guardia and the La Follettes. Naturally, since then I have watched and listened to him whenever I had the chance.) Well, I stayed up way past my bedtime to see him, and there he was, his own charming, lovely self. . . . He sat and seemed to be enjoying himself. He was relaxed, charming, and obviously amused as Carson started needling him in an attempt to get him to express himself about Vice-President Agnew. After sparring a bit, Lindsay took over and for about twenty-five minutes made one of the most wonderful speeches on leadership I've heard in ages. The gist of what he said was that leadership was moving people forward; it was guiding and leading the way. Negative leadership has no future, according to Lindsay. . . .

It is popular to say that New York is ungovernable, but Lindsay's work refutes this view. I recently asked a Milwaukee newspaperman if Milwaukee was still the best-governed big city in the United States, and he said it was. This worldwide reputation was built up by a succession of able Socialist mayors backed by an enlightened electorate. Milwaukee is a demonstration of what forward-looking leadership can achieve. . . .

Thank you.

RANNEY: Thank you very much, Mrs. La Follette.

Our fifth speaker, Charles Rice, was formerly an active leader of the Conservative party of New York, having been its vice-chairman for some time. He is now a professor of law at the University of Notre Dame, but he did not leave New York so soon that he was not able to give senator-elect Buckley some help. He apparently arrived in Indiana just a bit too late to do the cause there much good, but after all he hasn't been around there very long. Since the Conservative party of New York is, for reasons several of us have discussed here, one of the most impressively successful third-force movements in American politics today, I think we might look for a little action in Indiana. It is with particular interest that you should hear Professor Rice's remarks.

RICE: Thank you very much, Mr. Ranney.

I really find this symposium on third forces in American politics very congenial. I am delighted that the Fromkin family has done the wonderful thing of putting into this university a means for the systematic study of movements which did so much for our country, whether we agree or disagree with their ideas and what they did. . . .

Third parties and third forces have been very helpful and very useful in American life. On the drive up from South Bend I was thinking about what the conservative movement and the Conservative party and other third-force operations of various types today have in common with the groups that dominate the collection we are here today to inaugurate. I wonder if we can't say that a common denominator between the types of movements that inspired the formation of the Fromkin Collection and the movements I want to speak about today is a concern for the life and dignity of individuals. . . . This was certainly the concern that prompted the third-force movements in the early part of this century. Today we find a redoubled necessity for something to provide a forum for the protection of individual rights.

To the question of Professor Ranney . . . concerning whether third-force political movements are needed today, I would answer emphatically, yes. Not that we should go out and create them for their own sake, but they are needed, because, as he put it, there *are* some ideas that just can't find expression in the orthodox two-party system as it currently operates. And to his second question—Are such movements more necessary or less necessary than in the past?—I say that they are more necessary. One reason is the impact of instant communication. Political movements and public movements generally today have a larger opportunity than in the past to affect the lives and ideas of people much more quickly, and we must have some sort of counterforce to temper this power, and in this I'd agree with Mr. Ferry. . . .

There are two reasons that I think we should be concerned about third-force movements today. One is that we are running a risk in this country—now I'm a Conservative, and to some of you this may sound strange coming from me—but we are running a risk in this country of inviting undue repression in order to maintain the basic civil order. Therefore we must have a continuing force of the kind the Conservative party of New York is providing, for example, to urge a continuing, reasonable, and balanced enforcement of the law within the framework of a free society on behalf of the individual citizens who are directly affected.

There's another issue, too, which my mentioning as a third-force issue may surprise some of you. But I've found it popping up in various places around the country, and it has the potential to develop—and I hope it does develop—into a very important third-force movement. . . . I am speaking, of course, about the abortion issue. . . . If we're looking for a third-force movement which shares with the movements commemorated in the Fromkin Collection a motivating and abiding concern for the dignity of the individual and for individual rights, then . . . a third force organized around the abortion issue is something that is going to arrive fairly quickly. I frankly expect that by 1972 you're going to find a nationally organized operation putting candidates into all kinds of state and federal races or endorsing sympathetic candidates from the existing parties in order to present this issue to the people. . . . The American people should begin to think about the abortion issue, for if we adopt the idea that innocent human beings can be killed because their existence is inconvenient or uncomfortable to others or because others consider them unfit to live, then we really have compromised the very essence of liberty. . . .

It seems to me that we ought to get down to the very basics. That's why I think a collection like the one we are inaugurating today is so important. It demonstrates the legitimacy—I don't mean the contemporary legitimacy; any third-force movement is going to be derided in its own time—but the legitimacy in terms of what they were doing and in terms of their improving the welfare of people over the long run. . . .

I'm delighted to have the opportunity to be here. Thank you.

RANNEY: Thank you, Professor Rice.

The last speaker poses a very difficult problem for me. If ever there was an act of supererogation, it is introducing Frank Zeidler to a Milwaukee audience in Milwaukee. So I think all I will do here, Frank, is just set the historical record a little bit straight. In the biographical notes that were circulated to members of the panel for their mutual information I noticed that they said Frank Zeidler was the last Socialist mayor of Milwaukee. Now, this implies a prediction about the future that I'm not sure anyone can make, so I think perhaps we should rephrase that to say, the most recent Socialist mayor of Milwaukee, Frank Zeidler.

ZEIDLER: Thank you, Professor Ranney, for kicking off our next campaign.

I feel that I should put aside my notes and pick up where Professor Rice left off. I, too, am very much concerned about respect for human life, and I sort of share his position on the whole question of the ethical problems raised by abortion. But today I am very depressed because of what I heard last night. I heard that the Republican administration has once again commenced bombing North Vietnam. This has all the terrible implications of the continuation of this war, of the continuation of this conflict between the capitalists of the United States and the intransigent Communists of North Vietnam. Since I represent a party that has historically had as its major theme the whole question of peace, I cannot help but be depressed over this particular situation. Because of this situation I see a great need for a party like the Democratic Socialist party and other groups and individuals who share its concern for peace to continue being vocal and working for peace inside and outside the Republican and Democratic parties.

It is interesting to note that one of the reasons the Fromkin Collection has been created in this city is that Victor L. Berger lived and worked here. Berger was an Austrian immigrant who, after stopovers in several other places, wound up here in Milwaukee, where he organized a movement which ripened into a third party, the Democratic Socialist party. He was joined in this effort by labor people around the nation and by people who ardently desired a better-planned society, an end to the exploitation of human beings, and a system based on social justice. Out of this party emerged some great figures, great at least to some of us: Eugene Victor Debs and Norman Thomas, to name just two of them. In Wisconsin we have had many heroes of the sort I am talking about: for example, Frank J. Weber; Jake Friedrick, who is in the audience today; and many other people in the labor movement; Dan Hoan, who represented not so much "Sewer Socialism" as the improvement of the sewer system and the collection of rubbish, which is still an issue in this city, incidentally, and other improvements to make cities better places for people to live in. These men and many others represented the ideal of a better society. It is interesting to note that from this relatively tiny handful of men came much of the great social legislation and many of the programs which even the Conservative party accepts. Professor Rice, I would point out, came up from South Bend on a socialized highway system.

The need for a third party or for a multiparty system in the United States is to me now quite evident. If we look at the history of the major parties in the government, we see that since the end of Reconstruction about 1877 this nation has been ruled rather firmly by a coalition of southern Democrats and northern Republicans who have represented the corporate and financial interests of this country. This coalition has long been successful in imposing its will on the country, and it is beginning to dominate our thinking on many of today's major issues. Solutions to questions of social justice, of equal rights, of spending money for domestic needs instead of war are constantly being opposed and defeated by this coalition.

In Wisconsin we have voted recently for progressive Republicans or Progressives, and now we have voted for Democrats. We vote for them because of their liberal ideology, which is akin to Democratic Socialism. Unfortunately, once a party gains power nationally, people at the local level relax; and then at the local level all the goals of the national parties . . . go down to defeat or are watered down. National leaders of the Democratic party are for such things as housing and education; but when these goals are translated into working problems, too often by local politicians like the bosses of Newark or of Jersey City or of St. Louis, the goals are defeated. This is why I think third parties are needed—to keep up pressure so that good goals and good programs are adopted and translated into reality at all levels of government.

In many places in this nation a multiparty system cannot exist simply because the parties cannot get on the ballot. . . . Some of you will say that if there is a third party in this country, it will be a party of the Bill Buckley type or the George Wallace type and that these parties . . . will be concerned not about human dignity but mainly about maintaining a superior intellectual class or economic class or something of the sort. But those of us who are interested in a third-party system have to take that risk, the risk that such parties will come into existence. We who are Democratic Socialists also have to contend with third-party rumblings from totalitarians who, disgruntled and cynical about any chance for peaceful change in this country, have adopted an ideology and sometimes the practice of force as a means of bringing about change. So, even though the time is very risky for the emergence of third parties, . . . they are vitally needed to inject new ideas and programs into the American system so that it may be viable in the future.

I am happy that the Fromkin Collection has been created within the University of Wisconsin–Milwaukee, not only because of the origin of the Collection, but also because scholars studying the development of past third-force movements in the Fromkin Collection will be able to come up with new ideas for the creation of a better and more humane society today and tomorrow.

It is interesting to notice the heroes whose principles the two major parties have elevated to canon law. The Republican party now reveres Thomas Jefferson, who favored a weak central government, while the Democrats celebrate none other than Alexander Hamilton, who stood for a strong central government. So, since the time of their origins, the two parties have swapped heroes and ideologies. Perhaps the Socialist party is moving in the same direction. We are now talking about and relying more than we used to on community organization and participation of the people in the decisions that affect their lives. We no longer emphasize planning and a strong state. Something like the Fromkin Collection will, I hope, enable scholars to understand why reversals such as the ones I have mentioned have occurred, and this understanding may bring forth new ideas which will help prevent this world from perishing in a holocaust of totalitarian systems competing to impose their will on others.

I am very happy that the University of Wisconsin–Milwaukee is fulfilling our great tradition of progressive ideas here in the city and is in a position to carry out unfinished assignments and great new work.

RANNEY: Thank you, Mr. Zeidler.

Before we go fishing in the audience for questions and comments, I think we might toss a few onions, apples, and brickbats back and forth among ourselves. . . . I would like to ask Mr. Ferry and Mr. Zeidler what they think of this proposition, which I offer as a factual proposition: that the most powerful third-force movement in American politics within the next ten years is more likely to be the Wallace movement than any other; and if this is true, are they still as happy or as sanguine about or as eager for third forces as they were in their opening presentations? Mr. Ferry?

FERRY: Well, George Wallace can't make anyone of my persuasion very happy, but, you know, there is always a chance that he might be right. I think he is definitely one hundred percent wrong, but he certainly is appealing to something deep in American life. It's no accident that he polled all those votes, . . . but I think you have to accept the thick with the thin if you favor democracy and cultural pluralism, if you favor having many influences at work in American life.

I have a question I want to ask here, and I might as well put it in here before turning this over to Mr. Zeidler. Why is it that the people here who somehow represent, let us say, standard-brand politics have accepted today the need for third forces? I should have expected somebody at this table to say that they aren't necessary, that we have a good, healthy, two-party system in this country which can be made to work right without the so-called inputs from third forces. Everybody at this table seems to accept as a matter of fact that third forces are somehow required to keep the major parties morally honest . . . and enlightened.

RANNEY: Yes, that's a good question, and if I weren't so eager to hear what Mr. Zeidler has to say about my question we'd jump to that one immediately. I promise we will as soon as Mr. Zeidler is through.

ZEIDLER: My opinion is that the Wallace movement is going to gain in strength, especially with the rise of repressive police forces in the cities in response to proddings from the totalitarian Right. I believe the only way that the Wallace movement can be checked is by the rise of a fourth party or another third force, if you want to use that phrase. I think the reason the Wallace movement has succeeded is that there has been no counterbalancing movement to speak vigorously against it, with the result that Wallace has pulled both the Democratic party nationally and the Republican party nationally in his direction. It is almost too late now to do anything else but to launch a counterforce. As Victor Berger used to say many years ago, . . . we would work with anybody moving in our direction. We, the Democratic Socialists of America, will work with those groups which are seeking to check the rise of this native brand of fascism. We have been unsuccessful in persuading many of the Democratic city organizations to join us in opposition to the Wallace movement. And even the labor movement has been pulled in Mr. Wallace's direction. It seems to me that we now need a democratic movement to pull the whole spectrum or the whole center of balance in the United States in the direction of progressivism. I share with Mr. Ranney the fear that this Wallace movement is going to be a very powerful movement in the future.

RANNEY: Now to Mr. Ferry's question, which I'm going to direct to both Mr. Evans and Mr. Graven. The essence of the question is that each of you, active in major-party politics, has been saying all these sweet things about third forces—I'm embellishing your question a bit, Mr. Ferry. Is this because secretly you know third forces aren't very important and they're an all-right way to let kids have their fun? Or is it because you feel that in some way they are helpful to the major parties? Or is it because you feel that somehow there is a legitimacy, a positive contribution that third-force politics make, even though you yourselves don't participate? In other words, why, as leaders in the established major parties, do you say all these kind things about movements and leaders who do not believe that the major parties can ever be vehicles for social progress in this country?

GRAVEN: I want to come back to Professor Rice's abortion question later.

I guess I believe in third parties, third forces, or whatever you want to call the kind of maverick politics we're talking about today. I've spent the better part of my adult life working within the Minnesota DFL, and I've just flatly come to the conclusion that, no matter what they may say, the major established parties are really living on their myths, those great half-truths that kind of charge you all up. As instruments for raising and promoting new issues, the major established parties are conservative. . . . They will always tend to seek out the lowest common denominator, run the safest candidates, and campaign on the safest possible issues. People who because of their instincts and ambitions become involved in the political process are for the most part interested in the distribution and uses of power. While they may pay lip service to the issues and sincerely believe their own words, partly because of their allegiance to the myths of their party, basically they are interested in the distribution and uses of power.

In our DFL party in Minnesota we have a myth that we're gay, romantic, liberal *caballeros* who saunter forth every two or four years to slay the big-interest dragon. That's the way we like to think of ourselves and our party. But when we get down to articulating issues and setting our policies for achieving this or that, then, of course, we're lost. Where are we going to get our issues and policies? Where are the inputs going to come from? Usually they will come from outside the party structure. I could cite many examples from my own state where issues have been raised and developed and where pressures for solving problems have all been generated outside the established party structure. At some point the issues become so hot and the pressures so great that the major parties adopt the issues as their very own and either absorb the third force or third party or in some other way cancel its influence.

The New Democratic Coalition is an example of a third force fueled by high-energy emotionalism—based, of course, on the members' and the public's rage against the war. In our state the NDC is not a power for one very good reason: we just took it over. Today the Minnesota DFL is a peace party. The leadership and platform say so, and they mean it. Everybody knows the NDC is there, but it has no following to speak of. The peace advocates have found a home within the normal structure. But the pressure for the party to move to a peace platform and to elect a peace leadership never could have been generated within the regular party structure. We had to be shown by forces outside the regular structure that the peace issue had some political magic.

So I would say I am heartily in favor of third parties, or third forces, or, in some cases, just plain maverick politics. I just don't see any other way that the parties are going to move unless pressure is put on them from outside. My experience is that there will never be enough pressure from inside to force established parties to adopt new and controversial issues.

RANNEY: Mr. Evans?

EVANS: Well, I want to reaffirm my faith in third parties. I am not at all offended by the question which asked whether the established parties looked to third parties for inspiration. On the issues I think we do. I don't think we look to them for moral leadership, as someone suggested. I think there's nothing so common in politics as staking a claim to moral leadership. Everybody does it. I think we've got to look at the issues to see just what is being proposed and what proposals can best solve problems.

I think we're ignoring one premise in this discussion. I've stated that the two-party system is necessary and that it's the only thing that makes third parties viable and effective. If you look at the great populist issues—direct election of senators, postal reform, big government, control of the trusts—they weren't implemented by the populists anywhere but in random states. They were implemented nationally by the Republican party and the Democratic party.

One of the more worrisome suggestions that's come up today is Mr. Zeidler's that we should have a multiparty system in this country. We haven't had one in the sense of a host of parties, each of which cuts up the pie, each of which has some influence in selecting the national leadership, each of which has its tiny bloc in the national legislature constantly fighting and bickering with others. I give you the example of the French Third Republic and of many of the European democracies. I think that what we have is a good, solid two-party system where both parties have the good sense, the pragmatism, if you will, to embrace the ideas so regularly generated by third parties. Mr. Zeidler, if we were to go to a multiparty system, as you suggested, I think we'd lose a great deal. I think we still need the two major established parties. But they do need reinvigoration, and I've asked for suggestions as to how this might be done.

RANNEY: I asked Mr. Zeidler in a whisper whether he would like to respond to that, and he shot back a very loud *yes*, which you all must have heard. So now we'll hear from Mr. Zeidler.

ZEIDLER: Well, I merely want to say that, historically, Abraham Lincoln was elected in a four-party race.

EVANS: And I'm an alumnus of his party, and I think that's fine. That race was just one of the steps in the establishment of the Republicans as a permanent party.

RANNEY: I think that one problem every one of us has so far ignored is the role of the working class or organized labor, or however one wishes to talk about the organized and unorganized blue-collar population, in third-force politics. I am aware, of course, that the working class and organized labor are quite different, or at least distinguishable bodies. . . . The question that I want to ask . . . is: Is it possible to have in this country a truly powerful and truly effective progressive, liberal third force without substantial support from the working class, from wage earners; and is there any indication at all that the mass of American wage earners is any more ready today than it has been for the past sixty years to go the route of third-force or third-party politics? Mr. Zeidler.

ZEIDLER: In my opinion there's not much indication that the American worker is now prepared to do anything but vote Democratic, and by casting this kind of vote he is very consciously tending to support the existing system. But in looking at possible future actions of the labor movement, I do not think one can discount the division within the movement, especially the disaffection toward George Meany's international policies.

In looking at the politics of the future generally, one cannot ignore the fact that many of today's young people are sooner or later going to gain positions of power; and even though today they are bunched in minority groups, it seems to me that in the future some of these groups, or one of these groups, is going to emerge as a dominant party representing a dominant ideology. It is my opinion that the great concern of America now should not be with what the Democratic and Republican parties are fighting about, but with what's going on in these groups of young people where the finest intellectuals among the young are concerning themselves with the future. I think that here's where our attention should be focused, because nothing is more practical than a good theory, and out of some of these young people are going to come new theories of world organization, new theories of government, which will prove viable in the future.

In the future I'm not looking for the labor movement to furnish the leadership, as it did in the past. I'm looking for these young people to furnish the leadership, and I think that eventually they will convert labor to their side.

RANNEY: Professor Rice.

RICE: I think that in some ways we have not a generation gap but what one observer has called a campus gap. There have been surveys on this question showing that we tend to focus our attention on the extremely vocal minority of young people in college. The fact is that only a minority of young people is in college, and within this minority only a minority is involved in political activities which could be, loosely, labeled New Left. There is a wide gap between the vocal, New Left, college student and the wage-earning young person. . . . It seems to me that when we talk about the young, the best part of our generation, and all this business, we ought to be more specific than we usually are concerning which young people we're talking about. I think that sometimes we tend simply to give the most attention to those who make the most noise.

RANNEY: Anyone else care to comment on this?

Well, that brings us back to the party organization question. Having heard Mr. Zeidler's short but trenchant reminder that Abraham Lincoln, the first Republican president, was elected in a four-party race, I would simply like to add that it might be well to recall that the bloodiest civil war in history followed that election. If the war was a result of that kind of political division, perhaps we ought to think just a bit about the wisdom of having a multiparty system, even if it does produce an Abraham Lincoln.

But the larger question, the question that I think must concern anyone who is involved in any kind of third-force politics, is the whole problem of the most effective way to bring about the kind of social change you want. . . . I would like to address this question to Professor Rice first: What is there about organizing and operating as a political party that appeals to people of conservative philosophy and ideology in New York or elsewhere as opposed to attempting to accomplish their goals by organizing some kind of nonparty pressure group or protest movement?

RICE: When you look at the situation in New York, I think you can see why Conservatives organized themselves into a party rather than expressing their disagreements with the drift of state politics through other forms of political protest. New York did not have a two-party system before the Conservative party came along. It had a three-party system. There were the Democratic and Republican parties, as well as the highly influential Liberal party. The idea of the founders of the Conservative party was that it would operate on the Right as in our view the Liberal party had operated on the Left for many years. By its political pressure and by having a permanent line on the ballot, the Liberal party had over the years succeeded in pulling the two major established parties in a direction that Conservatives considered undesirable. The only way we could mount an effective counterweight was by using the same mechanism: a party. I don't think that this tactic is necessary in every part of the country. In many states you don't have a situation like New York's, where Conservatives regard the views of the two major established parties as identical. So, the peculiar conditions in New York demanded that the Conservative operation proceed as a political party, but I don't think you can generalize from our experience and say that political parties are *per se* preferable to pressure groups. It depends on the situation. In some areas you just might need a political party to run candidates on an *ad hoc* basis, such as, for example, on the abortion issue, which I mentioned earlier, but this doesn't have to be.

RANNEY: Mr. Evans, I really have not been trying to suppress your free speech. [Evans has been trying to say something, but Ranney has not given him the floor.] It's a question of my schedule, but if you would like to say what you were going to say a few minutes ago, or to speak to this question, or whatever, please go ahead.

EVANS: Excuse me. I think your point was well made. I was simply going to point out that the Republican party was the second party in 1856. I think perhaps we're over-historifying this particular question and not gaining so much from the point. I think, frankly, that your point was exceptionally well made and well taken.

RANNEY: One other question I wanted to raise, and then we'll invite questions from the audience.

I'm going to put Mrs. La Follette on the spot here because of her reference to a certain leading political figure. My question involves the individual version of the collective question we discussed earlier. Namely, what does one do if he is a person of considerable ability, force, attractiveness, and vote-getting ability who does not really fit very comfortably into the major established political parties? How can such a person act most effectively? This is certainly a question you know a good deal about from having observed your husband and brother-in-law and other Progressives in the late 1930s and early 1940s when they had some hard choices to make: whether they should continue as an independent party or return to the Republican party or move into the Democratic party. If Mayor Lindsay were to take a solemn oath to follow your political advice, what would you advise him to do in the immediate future?

LA FOLLETTE: I'd advise him to lead. The public expects leadership from people like him. He has had tremendous experience in New York. Other people say it's an impossible city to govern, but he doesn't think so. He's still at it. . . . It takes great persistence and courage to meet the constant challenges of governing New York.

You see, I know what it means to form a third party and get people to go out and get signatures. It's a very hard job that takes persistence and courage; that's why most people disappear after a while: not enough persistence and courage. But still I think they give a great deal.

The trouble with a lot of young people is that they're objecting, they're complaining about things, but they don't come up with anything in the way of a program. From the analysis I read of Mr. Buckley's senate campaign in New York, I gather that he attracted a great many young people to work for him, and the analysis said they were very enthusiastic and, it appears, successful. But in other places I've read that students didn't turn out to campaign the way everybody nine months ago thought they would. When the election came, most young people were indifferent.

I think a politician has got to command attention. I think that's why Lindsay goes on the Johnny Carson show. It has an enormous audience, though I don't know whether students watch it. I think that anybody who shows ability and has the courage to stick his neck out is going to attract attention among young people.

RANNEY: Thank you very much.

I should explain, if you'll forgive the personal reference, that although everybody else at this table has had considerable practical political experience, and the majority of them with third-party or third-force politics, my only personal venture outside the ivory tower as a candidate for public office was under the label of one of the two major parties. But I would argue that I finished so far behind my opponent that I didn't really finish second; in fact, I finished third, even though there were only two candidates on the ballot. So I've always thought of myself since then as having been a participant in third-party movements.

Mr. Ferry wants to say something.

FERRY: Yes, I'd like to say something before we bring the audience into this discussion. This has been really a rather curious experience. My view of the nation is that we are very ill. It's an illness that goes very deep. We've been in trouble in this country before, but we've never been in the kind of trouble it seems to me we are in now. Wallace is one expression of our trouble. The screams we are hearing from the ghettos and from the reservations and other places are expressions of it—the disenchantment of the young. (I speak of the unhappiness of the young despite Mr. Rice's notes on the subject, which I think are about 98 percent erroneous. They are factually correct; all the inferences are wrong. . . .) I'm almost sixty. I've been a newspaperman for much of my life, and I've been reporting on public events. I may even be mistaken about the present ailment in the United States. But it certainly is something that I've never before witnessed, and I was a reporter during the Great Depression, a newspaperman throughout that experience. . . .

But we're talking now about third forces around here as if they were a sort of pleasure—historical somethings that were nice to have had around, historically. They certainly have had some effect. I suggest that there's something about this discussion that is a little misleading, at least to me. We are in desperate difficulty in this country, it seems to me. I reject Mr. Evans' statement that no one should talk about particular moral inputs into the major established parties, that everybody strikes a moral stance. I agree that everybody strikes a moral stance, but I don't believe that real moral positions have been taken.

I don't know what's wrong with the country. I have a theory about why everybody, from the most affluent and best placed to the complaining student, is saying, "What in the name of heaven is wrong with this nation?" I won't go into it now; but I do want to say that, in view of the illness we are suffering, I think that the question of third forces before us is far more crucial than any of us here, including myself, have been making it. I think that we must listen to these voices a great deal more carefully than we have in the past. We're just tolerating the students. Some nice things, some amiable things, have been said here about the possibilities of allying with students and so on. I agree with Mr. Zeidler. But I think we have to take it a great deal more soberly, because as far as I can see the two-party system right now is a staggering wreck.

RANNEY: Professor Rice?

RICE: I disagree with Mr. Ferry that I am 98 percent wrong, as you might expect. I appreciate his concession that I am right factually. The comment about my inferences means that we disagree. I think that's all right, because that's what makes ball games. We draw different inferences from the same facts, and that's the way life goes.

I agree with Mr. Ferry on the infusion of morality into politics. Take, for example, the war, though I approach the morality of it a little differently from Mr. Ferry. I regard it as ambivalent and really unjustified to enter a war and make no provision for winning it. If you are not going to win it, you should be out of it. If you're going to win it, I think you *should* win it, provided you have the means, as I believe we've had, and provided you don't have to enlarge the conflict. It seems that we've been fatally ambivalent in Vietnam. . . . It seems to me that both parties have . . . ignored the realities. This is why I think third parties are essential—and not only third parties, but, as Professor Ranney mentioned before, third forces—to drive the major parties to deal with realities and the moral side of issues. On this point I'm glad to be able finally to agree with Mr. Ferry on something.

RANNEY: All right. As I say, it's not easy to distinguish hands out there, but I think I can. We will have the first comment from this lady.

QUESTIONER: Thank you.

I'm Myrtle Kastner. I am one of the six candidates for governor of Wisconsin; since we do not yet have the official vote, I have not yet conceded. I find it very odd that I was not invited to participate in this symposium on third-party forces, although I was in the campaign as a third-party candidate.

One of the panelists mentioned that third-party forces and third-party leaders are denounced while alive and honored when dead. An example is Eugene V. Debs, a great leader of the Socialist party in the early days when the party could still claim to be socialist. I would like to read just two sentences from Mr. Debs: "The Socialist party is not a capitalist party nor a middle-class party, but a revolutionary working-class party whose historic mission it is to conquer capitalism, to take possession of the means of wealth production, abolish wage slavery, and emancipate all workers and all humanity. We believe that the first step in this direction is to sever all relations with the capitalist parties." What calls itself the Socialist party today has endorsed Pat Lucey, a noted revolutionary in Wisconsin.

Now, I would like to point out, ladies and gentlemen, that as a panel on third forces in politics this program has been a farce. It has been a discussion of the various tendencies within the capitalist parties, the Democrat and Republican. Nobody has truly presented any opposition to a capitalist party of any kind or any name.

RANNEY: Mr. Zeidler, would you like to field this?

ZEIDLER: The speaker represents one group that calls itself socialist among the many groups that call themselves socialist. Some are totalitarian in character, and some are democratic. The speaker, I believe, represents a group which believes in the doctrine of Mao—namely, that the power needed to bring about a socialist society comes out of the barrel of a gun. The Debsian viewpoint, which I think I hold, is that the change to a socialist society must occur gradually through peaceful democratic processes. I think this is the major difference between her party and our party. And because of our belief in peaceful democratic processes, our group had to choose persons who represented progressive democratic tendencies, even though their philosophies included allegiance to many aspects of the capitalist system. We believe that even before the change to a socialist society occurs, government must be continuously in the hands of men and women dedicated to peaceful democratic methods of accomplishing change. Without this belief any group that is disposed to can seize power by force of arms.

I think that the modern Democratic Socialist is confronted with this kind of problem: He tends to reject totalitarianism, but he is today regularly confronted with requests for support from totalitarian groups which call themselves socialist to gain support and power. I think this is the difference between the questioner and me—that she represents totalitarian socialism disposed to use force to achieve its ends, whereas I represent democratic socialism dedicated to peaceful methods of change.

I hope that in the future Fromkin scholars will look into the problem of why certain elements of the socialist movement deserted the idea and use of democratic processes and took up the use of power and totalitarianism as means of achieving their ends.

QUESTIONER: Since my organization has been slandered, may I answer that? Mr. Zeidler should know better than to take quotations out of context. Power flowing from the barrel of a gun does not mean that you gain power by just going out and shooting everybody. But it does mean that when there is a movement for social justice, when the workers move to take over their own industries, when they are attacked, they have the right to fight back. . . . Marxists and Maoists and true socialists believe that capitalists are not going to permit the workers to take over the means of production peacefully or at the ballot box. I would argue that if the Socialist party felt that the only reason they *had* to support Pat Lucey was that there was no peaceful, democratic-minded, vote-oriented socialist running, you could have endorsed the campaign of Georgia Casini, who is even more peaceable than the Democratic party. Much more. It wouldn't have been an endorsement of our campaign, but you wouldn't have been stuck with Pat Lucey.

RANNEY: Yes, we're going to have Mr. Zeidler respond to that, and then I am going to impose cloture on this exchange and we'll go on to another question.

ZEIDLER: I merely want to suggest that the next symposium in this series, and a most interesting one it would be, might bring together all the brands of socialists to speak their piece.

RANNEY: Yes, I think that's a splendid idea. If such a program were held you could have the speakers out there and the audience up here.

This gentleman here. . . .

QUESTIONER: These third parties do their states good and the nation good, and then it all too often happens that the conservative forces, which have been sitting tight while the winds of reform were blowing, at some time move into action and, in Pogo-language, just swoggle up the liberals, who often are tired.

RANNEY: I myself think that's a good observation. Does anybody wish to deal with it?

GRAVEN: I think that is true. In my opening statement I remarked that third parties and third forces seem to need charismatic leaders. A lot of the power of a third party or third force is based on an individual; and when he goes, the movement seems to collapse. . . .

Minnesota presents a classic example of the dynamics of third forces in the case of the peace movement. We have an open party in Minnesota. People, many of them students, who in 1968 were saying that the system wasn't responsive, suddenly found themselves county chairmen and in control of the whole Minneapolis–St. Paul metropolitan area. By the time of the election in November no one was holding party offices but people from the McCarthy peace movement. That was two years ago. Those who are still in these positions forced the party to adopt basically the peace position. On the other hand, those who were just interested in the glamour and excitement of the crusade have faded away and have had very little long-run impact. . . .

QUESTIONER: Thank you.

Speaking as a retired worker, UAW, I just have come back from a trip to Siberia and Mongolia. If it were not for my union, my only trip would be to the Welfare Department. While abroad, I noticed that they had a national health care plan where everybody receives medicine and care from doctors. Now we have a big fight on our hands in the United States for a national health care plan. The workers do not yet know much about the many beautiful welfare programs we have for the rich; and when they do, . . . they are going to side with the students on these issues. . . .

I want to direct this to Professor Rice, please. He has such concern for the unborn children. How about the already born? The Conservatives here in Wisconsin have seen fit that the children who are already here have to be fed on sixteen cents a day.

RICE: As for the plight of needy human beings, I don't think it can be said that Conservatives are insensitive. We are dealing with the question of which type of economic system of distribution, production, etc., will most effectively provide the maximum advantages for everybody. I'm not opposed to welfare. I think government has an obligation to take care of people who can't take care of themselves. There's a question here, of course, as in other matters, as to how to go about it.

In my opening remarks I raised the abortion issue to indicate that this is a natural for a third force. We're dealing in this symposium with human beings at all stages of life, and I for one am concerned that we're entering a situation where we're saying that people can be killed because their existence is inconvenient. It seems to me that if a person can be killed, an innocent person, because he's too young, then one can be killed because he's too old or because he's too black or too stupid or too politically undesirable. This is the reason I raised that question, and certainly what I said does not imply that my concern for the quality of people's lives stops at birth. It certainly does not. But we're dealing with choices. I regard the abortion question as continuous with what we've been talking about here today. . . . We're dealing with a continuity among human beings, and we have to be concerned with the rights of innocent human beings at all stages of life.

RANNEY: Where did you get this . . . Pardon?

QUESTIONER: The conservatives in our state legislature have seen fit to think that sixteen cents a meal per child is a lot, and that's why I directed the question to you.

RICE: Well, I certainly do not hold myself responsible for the actions of people in Wisconsin or anywhere else who call themselves conservatives. Until last year I was the vice-chairman in New York state of the New York State Conservative party, which is a New York State operation. I can speak competently about that organization.

FERRY: Where did you guys get such a bad reputation?

RICE: From people like you.

FERRY: No, no. This is a serious question.

RICE: I know that.

FERRY: This is a serious question. It is asserted that the Conservative party represents property and privilege and hasn't very much time for questions of the kind this lady is raising. You say it's just a question of which is the most efficient way of taking care of people, but that's a pretty vague and unsatisfactory answer. Would you say that the reputation of Conservatives is entirely unmerited, that your concern for people has been a very wholesome one all these years, and that you've just been misunderstood?

RICE: My concern, yes. I'm just talking about myself.

FERRY: Oh no. Speak for the Conservative view. Go ahead.

RICE: All right. I think that, as with socialists, you have to distinguish among the various types of conservatives. You have a libertarian type of conservatism, with which I am not in sympathy. The libertarian point of view is primarily an economic conservatism giving insufficient consideration to the obligation of government and people to do certain things which may not jibe with the theoretical dynamics of the market economy but at times are absolutely necessary because people are involved. I believe in free enterprise; I believe in the capitalist system—yes. But I do not believe in the kind of conservatism espoused by the libertarian conservatives.

Now, concerning this bugaboo of the connection between conservatism and privilege and wealth, in New York State we had the experience of having to go around getting petitions signed—a chore Mrs. La Follette described so well with reference to her work in politics—and we found that we were drawing an almost complete blank in two types of areas. One was the area where the very wealthy lived, and there we drew a total blank; the other was where the very poor lived. The places where we were most successful in getting signatures and then votes was in the neighborhoods populated by the wage-earning, rent-paying, or home-owning guy. These are not the stereotyped fat-cat Conservatives. The very rich didn't want to have anything to do with us, because we were tending to upset the apple cart. I'm not saying that the reputation of conservatism is entirely without foundation, because there are all kinds of conservatives running around. But just as with liberalism and other political persuasions, with conservatism you have to discriminate various types.

I think we've got something to offer, and I think that it's something that should be listened to. . . .

RANNEY: Yes, in the front row.

QUESTIONER: Do you agree with the scientists of the world that the population cannot keep growing as it is without causing mass starvation around the world, that the world cannot sustain the kind of population growth we have now after the next century? Do you believe in birth control and in preventing the birth of babies born without a free choice?

RICE: To answer the first part of the question first, I do not believe in the so-called population explosion in the way it's usually talked about. I don't really want to get into this question, but let me say that the recently issued 1969 report of the United Nations Food and Agriculture Organization states that because of the new miracle grains, the most pressing problem now, particularly in the underdeveloped countries, is agricultural overproduction, a glut on the market—not underproduction. There is enough food being produced to feed the people of the world now and for the foreseeable future. You might recall that the Nobel Peace Prize was given to Dr. Norman E. Borlaug, who developed the genetic engineering for new strains of wheat, rice, corn, sorghum, and oats—what's called genetically "the green revolution." I don't believe that we are faced with an overwhelming population problem. I think that the population crisis has been exaggerated in three respects: first, as to the number of people around the world; second, as to our ability to feed them; and third, as to our ability to solve pollution problems in the face of an expanding population. I'd be delighted to go into these exaggerations at great length, but we can't here.

QUESTIONER: You don't believe in any population control?

RICE: [Small portion of comments unintelligible on tape] Abortion is a form of birth control. There are three forms: contraception, sterilization, and abortion. The reason I mentioned abortion here is because we're dealing with movements concerned with individual rights. We're dealing with individual persons who exist. I know some of you find it hard to believe that fetuses fit this description, but give them the benefit of the doubt. Abortion is very different from contraception and sterilization in that it involves snuffing out already existing life, while the other two prevent life from coming into being. Now, the power of government in the area of birth control has to be limited in order to protect individual rights. And there's no right higher than the right of an innocent life to live and not to be killed for the convenience of others. . . . Government cannot move in and punish the use of contraceptives without interfering—and the Supreme Court laid this down as law in 1965—without interfering with the right of privacy, certainly marital privacy. But when you have another human being already in existence, the question of birth control becomes a very different kind of problem. This is why I raised the question, because we are dealing here with individual rights, but I don't want to get off into this whole subject.

RANNEY: Mr. Zeidler also wishes to comment on that.

ZEIDLER: I'm deeply troubled by Professor Rice's remarks. I too am concerned about the whole question of birth control and the frightening possibility that it might be used by the state to kill people. I commend his university for looking into such problems. But I am also troubled by other problems of life and death that don't seem to concern him. One is the destruction of living people by bombing in Vietnam and elsewhere. Another he seems to avoid is the question of the mere starvation of people imposed by the conservatives of Wisconsin who operate under the name Republican but who, I think, heartily applauded the election of Buckley in New York. And he ignores the whole problem of what to do with the poverty-stricken people of the world. He just says there isn't such a problem so far as he can determine. I guess it's at this point that he and I would part company.

RICE: We certainly would, because I didn't say that. I didn't say there's no poverty problem. I said the population crisis was exaggerated. Of course there's a poverty problem, but it's a problem of distribution within our social and economic organization. I *am* concerned about the war in Vietnam. That's why I think that we should have gone in there and fought; and, as our military people told us years ago, we could have won that one in six months. But the decision was made not to do it; and as a result we have had more people killed on all sides. . . .

RANNEY: In the aisle.

QUESTIONER: You mention the subject of the two-party system as opposed to a multiparty system. As an official of the Democratic party here in Milwaukee County, I have noticed that only a fairly small number of people are active in our political parties and are seeking party nominations, so that if a group were well organized and active it could not only affect the politics of the major parties, but could actually take them over. As one example, in my own ward, the Fifth Ward of the city of Milwaukee, twenty-five people joined the Democratic unit. They took over. They controlled almost every meeting. The same thing could happen in other areas. So, in view of the fact that we have a system here, particularly here in Wisconsin, in which the parties are very open, in which party primaries are open, . . . isn't it clear that the political process within the two existing parties actually takes the place of a large number of narrow ideological parties?

RANNEY: Somebody answer that. Mr. Ferry?

FERRY: . . . I don't think there's any real answer to what he's said. I think he's made a simple statement of fact that just says that democracy hasn't been working very well in this country for a long while, and he's just illustrated one of the reasons why it doesn't in one of the most democratic parts of the country.

I'm intruding here because the time's running out, and I wanted to invite a comment from the audience or from a panel member on a proposition that was raised originally by Mr. Ranney in his opening remarks, that is, the role of television in politics. It seems to me that it would be very desirable to do away with television entirely during campaigns and to stop all this grousing about how much money it costs, the fairness doctrine, and so on, because as Mr. Ranney indicated, television is a third force in our political life of dimensions that no one really understands at all. This is a sort of McLuhan idea, that the medium here is the third force. I'd like to hear from someone on the panel or someone in the audience as to whether the drastic solution of keeping all the rascals off the tube for six to nine months might be one way at least of getting back to a little sanity. Give ourselves a furlough, so to speak, from this question.

GRAVEN: Well, the idea is an appealing one in a way, but in practice it would work out with the candidates at the mercy of the guys in the cutting room of the TV studio. I assume you're talking about commercially produced ads. We bar politics and cigarettes from the TV waves and good riddance to both.

FERRY: No, I'm talking about everything.

GRAVEN: If you start saying you can't put politics and politicians on the news, then you get into a very important First Amendment right. Newsmen say they've got the right to print and report the news. We're the news here, you know; and whatever else you might want to say about some guy running for office, he's news. Now if you're going to say that politicians can't be on the tube in news reports, then you would get opposition from me. I think that a political campaign, whatever else it may be, is news. But I have found that when you call a press conference, they take four shots of you, and what goes on the 10:00 o'clock news, which is the lifeblood of politics, is determined by some film editor who generally takes you at your worst. . . . You're at the mercy of the editors. So it's very comforting to be able to produce your own view of yourself; you know that if you don't do it right the first time, you can do it ten times till you get it just the way you want it. At least you have something you can live with. Coming back to the original point, I don't know how you can keep politics off the news.

FERRY: Well, I don't think we could keep it off the news, but it's a good idea, a way of sanitizing the process for a little while just to see whether it would work. I'm speaking now as a manager of a lot of forlorn hope organizations, political organizations, and others. We don't have your problems with television. You're a settled, successful, or nearly successful, politician, and you get on television not as often as you think you warrant getting on, but you get on regularly. None of my customers can get on at all. It's no problem for film editors, because nobody will ever take a picture of these blacks except when they are dead, none of these Chicanos except perhaps when they are being burned or evicted from their homes. I may just be speaking out of sheer frustration, because we can't get any attention for those third forces. . . .

RANNEY: Mr. Zeidler has something to say.

ZEIDLER: Mr. Ferry has pointed out something I think all third parties have worried about for a long time: that public opinion today is probably formed as much by television as by any other medium and that third parties cannot get on the air. The television stations hold channels which they do not own but which are owned by the United States government. These channels are often given to the stations, or stations may have purchased one from somebody who got it from somebody, but always at the beginning somebody got the channel virtually as a gift. It is my belief that if we're going to save the democratic process in America, prime time has to be made available on all the commercial stations, as well as on all the educational stations, for all parties, including minority parties. . . . And I think that if the two major parties really believed that third parties are good for something, they would initiate this kind of program.

RANNEY: Professor Rice.

RICE: I think the answer to this problem may lie in a more realistic interpretation of the Federal Communications Act's equal time provisions which allow more exposure for minority parties. But these provisions, of course, deal primarily with election campaigns. It's much more difficult to enforce them in the types of situations Mr. Ferry is talking about. But I don't agree that the answer is to stop televising the candidates during campaigns, because I just don't think that this would accord with the letter and spirit of the First Amendment in any way, and I believe you just have to accept free speech in this case, regardless of the fact that there may be some problems connected with it. We must work to try to insure some sort of equity in the use of these airwaves.

RANNEY: That's a very statesmanlike reply. I think that we all almost give in to the overwhelming temptation to demand that all political advertising be banned along about the last twelve hours before an election. But to resist this temptation for high democratic principles takes courage and should be applauded. Of course, if the proposition were simply to abolish television entirely . . .

RICE: I'd buy that.

RANNEY: . . . then we might be able to do some business.

We have, I think, time for one more question, and I don't think that I have neglected anybody else here. Yes.

QUESTIONER: I want to comment about the TV news situation. What we have is difficulty getting the opportunity to hear diverse opinions, because every one of the news broadcasts comes on at the same time and lasts the same amount of time. If the Communications Commission required that news broadcasts in an area be put on the air at different times, then we would have an opportunity to get a multiple choice of diversities of exposure to different opinions, say, in an election year. It would be very good if I wanted to listen to the news if I could listen to the *Journal*, the *Sentinel*, WISN/Channel 6. If I got exposure at different times, I could be exposed to different opinions. Now if I want to get the different opinions, I have to keep on switching channels. And this is a far easier way of controlling the news and political action.

RANNEY: Yes.

QUESTIONER: I should like to add that we are very fortunate to have such a diverse and intelligent panel here. All pretty sharp people. I was interested in coming here because I was the youngest delegate to the Progressive convention in 1933. I came here early because I thought all the seats would be filled and I wouldn't be able to get one. So I rushed down here. Now, what's bothering me—and I would like to ask your opinion—what can we do to get the young people to fill up these seats, the ones who are supposed to be a force, a third, or fourth, or a fifth force, the ones that want to ruin the establishment or wreck or change the establishment? How do we get them here to a wonderful panel of this kind to have a good interesting discussion?

RANNEY: Well, I can tell you how we do it in Madison: We tell them that a program is part of their regular classwork and that they may be asked questions on an exam about what was said at the program. They turn out very well.

QUESTIONER: I'd like to answer my friend's question about how to fill this room up. One way is by complying with the complaint of our socialist friend who said that we did not invite her party here. One way to fill this room up would be to invite a member of each and every party in the United States, regardless of what the cost might be. Then you would fill this place up. . . .

I would also like to make this statement. From what was said here, it is evident that a third force is absolutely essential. And I agree with Mr. Zeidler in that sense. Now what I want to state is this. I have known our absentee host, Mr. Morris Fromkin, for many, many years. I was an early member of the County Central of the Socialist party, representing the Eighteenth Ward, way before Mr. Zeidler's regime. And being friendly with him, I knew him very well. I read his biography in the program. It does not do him justice. Despite the fact that he was for individuals and individualism, he was for poor, he was for workers, he was for every person who suffered under each and every conceivable oppression. He was always a human being with sympathy for other human beings. Up to today I disbelieved in miracles. But from now on I believe that in his absence Morris Fromkin has accomplished a miracle. And I'll tell you what that miracle is. To have on one panel a leader of the Republican party, our first speaker today, followed by a Democratic leader, followed by a Farmer-Labor leader, then followed by a daughter-in-law of the founder of the Progressive party, and then of course followed by no less a gentleman (who calls himself faceless) than this Conservative—to have that kind of a panel almost in agreement with the kinds of causes Mr. Morris Fromkin believed in and almost in agreement with each other, that, I tell you, ladies and gentlemen, is the miracle our absentee host has performed. Everyone knows he can get a Republican and Democrat together. God forbid if he were to get together a Socialist or my friend ex-Mayor Zeidler and our interrogator who said she had just run for office. . . . [Small portion of comments unintelligible on tape]

I am an ex-member of YPSL, which is the Young People's Socialist League of New York. [Small portion of comments unintelligible on tape] I'm in accord with you who have good principles, whether they be practical or not. If you were to get those two together you would see two people practically at each other's throats. But here you see seven people almost in accord with each other. I say, again I reiterate, that a miracle has been performed.

In conclusion, Mr. Evans, please make no apologies for our ex-presidents you named at the commencement of your talk. I mean Mr. Hoover. You need make no apologies, because he did something that was inhuman: He got us used to starvation, hunger, and poverty and unemployment, which we're tolerating today very, very graciously. And you certainly don't have to make any apology for your president Mr. Harding, because the byword of youth today is permissiveness, and he certainly gave the inspiration for that.

RANNEY: Well, speaking on behalf of the members of the panel, I want to thank the speaker very much. I'm afraid one or two of us on the panel have some feeling that with this discussion today we might have killed third forces in American politics for all time to come, but your testimony as to their health is most welcome.

On behalf of all of us here, may I thank every member of the panel for this fascinating discussion, and this meeting is now adjourned.